Thomas Hobbes on Divers Topics

Heresy

"They that approve a private opinion, call it opinion; but they that mislike it, heresy: and yet heresy signifies no more than private opinion."

War

"Force and fraud are in war the two cardinal virtues."

Reading

"If I had spent as much time in reading as other men of learning, I should have been as ignorant as they."

Catholicism

"The Papacy is no other than the ghost of the deceased Roman Empire, sitting crowned upon the grave thereof."

Conscience

"A man's conscience and his judgement is the same thing, and as the judgement, so also the conscience, may be erroneous."

Leisure

"Leisure is the mother of Philosophy."

Collier Classics in the History of Thought

General Editors: CRANE BRINTON and PAUL EDWARDS
(Titles ready or in preparation)

THOMAS HOBBES

BODY, MAN, AND CITIZEN

Selections from **THOMAS HOBBES**, Edited with an
Introduction by **RICHARD S. PETERS**

COLLIER BOOKS
NEW YORK, N.Y.

Collier Books is a division of The Crowell-Collier Publishing Company

First Collier Books Edition 1962

Introduction

Thomas Hobbes was born in 1588 and educated at Magdalen Hall, Oxford. In 1608 he became tutor to the young son of William Cavendish, Earl of Devonshire. He spent the rest of his long life (he lived to the age of ninety) in similar employment, mainly with the Cavendish family. He was tutor to the future Charles II during the prince's exile in Paris in 1646 after the battle of Naseby.

Hobbes had been primarily a classical scholar, contributing nothing to philosophy until after he was forty when he seemed to develop a new lease on life due to his discovery of geometry. He had, however, encountered the growing dissatisfaction with the Aristotelian system of thought when he visited the continent in 1610. This dissatisfaction was probably increased by his meetings with Francis Bacon, whom he used to visit during the latter's retirement (1621–26). His naturally nervous disposition was provided with tangible enough objects; Hobbes reached his maturity at the time when the Civil War seemed almost inevitable. He therefore became very preoccupied with political problems. His earliest venture into the public field was with a translation of Thucydides in 1628, which was done partly to warn his fellow-countrymen of the dangers of democracy. Such warnings, however, were rather oblique and tentative. Hobbes' clarity of insight developed with his growing confidence; geometry seemed to present him with a method whereby he could convert the judicious warnings of Thucydides into clear-cut necessary truths. He had probably been inspired by Bacon's belief that knowledge meant power. Geometry appealed to him as a method for attaining knowledge and for demonstrating to his countrymen beyond any doubt the logic of their predicament. The ills of a sickening society might yet be cured if a clear-cut rationale of civil authority could be provided.

Hobbes' intellectual preoccupations, however, were never

distrust of the senses – neglect of physics 5
Geometry – one of the tools of reason that Bacon wanted
so for Hobbes sure deduction rather than induction.

purely political. He himself claimed originality for two main parts of his philosophy—his optics and his civil philosophy. Perhaps his greatest originality lay in the attempt to link the two together, which was, at that time, a considerable imaginative feat. Hobbes is often claimed as one of the founders of analytic philosophy. His remark, therefore, is often quoted: "For words are wise men's counters, they do but reckon by them; but they are the money of fools. . . ." It is, however, seldom realized what Hobbes thought wise men should do when they reckon with words, which was to spin out systems of thought in the manner of geometers. "When we calculate the magnitude and motions of heaven or earth" said Hobbes, "we do not ascend into heaven that we may divide it into parts, or measure the motions thereof, but we do it sitting still in our closets or in the dark." This striking quotation from Hobbes' *De Corpore* presents vividly the problem around which his philosophy of nature and mind revolved and intimated the kind of method by which he thought a solution could be found.

The problem that haunted Hobbes, and which was at the heart of his metaphysical speculations, was simply man's ability to sit in his closet and picture the world outside. "Of all the phenomena or appearances which are near to us, the most admirable" he said "is apparition itself, Τὸ φαίνεσθαι; namely, that some natural bodies have in themselves the pattern almost of all things, and others of none at all." It is recorded in his prose autobiography how he found himself in the study of some learned men who were discussing the cause of sensation. One of them asked what sensation was, and Hobbes was astonished to find that none of them could say. From that time onward Hobbes could not rest until he had given some sort of answer to these questions for himself. To answer such questions, however, required some kind of scientific method. Hobbes' picture of a man sitting in his closet calculating the magnitude of the heavens was the key to this, rather than Bacon's emphasis on the careful collection of data. Hobbes, as a matter of fact, flourished at a time when observation and experiment was extremely fashionable in English intellectual circles. The Royal Society, with its strong Baconian emphasis on observation and the method of induction, was to burst forth in 1662 from the chrysalis of the "invisible college." Yet Hobbes had nothing but contempt for the method of induction; his unswerving allegiance was to what was thought to be the rival method of deduction, as practiced by Descartes, Spinoza, Galileo and William Harvey. In Hobbes' view the followers of Bacon spent too much time on new-fangled devices and experiments and too little on deducing consequences from the fundamental theory of motion as pioneered by Galileo and his disciple, William Harvey. Hobbes' second journey to the continent in 1628 had already provided him with a rather rough and ready familiarity with the method of geometry. But it was his third journey to the continent (1634–36) which really provided the concepts for his imaginative scheme. In his verse autobiography Hobbes relates how, on this journey, he was obsessed by the omnipresence of motion. He was acclimatizing himself to the way of thinking he had learned from Galileo, to the audacious suggestion that motion was the natural state of bodies and that they continued in motion to infinity unless impeded. This went against the crude evidence of the senses as well as against the old Aristotelian world-view in which rest was regarded as the natural state.

Hobbes' solution to the problem about the cause of sensation was to look at a familiar process in the unfamiliar way which he had learned from Galileo. To quote his prose autobiography: ". . . it occurred to him that if bodies and all their parts were to be at rest, or were always to be moved by the same motion, our discrimination of all things would be removed, and (consequently) all sensation with it; and therefore the cause of all things must be sought in the variety of motion. Then he was led to geometry to learn the varieties and modes of motion. . . ." Apparition, which he found so wonderful, was to be viewed as a kind of meeting place of motions. Our sense-organs were agitated by external motions without which there could be no sensation. To give the entire cause of sensation would require an analysis of all motions in bodies external to us which were passed on by direct contact or via some medium. The answer to what was the cause of sensation must consist in deductions from a general mechanical theory.

Hobbes' first attempt at such a theory was in his *Little Treatise*,[1] which he wrote sometime between his discovery of geometry and his return to England in 1637. This little work was constructed in geometrical form and attempted in a very brief way to explain sensation in terms of a general theory of motion. Much of it was concerned with criticisms of the Aristotelian theory. Indeed it represents a transition in Hobbes' thought from the established Aristotelian opinions which he had learned at Oxford to the new way of looking at things made possible by the natural philosophy of Galileo. Even Aristotle's definition of "good" as that to which all things are moved was translated by Hobbes into his theory of local motion. This was a crude schematic anticipation of what was to come.

In 1637 Hobbes returned home stimulated by his first venture into philosophy and by his contact with continental thinkers. It is not clear whether it was at this period or at a later time that Hobbes conceived his ambitious plan of composing a trilogy of Body, Man, and Citizen, in which mechanical explanations would be extrapolated to the fields of psychology and politics. For, though it has been suggested that Galileo put the idea of an extrapolation to civil philosophy into Hobbes' head, it is not certain whether Hobbes envisaged such a trilogy at this period or later when he started on *De Corpore*. For, on returning to England, he found the country in such a state of upheaval that his thoughts turned naturally to politics. His discovery of geometry had provided him with a method of approach to such problems which would enable him to promulgate necessary truths to his countrymen about their plight. "The skill of making and maintaining commonwealths consisteth in certain rules, as doth arithmetic and geometry; not as tennis play, on practice only." The result of his thought about the contemporary situation was his *Elements of Law* which he published in

[1] Printed in this volume pp. 163-181.

1640, during the assembly of Parliament. This demonstrated the need for undivided sovereignty. (It was published later in 1650 in two parts, *Human Nature*[2] and *De Corpore Politico*.[3]) The first part, on Human Nature, is regarded by many as one of Hobbes' best works. It consists largely in traditional psychology coordinated and underpinned by a mechanical theory. In this respect it was a forerunner of the early sections in *Leviathan* on Man. The beginning of Chapter 7 states his theory in a nutshell:

In the eighth section of the second chapter is shewed, how conceptions or apparitions are nothing really, but motion in some internal substance of the head; which motion not stopping there, but proceeding to the heart, of necessity must there either help or hinder that motion which is called vital; when it helpeth, it is called DELIGHT, contentment, or pleasure, which is nothing really but motion about the heart, as conception is nothing but motion within the head; and the objects that cause it are called pleasant or delightful, or by some name equivalent; the Latins have *jucunda, a juvando,* from helping; and the same delight, with reference to the object, is called LOVE: but when such motion weakeneth or hindereth the vital motion, then it is called PAIN; and in relation to that which causeth it, HATRED, which the Latin expresseth sometimes by *odium,* and sometimes by *taedium.*

This motion, in which consisteth pleasure or pain, is also a solicitation or provocation either to draw near to the thing that pleaseth, or to retire from the thing that displeaseth. And this solicitation is the endeavour or internal beginning of animal motion, which when the object delighteth is called APPETITE; when it displeaseth, it is called AVERSION, in respect of the displeasure present; but in respect of the displeasure expected, FEAR. So that pleasure, love, and appetite, which is also called desire, are divers names for divers considerations of the same thing.

Every man, for his own part, calleth that which pleaseth,

[2] Printed in this volume pp. 182-244.
[3] Printed in this volume pp. 275-390.

and is delightful to himself, GOOD; and that EVIL which displeaseth him:[4]

Hobbes became increasingly excited by the prospect of deducing new consequences from the law of inertia. Harvey had tackled the circulation of the blood. Could not the theory of motion be extrapolated in considerable detail to psychology and politics? And so his imaginative idea gained momentum: "For seeing that life is but motion of limbs. . . . For what is the heart but a spring; and the nerves but so many strings; and the joints but so many wheels, giving motion to the whole body, such as was intended by the artificer?" Man is a natural machine and the state an artificial one. (The preceeding quotation is from the foreword to his later masterpiece *Leviathan*). There can be "no contentment but in proceeding." Liberty is "an absence of the lets and hindrances of motion." Individual differences in wits are due to differences in quickness or "swift succession of one thought to another." Desires and aversions are motions towards and away from objects. And so on. At the end of Chapter 9 of *Human Nature* Hobbes summed up his theory of the passions by relating them all to possible incidents in a race, which "we must suppose to have no other goal, nor other garland, but being foremost."

When Parliament impeached Strafford, Hobbes feared for his life and fled to the continent, priding himself later on being "the first of all that fled." His *De Cive* followed soon after, in 1642 (published in English in 1651 under the title *Philosophical Rudiments Concerning Government and Society*). In it he tried to demonstrate conclusively the proper purpose and extent of the civil power, and the relationship between church and state. Soon after the publication of his *De Cive* Hobbes started work on his *De Corpore*,[5] which was to be the foundation for his ambitious trilogy on Body, Man, and Citizen. It was not, however, completed until after his return to England much later; for after the advent of the

[4] Quoted from F. Tonnies' edition of *The Elements of Law* (Cambridge University Press, 1928) pp. 21-2.
[5] Printed in part in this volume pp. 23-162.

fugitive Charles II to Paris Hobbes turned aside from his physical speculations and started work on *Leviathan*,[6] which stated in a fuller and more pungent form the views on Man and Citizen he had stated earlier in his *Elements of Law*. (The treatment of religion in *Leviathan* was much more detailed.) It was published in 1651 and soon afterwards Hobbes was permitted by Cromwell to return home. For Hobbes, while conceding popular representation, used the social-contract theory to demonstrate the necessity of an absolute sovereign —by consent, not Divine Right. So his doctrine was one which could be used to justify any *de facto* government, provided that it governed—first that of Cromwell and later that of Charles II. The very fact that Hobbes could turn aside from his *De Corpore* and write up his views on Man and Citizen, which were not substantially different from views expressed earlier in his *Elements of Law* and *De Cive*, suggests that Hobbes did not view his trilogy as a strict deductive system. Indeed, he allowed for the possibility of constructing such theories without working out the basic postulates relating to Body in some remarks which he made about scientific method at the start of Part IV of *De Corpore*. He contrasts two types of scientific inquiry ". . . one from the generation of things to their possible effects; and the other, from their effects or appearances to some possible generation of the same." The former method he followed when dealing with parallel lines, refraction and reflection, circular and other forms of motion. But when starting on Part IV of *De Corpore*, which deals with physics, he admits that "The principles, therefore, upon which the following discourse depends, are not such as we ourselves make and pronounce in general terms, as definitions: but such, as being placed in the things themselves by the Author of Nature, are by us observed in them. . . ." This precedes his attempt to explain "apparition itself," which had puzzled him so much from the time when he witnessed the discussion by the learned men on the nature of sense. Such explanations as he gives may be true, but it cannot be demonstrated that they must

[6] See Hobbes: *Leviathan*, Ed. by Richard S. Peters, Collier Books, Classics in the History of Thought.

be so. With the state, however, the case is different. For the state is an artificial, not a natural body. We can therefore know with certainty the formula of its construction. To quote him in the Epistle Dedicatory to his *Six Lessons to the Professors of Mathematics* (written after *De Corpore* as part of the controversy which arose from his attempt to square the circle in Chapter 20), "Geometry, therefore is demonstrable, for the lines and figures from which we reason are drawn and described by ourselves; and civil philosophy is demonstrable because we make the commonwealth ourselves. But because of natural bodies we know not the construction, but seek it from effects, there lies no demonstration of what the causes be we seek for, but only of what they may be." In Hobbes' scheme, therefore, his physics occupied a position of indeterminate status as regards its certainty between geometry and politics. What in fact united these various sciences was the ubiquitousness of motion—even in his geometry. For he claimed that no one could understand the definitions of geometry unless he had performed experiments with motion like those involved in constructing a circle with "the motion of a compass or other equivalent means."

After geometry, in Hobbes' scheme, came mechanics which dealt with the effects of motions of bodies on each other, and physics which explained the generation of sensible qualities like heat and color out of the minute parts of bodies in contact with each other. For there could be no action at a distance, "no cause of motion, except in a body contiguous and moved." In his theory of action, Hobbes' great historical importance was to generalize this concept of the efficient cause and to apply it to man as well as to nature. "A final cause," he said, "has no place but in such things as have sense and will: and this also I shall prove hereafter to be an efficient cause." How then did he introduce such efficient causes, in the form of antecedent motions, into the sphere of human action? This transition from nature to man was effected by means of the concept of *conatus* or "endeavor." He defined "endeavor" as "motion made in less space and time than can be given; that is motion made through the length of a point and in an instant or part of time." In brief it was used to designate infinitely small motions. Hobbes took over this technical term from the physical scientists and generalized its application so that the gap between physics, physiology and psychology could be bridged. By means of this he was able to postulate minute unobservable motions in the medium between the object of sense and the brain, and he used it also to explain how movements coming from outside bodies were passed on through the body so that they eventually led to the gross movement observable in desire and aversion. An account of the initiation of actions, such as has been quoted above from his *Human Nature,* could thus be sketched in mechanical terms.

The transition from psychology to politics was rather ambiguously sketched by Hobbes. In his chapter called "Of Method" in *De Corpore,* after sketching his plan for geometry, the science of motion, physics, and moral philosophy, he says that men might attain knowledge of the passions and perturbations of the mind by reasoning synthetically from the first principles of philosophy and deduce from these the causes and necessity of constituting commonwealths; for the principles of politics consisted in the knowledge of the motions of the mind which comes from knowledge of sense and imagination. But he says, also, that even those who are ignorant of the principles of physics and geometry might attain knowledge of the principles of politics by the analytical method. For they could start, for instance, with the question whether an action be just or unjust; "unjust" could be resolved into "fact against law," and "law" into "command of him or them that have coercive power"; "power" could in its turn be derived from the wills of men that constituted such power to the end that they might live in peace. In the end the axiom would be reached that the appetites of men and the passions of their minds were such that, unless they were restrained by some power, they would always be making war on each other. If a man would look into his own mind he could confirm this analysis by introspection.

This line of argument suggests the possibility of a self-contained science of politics with a foundation of self-evident postulates reached by introspection. And, indeed, in *Levia-*

than, Hobbes not only followed this analytic method but also recommended it to his readers in the Introduction: "He that is to govern a whole nation, must read in himself, not this or that particular man; but mankind: which though it be hard to do, harder than to learn any language or science; yet when I shall have set down my own reading, orderly and perspicuously, the pains left another, will be only to consider, if he also find not the same in himself. For this kind of doctrine admitteth no other demonstration." It seems reasonable to conclude, in the light both of what Hobbes said about method and what he actually did, that he did not conceive of his trilogy in a strict deductive fashion. What united them was the use of mechanical notions in geometry, psychology and politics as well as in physics, physiology and mechanics. It is this which would justify the description of Hobbes as the great *metaphysician* of motion. For he generalized categories of description from one realm to cover all that is. It was not, however, simply Hobbes' attempt to introduce mechanical concepts into psychology and politics which will insure him an important place in the history of thought about human behaviour. It was also his attempt to establish psychology and political science as objective studies, untrammelled by theological assumptions and moralizing, to preserve a detached and uninvolved attitude towards man and society as well as towards nature. He tried to explain the behavior of men in the same sort of way as the behavior of bodies. Now probably most of the details of Hobbes' attempt were misconceived. There are fundamental differences between geometry and the empirical sciences as Hume was later to point out. Furthermore it is probably impossible—logically impossible—to describe and explain human *actions* (as distinct from mere movements of or within the body) in purely mechanical terms. But the objective attitude necessary for such an ambitious project was a considerable step forward in the attempt to understand man and society.

De Corpore is not of interest solely as the foundation stone of Hobbes' trilogy. It also contains many interesting points about logic. Hobbes made quite a niche for himself in the history of philosophy for his uncompromising nominalism. "A NAME is a word taken at pleasure to serve for a mark, which may raise in our mind a thought like to some thought we had before, and which being pronounced to others, may be to them a sign of what thought the speaker had, or had not before in his mind." Names may be either concrete or abstract. Concrete names can denote bodies, or their accidents or names. Abstract names only come into being with propositions and denote "the causes of concrete names." There are two classes of concrete names, proper names and universal names. Proper names like "Peter" are singular to one thing only; a universal name like "man" denotes each member of a class of things, though the uttering of it will give rise to an image of a particular member of this class in the mind. *cf. Berkeley*

This rather crude logical apparatus was sufficient for Hobbes' purposes, both negative and positive. Negatively he used it to launch polemics against the doctrines of the Schools whose adherence to Aristotelian essences not only, in Hobbes' view, fuddled men's minds with metaphysical vaporings, but also were a positive threat to peace by their encouragement of extra-mundane systems of beliefs and of the superstitions by means of which the priests maintained such a stranglehold on the population. "Universal" is the name of a type of name, not an extra sort of entity denoted by a name . . . "there being nothing in the world universal but names." The world is composed only of bodies in motion; there are no essences behind the appearances of things for universal names to designate. Names are called "universal" purely because they are *used* to refer to, *e.g.* different men rather than just one particular individual. The mistake of the Schoolmen was an example of the more general mistake of treating names for bodies, properties, or names in the same way. Redness, for instance, (which is a property) is not in blood in the same way as blood (which is a body) is in a bloody cloth (which is another body). Similar mistakes were generated by the failure to understand the different functions of the copula. For "is" can be used both to assign a date and a place to things and to express the relation of class-inclusion. Failure to see this can lead to the filling of the world with all sorts of strange entities. Indeed Hobbes went so far as to suggest that terms like "essence," "reality," and "quiddity" "could never have been heard of among such nations as do not copulate their names by the verb 'is' but by adjective verbs as runneth, sendeth. . . ." Hobbes, especially in his *Leviathan*, used this logical apparatus to expose all sorts of absurdities—especially those of the Schoolmen and Catholic Church. It is this which has led many to hail him as one of the fathers of modern analytic philosophy; for he supplemented his demand for clarity and concreteness of speech by a theory about how absurdities are generated through insufficient attention to the logical behavior of different classes of terms.

Positively Hobbes' theory of speech was important in so far as he insisted that speech was essential to reasoning and that it was reasoning, (as well as man's disinterested curiosity) in the sense of laying down definitions and drawing out the implications of general names, that distinguishes men from animals. His theory of abstract names, which figures prominently in science, was somewhat obscure; but it was interesting in that it was an attempt to combine an extreme form of nominalism with a stress on the role of abstract thought in the development of scientific systems.

Hobbes' *De Corpore* did not fall still-born from the press. But the attention it attracted was not for its contributions to logic and scientific method or for the boldness of the metaphysical scheme for which it laid the foundation. It was for Chapter 20 in which Hobbes had inserted his ill-fated attempt to square the circle. This did not then seem such a preposterous undertaking as it now seems; indeed circle-squaring contests sometimes took place at which patrons of the sciences presided. But Hobbes was not really a very competent geometer and his rather inept attempt was seized on by John Wallis, professor of geometry at Oxford and Seth Ward, the professor of astronomy. Both of them were Puritans and had been understandably irritated by Hobbes' criticisms of the Universities. A most unsavory wrangle started which lasted for about twenty years.

Hobbes had been engaged in another such intellectual controversy since his home-coming. In 1645 he had discussed the problem of free will with Bishop Bramhall (who had fled with Newcastle from Marston Moor,) in Newcastle's presence. At Newcastle's request they both wrote down their views on this matter soon afterwards. But a young disciple of Hobbes (John Davys) had managed to obtain a copy of the discussion and published Hobbes' contribution in 1654 without Hobbes' consent, under the title *Of Liberty and Necessity*.[7] Bramhall was understandably indignant and in 1655 published the whole controversy under the title *A Defense of the True Liberty of Human Actions from Antecedent or Extrinsic Necessity*. In 1656 Hobbes replied, printing Bramhall's book together with his own observations on it—his *Questions Concerning Liberty, Necessity, and Chance*. And so the controversy continued.

Hobbes' energy, which was remarkable for one so advanced in years (he played tennis up to the age of 70), was not completely absorbed in such controversies. In 1657, for instance, he published his *De Homine*. This was officially the second part of his proposed trilogy on Body, Man, and Citizen. It was in Latin and contained Hobbes' views on optics and a condensed version of Hobbes' views on the psychological foundations of politics. It contained little that Hobbes had not published before. Indeed his *Leviathan* and the first part on *Human Nature* of his *Elements of Law* state Hobbes' psychological theory much better. After the Restoration Hobbes was received at Court on account of his relationship with Charles II during exile. This royal patronage stood him in good stead when a Bill was brought before Parliament for the suppression of atheism on account of the hysteria provoked by the Plague and Great Fire and a committee was set up to look into *Leviathan*. It was probably only the intervention of the King that caused the matter to be dropped. However Hobbes was forbidden to publish his opinions. He turned to history and in 1668 completed his *Behemoth*, a history of the Civil War interpreted in the light of his opinions

[7] Printed in this volume pp. 245-274.

about man and society. It was published posthumously in 1682.

Even at this advanced age Hobbes was still capable of thinking in an acute and stimulating manner. When his biographer, John Aubrey, sent him Bacon's *Elements of Common Law* for his comments, Hobbes managed to produce his unfinished *Dialogue between a Philosopher and a Student of the Common Laws of England*[8] in 1666. (It was published posthumously in 1681.) Hobbes is famous for his advocacy of what is called the "command theory" of law and in many respects anticipated the Austinian school of analytical jurisprudence in the 19th century. Hobbes attacked the Common Law not simply because it had been constantly appealed to as a system of precedents that limited the prerogative of the King, but also because he considered it intellectually confused. Its fiction was that it was a declaration of the customs of the realm as interpreted by the trained reason of the judges. Hobbes held that, logically speaking, law had no necessary connection with either reason or custom. It was authority that made a law. Indeed law was simply the command of the sovereign. Hobbes thus emerged as an uncompromising advocate of Statute Law which was, at this time, beginning to emerge as the most important form of social control. Although it is difficult to defend the "command theory" as advocated by Hobbes, he did an extremely useful preliminary job in distinguishing the question "What do we mean by 'law'?" from other questions about the validity of law, the equitableness of law, and the justification of obedience to law.

At the age of 84 Hobbes wrote his own autobiography in Latin verse and two years later published a translation of the Odyssey and Iliad for want of something better to do. He died in 1679.

RICHARD S. PETERS

[8] Printed in part in this volume pp. 391-414.

Contents

PART 1

LOGIC AND METHODOLOGY

COMPUTATION OR LOGIC*

Chapter 1

Of Philosophy

1. Introduction. Philosophy seems to me to be amongst men now, in the same manner as corn and wine are said to have been in the world in ancient time. For from the beginning there were vines and ears of corn growing here and there in the fields; but no care was taken for the planting and sowing of them. Men lived therefore upon acorns; or if any were so bold as to venture upon the eating of those unknown and doubtful fruits, they did it with danger of their health. In like manner, every man brought Philosophy, that is, Natural Reason, into the world with him; for all men can reason to some degree, and concerning some things: but where there is need of a long series of reasons, there most men wander out of the way, and fall into error for want of method, as it were for want of sowing and planting, that is, of improving their reason. And from hence it comes to pass, that they who content themselves with daily experience, which may be likened to feeding upon acorns, and either reject, or not much regard philosophy, are commonly esteemed, and are, indeed, men of sounder judgment than those who, from opinions, though not vulgar, yet full of uncertainty, and carelessly received, do nothing but dispute and wrangle, like men that are not well in their wits. I confess, indeed, that that part of philosophy by which magnitudes and figures are computed, is highly improved. But because I have not observed the like advancement in the other parts of it, my purpose is, as far forth as I am able, to lay open the few and first Elements of Philosophy in general, as so many

*From *De Corpore* (Molesworth Ed. 1839, Vol. I of English Works), Chapters 1-6.

seeds from which pure and true Philosophy may hereafter spring up by little and little.

I am not ignorant how hard a thing it is to weed out of men's minds such inveterate opinions as have taken root there, and been confirmed in them by the authority of most eloquent writers; especially seeing true (that is, accurate) Philosophy professedly rejects not only the paint and false colors of language, but even the very ornaments and graces of the same; and the first grounds of all science are not only not beautiful, but poor, arid, and, in appearance, deformed. Nevertheless, there being certainly some men, though but few, who are delighted with truth and strength of reason in all things, I thought I might do well to take this pains for the sake even of those few. I proceed therefore to the matter, and take my beginning from the very definition of philosophy, which is this.

2. Definition of Philosophy explained. Philosophy *is such knowledge of effects or appearances, as we acquire by true ratiocination from the knowledge we have first of their causes or generation: And again, of such causes or generations as may be from knowing first their effects.*

For the better understanding of which definition, we must consider, first, that although Sense and Memory of things, which are common to man and all living creatures, be knowledge, yet because they are given us immediately by nature, and not gotten by ratiocination, they are not philosophy.

Secondly, seeing Experience is nothing but memory; and Prudence, or prospect into the future time, nothing but expectation of such things as we have already had experience of, Prudence also is not to be esteemed philosophy.

By RATIOCINATION, I mean *computation.* Now to compute, is either to collect the sum of many things that are added together, or to know what remains when one thing is taken out of another. *Ratiocination, therefore, is the same with addition* and *subtraction;* and if any man add *multiplication* and *division,* I will not be against it, seeing multiplication is nothing but addition of equals one to another, and division nothing but a subtraction of equals one from another, as often as is possible. So that all ratiocination is comprehended in these two operations of the mind, addition and subtraction.

3. Ratiocination of the Mind. But how by the *ratiocination* of our mind, we add and subtract in our silent thoughts, without the use of words, it will be necessary for me to make intelligible by an example or two. If therefore a man see something afar off and obscurely, although no appellation had yet been given to anything, he will, notwithstanding, have the same idea of that thing for which now, by imposing a name on it, we call it *body*. Again, when, by coming nearer, he sees the same thing thus and thus, now in one place and now in another, he will have a new idea thereof, namely, that for which we now call such a thing *animated*. Thirdly, when standing nearer, he perceives the figure, hears the voice, and sees other things which are signs of a rational mind, he has a third idea, though it have yet no appellation, namely, that for which we now call anything *rational*. Lastly, when, by looking fully and distinctly upon it, he conceives all that he has seen as one thing, the idea he has now is compounded of his former ideas, which are put together in the mind in the same order in which these three single names, *body*, *animated*, *rational*, are in speech compounded into this one name, *body-animated-rational*, or *man*. In like manner, of the several conceptions of *four sides, equality of sides, and right angles*, is compounded the conception of a *square*. For the mind may conceive a figure of four sides without any conception of their equality, and of that equality without conceiving a right angle; and may join together all these single conceptions into one conception or one idea of a square. And thus we see how the conceptions of the mind are compounded. Again, whosoever sees a man standing near him, conceives the whole idea of that man; and if, as he goes away, he follow him with his eyes only, he will lose the idea of those things which were signs of his being rational, whilst, nevertheless, the idea of a body-animated remains still before his eyes, so that the idea of rational is subtracted from the whole idea of man, that is to say, of body-animated-rational, and there remains

that of body-animated; and a while after, at a greater distance, the idea of animated will be lost, and that of body only will remain; so that at last, when nothing at all can be seen, the whole idea will vanish out of sight. By which examples, I think, it is manifest enough what is the internal ratiocination of the mind without words.

We must not therefore think that computation, that is, ratiocination, has place only in numbers, as if man were distinguished from other living creatures (which is said to have been the opinion of *Pythagoras*) by nothing but the faculty of numbering; for *magnitude, body, motion, time, degrees of quality, action, conception, proportion, speech and names* (in which all the kinds of philosophy consist) are capable of addition and subtraction. Now such things as we add or subtract, that is, which we put into an account, we are said to *consider,* in Greek λογίζεσθαι, in which language also συλλογίζεσθαι signifies to *compute, reason,* or *reckon.*

4. Properties, what they are. But *effects* and the *appearances* of things to sense, are faculties or powers of bodies, which make us distinguish them from one another; that is to say, conceive one body to be equal or unequal, like or unlike to another body; as in the example above, when by coming near enough to any body, we perceive the motion and going of the same, we distinguish it thereby from a tree, a column, and other fixed bodies; and so that motion or going is the *property* thereof, as being proper to living creatures, and a faculty by which they make us distinguish them from other bodies.

5. How Properties are known by Generation and contrariety. How the knowledge of any effect may be gotten from the knowledge of the generation thereof, may easily be understood by the example of a circle: for if there be set before us a plain figure, having, as near as may be, the figure of a circle, we cannot possibly perceive by sense whether it be a true circle or no; than which, nevertheless, nothing is more easy to be known to him that knows first the generation of the propounded figure. For let it be known that the figure was made by the circumduction of a body whereof one end remained unmoved, and we may reason thus; a body carried

about, retaining always the same length, applies itself first to one *radius,* then to another, to a third, a fourth, and successively to all; and, therefore, the same length, from the same point, toucheth the circumference in every part thereof, which is as much as to say, as all the *radii* are equal. We know, therefore, that from such generation proceeds a figure, from whose one middle point all the extreme points are reached unto by equal *radii.* And in like manner, by knowing first what figure is set before us, we may come by ratiocination to some generation of the same, though perhaps not that by which it was made, yet that by which it might have been made; for he that knows that a circle has the property above declared, will easily know whether a body carried about, as is said, will generate a circle or no.

6. Scope of Philosophy. The *end* or *scope* of philosophy is, that we may make use to our benefit of effects formerly seen; or that, by application of bodies to one another, we may produce the like effects of those we conceive in our mind, as far forth as matter, strength, and industry, will permit, for the commodity of human life. For the inward glory and triumph of mind that a man may have for the mastering of some difficult and doubtful matter, or for the discovery of some hidden truth, is not worth so much pains as the study of Philosophy requires; nor need any man care much to teach another what he knows himself, if he think that will be the only benefit of his labor. The end of knowledge is power; and the use of theorems (which, among geometricians, serve for the finding out of properties) is for the construction of problems; and, lastly, the scope of all speculation is the performing of some action, or thing to be done.

7. Utility of Philosophy. But what the *utility* of philosophy is, especially of natural philosophy and geometry, will be best understood by reckoning up the chief commodities of which mankind is capable, and by comparing the manner of life of such as enjoy them, with that of others which want the same. Now, the greatest commodities of mankind are the arts; namely, of measuring matter and motion; of moving ponderous bodies; of architecture; of navigation; of making instruments for all uses; of calculating the celestial motions,

↳ Rejection of the classical position on the primacy of contemplation,

the aspects of the stars, and the parts of time; of geography, &c. By which sciences, how great benefits men receive is more easily understood than expressed. These benefits are enjoyed by almost all the people of Europe, by most of those of Asia, and by some of Africa: but the Americans, and they that live near the Poles, do totally want them. But why? Have they sharper wits than these? Have not all men one kind of soul, and the same faculties of mind? What, then, makes this difference, except philosophy? Philosophy, therefore, is the cause of all these benefits. But the utility of moral and civil philosophy is to be estimated, not so much by the commodities we have by knowing these sciences, as by the calamities we receive from not knowing them. Now, all such calamities as may be avoided by human industry, arise from war, but chiefly from civil war; for from this proceed slaughter, solitude, and the want of all things. But the cause of war is not that men are willing to have it; for the will has nothing for object but good, at least that which seemeth good. Nor is it from this, that men know not that the effects of war are evil; for who is there that thinks not poverty and loss of life to be great evils? The cause, therefore, of civil war is, that men know not the causes neither of war nor peace, there being but few in the world that have learned those duties which unite and keep men in peace, that is to say, that have learned the rules of civil life sufficiently. Now, the knowledge of these rules is moral philosophy. But why have they not learned them, unless for this reason, that none hitherto have taught them in a clear and exact method? For what shall we say? Could the ancient masters of Greece, Egypt, Rome, and others, persuade the unskilful multitude to their innumerable opinions concerning the nature of their gods, which they themselves knew not whether they were true or false, and which were indeed manifestly false and absurd; and could they not persuade the same multitude to civil duty, if they themselves had understood it? Or shall those few writings of geometricians which are extant, be thought sufficient for the taking away of all controversy in the matters they treat of, and shall those innumerable and huge volumes of *ethics* be thought unsufficient, if what they teach had been certain and well demonstrated? What, then, can be imagined to be the cause that the writings of those men have increased science, and the writings of these have increased nothing but words, saving that the former were written by men that knew, and the latter by such as knew not, the doctrine they taught only for ostentation of their wit and eloquence? Nevertheless, I deny not but the reading of some such books is very delightful; for they are most eloquently written, and contain many clear, wholesome and choice sentences, which yet are not universally true, though by them universally pronounced. From whence it comes to pass, that the circumstances of times, places, and persons being changed, they are no less frequently made use of to confirm wicked men in their purposes, than to make them understand the precepts of civil duties. Now that which is chiefly wanting in them, is a true and certain rule of our actions, by which we might know whether that we undertake be just or unjust. For it is to no purpose to be bidden in every thing to do right, before there be a certain rule and measure of right established, which no man hitherto hath established. Seeing, therefore, from the not knowing of civil duties, that is, from the want of moral science, proceed civil wars, and the greatest calamities of mankind, we may very well attribute to such science the production of the contrary commodities. And thus much is sufficient, to say nothing of the praises and other contentment proceeding from philosophy, to let you see the utility of the same in every kind thereof.

8. Subject of Philosophy. The *subject* of Philosophy, or the matter it treats of, is every body of which we can conceive any generation, and which we may, by any consideration thereof, compare with other bodies, or which is capable of composition and resolution; that is to say, every body of whose generation or properties we can have any knowledge. And this may be deduced from the definition of philosophy, whose profession it is to search out the properties of bodies from their generation, or their generation from their properties; and, therefore, where there is no generation or property, there is no philosophy. Therefore it excludes *Theology*, I mean the doctrine of God, eternal, ingenerable, incompre-

hensible, and in whom there is nothing neither to divide nor compound, nor any generation to be conceived.

It excludes the doctrine of *angels*, and all such things as are thought to be neither bodies nor properties of bodies; there being in them no place neither for composition nor division, nor any capacity of more and less, that is to say, no place for ratiocination.

It excludes *history*, as well *natural* as *political*, though most useful (nay necessary) to philosophy; because such knowledge is but experience, or authority, and not ratiocination.

It excludes all such knowledge as is acquired by Divine inspiration, or revelation, as not derived to us by reason, but by Divine grace in an instant, and, as it were, by some sense supernatural.

It excludes not only all doctrines which are false, but such also as are not well-grounded; for whatsoever we know by right ratiocination, can neither be false nor doubtful; and, therefore, *astrology*, as it is now held forth, and all such divinations rather than sciences, are excluded.

Lastly, the doctrine of *God's worship* is excluded from philosophy, as being not to be known by natural reason, but by the authority of the Church; and as being the object of faith, and not of knowledge.

9. Parts of Philosophy. The principal parts of philosophy are two. For two chief kinds of bodies, and very different from one another, offer themselves to such as search after their generation and properties; one whereof being the work of nature, is called a *natural body*, the other is called a *commonwealth*, and is made by the wills and agreement of men. And from these spring the two parts of philosophy, called *natural* and *civil*. But seeing that, for the knowledge of the properties of a commonwealth, it is necessary first to know the dispositions, affections, and manners of men, civil philosophy is again commonly divided into two parts, whereof one, which treats of men's dispositions and manners, is called *ethics;* and the other, which takes cognizance of their civil duties, is called *politics*, or simply *civil philosophy*. In the first place, therefore (after I have set down such premises as appertain to the nature of philosophy in general),

I will discourse of *bodies natural;* in the second, of the *dispositions and manners of men;* and in the third, of the *civil duties of subjects.*

10. Epilogue. To conclude; seeing there may be many who will not like this my definition of philosophy, and will say, that, from the liberty which a man may take of so defining as seems best to himself, he may conclude any thing from any thing (though I think it no hard matter to demonstrate that this definition of mine agrees with the sense of all men); yet, lest in this point there should be any cause of dispute betwixt me and them, I here undertake no more than to deliver the elements of that science by which the effects of anything may be found out from the known generation of the same, or contrarily, the generation from the effects; to the end that they who search after other philosophy, may be admonished to seek it from other principles.

Chapter 2

Of Names

1. **Necessity of sensible Moniments or Marks for the help of Memory: a Mark defined.** How unconstant and fading men's thoughts are, and how much the recovery of them depends upon chance, there is none but knows by infallible experience in himself. For no man is able to remember quantities without sensible and present measures, nor colors without sensible and present patterns, nor number without the names of numbers disposed in order and learned by heart. So that whatsoever a man has put together in his mind by ratiocination without such helps, will presently slip from him, and not be revocable but by beginning his ratiocination anew. From which it follows, that, for the acquiring of philosophy, some sensible moniments are necessary, by which our past thoughts may be not only reduced, but also registered every one in its own order. These moniments I call MARKS, namely, sensible things taken at pleasure, that, by the sense of them, such thoughts may be recalled to our mind as are like those thoughts for which we took them.

2. **Necessity of Marks for the signification of the conceptions of the Mind.** Again, though some one man, of how excellent a wit soever, should spend all his time partly in reasoning, and partly in inventing marks for the help of his memory, and advancing himself in learning; who sees not that the benefit he reaps to himself will not be much, and to others none at all? For unless he communicate his notes with others, his science will perish with him. But if the same notes be made common to many, and so one man's inventions be taught to others, sciences will thereby be increased to the general good of mankind. It is therefore necessary, for the acquiring of philosophy, that there be certain

signs, by which what one man finds out may be manifested and made known to others. Now, those things we call SIGNS are the *antecedents of their consequents, and the consequents of their antecedents, as often as we observe them to go before or follow after in the same manner.* For example, a thick cloud is a sign of rain to follow, and rain a sign that a cloud has gone before, for this reason only, that we seldom see clouds without the consequence of rain, nor rain at any time but when a cloud has gone before. And of signs, some are *natural,* whereof I have already given an example, others are *arbitrary,* namely, those we make choice of at our own pleasure, as a bush hung up, signifies that wine is to be sold there; a stone set in the ground signifies the bound of a field; and words so and so connected, signify the cogitations and motions of our mind. The difference, therefore, betwixt marks and signs is this, that we make those for our own use, but these for the use of others.

3. Names supply both those necessities. Words so connected as that they become signs of our thoughts, are called SPEECH, of which every part is a *name.* But seeing (as is said) both marks and signs are necessary for the acquiring of philosophy (marks by which we may remember our own thoughts, and signs by which we may make our thoughts known to others), names do both these offices; but they serve for marks before they be used as signs. For though a man were alone in the world, they would be useful to him in helping him to remember; but to teach others, (unless there were some others to be taught) of no use at all. Again, names, though standing singly by themselves, are marks, because they serve to recall our own thoughts to mind; but they cannot be signs, otherwise than by being disposed and ordered in speech as parts of the same. For example, a man may begin with a word, whereby the hearer may frame an idea of something in his mind, which, nevertheless, he cannot conceive to be the idea which was in the mind of him that spake, but that he would say something which began with that word, though perhaps not as by itself, but as part of another word. So that the nature of a name consists principally in this, that it is a

mark taken for memory's sake; but it serves also by accident to signify and make known to others what we remember ourselves, and, therefore, I will define it thus:

4. Definition of a Name. *A* NAME *is a word taken at pleasure to serve for a mark, which may raise in our mind a thought like to some thought we had before, and which being pronounced to others, may be to them a sign of what thought the speaker had, or had not before in his mind.* And it is for brevity's sake that I suppose the original of names to be arbitrary, judging it a thing that may be assumed as unquestionable. For considering that new names are daily made, and old ones laid aside; that diverse nations use different names, and how impossible it is either to observe similitude, or make any comparison betwixt a name and a thing, how can any man imagine that the names of things were imposed from their natures? For though some names of living creatures and other things, which our first parents used, were taught by God himself; yet they were by him arbitrarily imposed, and afterwards, both at the Tower of Babel, and since, in process of time, growing everywhere out of use, are quite forgotten, and in their room have succeeded others, invented and received by men at pleasure. Moreover, whatsoever the common use of words be, yet philosophers, who were to teach their knowledge to others, had always the liberty, and sometimes they both had and will have a necessity, of taking to themselves such names as they please for the signifying of their meaning, if they would have it understood. Nor had mathematicians need to ask leave of any but themselves to name the figures they invented, *parabolas, hyperboles, cissoeides, quadratices,* &c. or to call one magnitude A, another B.

5. Names are signs not of things, but of our cogitations. But seeing names ordered in speech (as is defined) are signs of our conceptions, it is manifest they are not signs of the things themselves; for that the sound of this word *stone* should be the sign of a stone, cannot be understood in any sense but this, that he that hears it collects that he that pronounces it thinks of a stone. And, therefore, that disputation, whether names signify the matter or form, or something com-

pounded of both, and other like subtleties of the *metaphysics*, is kept up by erring men, and such as understand not the words they dispute about.

6. What it is we give names to. Nor, indeed, is it at all necessary that every name should be the name of something. For as these, a *man*, a *tree*, a *stone*, are the names of the things themselves, so the images of a man, of a tree, and of a stone, which are represented to men sleeping, have their names also, though they be not things, but only fictions and phantasms of things. For we can remember these; and, therefore, it is no less necessary that they have names to mark and signify them, than the things themselves. Also this word *future* is a name, but no future thing has yet any being, nor do we know whether that which we call future, shall ever have a being or no. Nevertheless, seeing we use in our mind to knit together things past with those that are present, the name *future* serves to signify such knitting together. Moreover, that which neither is, nor has been, nor ever shall, or ever can be, has a name, namely, *that which neither is nor has been*, &c.; or more briefly this, *impossible*. To conclude; this word *nothing* is a name, which yet cannot be the name of any thing: for when, for example, we subtract 2 and 3 from 5, and so nothing remaining, we would call that subtraction to mind, this speech *nothing remains*, and in it the word *nothing* is not unuseful. And for the same reason we say truly, *less than nothing* remains, when we subtract more from less; for the mind feigns such remains as these for doctrine's sake, and desires, as often as is necessary, to call the same to memory. But seeing every name has some relation to that which is named, though that which we name be not always a thing that has a being in nature, yet it is lawful for doctrine's sake to apply the word *thing* to whatsoever we name; as if it were all one whether that thing be truly existent, or be only feigned.

7. Names Positive and Negative. The first distinction of names is, that some are *positive*, or *affirmative*, others *negative*, which are also called *privative* and *indefinite*. Positive are such as we impose for the likeness, equality, or identity of the things we consider; *negative*, for the diversity, unlike-

ness, or inequality of the same. Examples of the former are, *a man, a philosopher;* for a *man* denotes any one of a multitude of men, and a *philosopher*, any one of many philosophers, by reason of their similitude; also, *Socrates* is a positive name, because it signifies always one and the same man. Examples of *negatives* are such positives as have the negative particle *not* added to them, as *not-man, not-philosopher*. But positives were before negatives; for otherwise there could have been no use at all of these. For when the name of *white* was imposed upon certain things, and afterwards upon other things, the names of *black, blue, transparent,* &c. the infinite dissimilitudes of these with *white* could not be comprehended in any one name, save that which had in it the negation of white, that is to say, the name *not-white,* or some other equivalent to it, in which the word *white* is repeated, such as *unlike to white,* &c. And by these *negative names,* we take notice ourselves, and signify to others what we have not thought of.

8. Contradictory names. Positive and negative names are *contradictory* to one another, so that they cannot both be the name of the same thing. Besides, of contradictory names, one is the name of anything whatsoever; for whatsoever is, is either man, or not-man, white or not-white, and so of the rest. And this is so manifest, that it needs no farther proof or explication; for they that say *the same thing cannot both be, and not be,* speak obscurely; but they that say, *whatsoever is, either is, or is not,* speak also absurdly and ridiculously. The certainty of this axiom, viz. *of two contradictory names, one is the name of anything whatsoever, the other not,* is the original and foundation of all ratiocination, that is, of all philosophy; and therefore it ought to be so exactly propounded, that it may be of itself clear and perspicuous to all men; as indeed it is, saving to such, as reading the long discourses made upon this subject by the writers of *metaphysics* (which they believe to be some egregious learning) think they understand not, when they do.

9. A common name. Secondly, of names, some are *common* to many things, as a *man, a tree;* others *proper* to one thing, as *he that writ the Iliad, Homer, this man, that man.*

And a common name, being the name of many things severally taken, but not collectively of all together (as man is not the name of all mankind, but of every one, as of Peter, John, and the rest severally) is therefore called a *universal name;* and therefore this word *universal* is never the name of any thing existent in nature, nor of any idea or phantasm formed in the mind, but always the name of some word or name; so that when *a living creature, a stone, a spirit,* or any other thing, is said to be *universal,* it is not to be understood, that any man, stone, &c. ever was or can be universal, but only that these words, *living creature, stone,* &c. are *universal names,* that is, names common to many things; and the conceptions answering them in our mind, are the images and phantasms of several living creatures, or other things. And therefore, for the understanding of the extent of a universal name, we need no other faculty but that of our imagination, by which we remember that such names bring sometimes one thing, sometimes another, into our mind. Also of common names, some are more, some less common. *More common,* is that which is the name of more things; *less common,* the name of fewer things; as *living creature* is more common than *man,* or *horse,* or *lion,* because it comprehends them all: and therefore a more common name, in respect of a less common, is called the *genus,* or a *general name;* and this in respect of that, the *species,* or a *special name.*

10. Names of the first and second intention. And from hence proceeds the third distinction of names, which is, that some are called names of the *first,* others of the *second intention.* Of the *first intention* are the names of things, a *man, stone,* &c.: of the *second* are the names of names and speeches, as *universal, particular, genus, species, syllogism,* and the like. But it is hard to say why those are called names of the *first,* and these of the *second intention,* unless perhaps it was first intended by us to give names to those things which are of daily use in this life, and afterwards to such things as appertain to science, that is, that our second intention was to give names to names. But whatsoever the cause hereof may be, yet this is manifest, that *genus, species, definition,* &c., are names of words and names only; and there-

fore to put *genus* and *species* for things, and *definition* for the nature of any thing, as the writers of *metaphysics* have done, is not right, seeing they be only significations of what we think of the nature of things.

11. Universal, particular, individual, and indefinite names. Fourthly, some names are of *certain* and *determined*, others of *uncertain* and *undetermined* signification. Of *determined* and *certain* signification is, first, that name which is given to any one thing by itself, and is called an *individual name;* as *Homer, this tree, that living creature,* &c. Secondly that which has any of these words, *all, every, both, either,* or the like added to it; and it is therefore called a universal name. because it signifies every one of those things to which it is common; and of *certain* signification for this reason, that he which hears, conceives in his mind the same thing that he which speaks would have him conceive. Of *indefinite* signification is, first, that name which has the word *some,* or the like added to it, and is called a *particular name;* secondly, a common name set by itself without any note either of universality or particularity, as *man, stone,* and is called an *indefinite name;* but both *particular* and *indefinite* names are of uncertain signification, because the hearer knows not what thing it is the speaker would have him conceive; and therefore in speech, particular and indefinite names are to be esteemed equivalent to one another. But these words, *all, every, some,* &c. which denote universality and particularity, are not names, but parts only of names; so that *every man,* and *that man which the hearer conceives in his mind,* are all one; and *some man,* and *that man which the speaker thought of,* signify the same. From whence it is evident, that the use of signs of this kind, is not for a man's own sake, or for his getting of knowledge by his own private meditation (for every man has his own thoughts sufficiently determined without such helps as these) but for the sake of others; that is, for the teaching and signifying of our conceptions to others; nor were they invented only to make us remember, but to make us able to discourse with others.

12. Names univocal and equivocal. Fifthly, names are

usually distinguished into *univocal* and *equivocal*. *Univocal* are those which in the same train of discourse signify always the same thing; but *equivocal* those which mean sometimes one thing and sometimes another. Thus, the name *triangle* is said to be *univocal*, because it is always taken in the same sense; and *parabola* to be *equivocal*, for the signification it has sometimes of allegory or similitude, and sometimes of a certain geometrical figure. Also every *metaphor* is by profession *equivocal*. But this distinction belongs not so much to names, as to those that use names, for some use them properly and accurately for the finding out of truth; others draw them from their proper sense, for ornament or deceit.

13. Absolute and relative names. Sixthly, of names, some are *absolute*, others *relative*. *Relative* are such as are imposed for some comparison, as *father, son, cause, effect, like, unlike, equal, unequal, master, servant,* &c. And those that signify no comparison at all are *absolute names*. But, as it was noted above, that universality is to be attributed to words and names only, and not to things, so the same is to be said of other distinctions of names; for no things are either *univocal* or *equivocal*, or *relative* or *absolute*. There is also another distinction of names into *concrete* and *abstract;* but because abstract names proceed from proposition, and can have no place where there is no affirmation, I shall speak of them hereafter.

14. Simple and compounded names. Lastly, there are *simple* and *compounded names*. But here it is to be noted, that a name is not taken in philosophy, as in grammar, for one single word, but for any number of words put together to signify one thing; for among philosophers *sentient animated body* passes but for one name, being the name of every living creature, which yet, among grammarians, is accounted three names. Also a *simple name* is not here distinguished from a *compounded name* by a preposition, as in grammar. But I call a *simple name*, that which in every kind is the most common or most universal; and that a *compounded name*, which by the joining of another name to it, is made less universal, and signifies that more conceptions than one were

in the mind, for which that latter name was added. For example, in the conception of *man* (as is shown in the former chapter). First, he is conceived to be something that has extension, which is marked by the word *body*. *Body*, therefore, is a *simple name*, being put for that first single conception; afterwards, upon the sight of such and such motion, another conception arises, for which he is called an *animated body;* and this I here call a *compounded name*, as I do also the name *animal*, which is equivalent to an *animated body*. And, in the same manner, an *animated rational body*, as also a *man*, which is equivalent to it, is a more compounded name. And by this we see how the composition of conceptions in the mind is answerable to the composition of names; for, as in the mind one idea or phantasm succeeds to another, and to this a third; so to one name is added another and another successively, and of them all is made one *compounded* name. Nevertheless we must not think bodies which are without the mind, are compounded in the same manner, namely, that there is in nature a body, or any other imaginable thing existent, which at the first has no magnitude, and then, by the addition of magnitude, comes to have quantity, and by more or less quantity to have density or rarity; and again, by the addition of figure, to be figurate, and after this, by the injection of light or color, to become lucid or colored; though such has been the philosophy of many.

15. *A predicament described.* The writers of *logic* have endeavored to digest the names of all the kinds of things into certain *scales* or degrees, by the continual subordination of names less common, to names more common. In the scale of *bodies* they put in the first and highest place *body* simply, and in the next place under it less common names, by which it may be more limited and determined, namely *animated* and *inanimated*, and so on till they come to *individuals*. In like manner, in the scale of *quantities*, they assign the first place to *quantity*, and the next to *line, superficies*, and *solid*, which are names of less latitude; and these orders or scales of names they usually call *predicaments* and *categories*. And of this ordination not only positive, but negative names also are

capable; which may be exemplified by such forms of the predicaments as follow:

THE FORM OF THE PREDICAMENT OF BODY

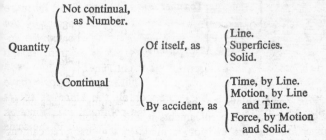

Not-Body, or
  Accident.

Body
  { Not animated.
  { Animated
      { Not living Creature.
      { Living Creature
          { Not Man.
          { Man
              { Not Peter.
              { Peter.

Both Accident and Body are considered
  { Absolutely, as { Quantity, or so much.
                   { Quality, or such.
  { or
  { Comparatively, which is called their Relation.

THE FORM OF THE PREDICAMENT OF QUANTITY

Quantity
  { Not continual, as Number.
  { Continual
      { Of itself, as { Line.
                      { Superficies.
                      { Solid.
      { By accident, as { Time, by Line.
                        { Motion, by Line and Time.
                        { Force, by Motion and Solid.

Where, it is to be noted, that *line, superficies,* and *solid,* may be said to be of such and such quantity, that is, to be originally and of their own nature capable of equality and inequality; but we cannot say there is either majority or minority, or equality, or indeed any quantity at all, in *time,* without the help of *line* and *motion;* nor in *motion,* without *line* and *time;* nor in *force,* otherwise than by *motion* and *solid.*

THE FORM OF THE PREDICAMENT OF QUALITY

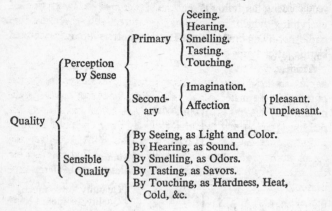

THE FORM OF THE PREDICAMENT OF RELATION

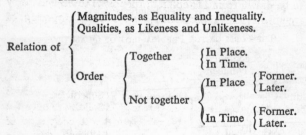

16. **Some things to be noted concerning predicaments.** Concerning which predicaments it is to be noted, in the first place, that as the division is made in the first predicament into contradictory names, so it might have been done in the rest. For, as there, *body* is divided into *animated* and *not-animated,* so, in the second predicament, *continual quantity* may be divided into *line* and *not-line,* and again, *not-line* into *superficies* and *not-superficies,* and so in the rest; but it was not necessary.

Secondly, it is to be observed, that of *positive* names the former comprehends the latter; but of *negatives* the former is comprehended by the latter. For example, *living-creature* is the name of every man, and therefore it comprehends the name *man;* but, on the contrary, *not-man* is the name of everything which is not-living-creature, and therefore the name *not-living-creature,* which is put first, is comprehended by the latter name *not-man.*

Thirdly, we must take heed that we do not think, that as names, so the diversities of things themselves may be searched out and determined by such distinctions as these; or that arguments may be taken from hence (as some have done ridiculously) to prove that the kinds of things are not infinite.

Fourthly, I would not have any man think I deliver the forms above for a true and exact ordination of names; for this cannot be performed as long as philosophy remains imperfect; nor that by placing (for example) *light* in the predicament of *qualities,* while another places the same in the predicament of bodies, I pretend that either of us ought for this to be drawn from his opinion; for this is to be done only by arguments and ratiocination, and not by disposing of words into *classes.*

Lastly, I confess I have not yet seen any great use of the predicaments in philosophy. I believe *Aristotle* when he saw he could not digest the things themselves into such orders, might nevertheless desire out of his own authority to reduce words to such forms, as I have done; but I do it only for this end, that it may be understood what this ordination of words is, and not to have it received for true, till it be demonstrated by good reason to be so.

Chapter 3

Of Proposition

1. **Divers kinds of speech.** From the connection or contexture of names arise divers kinds of speech, whereof some signify the desires and affections of men; such are, first, *interrogations*, which denote the desire of knowing: as, *Who is a good man?* In which speech there is one name expressed, and another desired and expected from him of whom we ask the same. Then *prayers*, which signify the desire of having something; *promises, threats, wishes, commands, complaints*, and other significations of other affections. Speech may also be absurd and insignificant; as when there is a succession of words, to which there can be no succession of thoughts in mind to answer them; and this happens often to such, as, understanding nothing in some subtle matter, do, nevertheless, to make others believe they understand, speak of the same incoherently; for the connection of incoherent words, though it want the end of speech (which is signification) yet it is speech; and is used by writers of *metaphysics* almost as frequently as speech significative. In philosophy, there is but one kind of speech useful, which some call in Latin *dictum*, others *enuntiatum et pronunciatum;* but most men call it *proposition*, and is the speech of those that affirm or deny, and expresseth truth or falsity.

2. **Proposition defined.** *A* PROPOSITION *is a speech consisting of two names copulated, by which he that speaketh signifies he conceives the latter name to be the name of the same thing whereof the former is the name; or* (which is all one) *that the former name is comprehended by the latter.* For example, this speech, *man is a living creature*, in which two names are copulated by the verb, *is*, is a *proposition*, for this reason, that he that speaks it conceives both *living creature* and *man* to be names of the same thing, or that the former

name, *man,* is comprehended by the latter name, *living crea-ture.* Now the former name is commonly called the *subject,* or *antecedent,* or the *contained name,* and the latter the *predi-cate, consequent,* or *containing name.* The sign of connection amongst most nations is either some word, as the word *is* in the proposition *man is a living creature,* or some case or termination of a word, as in this proposition, *man walketh* (which is equivalent to this, *man is walking*); the termination by which it is said he *walketh,* rather than he *is walking,* sig-nifieth that those two are understood to be copulated, or to be names of the same thing.

But there are, or certainly may be, some nations that have no word which answers to our verb *is,* who nevertheless form propositions by the position only of one name after another, as if instead of *man is a living creature,* it should be said *man a living creature;* for the very order of the names may sufficiently show their connection; and they are as apt and useful in philosophy, as if they were copulated by the verb *is.*

3. Subject, predicate, and copula, what they are, and ab-stract and concrete what. Wherefore, in every proposition three things are to be considered, *viz.* the two names, which are the *subject,* and the *predicate,* and their *copulation;* both which names raise in our mind the thought of one and the same thing; but the copulation makes us think of the cause for which those names were imposed on that thing. As, for example, when we say *a body is moveable,* though we con-ceive the same thing to be designed by both those names, yet our mind rests not there, but searches farther what it is *to be a body,* or *to be moveable,* that is, wherein consists the dif-ference betwixt these and other things, for which these are so called, others are not so called. They, therefore, that seek what it is *to be* any thing, as *to be moveable, to be hot, &c.* seek in things the causes of their names.

And from hence arises that distinction of names (touched in the last chapter) into *concrete* and *abstract.* For *concrete* is the name of any thing which we suppose to have a being, and is therefore called the *subject,* in Latin *suppositum,* and in Greek ὑποκείμενον; as *body, moveable, moved, figurate, a cubit high, hot, cold, like, equal, Appius, Lentulus,* and the like; and, *abstract* is that which in any subject denotes the cause of the concrete name, as *to be a body, to be moveable, to be moved, to be figurate, to be of such quantity, to be hot, to be cold, to be like, to be equal, to be Appius, to be Lentulus,* &c. Or names equivalent to these, which are most commonly called *abstract* names, as *corporiety, mobility, motion, figure, quantity, heat, cold, likeness, equality,* and (as Cicero has it) *Appiety* and *Lentulity.* Of the same kind also are infinitives; for *to live* and *to move* are the same with *life* and *motion,* or *to be living* and *to be moved.* But *abstract names* denote only the causes of *concrete names,* and not the things themselves. For example, when we see any thing, or conceive in our mind any visible thing, that thing appears to us, or is conceived by us, not in one point, but as having parts distant from one another, that is, as being extended and filling some space. Seeing therefore we call the thing so conceived *body,* the cause of that name is, that that thing is *extended,* or the *extension* or *corporiety* of it. So when we see a thing appear sometimes here, sometimes there, and call it *moved* or *removed,* the cause of that name is that it *is moved* or the *motion* of the same.

And these causes of names are the same with the causes of our conceptions, namely, some power of action, or affection of the thing conceived, which some call the manner by which any thing works upon our senses, but by most men they are called *accidents;* I say accidents, not in that sense in which accident is opposed to necessary; but so, as being neither the things themselves, nor parts thereof, do nevertheless accompany the things in such manner, that (saving extension) they may all perish, and be destroyed, but can never be abstracted.

4. *The use and abuse of names abstract.* There is also this difference betwixt *concrete* and *abstract* names, that those were invented before propositions, but these after; for these could have no being till there were propositions, from whose *copula* they proceed. Now in all matters that concern this life, but chiefly in philosophy, there is both great use and great abuse of *abstract names;* and the use consists in this, that without them we cannot, for the most part, either rea-

son, or compute the properties of bodies; for when we would multiply, divide, add, or subtract heat, light, or motion, if we should double or add them together by concrete names, saying (for example) hot is double to hot, light double to light, or moved double to moved, we should not double the properties, but the bodies themselves that are hot, light, moved, &c. which we would not do. But the abuse proceeds from this, that some men seeing they can consider, that is (as I said before) bring into account the increasings and decreasings of quantity, heat and other accidents, without considering their bodies or subjects (which they call *abstracting,* or making to exist apart by themselves) they speak of accidents, as if they might be separated from all bodies. And from hence proceed the gross errors of writers of metaphysics; for, because they can consider thought without the consideration of body, they infer there is no need of a thinking-body; and because quantity may be considered without considering body, they think also that quantity may be without body, and body without quantity; and that a body has quantity by the addition of quantity to it. From the same fountain spring those insignificant words, *abstract substance, separated essence,* and the like; as also that confusion of words derived from the Latin verb *est,* as *essence, essentiality, entity, entitative;* besides *reality, aliquiddity, quiddity, &c.* which could never have been heard of among such nations as do not copulate their names by the very *is,* but by adjective verbs, as runneth, readeth, &c. or by the mere placing of one name after another; and yet seeing such nations compute and reason, it is evident that philosophy has no need of those words *essence, entity,* and other the like barbarous terms.

5. *Proposition, universal and particular.* There are many distinctions of propositions, whereof the first is, that some are *universal,* others *particular,* others *indefinite,* and others *singular;* and this is commonly called the distinction of *quantity.* A *universal* proposition is that whose subject is affected with the sign of a universal name, as *every man is a living creature. Particular,* that whose subject is affected with the sign of a particular name, as *some man is learned.*

An *indefinite* proposition has for its subject a common name, and put without any sign, as *man is a living creature, man is learned*. And a *singular* proposition is that whose subject is a singular name, as *Socrates is a philosopher, this man is black*.

6. Affirmative and negative. The second distinction is into *affirmative* and *negative,* and is called the distinction of *quality*. An *affirmative* proposition is that whose predicate is a positive name, as *man is a living creature. Negative,* that whose predicate is a negative name, as *man is not a stone.*

7. True & false. The third distinction is, that one is *true,* another *false.* A *true* proposition is that, whose predicate contains, or comprehends its subject, or whose predicate is the name of every thing, of which the subject is the name; as *man is a living creature* is therefore a true proposition, because whatsoever is called *man,* the same is also called *living creature;* and *some man is sick,* is true, because *sick* is the name of *some man.* That which is not true, or that whose predicate does not contain its subject, is called a *false* proposition, as *man is a stone.*

Now these words *true, truth,* and *true proposition,* are equivalent to one another; for truth consists in speech, and not in the things spoken of; and though *true* be sometimes opposed to *apparent* or *feigned,* yet it is always to be referred to the truth of proposition; for the image of a man in a glass, or a ghost, is therefore denied to be a very man, because this proposition, *a ghost is a man,* is not true; for it cannot be denied but that a ghost is a very ghost. And therefore truth or verity is not any affection of the thing, but of the proposition concerning it. As for that which the writers of metaphysics say, that *a thing, one thing,* and *a very thing,* are equivalent to one another, it is but trifling and childish; for who does not know, that *a man, one man,* and *a very man,* signify the same.

8. True & false belongs to speech, and not to things. And from hence it is evident, that truth and falsity have no place but amongst such living creatures as use speech. For though some brute creatures, looking upon the image of a man in a

glass, may be affected with it, as if it were the man himself, and for this reason fear it or fawn upon it in vain; yet they do not apprehend it as true or false, but only as like; and in this they are not deceived. Wherefore, as men owe all their true ratiocination to the right understanding of speech; so also they owe their errors to the misunderstanding of the same; and as all the ornaments of philosophy proceed only from man, so from man also is derived the ugly absurdity of false opinions. For speech has something in it like to a spider's web, (as it was said of old of *Solon's* laws) for by contexture of words tender and delicate wits are ensnared and stopped; but strong wits break easily through them.

From hence also this may be deduced, that the first truths were arbitrarily made by those that first of all imposed names upon things, or received them from the imposition of others. For it is true (for example) that *man is a living creature,* but it is for this reason, that it pleased men to impose both those names on the same thing.

9. Proposition, primary, not primary, definition, axiom, petition. Fourthly, propositions are distinguished into *primary* and *not primary. Primary* is that wherein the subject is explicated by a predicate of many names, as *man is a body, animated, rational;* for that which is comprehended in the name *man,* is more largely expressed in the names *body, animated,* and *rational,* joined together; and it is called *primary,* because it is first in ratiocination; for nothing can be proved, without understanding first the name of the thing in question. Now *primary* propositions are nothing but definitions, or parts of definitions, and these only are the principles of demonstration, being truths constituted arbitrarily by the inventors of speech, and therefore not to be demonstrated. To these propositions, some have added others, which they call *primary* and *principles,* namely, *axioms,* and *common notions;* which, (though they be so evident that they need no proof) yet, because they may be proved, are not truly principles; and the less to be received for such, in regard propositions not intelligible, and sometimes manifestly false, are thrust on us under the name of *principles* by the clamor of men, who ob-

trude for evident to others, all that they themselves think true. Also certain petitions are commonly received into the number of principles; as, for example, *that a straight line may be drawn between two points,* and other petitions of the writers of geometry; and these are indeed the principles of art or construction, but not of science and demonstration.

10. Proposition necessary & contingent. Fifthly, propositions are distinguished into *necessary,* that is, necessarily true; and true, but not necessarily, which they call *contingent.* A *necessary* proposition is when nothing can at any time be conceived or feigned, whereof the subject is the name, but the predicate also is the name of the same thing; as *man is a living creature* is a necessary proposition, because at what time soever we suppose the name *man* agrees with any thing, at that time the name *living-creature* also agrees with the same. But a *contingent* proposition is that, which at one time may be true, at another time false; as *every crow is black;* which may perhaps be true now, but false hereafter. Again, in every *necessary* proposition, the predicate is either equivalent to the subject, as in this, *man is a rational living creature;* or part of an equivalent name, as in this, *man is a living creature,* for the name *rational-living-creature,* or *man,* is compounded of these two, *rational* and *living-creature.* But in a *contingent* proposition this cannot be; for though this were true, *every man is a liar,* yet because the word *liar* is no part of a compounded name equivalent to the name *man,* that proposition is not to be called *necessary,* but *contingent,* though it should happen to be true always. And therefore those propositions only are *necessary,* which are of sempiternal truth, that is, true at all times. From hence also it is manifest, that truth adheres not to things, but to speech only, for some truths are eternal; for it will be eternally true, *if man, then living-creature;* but that any *man,* or *living-creature,* should exist eternally, is not necessary.

11. Categorical & hypothetical. A sixth distinction of propositions is into *categorical* and *hypothetical.* A *categorical* proposition is that which is simply or absolutely pronounced, as *every man is a living-creature, no man is a tree;* and *hypo-*

thetical is that which is pronounced conditionally, as, *if any thing be a man, the same is also a living-creature, if any thing be a man, the same is also not-a-stone.*

A *categorical* proposition, and a *hypothetical* answering it, do both signify the same, if the propositions be necessary; but not if they be contingent. For example, if this, *every man is a living-creature,* be true, this also will be true, *if any thing be a man, the same is also a living-creature;* but in contingent propositions, though this be true, *every crow is black,* yet this, *if any thing be a crow, the same is black,* is false. But a *hypothetical* proposition is then rightly said to be true, when the consequence is true, as *every man is a living-creature,* is rightly said to be a true proposition, because of whatsoever it is truly said *that is a man,* it cannot but be truly said also, *the same is a living creature.* And therefore whensoever a *hypothetical proposition* is true, the *categorical* answering it, is not only true, but also necessary; which I thought worth the noting, as an argument, that philosophers may in most things reason more solidly by *hypothetical* than *categorical* propositions.

12. The same proposition diversely pronounced. But seeing every proposition may be, and used to be, pronounced and written in many forms, and we are obliged to speak in the same manner as most men speak, yet they that learn philosophy from masters, had need to take heed they be not deceived by the variety of expressions. And therefore, whensoever they meet with any obscure proposition, they ought to reduce it to its most simple and categorical form; in which the copulative word *is* must be expressed by itself, and not mingled in any manner either with the subject or predicate, both which must be separated and clearly distinguished one from another. For example, if this proposition, *man can not sin,* be compared with this, *man cannot sin,* their difference will easily appear if they be reduced to these, *man is able not to sin,* and, *man is not able to sin,* where the predicates are manifestly different. But they ought to do this silently by themselves, or betwixt them and their masters only; for it will be thought both ridiculous and absurd, for a man to use such

language publicly. Being therefore to speak of *equipollent* propositions, I put in the first place all those for *equipollent*, that may be reduced purely to one and the same categorical proposition.

13. Propositions that may be reduced to the same categorical proposition, are equipollent. Secondly, that which is categorical and necessary, is *equipollent* to its hypothetical proposition; as this categorical, *a right-lined triangle has its three angles equal to two right angles,* to this hypothetical, *if any figure be a right-lined triangle, the three angles of it are equal to two right angles.*

14. Universal propositions converted by contradictory names, are equipollent. Also, any two universal propositions, of which the terms of the one (that is, the subject and predicate) are contradictory to the terms of the other, and their order inverted, as these, *every man is a living creature,* and *every thing that is not a living-creature is not a man,* are *equipollent.* For seeing *every man is a living creature* is a true proposition, the name *living creature* contains the name *man;* but they are both positive names, and therefore (by the last article of the precedent chapter) the negative name *not man,* contains the negative name *not living-creature;* wherefore *every thing that is not a living-creature, is not a man,* is a true proposition. Likewise these, *no man is a tree, no tree is a man,* are *equipollent.* For if it be true that *tree* is not the name of any *man,* then no one thing can be signified by the two names *man* and *tree,* wherefore *no tree is a man* is a true proposition. Also to this, *whatsoever is not a living-creature is not a man,* where both the terms are negative, this other proposition is equipollent, *only a living creature is a man.*

15. Negative propositions are the same, whether the negation be before or after the copula. Fourthly, negative propositions, whether the particle of negation be set after the copula as some nations do, or before it, as it is in Latin and Greek, if the terms be the same, as equipollent: as, for example, *man is not a tree,* and, *man is not-a-tree,* are equipollent, though Aristotle deny it. Also these, *every man is not a tree,* and *no*

man is a tree, are equipollent, and that so manifestly, as it needs not be demonstrated.

16. Particular propositions simply converted, are equipollent. Lastly, all particular propositions that have their terms inverted, as these, *some man is blind, some blind thing is a man* are equipollent; for either of the two names, is the name of some one and the same man; and therefore in which soever of the two orders they be connected, they signify the same truth.

17. What are subaltern, contrary, subcontrary, and contradictory propositions. Of propositions that have the same terms, and are placed in the same order, but varied either by quantity or quality, some are called *subaltern,* others *contrary,* others *subcontrary,* and others *contradictory.*

Subaltern, are universal and particular propositions of the same quality; as *every man is a living creature, some man is a living creature;* or *no man is wise, some man is not wise.* Of these, if the universal be true, the particular will be true also.

Contrary, are universal propositions of different quality; as, *every man is happy, no man is happy.* And of these, if one be true, the other is false: also, they may both be false, as in the example given.

Subcontrary, are particular propositions of different quality; as, *some man is learned, some man is not learned;* which cannot be both false, but they may be both true.

Contradictory are those that differ both in quantity and quality; as, *every man is a living creature, some man is not a living-creature;* which can neither be both true, nor both false.

18. Consequence, what it is. A proposition is said to *follow* from two other propositions, when these being granted to be true, it cannot be denied but the other is true also. For example, let these two propositions, *every man is a living creature,* and, *every living creature is a body,* be supposed true, that is, that *body* is the name of *every living creature,* and *living creature* the name of *every man.* Seeing therefore, if these be understood to be true, it cannot be

understood that *body* is not the name of *every man*, that is, that *every man is a body* is false, this proposition will be said to *follow* from those two, or to be necessarily *inferred* from them.

19. Falsity cannot follow from truth. That a true proposition may follow from false propositions, may happen sometimes; but false from true, never. For if these, *every man is a stone*, and *every stone is a living creature*, (which are both false) be granted to be true, it is granted also that *living creature* is the name of *every stone*, and *stone* of *every man*, that is, that *living creature* is the name of *every man;* that is to say, this proposition *every man is a living creature*, is true, as it is indeed true. Wherefore a true proposition may sometimes follow from false. But if any two propositions be true, a false one can never follow from them. For if true follow from false, for this reason only, that the false are granted to be true, then truth from two truths granted will follow in the same manner.

20. How one proposition is the cause of another. Now, seeing none but a true proposition will follow from true, and that the understanding of two propositions to be true, is the cause of understanding that also to be true which is deduced from them; the two antecedent propositions are commonly called the causes of the inferred proposition, or conclusion. And from hence it is that logicians say, the *premises* are causes of the *conclusion;* which may pass, though it be not properly spoken; for though understanding be the cause of understanding, yet speech is not the cause of speech. But when they say, the cause of the properties of any thing, is the thing itself, they speak absurdly. For example, if a figure be propounded which is triangular; seeing every triangle has all its angles together equal to two right angles, from whence it follows that all the angles of that figure are equal to two right angles, they say, for this reason, that that figure is the cause of that equality. But seeing the figure does not itself make its angles, and therefore cannot be said to be the *efficient-cause*, they call it the *formal-cause;* whereas indeed it is no cause at all; nor does the property of any figure follow

the figure, but has its being at the same time with it; only the knowledge of the figure goes before the knowledge of the properties; and one knowledge is truly the cause of another knowledge, namely the *efficient cause*.

And thus much concerning *proposition;* which in the progress of philosophy is the first step, like the moving towards of one foot. By the due addition of another step I shall proceed to *syllogism*, and make a complete pace. Of which in the next chapter.

Chapter 4

Of Syllogism

1. Definition of syllogism. A SPEECH, consisting of three propositions, from two of which the third follows, is called a SYLLOGISM; and that which follows is called the *conclusion;* the other two *premises.* For example, this speech, *every man is a living creature, every living creature is a body*, therefore, *every man is a body,* is a *syllogism,* because the third proposition follows from the two first; that is, if those be granted to be true, this must also be granted to be true.

2. In a syllogism there are but three terms. From two propositions which have not one term common, no conclusion can follow; and therefore no *syllogism* can be made of them. For let any two premises, *a man is a living creature, a tree is a plant,* be both of them true, yet because it cannot be collected from them that *plant* is the name of a *man,* or *man* the name of a *plant,* it is not necessary that this conclusion, *a man is a plant,* should be true. Corollary: therefore, in the *premises* of a *syllogism* there can be but three *terms.*

Besides, there can be no term in the *conclusion,* which was not in the *premises.* For let any two premises be, *a man is a living creature, a living creature is a body,* yet if any other term be put in the conclusion, as *man is two-footed;* though it be true, it cannot follow from the premises, because from them it cannot be collected, that the name *two-footed* belongs to a *man;* and therefore, again, in every *syllogism* there can be but three *terms.*

3. Major, minor and middle term; also major & minor proposition, what they are. Of these terms, that which is the *predicate* in the conclusion, is commonly called the *major;* that which is the *subject* in the conclusion, the *minor,* and the other is the *middle term;* as in this syllogism, *a man is a living creature, a living creature is a body,* therefore, *a man is a body, body* is the *major, man* the *minor,* and *living crea-*

ture the *middle term*. Also of the premises, that in which the *major term* is found, is called the *major proposition*, and that which has the *minor term*, the *minor proposition*.

4. The middle term in every syllogism to be determined in both propositions to one and the same thing. If the middle term be not in both the premises determined to one and the same singular thing, no conclusion will follow, nor syllogism be made. For let the minor term be *man*, the middle term *living creature*, and the major term *lion*; and let the premises be, *man is a living creature, some living creature is a lion*, yet it will not follow that *every* or *any man is a lion*. By which it is manifest, that in every syllogism, that proposition which has the middle term for its *subject*, ought to be either *universal* or *singular*, but not *particular* nor *indefinite*. For example, this syllogism, *every man is a living creature, some living creature is four-footed*, therefore *some man is four-footed*, is therefore faulty, because the middle term, *living creature*, is in the first of the premises determined only to *man*, for there the name of *living creature* is given to man only, but in the latter premise it may be understood of some other living creature besides man. But if the latter premise had been *universal*, as here, *every man is a living creature, every living creature is a body*, therefore *every man is a body*, the syllogism had been true; for it would have followed that *body* had been the name of *every living creature*, that is of *man;* that is to say, the conclusion *every man is a body* had been true. Likewise, when the middle term is a *singular* name, a syllogism may be made, I say a true syllogism, though useless in philosophy, as this, *some man is Socrates, Socrates is a philosopher*, therefore, *some man is a philosopher;* for the premises being granted, the conclusion cannot be denied.

5. From two particular propositions nothing can be concluded. And therefore of two premises, in both which the middle term is particular, a syllogism cannot be made; for whether the middle term be the *subject* in both the premises, or the *predicate* in both, or the *subject* in one, and the *predicate* in the other, it will not be necessarily determined to the same thing. For let the premises be,

Some man is blind,   }In both which the middle
Some man is learned,   } term is the *subject,*

it will not follow that *blind* is the name of any *learned man,*
or *learned* the name of any *blind man,* seeing the name
learned does not contain the name *blind,* nor this that; and
therefore it is not necessary that both should be names of
the same man. So from these premises,

Every man is a living-creature, }In both which the middle
Every horse is a living-creature, } term is the *predicate,*

nothing will follow. For seeing *living creature* is in both of
them *indefinite,* which is equivalent to *particular,* and that
man may be one kind of *living creature,* and *horse* another
kind, it is not necessary that *man* should be the name of
horse, or *horse* of *man.* Or if the premises be,

Every man is a living-
creature,   }In one of which the middle
Some living creature is }term is the *subject, and in*
four-footed,   }the other the *predicate,*

the conclusion will not follow, because the name *living crea-*
ture being not determined, it may in one of them be understood of *man,* in the other of *not-man.*

6. A syllogism is the collection of two propositions into
one sum. Now it is manifest from what has been said, that
a syllogism is nothing but a collection of the sum of two
propositions, joined together by a common term, which is
called the *middle term.* And as proposition is the addition of
two names, so syllogism is the adding together of three.

7. The figure of a syllogism, what it is. Syllogisms are
usually distinguished according to their diversity of *figures,*
that is, by the diverse position of the middle term. And again
in figure there is a distinction of certain *moods,* which consist of the differences of propositions in *quantity* and *quality.*
The first figure is that, in which the terms are placed one

after another according to their latitude of signification; in which order the *minor term* is first, the *middle term* next, and the *major* last; as, if the minor term be *man*, the middle term, *living creature*, and the major term, *body*, then, *man is a living-creature, is a body*, will be a syllogism in the first figure: in which, *man is a living creature* is the minor proposition; the major, *living creature is a body*, and the conclusion, or sum of both, *man is a body*. Now this figure is called *direct*, because the terms stand in direct order; and it is varied by *quantity* and *quality* into four *moods:* of which the first is that wherein all the terms are *positive*, and the minor term *universal*, as *every man is a living creature, every living creature is a body:* in which all the propositions are affirmative, and universal. But if the major term be a negative name, and the minor a universal name, the *figure* will be in the second *mood*, as, *every man is a living creature, every living creature is not a tree*, in which the major proposition and conclusion are both universal and negative. To these two, are commonly added two more, by making the minor term particular. Also it may happen that both the major and middle terms are negative terms, and then there arises another *mood*, in which all the propositions are negative, and yet the syllogism will be good; as, if the minor term be *man*, the middle term *not a stone*, and the major term *not a flint*, this syllogism, *no man is a stone, whatsoever is not a stone is not a flint*, therefore, *no man is a flint*, is true, though it consists of three negatives. But in philosophy, the profession whereof is to establish universal rules concerning the properties of things, seeing the difference betwixt negatives and affirmatives is only this, that in the former the subject is affirmed by a negative name, and by a positive in the latter, it is superfluous to consider any other *mood* in direct *figure*, besides that, in which all the propositions are both universal and affirmative.

8. What is in the mind answering to a syllogism. The thoughts in the mind answering to a direct syllogism, proceed in this manner; first, there is conceived a phantasm of the thing named, with that accident or quality thereof, for which it is in the minor proposition called by that name

which is the subject; next, the mind has a phantasm of the same thing with that accident, or quality, for which it hath the name, that in the same proposition is the predicate; thirdly, the thought returns of the same thing as having that accident in it, for which it is called by the name, that is the predicate of the major proposition; and lastly, remembering that all those are the accidents of one and the same thing, it concludes that those three names are also names of one and the same thing; that is to say, the conclusion is true. For example, when this syllogism is made, *man is a living creature, a living creature is a body,* therefore, *man is a body,* the mind conceives first an image of a man speaking or discoursing, and remembers that that, which so appears, is called *man;* then it has the image of the same man moving, and remembers that that, which appears so, is called *living creature;* thirdly, it conceives an image of the same man, as filling some place or space, and remembers that what appears so is called *body;* and lastly, when it remembers that that thing, which was extended, and moved and spake, was one and the same thing, it concludes that the three names, *man, living creature,* and *body,* are names of the same thing, and that therefore *man is a living creature* is a true proposition. From whence it is manifest, that living creatures that have not the use of speech, have no conception or thought in the mind, answering to a syllogism made of universal propositions; seeing it is necessary to think not only of the thing, but also by turns to remember the divers names, which for divers considerations thereof are applied to the same.

9. *The first indirect figure, how made.* The rest of the figures arise either from the inflection, or inversion of the first or direct figure; which is done by changing the major, or minor, or both the propositions, into converted propositions equipollent to them.

From whence follow three other figures; of which, two are *inflected,* and the third *inverted.* The first of these three is made by the conversion of the major proposition. For let the minor, middle, and major terms stand in direct order, thus, *man is a living creature, is not a stone,* which is the first or direct figure; the inflection will be by converting the major proposition in this manner, *man is a living creature, a stone is not a living creature;* and this is the second figure, or the first of the indirect figures; in which the conclusion will be, *man is not a stone.* For (having shown in the last chapter, art. 14, that universal propositions, converted by contradiction of the terms, are equipollent) both those syllogisms conclude alike; so that if the major be read (like Hebrew) backwards, thus, *a living creature is not a stone,* it will be direct again, as it was before. In like manner this direct syllogism, *man is not a tree, is not a pear-tree,* will be made indirect by converting the major proposition (by contradiction of the terms) into another equipollent to it, thus, *man is not a tree, a pear-tree is a tree;* for the same conclusion will follow, *man is not a pear-tree.*

But for the conversion of the direct figure into the first indirect figure, the major term in the direct figure ought to be negative. For though this direct, *man is a living creature, is a body,* be made indirect, by converting the major proposition, thus,

> Man is a living creature,
> Not a body is not a living creature,
> Therefore, Every man is a body;

Yet this conversion appears so obscure, that this mood is of no use at all. By the conversion of the major proposition, it is manifest, that in this figure, the middle term is always the predicate in both the premises.

10. Second indirect figure, how made. The second indirect figure is made by converting the minor proposition, so as that the middle term is the subject in both. But this never concludes universally, and therefore is of no use in philosophy. Nevertheless I will set down an example of it; by which this direct

> Every man is a living creature,
> Every living creature is a body,

by conversion of the minor proposition, will stand thus,

Some living creature is a man,
Every living creature is a body,
Therefore, *Some man is a body.*

For *every man is a living creature* cannot be converted into this, *every living creature is a man:* and therefore if this syllogism be restored to its direct form, the minor proposition will be *some man is a living creature,* and consequently the conclusion will be *some man is a body,* seeing the minor term *man,* which is the subject in the conclusion, is a particular name.

11. How the third indirect figure is made. The third indirect or inverted figure, is made by the conversion of both the premises. For example, this direct syllogism,

Every man is a living creature,
Every living creature is not a stone,
Therefore, *Every man is not a stone,*

being inverted, will stand thus,

Every stone is not a living creature,
Whatsoever is not a living creature, is not a man,
Therefore, *Every stone is not a man,*

which conclusion is the converse of the direct conclusion, and equipollent to the same.

The figures, therefore, of syllogisms, if they be numbered by the diverse situation of the middle term only, are but three; in the first whereof, the middle term has the middle place; in the second, the last; and in the third, the first place. But if they be numbered according to the situation of the terms simply, they are four; for the first may be distinguished again into two, namely, into direct and inverted. From whence it is evident, that the controversy among logicians concerning the fourth figure, is a mere λογόμαχια, or contention about the name thereof; for, as for the thing itself, it is plain that the situation of the terms (not considering the quantity or quality by which the moods are distinguished) makes four differences of syllogisms, which may be called figures, or have any other name at pleasure.

12. There are many moods in every figure, but most of them useless in philosophy. In every one of these figures there are many moods, which are made by varying the premises according to all the differences they are capable of, by quantity and quality; as namely, in the direct figure there are six moods; in the first indirect figure, four; in the second, fourteen; and in the third, eighteen. But because from the direct figure I rejected as superfluous all moods besides that which consists of universal propositions, and whose minor proposition is affirmative, I do, together with it, reject the moods of the rest of the figures which are made by conversion of the premises in the direct figure.

13. A hypothetical syllogism when equipollent to a categorical. As it was showed before, that in necessary propositions a categorical and hypothetical proposition are equipollent; so likewise it is manifest that a categorical and hypothetical syllogism are equivalent. For every categorical syllogism, as this,

> *Every man is a living creature,*
> *Every living creature is a body,*
> Therefore, *Every man is a body,*

is of equal force with this hypothetical syllogism:

If any thing be a man, the same is also a living creature,
If any thing be a living creature, the same is a body,
Therefore, *If any thing be a man, the same is a body.*

In like manner, this categorical syllogism in an indirect figure,

> *No stone is a living creature,*
> *Every man is a living creature,*
> Therefore, *No man is a stone,*
> Or, *No stone is a man,*

is equivalent to this hypothetical syllogism:

If any thing be a man, the same is also a living creature,
If any thing be a stone, the same is not a living creature,
Therefore, *If any thing be a stone, the same is not a man,*
Or, *If any thing be a man, the same is not a stone.*

And thus much seems sufficient for the nature of syllogisms; (for the doctrine of moods and figures is clearly delivered by others that have written largely and profitably of the same). Nor are precepts so necessary as practice for the attaining of true ratiocination; and they that study the demonstrations of mathematicians, will sooner learn true logic, than they that spend time in reading the rules of syllogizing which logicians have made; no otherwise than little children learn to go, not by precepts, but by exercising their feet. This, therefore, may serve for the first pace in the way to Philosophy.

In the next place I shall speak of the faults and errors into which men that reason unwarily are apt to fall; and of their kinds and causes.

Chapter 5

Of Erring, Falsity, and Captions

1. Erring & falsity, how they differ. Error of the mind by itself, without the use of words, how it happens. Men are subject to *err* not only in affirming and denying, but also in perception, and in silent cogitation. In affirming and denying, when they call any thing by a name, which is not the name thereof; as if from seeing the sun first by reflection in water, and afterwards again directly in the firmament, we should to both those appearances give the name of sun, and say there are two suns; which none but men can do, for no other living creatures have the use of names. This kind of error only deserves the name of *falsity*, as arising, not from sense, nor from the things themselves, but from pronouncing rashly; for names have their constitution, not from the species of things, but from the will and consent of men. And hence it comes to pass, that men pronounce *falsely*, by their own negligence, in departing from such appellations of things as are agreed upon, and are not deceived neither by the things, nor by the sense; for they do not perceive that the thing they see is called sun, but they give it that name from their own will and agreement. Tacit errors, or the errors of sense and cogitation, are made, by passing from one imagination to the imagination of another different thing; or by feigning that to be past, or future, which never was, nor ever shall be; as when, by seeing the image of the sun in water, we imagine the sun itself to be there; or by seeing swords, that there has been or shall be fighting, because it uses to be so for the most part; or when from promises we feign the mind of the promiser to be such and such; or lastly, when from any sign we vainly imagine something to be signified, which is not. And errors of this sort are common to all things that have sense; and yet the deception proceeds neither from our senses, nor from the things we perceive; but from ourselves

65

while we feign such things as are but mere images to be something more than images. But neither things, nor imaginations of things, can be said to be false, seeing they are truly what they are; nor do they, as signs, promise any thing which they do not perform; for they indeed do not promise at all, but we from them; nor do the clouds, but we, from seeing the clouds, say it shall rain. The best way, therefore, to free ourselves from such errors as arise from natural signs, is first of all, before we begin to reason concerning such conjectural things, to suppose ourselves ignorant, and then to make use of our ratiocination; for these errors proceed from the want of ratiocination; whereas, errors which consist in affirmation and negation, (that is, the falsity of propositions) proceed only from reasoning amiss. Of these, therefore, as repugnant to philosophy, I will speak principally.

2. A sevenfold incoherency of names, all of which make always a false proposition. Errors which happen in reasoning, that is, in syllogizing, consist either in the falsity of the premises, or of the inference. In the first of these cases, a syllogism is said to be faulty in the *matter* of it; and in the second case, in the *form*. I will first consider the matter, namely, how many ways a proposition may be false; and next the form, and how it comes to pass, that when the premises are true, the inference is, notwithstanding, false.

Seeing, therefore, that proposition only is true, (chap. 3, art. 7) in which are copulated two names of one and the same thing; and that always false, in which names of different things are copulated, look how many ways names of different things may be copulated, and so many ways a false proposition may be made.

Now, all thing to which we give names, may be reduced to these four kinds, namely, *bodies, accidents, phantasms,* and *names* themselves; and therefore, in every true proposition, it is necessary that the names copulated, be both of them names of *bodies,* or both names of *accidents,* or both names of *phantasms,* or both names of *names.* For names otherwise copulated are incoherent, and constitute a false proposition. It may happen, also, that the name of a *body,* of an *accident*, or of a *phantasm*, may be copulated with the name of a *speech*. So that copulated names may be incoherent seven manner of ways.

1. If the name of a Body		the name of an Accident.
2. If the name of a Body		the name of a Phantasm.
3. If the name of a Body		the name of a Name.
4. If the name of an Accident	be copulated with	the name of a Phantasm.
5. If the name of an Accident		the name of a Name.
6. If the name of a Phantasm		the name of a Name.
7. If the name of a Body, Accident, or Phantasm		the name of a Speech.

Of all which I will give some examples.

3. Examples of the first manner of incoherency. After the first of these ways propositions are false, when abstract names are copulated with concrete names; as (in Latin and Greek) *esse est ens, essentia est ens, τὸ τί ἦν εἶναι* (i.); *quidditas est ens,* and many the like, which are found in Aristotle's *Metaphysics.* Also, the *understanding worketh,* the *understanding understandeth,* the *sight seeth;* a *body* is *magnitude,* a *body* is *quantity,* a *body* is *extension;* to *be a man* is a *man, whiteness* is a *white thing,* &c.; which is as if one should say, the *runner* is the *running,* or the *walk walketh.* Moreover, *essence* is *separated,* substance is *abstracted:* and others like these, or derived from these (with which common philosophy abounds). For seeing no *subject* of an *accident* (that is, no *body*) is an *accident:* no name of an *accident* ought to be given to a *body,* nor of a *body* to an *accident.*

4. The second. False, in the second manner, are such propositions as these; a *ghost is a body,* or a *spirit,* that is, a thin body; *sensible species fly up and down in the air,* or *are moved hither and thither,* which is proper to bodies; also, a *shadow is moved,* or *is a body; light is moved,* or *is a body; color is the object of sight, sound of hearing; space* or *place is extended;* and innumerable others of this kind. For seeing ghosts, sensible species, a shadow, light, color, sound, space, &c. appear to us no less sleeping than waking, they cannot be things without us, but only phantasms of the mind that imagines them; and therefore the names of these, copulated

with the names of bodies, cannot constitute a true proposition.

5. The third. False propositions of the third kind, are such as these; *genus est ens, universale est ens, ens de ente prædicatur.* For *genus,* and *universale,* and *predicare,* are names of names, and not of things. Also, *number is infinite,* is a false proposition; for no number can be infinite, but only the word *number* is then called an indefinite name when there is no determined number answering to it in the mind.

6. The fourth. To the fourth kind belong such false propositions as these, *an object is of such magnitude or figure as appears to the beholders; color, light, sound, are in the object;* and the like. For the same object appears sometimes greater, sometimes lesser, sometimes square, sometimes round, according to the diversity of the distance and medium; but the true magnitude and figure of the thing seen is always one and the same; so that the magnitude and figure which appears, is not the true magnitude and figure of the object, nor anything but phantasm; and therefore, in such propositions as these, the names of accidents are copulated with the names of phantasms.

7. The fifth. Propositions are false in the fifth manner, when it is said that *the definition is the essence of a thing; whiteness,* or some other accident, *is the genus, or universal.* For definition is not the essence of any thing, but a speech signifying what we conceive of the essence thereof; and so also not whiteness itself, but the word whiteness, is a genus, or a universal name.

8. The sixth. In the sixth manner they err, that say the *idea of anything is universal;* as if there could be in the mind an image of a man, which were not the image of some one man, but a man simply, which is impossible; for every idea is one, and of one thing; but they are deceived in this, that they put the *name* of the thing for the *idea* thereof.

9. The seventh. They err in the seventh manner, that make this distinction between things that have being, that some of them *exist by themselves,* others by *accident;* namely, because *Socrates is a man* is a necessary proposition, and *Socrates is a musician* a contingent proposition, therefore they say some

things exist necessarily or by themselves, others contingently or by accident; whereby, seeing *necessary, contingent, by itself, by accident,* are not names of things, but of propositions, they that say *any thing that has being, exists by accident,* copulate the name of a proposition with the name of a thing. In the same manner also, they err, which place some ideas in the understanding, others in the fancy; as if from the understanding of this proposition, *man is a living creature,* we had one idea or image of a man derived from sense to the memory, and another to the understanding; wherein that which deceives them is this, that they think one idea should be answerable to a name, another to a proposition, which is false; for proposition signifies only the order of those things one after another, which we observe in the same idea of man; so that this proposition, *man is a living creature* raises but one idea in us, though in that idea we consider that first, for which he is called man, and next that, for which he is called living creature. The falsities of propositions in all these several manners, is to be discovered by the definitions of the copulated names.

10. Falsity of propositions detected by resolving the terms with definitions. But when names of bodies are copulated with names of bodies, names of accidents with names of accidents, names of names with names of names, and names of phantasms with names of phantasms, if we, nevertheless, remain still doubtful whether such propositions are true, we ought then in the first place to find out the definition of both those names, and again the definitions of such names as are in the former definition, and so proceed by a continual resolution till we come to a simple name, that is, to the most general or most universal name of that kind; and if after all this, the truth or falsity thereof be not evident, we must search it out by philosophy, and ratiocination, beginning from definitions. For every proposition, universally true, is either a definition, or part of a definition, or the evidence of it depends upon definitions.

11. Of the fault of a syllogism consisting in implication of the terms with the copula. That fault of a syllogism which lies hid in the form thereof, will always be found either in

the implication of the copula with one of the terms, or in the equivocation of some word; and in either of these ways there will be four terms, which (as I have shown) cannot stand in a true syllogism. Now the implication of the copula with either term, is easily detected by reducing the propositions to plain and clear predication; as (for example) if any man should argue thus,

> *The hand toucheth the pen,*
> *The pen toucheth the paper,*
> Therefore, *The hand toucheth the paper;*

the fallacy will easily appear by reducing it, thus:

> *The hand, is, touching the pen,*
> *The pen, is, touching the paper,*
> Therefore, *The hand, is, touching the paper;*

where there are manifestly these four terms, *the hand, touching the pen, the pen,* and *touching the paper.* But the danger of being deceived by sophisms of this kind, does not seem to be so great, as that I need insist longer upon them.

12. Of the fault which consists in equivocation. And though there may be fallacy in equivocal terms, yet in those that be manifestly such, there is none at all; nor in metaphors, for they profess the transferring of names from one thing to another. Nevertheless, sometimes equivocals (and those not very obscure) may deceive; as in this argumentation:— *It belongs to metaphysics to treat of principles; but the first principle of all, is, that the same thing cannot both exist and not exist at the same time; and therefore it belongs to metaphysics to treat whether the same thing may both exist and not exist at the same time;* where the fallacy lies in the equivocation of the word principle; for whereas Aristotle in the beginning of his *Metaphysics,* says, that *the treating of principles belongs to primary science,* he understands by principles, causes of things, and certain existences which he calls primary; but where he says *a primary proposition is a principle,* by principle, there, he means the beginning and

cause of knowledge, that is, the understanding of words, which, if any man want, he is incapable of learning.

13. Sophistical captions are oftener faulty in the matter than in the form of syllogisms. But the *captions* of sophists and sceptics, by which they were wont, of old, to deride and oppose truth, were faulty for the most part, not in the form, but in the matter of syllogism; and they deceived not others oftener than they were themselves deceived. For the force of that famous argument of Zeno against motion, consisted in this proposition, *whatsoever may be divided into parts, infinite in number, the same is infinite;* which he, without doubt, thought to be true, yet nevertheless is false. For to be divided into infinite parts, is nothing else but to be divided into as many parts as any man will. But it is not necessary that a line should have parts infinite in number, or be infinite, because I can divide and subdivide it as often as I please; for how many parts soever I make, yet their number is finite; but because he that says parts, simply, without adding how many, does not limit any number, but leaves it to the determination of the hearer, therefore we say commonly, a line may be divided infinitely; which cannot be true in any other sense.

And thus much may suffice concerning syllogism, which is, at it were, the first pace towards philosophy; in which I have said as much as is necessary to teach any man from whence all true argumentation has its force. And to enlarge this treatise with all that may be heaped together, would be as superfluous, as if one should (as I said before) give a young child precepts for the teaching of him to go; for the art of reasoning is not so well learned by precepts as by practice, and by the reading of those books in which the conclusions are all made by severe demonstration. And so I pass on to the way of philosophy, that is, to the method of study.

Chapter 6

Of Method

1. *Method and science defined.* For the understanding of *method*, it will be necessary for me to repeat the definition of philosophy, delivered above (Chap. 1, art. 2.) in this manner, *Philosophy is the knowledge we acquire, by true ratiocination, of appearances, or apparent effects, from the knowledge we have of some possible production or generation of the same; and of such production, as has been or may be, from the knowledge we have of the effects.* METHOD, therefore, in the study of philosophy, *is the shortest way of finding out effects by their known causes, or of causes by their known effects.* But we are then said to know any effect, when we know *that there be causes of the same,* and *in what subject those causes are,* and *in what subject they produce that effect,* and *in what manner they work the same.* And this is the science of causes, or, as they call it, of the διότι. All other science, which is called the ὅτι, is either perception by sense, or the imagination, or memory remaining after such perception.

The first beginnings, therefore, of knowledge, are the phantasms of sense and imagination; and that there be such phantasms we know well enough by nature; but to know why they be, or from what causes they proceed, is the work of ratiocination; which consists (as is said above, in the 1st Chapter, art. 2) in *composition* and *division* or *resolution.* There is therefore no method, by which we find out the causes of things, but is either *compositive* or *resolutive,* or *partly compositive,* and *partly resolutive.* And the resolutive is commonly called *analytical* method, as the compositive is called *synthetical.*

2. It is easier known concerning singular than universal things, that they are; and contrarily it is easier known con-

cerning universal than singular things, why they are, or what are their causes. It is common to all sorts of method, to proceed from known things to unknown; and this is manifest from the cited definition of philosophy. But in knowledge by sense, the whole object is more known, than any part thereof; as when we see a man, the conception or whole idea of that man is first or more known, than the particular ideas of his being *figurate, animate,* and *rational;* that is, we first see the whole man, and take notice of his being, before we observe in him those other particulars. And therefore in any knowledge of the ὅτι, or that any thing *is,* the beginning of our search is from the whole idea; and contrarily, in our knowledge of the διότι, or of the causes of anything, that is in the sciences, we have more knowledge of the causes of the parts than of the whole. For the cause of the whole is compounded of the causes of the parts; but it is necessary that we know the things that are to be compounded, before we can know the whole compound. Now, by parts, I do not here mean parts of the thing itself, but parts of its nature; as, by the parts of man, I do not understand his head, his shoulders, his arms, &c. but his figure, quantity, motion, sense, reason, and the like; which accidents being compounded or put together, constitute the whole nature of man, but not the man himself. And this is the meaning of that common saying, namely, that some things are more known to us, others more known to nature; for I do not think that they, which so distinguish, mean that something is known to nature, which is known to no man; and therefore, by those things, that are more known to us, we are to understand things we take notice of by our senses, and, by more known to nature, those we acquire the knowledge of by reason; for in this sense it is, that the *whole,* that is, those things that have universal names, (which, for brevity's sake, I call *universal*) are more known to us than the *parts,* that is, such things as have names less universal, (which I therefore call *singular*); and the causes of the parts are more known to nature than the cause of the whole; that is, universals than singulars.

3. *What it is philosophers seek to know.* In the study of philosophy, men search after science either simply or in-

definitely; that is, to know as much as they can, without propounding to themselves any limited question; or they inquire into the cause of some determined appearance, or endeavor to find out the certainty of something in question, as what is the cause of *light,* of *heat,* of *gravity,* of a *figure* propounded, and the like; or in what *subject* any propounded *accident* is inherent; or what may conduce most to the *generation* of some propounded *effect* from many *accidents;* or in what manner particular causes ought to be compounded for the production of some certain effect. Now, according to this variety of things in question, sometimes the *analytical method* is to be used, and sometimes the *synthetical.*

4. The first part, by which principles are discovered, is purely analytical. But to those that search after science indefinitely, which consists in the knowledge of the causes of all things, as far forth as it may be attained, (and the causes of singular things are compounded of the causes of universal or simple things) it is necessary that they know the causes of universal things, or of such accidents as are common to all bodies, that is, to all matter, before they can know the causes of singular things, that is, of those accidents by which one thing is distinguished from another. And, again, they must know what those universal things are, before they can know their causes. Moreover, seeing universal things are contained in the nature of singular things, the knowledge of them is to be acquired by reason, that is, by resolution. For example, if there be propounded a conception or *idea* of some singular thing, as of a *square,* this square is to be resolved into a *plane, terminated with a certain number of equal and straight lines and right angles.* For by this resolution we have these things universal or agreeable to all matter, namely, *line, plane,* (which contains *superficies*) *terminated, angle, straightness, rectitude,* and *equality;* and if we can find out the causes of these, we may compound them altogether into the cause of a square. Again, if any man propound to himself the conception of *gold,* he may, by resolving, come to the ideas of *solid, visible, heavy,* (that is, tending to the center of the earth, or downwards) and many other more universal than gold itself; and these he may resolve again, till he come to such things as are

most universal. And in this manner, by resolving continually, we may come to know what those things are, whose causes being first known severally, and afterwards compounded, bring us to the knowledge of singular things. I conclude, therefore, that the method of attaining to the universal knowledge of things, is purely *analytical*.

5. The highest causes, and most universal in every kind, are known by themselves. But the causes of universal things (of those, at least, that have any cause) are manifest of themselves, or (as they say commonly) known to nature; so that they need no method at all; for they have all but one universal cause, which is motion. For the variety of all figures arises out of the variety of those motions by which they are made; and motion cannot be understood to have any other cause besides motion; nor has the variety of those things we perceive by sense, as of *colors, sounds, savors*, &c., any other cause than motion, residing partly in the objects that work upon our senses, and partly in ourselves, in such manner, as that it is manifestly some kind of motion, though we cannot, without ratiocination, come to know what kind. For though many cannot understand till it be in some sort demonstrated to them, that all mutation consists in motion; yet this happens not from any obscurity in the thing itself (for it is not intelligible that anything can depart either from rest, or from the motion it has, except by motion), but either by having their natural discourse corrupted with former opinions received from their masters, or else for this, that they do not at all bend their mind to the inquiring out of truth. .

6. Method from principles found out, tending to science simply, what it is. By the knowledge therefore of universals, and of their causes (which are the first principles by which we know the $\delta\iota\acute{o}\tau\iota$ of things) we have in the first place their definitions (which are nothing but the explication of our simple conceptions). For example, he that has a true conception of *place*, cannot be ignorant of this definition, *place is that space which is possessed or filled adequately by some body;* and so, he that conceives *motion* aright, cannot but know that *motion is the privation of one place, and the acquisition of another*. In the next place, we have their gene-

rations or descriptions; as (for example) that *a line is made by the motion of a point, superficies by the motion of a line,* and *one motion by another motion,* &c. It remains, that we inquire what motion begets such and such effects; as, what motion makes a straight line, and what a circular; what motion thrusts, what draws, and by what way; what makes a thing which is seen or heard, to be seen or heard sometimes in one manner, sometimes in another. Now the method of this kind of inquiry, is *compositive.* For first we are to observe what effect a body moved produceth, when we consider nothing in it besides its motion; and we see presently that this makes a line, or length; next, what the motion of a long body produces, which we find to be superficies; and so forwards, till we see what the effects of simple motion are; and then, in like manner, we are to observe what proceeds from the addition, multiplication, subtraction, and division, of these motions, and what effects, what figures, and what properties, they produce; from which kind of contemplation sprung that part of philosophy which is called *geometry.*

From this consideration of what is produced by simple motion, we are to pass to the consideration of what effects one body moved worketh upon another; and because there may be motion in all the several parts of a body, yet so as that the whole body remain still in the same place, we must inquire first, what motion causeth such and such motion in the whole, that is, when one body invades another body which is either at rest or in motion, what way, and with what swiftness, the invaded body shall move; and, again, what motion this second body will generate in a third, and so forwards. From which contemplation shall be drawn that part of philosophy which treats of motion.

In the third place we must proceed to the inquiry of such effects as are made by the motion of the parts of any body, as, how it comes to pass, that things when they are the same, yet seem not to be the same, but changed. And here the things we search after are sensible qualities, such as *light, color, transparency, opacity, sound, odor, savor, heat, cold,* and the like; which because they cannot be known till we know the causes of sense itself, therefore the consideration of the causes of *seeing, hearing, smelling, tasting,* and *touching,* belongs to this third place; and all those qualities and changes, above mentioned, are to be referred to the fourth place; which two considerations comprehend that part of philosophy which is called *physics.* And in these four parts is contained whatsoever in natural philosophy may be explicated by demonstration, properly so called. For if a cause were to be rendered of natural appearances in special, as, what are the motions and influences of the heavenly bodies, and of their parts, the reason hereof must either be drawn from the parts of the sciences above mentioned, or no reason at all will be given, but all left to uncertain conjecture.

After *physics* we must come to *moral philosophy;* in which we are to consider the motions of the mind, namely, *appetite, aversion, love, benevolence, hope, fear, anger, emulation, envy, &c.;* what causes they have, and of what they be causes. And the reason why these are to be considered after *physics* is, that they have their causes in sense and imagination, which are the subject of *physical* contemplation. Also the reason, why all these things are to be searched after in the order above-said, is, that physics cannot be understood, except we know first what motions are in the smallest parts of bodies; nor such motion of parts, till we know what it is that makes another body move; nor this, till we know what simple motion will effect. And because all appearance of things to sense is determined, and made to be of such and such quality and quantity by compounded motions, every one of which has a certain degree of velocity, and a certain and determined way; therefore, in the first place, we are to search out the ways of motion simply (in which geometry consists); next the ways of such generated motions as are manifest; and, lastly, the ways of internal and invisible motions (which is the inquiry of natural philosophers). And, therefore, they that study natural philosophy, study in vain, except they begin at geometry; and such writers or disputers thereof, as are ignorant of geometry, do but make their readers and hearers lose their time.

7. That method of civil and natural science, proceeding from sense to principles, is analytical; and again, that which begins at principles is synthetical. *Civil* and *moral philosophy*

do not so adhere to one another, but that they may be severed. For the causes of the motions of the mind are known, not only by ratiocination, but also by the experience of every man that takes the pains to observe those motions within himself. And, therefore, not only they that have attained the knowledge of the passions and perturbations of the mind, by the *synthetical method*, and from the very first principles of philosophy, may by proceeding in the same way, come to the causes and necessity of constituting commonwealths, and to get the knowledge of what is natural right, and what are civil duties; and, in every kind of government, what are the rights of the commonwealth, and all other knowledge appertaining to civil philosophy; for this reason, that the principles of the politics consist in the knowledge of the motions of the mind, and the knowledge of these motions from the knowledge of sense and imagination; but even they also that have not learned the first part of philosophy, namely, *geometry* and *physics*, may, notwithstanding, attain the principles of civil philosophy, by the *analytical method*. For if a question be propounded, as, *whether such an action be just or unjust;* if that *unjust* be resolved into *fact against law,* and that notion *law* into the *command* of him or them that have *coercive power;* and that *power* be derived from the *wills* of men that constitute such power, to the end they may live in peace, they may at last come to this, that the appetites of men and the passions of their minds are such, that, unless they be restrained by some power, they will always be making war upon one another; which may be known to be so by any man's experience, that will but examine his own mind. And, therefore, from hence he may proceed, by compounding, to the determination of the justice or injustice of any propounded action. So that it is manifest, by what has been said, that the method of philosophy, to such as seek science simply, without propounding to themselves the solution of any particular question, is partly analytical, and partly synthetical; namely, that which proceeds from sense to the invention of principles, analytical; and the rest synthetical.

8. The method of searching out, whether anything propounded be matter or accident. To those that seek the cause

of some certain and propounded appearance or effect, it happens, sometimes, that they know not whether the thing, whose cause is sought after, be matter or body, or some accident of a body. For though in geometry, when the cause is sought of magnitude, or proportion, or figure, it be certainly known that these things, namely magnitude, proportion, and figure, are accidents; yet in natural philosophy, where all questions are concerning the causes of the phantasms of sensible things, it is not so easy to discern between the things themselves, from which those phantasms proceed, and the appearances of those things to the sense; which have deceived many, especially when the phantasms have been made by light. For example, a man that looks upon the sun, has a certain shining idea of the magnitude of about a foot over, and this he calls the sun, though he know the sun to be truly a great deal bigger; and, in like manner, the phantasm of the same thing appears sometimes round, by being seen afar off, and sometimes square, by being nearer. Whereupon it may well be doubted, whether that phantasm be matter, or some body natural, or only some accident of a body; in the examination of which doubt we may use this method. The properties of matter and accidents already found out by us, by the synthetical method, from their definitions, are to be compared with the idea we have before us; and if it agree with the properties of matter or body, then it is a body; otherwise it is an accident. Seeing, therefore, matter cannot by any endeavor of ours be either made or destroyed, or increased, or diminished, or moved out of its place, whereas that idea appears, vanishes, is increased and diminished, and moved hither and thither at pleasure; we may certainly conclude that it is not a body, but an accident only. And this method is *synthetical*.

9. The method of seeking whether any accident be in this or in that subject. But if there be a doubt made concerning the subject of any known accident (for this may be doubted sometimes, as in the precedent example, doubt may be made in what subject that splendor and apparent magnitude of the sun is), then our inquiry must proceed in this manner. First, matter in general must be divided into parts, as, into object, medium, and the sentient itself, or such other parts as seem

most conformable to the thing propounded. Next, these parts are severally to be examined how they agree with the definition of the subject; and such of them as are not capable of that accident are to be rejected. For example, if by any true ratiocination the sun be found to be greater than its apparent magnitude, then that magnitude is not in the sun; if the sun be in one determined straight line, and one determined distance, and the magnitude and splendor be seen in more lines and distances than one, as it is in reflection or refraction, then neither that splendor nor apparent magnitude are in the sun itself, and, therefore, the body of the sun cannot be the subject of that splendor and magnitude. And for the same reasons the air and other parts will be rejected, till at last nothing remain which can be the subject of that splendor and magnitude but the sentient itself. And this method, in regard the subject is divided into parts, is analytical; and in regard the properties, both of the subject and accident, are compared with the accident concerning whose subject the inquiry is made, it is synthetical.

10. Method of searching for the cause of any effect, propounded. But when we seek after the cause of any propounded effect, we must in the first place get into our mind an exact notion or idea of that which we call cause, namely, that *a cause is the sum or aggregate of all such accidents, both in the agents and the patient, as concur to the producing of the effect propounded; all which existing together, it cannot be understood but that the effect existeth with them; or that it can possibly exist if any one of them be absent.* This being known, in the next place we must examine singly every accident that accompanies or precedes the effect, as far forth as it seems to conduce in any manner to the production of the same, and see whether the propounded effect may be conceived to exist, without the existence of any of those accidents; and by this means separate such accidents, as do not concur, from such as concur to produce the said effect; which being done, we are to put together the concurring accidents, and consider whether we can possibly conceive, that when these are all present, the effect propounded will not follow; and if it be evident that the effect will follow, then that aggregate of acci-

dents is the entire cause, otherwise not; but we must still search out and put together other accidents. For example, if the cause of light be propounded to be sought out; first, we examine things without us, and find that whensoever light appears, there is some principal object, as it were the fountain of light, without which we cannot have any perception of light; and, therefore, the concurrence of that object is necessary to the generation of light. Next we consider the medium, and find, that unless it be disposed in a certain manner, namely, that it be transparent, though the object remain the same, yet the effect will not follow; and, therefore, the concurrence of transparency is also necessary to the generation of light. Thirdly, we observe our own body, and find that by the indisposition of the eyes, the brain, the nerves, and the heart, that is, by obstructions, stupidity, and debility, we are deprived of light, so that a fitting disposition of the organs to receive impressions from without is likewise a necessary part of the cause of light. Again, of all the accidents inherent in the object, there is none that can conduce to the effecting of light, but only action (or a certain motion), which cannot be conceived to be wanting, whensoever the effect is present; for, that anything may shine, it is not requisite that it be of such or such magnitude or figure, or that the whole body of it be moved out of the place it is in (unless it may perhaps be said, that in the sun, or other body, that which causes light is the light it hath in itself; which yet is but a trifling exception, seeing nothing is meant thereby but the cause of light; as if any man should say that the cause of light is that in the sun which produceth it); it remains, therefore, that the action, by which light is generated, is motion only in the parts of the object. Which being understood, we may easily conceive what it is the medium contributes, namely, the continuation of that motion to the eye; and, lastly, what the eye and the rest of the organs of the sentient contribute, namely, the continuation of the same motion to the last organ of sense, the heart. And in this manner the cause of light may be made up of motion continued from the original of the same motion, to the original of vital motion, light being nothing but the alteration of vital motion, made by the impression upon it of motion continued from the object. But I give this only for an example, for I shall speak more at large of light, and the generation of it, in its proper place. In the mean time it is manifest, that in the searching out of causes, there is need partly of the analytical, and partly of the synthetical method; of the analytical, to conceive how circumstances conduce severally to the production of effects; and of the synthetical, for the adding together and compounding of what they can effect singly by themselves. And thus much may serve for the method of invention. It remains that I speak of the method of teaching, that is, of demonstration, and of the means by which we demonstrate.

11. Words serve to invention as marks; to demonstration as signs. In the method of invention, the use of words consists in this, that they may serve for marks, by which, whatsoever we have found out may be recalled to memory; for without this all our inventions perish, nor will it be possible for us to go on from principles beyond a syllogism or two, by reason of the weakness of memory. For example, if any man, by considering a triangle set before him, should find that all its angles together taken are equal to two right angles, and that by thinking of the same tacitly, without any use of words either understood or expressed; and it should happen afterwards that another triangle, unlike the former, or the same in different situation, should be offered to his consideration, he would not know readily whether the same property were in this last or no, but would be forced, as often as a different triangle were brought before him (and the difference of triangles is infinite) to begin his contemplation anew; which he would have no need to do if he had the use of names, for every universal name denotes the conceptions we have of infinite singular things. Nevertheless, as I said above, they serve as *marks* for the help of our memory, whereby we register to ourselves our own inventions; but not as *signs* by which we declare the same to others; so that a man may be a philosopher alone by himself, without any master; Adam had this capacity. But to teach, that is, to demonstrate, supposes two at the least, and syllogistical speech.

12. The method of demonstration is synthetical. And seeing teaching is nothing but leading the mind of him we teach, to

the knowledge of our inventions, in that track by which we attained the same with our own mind; therefore, the same method that served for our invention, will serve also for demonstration to others, saving that we omit the first part of method which proceeded from the sense of things to universal principles, which, because they are principles, cannot be demonstrated; and seeing they are known by nature, (as was said above in the 5th article) they need no demonstration, though they need explication. The whole method, therefore, of demonstration, is *synthetical*, consisting of that order of speech which begins from primary or most universal propositions, which are manifest of themselves, and proceeds by a perpetual composition of propositions into syllogisms, till at last the learner understand the truth of the conclusion sought after.

13. Definitions only are primary, & universal propositions. Now, such principles are nothing but definitions, whereof there are two sorts; one of names, that signify such things as have some conceivable cause, and another of such names as signify things of which we can conceive no cause at all. Names of the former kind are, *body,* or *matter, quantity,* or *extension, motion,* and whatsoever is common to all matter. Of the second kind, are *such a body, such and so great motion, so great magnitude, such figure,* and whatsoever we can distinguish one body from another by. And names of the former kind are well enough defined, when, by speech as short as may be, we raise in the mind of the hearer perfect and clear ideas or conceptions of the things named, as when we define motion to be *the leaving of one place, and the acquiring of another continually;* for though no thing moved, nor any cause of motion be in that definition, yet, at the hearing of that speech, there will come into the mind of the hearer an *idea* of motion clear enough. But definitions of things, which may be understood to have some cause, must consist of such names as express the cause or manner of their generation, as when we define a circle to be a figure made by the circumduction of a straight line in a plane, &c. Besides definitions, there is no other proposition that ought to be called primary, or (according to severe truth) be received into the number of principles. For those *axioms of Euclid,* seeing they may be demonstrated, are no principles of

demonstration, though they have by the consent of all men gotten the authority of principles, because they need not be demonstrated. Also, those *petitions,* or *postulata,* (as they call them) though they be principles, yet they are not principles of demonstration, but of construction only; that is, not of science, but of power; or (which is all one) not of *theorems,* which are speculations, but of *problems,* which belong to practice, or the doing of something. But as for those common received opinions, *Nature abhors vacuity, Nature doth nothing in vain,* and the like, which are neither evident in themselves, nor at all to be demonstrated, and which are oftener false than true, they are much less to be acknowledged for principles.

To return, therefore, to definitions; the reason why I say that the cause and generation of such things, as have any cause or generation, ought to enter into their definitions, is this. The end of science is the demonstration of the causes and generations of things; which if they be not in the definitions, they cannot be found in the conclusion of the first syllogism, that is made from those definitions; and if they be not in the first conclusion, they will not be found in any further conclusion deduced from that; and, therefore, by proceeding in this manner, we shall never come to science; which is against the scope and intention of demonstration.

14. The nature & definition of a definition. Now, seeing definitions (as I have said) are principles, or primary propositions, they are therefore speeches; and seeing they are used for the raising of an *idea* of some thing in the mind of the learner, whensoever that thing has a name, the definition of it can be nothing but the explication of that name by speech; and if that name be given it for some compounded conception, the definition is nothing but a resolution of that name into its most universal parts. As when we define man, saying *man is a body animated, sentient, rational,* those names, *body animated, &c.* are parts of that whole name *man;* so that definitions of this kind always consist of *genus* and *difference;* the former names being all, till the last, *general;* and the last of all, *difference.* But if any name be the most universal in its kind, then the definition of it cannot consist of *genus* and *difference,* but is to be made by such circumlocution, as best explicateth the

force of that name. Again, it is possible, and happens often, that the *genus* and *difference* are put together, and yet make no definition; as these words, *a straight line*, contain both the *genus* and *difference;* but are not a definition, unless we should think a straight line may be thus defined, *a straight line is a straight line:* and yet if there were added another name, consisting of different words, but signifying the same thing which these signify, then these might be the definition of that name. From what has been said, it may be understood how a definition ought to be defined, namely, *that it is a proposition, whose predicate resolves the subject, when it may; and when it may not, it exemplifies the same.*

15. Properties of a definition. The properties of a definition are:

First, that it takes away equivocation, as also all that multitude of distinctions, which are used by such as think they may learn philosophy by disputation. For the nature of a definition is to define, that is, to determine the signification of the defined name, and to pare from it all other signification besides what is contained in the definition itself; and therefore one definition does as much, as all the distinctions (how many soever) that can be used about the name defined.

Secondly, that it gives a universal notion of the thing defined, representing a certain universal picture thereof, not to the eye, but to the mind. For as when one paints a man, he paints the image of some man; so he, that defines the name man, makes a representation of some man to the mind.

Thirdly, that it is not necessary to dispute whether definitions are to be admitted or no. For when a master is instructing his scholar, if the scholar understand all the parts of the thing defined, which are resolved in the definition, and yet will not admit of the definition, there needs no further controversy betwixt them, it being all one as if he refused to be taught. But if he understand nothing, then certainly the definition is faulty; for the nature of a definition consists in this, that it exhibit a clear idea of the thing defined; and principles are either known by themselves, or else they are not principles.

Fourthly, that, in philosophy, definitions are before defined names. For in teaching philosophy, the first beginning is from definitions; and all progression in the same, till we come to the knowledge of the thing compounded, is compositive. Seeing, therefore, definition is the explication of a compounded name by resolution, and the progression is from the parts to the compound, definitions must be understood before compounded names; nay, when the names of the parts of any speech be explicated, it is not necessary that the definition should be a name compounded of them. For example, when these names, *equilateral, quadrilateral, right-angled,* are sufficiently understood, it is not necessary in geometry that there should be at all such a name as *square;* for defined names are received in philosophy for brevity's sake only.

Fifthly, that compounded names, which are defined one way in some one part of philosophy, may in another part of the same be otherwise defined; as a *parabola* and a *hyperbole* have one definition in geometry, and another in rhetoric; for definitions are instituted and serve for the understanding of the doctrine which is treated of. And, therefore, as in one part of philosophy, a definition may have in it some one fit name for the more brief explanation of some proposition in geometry; so it may have the same liberty in other parts of philosophy; for the use of names is particular (even where many agree to the settling of them) and arbitrary.

Sixthly, that no name can be defined by any one word; because no one word is sufficient for the resolving of one or more words.

Seventhly, that a defined name ought not to be repeated in the definition. For a defined name is the whole compound, and a definition is the resolution of that compound into parts; but no total can be part of itself.

16. Nature of a demonstration. Any two definitions, that may be compounded into a syllogism, produce a conclusion; which, because it is derived from principles, that is, from definitions, is said to be demonstrated; and the derivation or composition itself is called a demonstration. In like manner, if a syllogism be made of two propositions, whereof one is a definition, the other a demonstrated conclusion, or neither of them is a definition, but both formerly demonstrated, that syllogism is also called a demonstration, and so successively.

The definition therefore of a demonstration is this, *a demonstration is a syllogism, or series of syllogisms, derived and continued, from the definitions of names, to the last conclusion.* And from hence it may be understood, that all true ratiocination, which taketh its beginning from true principles, produceth science, and is true demonstration. For as for the original of the name, although that, which the Greeks called ὁποδέιξις, and the Latins *demonstratio*, was understood by them for that sort only of ratiocination, in which, by the describing of certain lines and figures, they placed the thing they were to prove, as it were before men's eyes, which is properly ἀποδεικνύειν, or to *show* by the figure; yet they seem to have done it for this reason, that unless it were in geometry, (in which only there is place for such figures) there was no ratiocination certain, and ending in science, their doctrines concerning all other things being nothing but controversy and clamor; which, nevertheless, happened, not because the truth to which they pretended could not be made evident without figures, but because they wanted true principles, from which they might derive their ratiocination; and, therefore, there is no reason but that if true definitions were premised in all sorts of doctrines, the demonstrations also would be true.

17. *Properties of a demonstration, and order of things to be demonstrated.* It is proper to methodical demonstration:

First, that there be a true succession of one reason to another, according to the rules of syllogizing delivered above.

Secondly, that the premises of all syllogisms be demonstrated from the first definitions.

Thirdly, that after definitions, he that teaches or demonstrates any thing, proceed in the same method by which he found it out; namely, that in the first place those things be demonstrated, which immediately succeed to universal definitions (in which is contained that part of philosophy which is called *philosophia prima*). Next, those things which may be demonstrated by simple motion (in which geometry consists). After geometry, such things as may be taught or showed by manifest action, that is, by thrusting from, or pulling towards. And after these, the motion or mutation of the invisible parts of things, and the doctrine of sense and imaginations, and of the internal passions, especially those of men, in which are comprehended the grounds of civil duties, or civil philosophy; which takes up the last place. And that this method ought to be kept in all sorts of philosophy, is evident from hence, that such things as I have said are to be taught last, cannot be demonstrated, till such as are propounded to be first treated of, be fully understood. Of which method no other example can be given, but that treatise of the elements of philosophy, which I shall begin in the next chapter, and continue to the end of the work.

18. Faults of a demonstration. Besides those *paralogisms*, whose fault lies either in the falsity of the premises, or the want of true composition, of which I have spoken in the precedent chapter, there are two more, which are frequent in demonstration; one whereof is commonly called *petitio principii;* the other is the supposing of a *false cause;* and these do not only deceive unskilful learners, but sometimes masters themselves, by making them take that for well demonstrated, which is not demonstrated at all. *Petitio principii* is, when the conclusion to be proved is disguised in other words, and put for the definition or principle from whence it is to be demonstrated; and thus, by putting for the cause of the thing sought, either the thing itself or some effect of it, they make a circle in their demonstration. As for example, he that would demonstrate that the earth stands still in the center of the world, and should suppose the earth's gravity to be the cause thereof, and define gravity to be a quality by which every heavy body tends towards the center of the world, would lose his labor; for the question is, what is the cause of that quality in the earth? and, therefore, he that supposes gravity to be the cause, puts the thing itself for its own cause.

Of a *false cause* I find this example in a certain treatise where the thing to be demonstrated is the motion of the earth. He begins, therefore, with this, that seeing the earth and the sun are not always in the same situation, it must needs be that one of them be locally moved, which is true; next, he affirms that the vapors, which the sun raises from the earth and sea, are, by reason of this motion, necessarily moved, which also is true; from whence he infers the winds are made, and this may pass for granted; and by these winds he says, the waters of the sea are moved, and by their motion the bottom of the sea, as if it were beaten forwards, moves round; and let this also be granted; wherefore, he concludes, the earth is moved; which is, nevertheless, a paralogism. For, if that wind were the cause why the earth was, from the beginning, moved round, and the motion either of the sun or the earth were the cause of that wind, then the motion of the sun or the earth was before the wind itself; and if the earth were moved, before the wind was made, then the wind could not be the cause of the earth's revolution; but, if the sun were moved, and the earth stand still, then it is manifest the earth might remain unmoved, notwithstanding that wind; and therefore that motion was not made by the cause which he allegeth. But paralogisms of this kind are very frequent among the writers of *physics,* though none can be more elaborate than this in the example given.

19. Why the analytical method of geometricians cannot be treated of in this place. It may to some men seem pertinent to treat in this place of that art of the geometricians, which they call *logistica,* that is, the art, by which, from supposing the thing in question to be true, they proceed by ratiocination, till either they come to something known, by which they may demonstrate the truth of the thing sought for; or to something which is impossible, from whence they collect that to be false, which they supposed true. But this art cannot be explicated here, for this reason, that the method of it can neither be practiced, nor understood, unless by such as are well versed in geometry; and among geometricians themselves, they, that have most theorems in readiness, are the most ready in the use of this *logistica;* so that, indeed, it is not a distinct thing from geometry itself; for there are, in the method of it, three parts; the first whereof consists in the finding out of equality betwixt known and unknown things, which they call equation; and this equation cannot be found out, but by such as know perfectly the nature, properties, and transpositions of proportion, as also the addition, subtraction, multiplication, and division of lines and superficies, and the extraction of roots; which are the parts of no mean geometrician. The second is,

when an equation is found, to be able to judge whether the truth or falsity of the question may be deduced from it, or no; which yet requires greater knowledge. And the third is, when such an equation is found, as is fit for the solution of the question, to know how to resolve the same in such manner, that the truth or falsity may thereby manifestly appear; which, in hard questions, cannot be done without the knowledge of the nature of crooked-lined figures; but he that understands readily the nature and properties of these, is a complete geometrician. It happens besides, that for the finding out of equations, there is no certain method, but he is best able to do it, that has the best natural wit.

PART 2

BODY AND MOTION

THE FIRST GROUNDS OF PHILOSOPHY*

Chapter 7

Of Place and Time

1. Things that have no existence, may nevertheless be understood and computed. In the teaching of natural philosophy, I cannot begin better (as I have already shown) than from *privation;* that is, from feigning the world to be annihilated. But, if such annihilation of all things be supposed, it may perhaps be asked, what would remain for any man (whom only I except from this universal annihilation of things) to consider as the subject of philosophy, or at all to reason upon; or what to give names unto for ratiocination's sake.

I say, therefore, there would remain to that man ideas of the world, and of all such bodies as he had, before their annihilation, seen with his eyes, or perceived by any other sense; that is to say, the memory and imagination of magnitudes, motions, sounds, colors, &c. as also of their order and parts. All which things, though they be nothing but ideas and phantasms, happening internally to him that imagineth; yet they will appear as if they were external, and not at all depending upon any power of the mind. And these are the things to which he would give names, and subtract them from, and compound them with one another. For seeing, that after the destruction of all other things, I suppose man still remaining, and namely that he thinks, imagines, and remembers, there can be nothing for him to think of but what is past; nay, if we do but observe diligently what it is we do when we consider and reason, we shall find, that though all things be still remaining in the world, yet we compute nothing but our own phantasms. For when

---

*From *De Corpore* (Molesworth Ed.) 1839, Vol. I of English Works, Chapters 7-11.

we calculate the magnitude and motions of heaven or earth, we do not ascend into heaven that we may divide it into parts, or measure the motions thereof, but we do it sitting still in our closets or in the dark. Now things may be considered, that is, be brought into account, either as internal accidents of our mind, in which manner we consider them when the question is about some faculty of the mind; or as species of external things, not as really existing, but appearing only to exist, or to have a being without us. And in this manner we are now to consider them.

2. What is Space. If therefore we remember, or have a phantasm of any thing that was in the world before the supposed annihilation of the same; and consider, not that the thing was such or such, but only that it had a being without the mind, we have presently a conception of that we call *space:* an imaginary space indeed, because a mere phantasm, yet that very thing which all men call so. For no man calls it space for being already filled, but because it may be filled; nor does any man think bodies carry their places away with them, but that the same space contains sometimes one, sometimes another body; which could not be if space should always accompany the body which is once in it. And this is of itself so manifest, that I should not think it needed any explaining at all, but that I find space to be falsely defined by certain philosophers, who infer from thence, one, that the world is infinite (for taking *space* to be the extension of bodies, and thinking extension may increase continually, he infers that bodies may be infinitely extended); and, another, from the same definition, concludes rashly, that it is impossible even to God himself to create more worlds than one; for, if another world were to be created, he says, that seeing there is nothing without this world, and therefore (according to his definition) no space, that new world must be placed in nothing; but in nothing nothing can be placed; which he affirms only, without showing any reason for the same; whereas the contrary is the truth: for more cannot be put into a place already filled, so much is empty space fitter than that, which is full, for the receiving of new bodies. Having therefore spoken thus much

for these men's sakes, and for theirs that assent to them, I return to my purpose, and define *space* thus: SPACE *is the phantasm of a thing existing without the mind simply;* that is to say, that phantasm, in which we consider no other accident, but only that it appears without us.

3. Time. As a body leaves a phantasm of its magnitude in the mind, so also a moved body leaves a phantasm of its motion, namely, an idea of that body passing out of one space into another by continual succession. And this idea, or phantasm, is that, which (without receding much from the common opinion, or from *Aristotle's* definition) I call *Time*. For seeing all men confess a year to be time, and yet do not think a year to be the accident or affection of any body, they must needs confess it to be, not in the things without us, but only in the thought of the mind. So when they speak of the times of their predecessors, they do not think after their predecessors are gone, that their times can be any where else than in the memory of those that remember them. And as for those that say, days, years, and months are the motions of the sun and moon, seeing it is all one to say, motion *past* and motion *destroyed,* and that *future* motion is the same with motion which *is not yet begun,* they say that, which they do not mean, that there neither is, nor has been, nor shall be any time: for of whatsoever it may be said, *it has been* or *it shall be,* of the same also it might have been said heretofore, or may be said hereafter, *it is.* What then can days, months, and years, be, but the names of such computations made in our mind? *Time* therefore is a phantasm, but a phantasm of motion, for if we would know by what moments time passes away, we make use of some motion or other, as of the sun, of a clock, of the sand in an hourglass, or we mark some line upon which we imagine something to be moved, there being no other means by which we can take notice of any time at all. And yet, when I say *time* is a phantasm of motion, I do not say this is sufficient to define it by; for this word *time* comprehends the notion of *former* and *latter,* or of *succession* in the motion of a body, in as much as it is first *here* then *there.* Wherefore a complete definition of *time* is such as this, TIME *is the phantasm of be-*

fore and after in motion; which agrees with this definition of
Aristotle, *time is the number of motion according to former
and latter;* for that numbering is an act of the mind; and
therefore it is all one to say, *time is the number of motion
according to former and latter;* and *time is a phantasm of
motion numbered.* But that other definition, *time is the measure of motion,* is not so exact, for we measure time by motion
and not motion by time.

4. Part. One space is called *part* of another space, and one
time *part* of another time, when this contains that and something besides. From whence it may be collected, that nothing
can rightly be called a PART, but that which is compared with
something that contains it.

5. Division. And therefore to *make parts,* or to *part* or
DIVIDE space or *time,* is nothing else but to consider one and
another within the same; so that if any man *divide* space or
time, the diverse conceptions he has are more, by one, than
the parts he makes; for his first conception is of that which is
to be divided, then of some part of it, and again of some other
other part of it, and so forwards as long as he goes on in
dividing.

But it is to be noted, that here, by *division,* I do not mean
the severing or pulling asunder of one space or time from
another (for does any man think that one hemisphere may be
separated from the other hemisphere, or the first hour from
the second?) but diversity of consideration; so that division is
not made by the operation of the hands but of the mind.

6. One. When space or time is considered among other
spaces or times, it is said to be ONE, namely *one of them;* for
except one space might be added to another, and subtracted
from another space, and so of time, it would be sufficient to
say space or time simply, and superfluous to say one space or
one time, if it could not be conceived that there were another.
The common definition of *one,* namely, that *one is that which
is undivided,* is obnoxious to an absurd consequence; for it
may thence be inferred, that whatsoever is divided is many
things, that is, that every divided thing, is divided things, which
is insignificant.

7. Number. Number is *one* and *one,* or *one one* and *one,* and so forwards; namely, *one* and *one* make the number *two,* and *one one* and *one* the number *three;* so are all other numbers made; which is all one as if we should say, *number is unities.*

8. Composition. To compound space of spaces, or time of times, is first to consider them one after another, and then altogether as one; as if one should reckon first the head, the feet, the arms, and the body, severally, and then for the account of them all together put *man.* And that which is so put for all the severals of which it consists, is called the WHOLE; and those severals, when by the division of the whole they come again to be considered singly, are parts thereof; and therefore the *whole* and *all the parts taken together* are the same thing. And as I noted above, that in *division* it is not necessary to pull the parts asunder; so in *composition,* it is to be understood, that for the making up of a whole there is no need of putting the parts together, so as to make them touch one another, but only of collecting them into one sum in the mind. For thus all men, being considered together, make up the whole of mankind, though never so much dispersed by time and place; and twelve hours, though the hours of several days, may be compounded into one number of twelve.

9. The whole. This being well understood, it is manifest, that nothing can rightly be called a whole, that is not conceived to be compounded of parts, and that it may be divided into parts; so that if we deny that a thing has parts; we deny the same to be a whole. For example, if we say the soul can have no parts, we affirm that no soul can be a whole soul. Also it is manifest, that nothing has parts till it be divided; and when a thing is divided, the parts are only so many as the division makes them. Again, that a part of a part is a part of the whole; and thus any part of the number *four,* as *two,* is a part of the number *eight;* for *four* is made of *two* and *two;* but *eight* is compounded of *two, two,* and *four,* and therefore *two,* which is a part of the part *four,* is also a part of the whole *eight.*

10. Spaces and times contiguous and continual. Two spaces are said to be CONTIGUOUS, when there is no other space be-

twixt them. But two times, betwixt which there is no other
time, are called immediate, as AB, BC.

And any two spaces, as well as times, A B C
are said to be CONTINUAL, when they have one common part,
as AC, BD, where the part BC is com-
mon; and more spaces and times are A B C D
continual, when every two which are next one another are
continual.

11. *Beginning, end, way, finite, infinite.* That part which is
between two other parts, is called a MEAN; and that which is
not between two other parts, an EXTREME. And of extremes,
that which is first reckoned is the BEGINNING, and that which
last, the END; and all the means together taken are the WAY.
Also, *extreme parts* and *limits* are the same thing. And from
hence it is manifest, that *beginning* and *end* depend upon the
order in which we number them; and that to *terminate* or *limit*
space and time, is the same thing with *imagining their beginning and end;* as also that every thing is FINITE or INFINITE,
according as we imagine or not imagine it *limited* or *terminated* every way; and that the *limits* of any number are
unities, and of these, that which is the first in our numbering
is the *beginning,* and that which we number last, is the *end.*
When we say number is *infinite,* we mean only that no number
is expressed; for when we speak of the numbers *two, three, a
thousand,* &c. they are always *finite.* But when no more is said
but this, *number is infinite,* it is to be understood as if it were
said, this name *number* is an *indefinite* name.

12. *What is infinite in power.* Nothing infinite can be truly
said to be either whole or one; nor infinite spaces or times,
many. Space or time is said to be *finite in power,* or *terminable,*
when there may be assigned a number of finite spaces or times,
as of paces or hours, than which there can be no greater number of the same measure in that space or time; and *infinite
in power* is that space or time, in which a greater number of
the said paces or hours may be assigned, than any number that
can be given. But we must note, that, although in that space
or time which is infinite in power, there may be numbered
more paces or hours than any number that can be assigned,
yet their number will always be finite; for every number is

finite. And therefore his ratiocination was not good, that undertaking to prove the world to be finite, reasoned thus; *If the world be infinite, then there may be taken in it some part which is distant from us an infinite number of paces: but no such part can be taken; wherefore the world is not infinite;* because that consequence of the major proposition is false; for in an infinite space, whatsoever we take or design in our mind, the distance of the same from us is a finite space; for in the very designing of the place thereof, we put an end to that space, of which we ourselves are the beginning; and whatsoever any man with his mind cuts off both ways from infinite, he determines the same, that is, he makes it finite.

Of infinite space or time, it cannot be said that it is a *whole* or *one:* not a *whole,* because not compounded of parts; for seeing parts, how many soever they be, are severally finite, they will also, when they are all put together, make a whole finite: nor *one,* because nothing can be said to be one, except there be another to compare it with; but it cannot be conceived that there are two spaces, or two times, infinite. Lastly, when we make question whether the world be finite or infinite, we have nothing in our mind answering to the name *world*; for whatsoever we imagine, is therefore finite, though our computation reach the fixed stars, or the ninth or tenth, nay, the thousandth sphere. The meaning of the question is this only, whether God has actually made so great an addition of body to body, as we are able to make of space to space.

13. *Division proceeds not to the least.* And, therefore, that which is commonly said, that space and time may be divided infinitely, is not to be so understood, as if there might be any infinite or eternal division; but rather to be taken in this sense, *whatsoever is divided, is divided into such parts as may again be divided*; or thus, *the least divisible thing is not to be given*; or, as geometricians have it, *no quantity is so small, but a less may be taken*; which may easily be demonstrated in this manner. Let any space or time, that which was thought to be the least divisible, be divided into two equal parts, A and B. I say either of them, as A, may be divided again. For suppose the part A to be con-

tiguous to the part B of one side, and of the other side to some other space equal to B. This whole space, therefore, being greater than the space given, is divisible. Wherefore, if it be divided into two equal parts, the part in the middle, which is A, will be also divided into two equal parts; and therefore A was divisible.

Chapter 8

Of Body and Accident

1. Body defined. Having understood what imaginary space is, in which we supposed nothing remaining without us, but all those things to be destroyed, that, by existing heretofore, left images of themselves in our minds; let us now suppose some one of those things to be placed again in the world, or created anew. It is necessary, therefore, that this new-created or replaced thing do not only fill some part of the space above mentioned, or be coincident and coextended with it, but also that it have no dependence upon our thought. And this is that which, for the extension of it, we commonly call *body*; and because it depends not upon our thought, we say is *a thing subsisting of itself*; as also *existing*, because without us; and, lastly, it is called the *subject*, because it is so placed in and *subjected* to imaginary space, that it may be understood by reason, as well as perceived by sense. The definition, therefore, of *body* may be this, a *body is that, which having no dependence upon our thought, is coincident or coextended with some part of space.*

2. Accident defined. But what an *accident* is cannot so easily be explained by any definition, as by examples. Let us imagine, therefore, that a body fills any space, or is coextended with it; that coextension is not the coextended body: and, in like manner, let us imagine that the same body is removed out of its place; that removing is not the removed body: or let us think the same not removed; that not removing or rest is not the resting body. What, then, are these things? They are *accidents* of that body. But the thing in question is, *what is an accident?* which is an inquiry after that which we know already, and not that which we should inquire after. For who does not always and in the same manner understand him that says any thing is extended, or moved, or not moved? But most men will have it be said that *an accident is something*, namely, some part of

101

a natural thing, when, indeed, it is no part of the same. To satisfy these men, as well as may be, they answer best that define an *accident* to be *the manner by which any body is conceived*; which is all one as if they should say, *an accident is that faculty of any body, by which it works in us a conception of itself*. Which definition, though it be not an answer to the question propounded, yet it is an answer to that question which should have been propounded, namely, *whence does it happen that one part of any body appears here, another there?* For this is well answered thus: *it happens from the extension of that body*. Or, *how comes it to pass that the whole body, by succession, is seen now here, now there?* and the answer will be, *by reason of its motion*. Or, lastly, *whence is it that any body possesseth the same space for sometime?* and the answer will be, *because it is not moved*. For if concerning the name of a body, that is, concerning a concrete name, it be asked, *what is it?* the answer must be made by definition; for the question is concerning the signification of the name. But if it be asked concerning an abstract name, *what is it?* the cause is demanded why a thing appears so or so. As if it be asked, *what is hard?* The answer will be, hard is that, whereof no part gives place, but when the whole gives place. But if it be demanded, *what is hardness?* a cause must be shown why a part does not give place, except the whole give place. Wherefore, I define an *accident* to be *the manner of our conception of body*.

3. How an accident may be understood to be in its subject. When an *accident* is said *to be in a body*, it is not so to be understood, as if any thing were contained in that body; as if, for example, redness were in blood, in the same manner, as blood is in a bloody cloth, that is, as a part in the whole; for so, an accident would be a body also. But, as magnitude, or rest, or motion, is in that which is great, or which resteth, or which is moved, (which, how it is to be understood, every man understands) so also, it is to be understood, that every other accident *is in* its subject. And this, also, is explicated by *Aristotle* no otherwise than negatively, namely, that *an accident is in its subject, not as any part thereof, but so as that it may be away, the subject still remaining*; which is

ight, saving that there are certain accidents which can never
perish except the body perish also; for no body can be conceived to be without extension, or without figure. All other
accidents, which are not common to all bodies, but peculiar to
some only, as *to be at rest, to be moved, color, hardness*, and
the like, do perish continually, and are succeeded by others;
yet so, as that the body never perisheth. And as for the
opinion that some may have, that all other accidents are not in
their bodies in the same manner that extension, motion, rest,
or figure, are in the same; for example, that color, heat, odor,
virtue, vice, and the like, are otherwise in them, and, as they
say, *inherent*; I desire they would suspend their judgment for
the present, and expect a little, till it be found out by ratiocination, whether these very accidents are not also certain motions either of the mind of the perceiver, or of the bodies
themselves which are perceived; for in the search of this, a
great part of natural philosophy consists.

4. *Magnitude, what it is.* The *extension* of a body, is the
same thing with the *magnitude* of it, or that which some call
real space. But this *magnitude* does not depend upon our cogitation, as imaginary space doth; for this is an effect of our
imagination, but *magnitude* is the cause of it; this is an accident of the mind, that of a body existing out of the mind.

5. *Place, what it is, and that it is immovable.* That
space, by which word I here understand imaginary space,
which is coincident with the magnitude of any body, is
called the *place* of that body; and the body itself is that which
we call the *thing placed*. Now *place*, and the *magnitude* of the
thing placed, differ. First in this, that a body keeps always the
same *magnitude*, both when it is at rest, and when it is moved;
but when it is moved, it does not keep the same *place*. Secondly in this, that *place* is a phantasm of any body of such
and such quantity and figure; but *magnitude* is the peculiar
accident of every body; for one body may at several times
have several places, but has always one and the same magnitude. Thirdly in this, that *place* is nothing out of the mind, nor
magnitude any thing within it. And lastly, *place* is feigned
extension, but *magnitude* true extension; and a placed body is
not extension, but a thing extended. Besides, *place is immova-*

ble; for, seeing that which is moved, is understood to be carried from place to place, if place were moved, it would also be carried from place to place, so that one place must have another place, and that place another place, and so on infinitely, which is ridiculous. And as for those, that, by making *place* to be of the same nature with *real space*, would from thence maintain it to be immovable, they also make place, though they do not perceive they make it so, to be a mere phantasm. For whilst one affirms that place is therefore said to be immovable, because space in general is considered there; if he had remembered that nothing is general or universal besides names or signs, he would easily have seen that that space, which he says is considered in general, is nothing but a phantasm, in the mind or the memory, of a body of such magnitude and such figure. And whilst another says: real space is made immovable by the understanding; as when, under the superficies of running water, we imagine other and other water to come by continual succession, that superficies fixed there by the understanding, is the *immovable place* of the river: what else does he make it to be but a phantasm, though he do it obscurely and in perplexed words? Lastly, the nature of *place* does not consist in the *superficies of the ambient*, but in *solid space*; for the whole placed body is coextended with its whole place, and every part of it with every answering part of the same place; but seeing every placed body is a solid thing, it cannot be understood to be coextended with superficies. Besides, how can any whole body be moved, unless all its parts be moved together with it? Or how can the internal parts of it be moved, but by leaving their place? But the internal parts of a body cannot leave the superficies of an external part contiguous to it; and, therefore, it follows, that if place be the superficies of the ambient, then the parts of a body moved, that is, bodies moved, are not moved.

6. What is full and empty. Space, or place, that is possessed by a body, is called *full*, and that which is not so possessed, is called *empty*.

7. Here, there, somewhere, what they signify. *Here, there, in the country, in the city*, and other the like

names, by which answer is made to the question *where is it?* are not properly names of place, nor do they of themselves bring into the mind the place that is sought; for *here* and *there* signify nothing, unless the thing be shown at the same time with the finger or something else; but when the eye of him that seeks, is, by pointing or some other sign, directed to the thing sought, the place of it is not hereby defined by him that answers, but found out by him that asks the question. Now such showings as are made by words only, as when we say, *in the country,* or *in the city,* are some of greater latitude than others, as when we say, *in the country, in the city, in such a street, in a house, in the chamber, in bed,* &c. For these do, by little and little, direct the seeker nearer to the proper place; and yet they do not determine the same, but only restrain it to a lesser space, and signify no more, than that the place of the thing is within a certain space designed by those words, as a part is in the whole. And all such names, by which answer is made to the question *where?* have, for their highest *genus,* the name *somewhere.* From whence it may be understood, that whatsoever is somewhere, is in some place properly so called, which place is part of that greater space that is signified by some of these names, *in the country, in the city,* or the like.

8. Many bodies cannot be in one place, nor one body in many places. A body, and the magnitude, and the place thereof, are divided by one and the same act of the mind; for, to divide an extended body, and the extension thereof, and the idea of that extension, which is place, is the same with dividing any one of them; because they are coincident, and it cannot be done but by the mind, that is by the division of space. From whence it is manifest, that neither two bodies can be together in the same place, nor one body be in two places at the same time. Not two bodies in the same place; because when a body that fills its whole place is divided into two, the place itself is divided into two also, so that there will be two places. Not one body in two places; for the place that a body fills being divided into two, the placed body will be also divided into two; for, as I said, a place and the body that fills that place, are divided both together; and so there will be two bodies.

9. Contiguous and continual, what they are. Two bodies are said to be *contiguous* to one another, and *continual*, in the same manner as spaces are; namely, *those are contiguous, between which there is no space*. Now, by space I understand, here as formerly, an idea or phantasm of a body. Wherefore, though between two bodies there be put no other body, and consequently no magnitude, or, as they call it, real space, yet if another body may be put between them, that is, if there intercede any imagined space which may receive another body, then those bodies are not contiguous. And this is so easy to be understood, that I should wonder at some men, who being otherwise skilful enough in philosophy, are of a different opinion, but that I find that most of those that affect metaphysical subtleties wander from truth, as if they were led out of their way by an *ignis fatuus*. For can any man that has his natural senses, think that two bodies must therefore necessarily touch one another, because no other body is between them? Or that there can be no *vacuum*, because *vacuum* is nothing, or as they call it, *non ens?* Which is as childish, as if one should reason thus; no man can fast, because to fast is to eat nothing; but nothing cannot be eaten. *Continual, are any two bodies that have a common part; and more than two are continual, when every two, that are next to one another, are continual.*

10. The definition of motion. No motion intelligible but with time. MOTION *is a continual relinquishing of one place, and acquiring of another*; and that place which is relinquished is commonly called the *terminus a quo,* as that which is acquired is called the *terminus ad quem*, I say a continual relinquishing, because no body, how little soever, can totally and at once go out of its former place into another, so, but that some part of it will be in a part of a place which is common to both, namely, to the relinquished and the acquired places. For example, let any body be in the place A C B D; the same body cannot come into the place B D E F, but it must first be in G H I K, whose part G H B D is common to both the places A C B D, and G H I K, and whose part B D I K, is common to both

A	G	B	I	E
:				:
:				:
C	H	D	K	F

the places G H I K, and B D E F. Now it cannot be conceived that any thing can be moved without time; for time is, by the definition of it, a phantasm, that is, a conception of motion; and, therefore, to conceive that any thing may be moved without time, were to conceive motion without motion, which is impossible.

11. *What it is to be at rest, to have been moved, and to be moved. No motion to be conceived without the conception of past and future.* *That is said to be at rest, which, during any time, is in one place; and that to be moved, or to have been moved, which, whether it be now at rest or moved, was formerly in another place than that which it is now in.* From which definitions it may be inferred, first, that *whatsoever is moved, has been moved*; for if it be still in the same place in which it was formerly, it is at rest, that is, it is not moved, by the definition of *rest*; but if it be in another place, it has been moved, by the definition of *moved*. Secondly, that *what is moved, will yet be moved*; for that which is moved, leaveth the place where it is, and therefore will be in another place, and consequently will be moved still. Thirdly, that *whatsoever is moved, is not in one place during any time, how little soever that time be*; for by the definition of rest, that which is in one place during any time, is at rest.

There is a certain sophism against motion, which seems to spring from the not understanding of this last proposition. For they say, that, *if any body be moved, it is moved either in the place where it is, or in the place where it is not; both which are false; and therefore nothing is moved.* But the falsity lies in the major proposition; for that which is moved, is neither moved in the place where it is, nor in the place where it is not; but from the place where it is, to the place where it is not. Indeed it cannot be denied but that whatsoever is moved, is moved somewhere, that is, within some space; but then the place of that body is not that whole space, but a part of it, as is said above in the seventh article. From what is above demonstrated, namely, that whatsoever is moved, has also been moved, and will be moved, this also may be collected, that there can be no conception of motion, without conceiving past and future time.

12. *A point, a line, superficies, and solid, what they are.* Though there be no body which has not some magnitude, yet if, when any body is moved, the magnitude of it be not at all considered, the way it makes is called a *line*, or one single dimension; and the space, through which it passeth, is called *length*; and the body itself, a *point*; in which sense the earth is called a *point*, and the way of its yearly revolution, the *ecliptic line*. But if a body, which is moved, be considered as *long*, and be supposed to be so moved, as that all the several parts of it be understood to make several lines, then the way of every part of that body is called *breadth*, and the space which is made is called *superficies*, consisting of two dimensions, one whereof to every several part of the other is applied whole. Again, if a body be considered as having *superficies*, and be understood to be so moved, that all the several parts of it describe several lines, then the way of every part of that body is called *thickness* or *depth*, and the space which is made is called *solid*, consisting of three dimensions, any two whereof are applied whole to every several part of the third.

But if a body be considered as *solid*, then it is not possible that all the several parts of it should describe several lines; for what way soever it be moved, the way of the following part will fall into the way of the part before it, so that the same solid will still be made which the foremost superficies would have made by itself. And therefore there can be no other dimension in any body, as it is a body, than the three which I have now described; though, as it shall be shown hereafter, *velocity*, which is motion according to *length*, may, by being applied to all the parts of a *solid*, make a magnitude of motion, consisting of four dimensions; as the goodness of gold, computed in all the parts of it, makes the price and value thereof.

13. *Equal, great, greater, and less, in bodies and magnitudes, what they are.* *Bodies*, how many soever they be, that can fill every one the place of every one, are said to be *equal* every one to every other. Now, one body may fill the same place which another body filleth, though it be not of the same figure with that other body, if so be that it may be understood to be reducible to the same figure, either by flexion or transposition

of the parts. And *one body is greater than another body, when a part of that is equal to all this; and less, when all that is equal to a part of this*. Also, *magnitudes* are *equal*, or *greater*, or *lesser*, than one another, for the same consideration, namely, when the bodies, of which they are the magnitudes, are either *equal*, or *greater*, or *less*, &c.

14. One and the same body has always one and the same magnitude. One and the same body is always of one and the same magnitude. For seeing a body and the magnitude and place thereof cannot be comprehended in the mind otherwise than as they are coincident, if any body be understood to be at rest, that is, to remain in the same place during some time, and the magnitude thereof be in one part of that time greater, and in another part less, that body's place, which is one and the same, will be coincident sometimes with greater, sometimes with less magnitude, that is, the same place will be greater and less than itself, which is impossible. But there would be no need at all of demonstrating a thing that is in itself so manifest, if there were not some, whose opinion concerning bodies and their magnitudes is, that a body may exist separated from its magnitude, and have greater or less magnitude bestowed upon it, making use of this principle for the explication of the nature of *rarum* and *densum*.

15. Velocity, what it is. Motion, in as much as a certain length may in a certain time be transmitted by it, is called VELOCITY or *swiftness*: &c. For though *swift* be very often understood with relation to *slower* or *less swift*, as great as in respect of less, yet nevertheless, as magnitude is by philosophers taken absolutely for extension, so also *velocity* or *swiftness* may be put absolutely for motion according to length.

16. Equal, greater, and less, in times, what they are. Many motions are said to be made in equal times, when every one of them begins and ends together with some other motion, or if it had begun together, would also have ended together with the same. For time, which is a phantasm of motion, cannot be reckoned but by some exposed motion; as in dials by the motion of the sun or of the hand; and if two or more motions begin and end with this motion, they are

said to be made in equal times; from whence also it is easy to understand what it is to be moved in greater or longer time, and in less time or not so long; namely, that that is longer moved, which beginning with another, ends later; or ending together, began sooner.

17. Equal, greater, and less, in velocity, what. Motions are said to be equally swift, when equal lengths are transmitted in equal times; and greater swiftness is that, wherein greater length is passed in equal time, or equal length in less time. Also that swiftness by which equal lengths are passed in equal parts of time, is called *uniform* swiftness or motion; and of motions *not uniform*, such as become swifter or slower by equal increasings or decreasings in equal parts of time, are said to be *accelerated* or *retarded uniformly*.

18. Equal, greater, and less, in motion, what. But motion is said to be greater, less, and equal, not only in regard of the length which is transmitted in a certain time, that is, in regard of swiftness only, but of swiftness applied to every smallest particle of magnitude; for when any body is moved, every part of it is also moved; and supposing the parts to be halves, the motions of those halves have their swiftness equal to one another, and severally equal to that of the whole; but the motion of the whole is equal to those two motions, either of which is of equal swiftness with it; and therefore it is one thing for two motions to be equal to one another, and another thing for them to be equally swift. And this is manifest in two horses that draw abreast, where the motion of both the horses together is of equal swiftness with the motion of either of them singly; but the motion of both is greater than the motion of one of them, namely, double. Wherefore *motions are said to be simply equal to one another, when the swiftness of one, computed in every part of its magnitude, is equal to the swiftness of the other computed also in every part of its magnitude: and greater than one another, when the swiftness of one computed as above, is greater than the swiftness of the other so computed; and less, when*

less. Besides, the magnitude of motion computed in this manner is that which is commonly called FORCE.

19. That which is at rest will always be at rest, except it be moved by some external thing. *Whatsoever is at rest will always be at rest, unless there be some other body besides it, which, by endeavoring to get into its place by motion, suffers it no longer to remain at rest*. For suppose that some finite body exist and be at rest, and that all space besides be empty; if now this body begin to be moved, it will certainly be moved some way; seeing therefore there was nothing in that body which did not dispose it to rest, the reason why it is moved this way is in something out of it; and in like manner, if it had been moved any other way, the reason of motion that way had also been in something out of it; but seeing it was supposed that nothing is out of it, the reason of its motion one way would be the same with the reason of its motion every other way, wherefore it would be moved alike all ways at once; which is impossible.

In like manner, *whatsoever is moved, will always be moved, except there be some other body besides it, which causeth it to rest*. For if we suppose nothing to be without it, there will be no reason why it should rest now, rather than at another time; wherefore its motion would cease in every particle of time alike; which is not intelligible.

20. Accidents are generated and destroyed, but bodies not so. When we say a living creature, a tree, or any other specified body is *generated* or *destroyed*, it is not to be so understood as if there were made a body of that which is not-body, or not a body of a body, but of a living creature not a living creature, of a tree not a tree, &c. that is, that those accidents for which we call one thing a living creature, another thing a tree, and another by some other name, are generated and destroyed; and that therefore the same names are not to be given to them now, which were given them before. But that magnitude for which we give to any thing the name of body is neither generated nor destroyed. For though we may feign in our mind that a point may swell to a huge bulk, and that this may again contract itself to a point; that is, though we may imagine something to arise where

before was nothing, and nothing to be there where before was something, yet we cannot comprehend in our mind how this may possibly be done in nature. And therefore philosophers, who tie themselves to natural reason, suppose that a body can neither be generated nor destroyed, but only that it may appear otherwise than it did to us, that is, under different *species*, and consequently be called by other and other names; so that that which is now called man, may at another time have the name of not-man; but that which is once called body, can never be called not-body. But it is manifest, that all other accidents besides magnitude or extension may be generated and destroyed; as when a white thing is made black, the whiteness that was in it perisheth, and the blackness that was not in it is now generated; and therefore bodies, and the accidents under which they appear diversely, have this difference, that bodies are things, and not generated; accidents are generated, and not things.

21. An accident cannot depart from its subject and therefore, when any thing appears otherwise than it did by reason of other and other accidents, it is not to be thought that an accident goes out of one subject into another, (for they are not, as I said above, in their subjects as a part in the whole, or as a contained thing in that which contains it, or as a master of a family in his house,) but that one accident perisheth, and another is generated. For example, when the hand, being moved, moves the pen, motion does not go out of the hand into the pen; for so the writing might be continued though the hand stood still; but a new motion is generated in the pen, and is the pen's motion.

22. Nor be moved. And therefore also it is improper to say, an accident is moved; as when, instead of saying, *figure is an accident of a body carried away*, we say, *a body carries away its figure*.

23. Essence, form, and matter, what they are. Now that accident for which we give a certain name to any body, or the accident which denominates its subject, is commonly called the ESSENCE thereof; as rationality is the essence of a man; whiteness, of any white thing, and extension the essence of a body. And the same essence, in as much as it

is generated, is called the FORM. Again, a body, in respect of any accident, is called the SUBJECT, and in respect of the form it is called the MATTER.

Also, the production or perishing of any accident makes its subject be said *to be changed*; only the production or perishing of form makes it be said it is *generated* or *destroyed*; but in all generation and mutation, the name of *matter* still remains. For a table made of wood is not only wooden, but wood; and a statue of brass is brass as well as brazen; though Aristotle, in his *Metaphysics*, says, that whatsoever is made of any thing ought not to be called ἐκεινὸ, but ἐκέινινον; as that which is made of wood, not ξύλον, but ξύλινον, that is, not wood, but wooden.

24. First matter, what. And as for that matter which is common to all things, and which philosophers, following Aristotle, usually call *materia prima*, that is, *first matter*, it is not any body distinct from all other bodies, nor is it one of them. What then is it? A mere name; yet a name which is not of vain use; for it signifies a conception of body without the consideration of any form or other accident except only magnitude or extension, and aptness to receive form and other accident. So that whensoever we have use of the name *body in general*, if we use that of *materia prima*, we do well. For as when a man not knowing which was first, water or ice, would find out which of the two were the matter of both, he would be fain to suppose some third matter which were neither of these two; so he that would find out what is the matter of all things, ought to suppose such as is not the matter of anything that exists. Wherefore *materia prima* is nothing; and therefore they do not attribute to it either form or any other accident besides quantity; whereas all singular things have their forms and accidents certain.

Materia prima, therefore, is body in general, that is, body considered universally, not as having neither form nor any accident, but in which no form nor any other accident but quantity are at all considered, that is, they are not drawn into argumentation.

25. That the whole is greater than any part thereof, why

demonstrated. From what has been said, those axioms may be demonstrated, which are assumed by Euclid in the beginning of his first element, about the equality and inequality of magnitudes; of which, omitting the rest, I will here demonstrate only this one, *the whole is greater than any part thereof*; to the end that the reader may know that those axioms are not indemonstrable, and therefore not principles of demonstration; and from hence learn to be wary how he admits any thing for a principle, which is not at least as evident as these are. *Greater* is defined to be that, whose part is equal to the whole of another. Now if we suppose any whole to be A, and a part of it to be B; seeing the whole B is equal to itself, and the same B is a part of A; therefore a part of A will be equal to the whole B. Wherefore, by the definition above, A is greater than B; which was to be proved.

Chapter 9

Of Cause and Effect

1. *Action and Passion, what they are.* A body is said to work upon or *act,* that is to say, *do* something to another body, when it either generates or destroys some accident in it: and the body in which an accident is generated or destroyed is said to *suffer,* that is, to have something *done* to it by another body; as when one body by putting forwards another body generates motion in it, it is called the AGENT; and the body in which motion is so generated, is called the PATIENT; so fire that warms the hand is the *agent,* and the hand, which is warmed, is the *patient.* That accident, which is generated in the patient, is called the EFFECT.

2. *Action and passion, mediate and immediate.* When an agent and patient are contiguous to one another, their action and passion are then said to be *immediate,* otherwise, *mediate;* and when another body, lying betwixt the agent and patient, is contiguous to them both, it is then itself both an agent and a patient; an agent in respect of the body next after it, upon which it works, and a patient in respect of the body next before it, from which it suffers. Also, if many bodies be so ordered that every two which are next to one another be contiguous, then all those that are betwixt the first and the last are both agents and patients, and the first is an agent only, and the last a patient only.

3. *Cause simply taken.* An agent is understood to *produce* its determined or certain effect in the patient, according to some certain accident or accidents, with which both it and the patient are affected; that is to say, the agent hath its effect precisely such, not because it is a body, but because such a body, or so moved. For otherwise all agents, seeing they are all bodies alike, would produce like effects in all patients. And therefore the fire, for example, does not warm, because it is a body, but because it is hot; nor does one

body put forward another body because it is a body, but because it is moved into the place of that other body. The cause, therefore, of all effects consists in certain accidents both in the agents and in the patients; which when they are all present, the effect is produced; but if any one of them be wanting, it is not produced; and that accident either of the agent or patient, without which the effect cannot be produced, is called *causa sine qua non,* or *cause necessary by supposition,* as also the *cause requisite for the production of the effect.* But a CAUSE simply, or *an entire cause, is the aggregate of all the accidents both of the agents how many soever they be, and of the patient, put together; which when they are all supposed to be present, it cannot be understood but that the effect is produced at the same instant; and if any one of them be wanting, it cannot be understood but that the effect is not produced.*

4. Cause efficient, and material. The aggregate of accidents in the agent or agents, requisite for the production of the effect, the effect being produced, is called the *efficient cause* thereof; and the aggregate of accidents in the patient, the effect being produced, is usually called the *material cause;* I say the effect being produced; for where there is no effect, there can be no cause; for nothing can be called a cause, where there is nothing that can be called an effect. But the efficient and material causes are both but partial causes, or parts of that cause, which in the next precedent article I called an entire cause. And from hence it is manifest, that the effect we expect, though the agents be not defective on their part, may nevertheless be frustrated by a defect in the patient; and when the patient is sufficient, by a defect in the agents.

5. An entire cause is always sufficient to produce its effect. An entire cause is always sufficient for the production of its effect, if the effect be at all possible. For let any effect whatsoever be propounded to be produced; if the same be produced, it is manifest that the cause which produced it was a sufficient cause; but if it be not produced, and yet be possible, it is evident that something was wanting either in some agent, or in the patient, without which it could not be pro-

duced; that is, that some accident was wanting which was requisite for its production; and therefore, that cause was not *entire*, which is contrary to what was supposed.

It follows also from hence, that in whatsoever instant the cause is entire, in the same instant the effect is produced. For if it be not produced, something is still wanting, which is requisite for the production of it; and therefore the cause was not entire, as was supposed.

And seeing a necessary cause is defined to be that, which being supposed, the effect cannot but follow; this also may be collected, that whatsoever effect is produced at any time, the same is produced by a necessary cause. For whatsoever is produced, in as much as it is produced, had an entire cause, that is, had all those things, which being supposed, it cannot be understood but that the effect follows; that is, it had a necessary cause. And in the same manner it may be shown, that whatsoever effects are hereafter to be produced, shall have a necessary cause; so that all the effects that have been, or shall be produced, have their necessity in things antecedent.

6. The generation of effects is continual. What is the beginning in causation. And from this, that whensoever the cause is entire, the effect is produced in the same instant, it is manifest that causation and the production of effects consist in a certain continual progress; so that as there is a continual mutation in the agent or agents, by the working of other agents upon them, so also the patient, upon which they work, is continually altered and changed. For example: as the heat of the fire increases more and more, so also the effects thereof, namely, the heat of such bodies as are next to it, and again, of such other bodies as are next to them, increase more and more accordingly; which is already no little argument that all mutation consists in motion only; the truth whereof shall be further demonstrated in the ninth article. But in this progress of causation, that is, of action and passion, if any man comprehend in his imagination a part thereof, and divide the same into parts, the first part or beginning of it cannot be considered otherwise than as action or cause; for, if it should be considered as effect or passion,

then it would be necessary to consider something before it, for its cause or action; which cannot be, for nothing can be before the beginning. And in like manner, the last part is considered only as effect; for it cannot be called cause, if nothing follow it; but after the last, nothing follows. And from hence it is, that in all action the beginning and cause are taken for the same thing. But every one of the intermediate parts are both action and passion, and cause and effect, according as they are compared with the antecedent or subsequent part.

7. *No cause of motion but in a body contiguous and moved.* There can be no cause of motion, except in a body contiguous and moved. For let there be any two bodies which are not contiguous, and betwixt which the intermediate space is empty, or, if filled, filled with another body which is at rest; and let one of the propounded bodies be supposed to be at rest; I say it shall always be at rest. For if it shall be moved, the cause of that motion, by the 8th chapter, article 19, will be some external body; and, therefore, if between it and that external body there be nothing but empty space, then whatsoever the disposition be of that external body or of the patient itself, yet if it be supposed to be now at rest, we may conceive it will continue so till it be touched by some other body. But seeing cause, by the definition, is the aggregate of all such accidents, which being supposed to be present, it cannot be conceived but that the effect will follow, those accidents, which are either in external bodies, or in the patient itself, cannot be the cause of future motion. And in like manner, seeing we may conceive that whatsoever is at rest will still be at rest, though it be touched by some other body, except that other body be moved; therefore in a contiguous body, which is at rest, there can be no cause of motion. Wherefore there is no cause of motion in any body, except it be contiguous and moved.

The same reason may serve to prove that whatsoever is moved, will always be moved on in the same way and with the same velocity, except it be hindered by some other contiguous and moved body; and consequently that no bodies, either when they are at rest, or when there is an interposition of vacuum, can generate or extinguish or lessen motion in other bodies. There is one that has written that things moved are more resisted by things at rest, than by things contrarily moved; for this reason, that he conceived motion not to be so contrary to motion as rest. That which deceived him was, that the words *rest* and *motion* are but contradictory names; whereas motion, indeed, is not resisted by rest, but by contrary motion.

8. The same agents and patients, if alike disposed, produce like effects, though at different times. But if a body work upon another body at one time, and afterwards the same body work upon the same body at another time, so that both the agent and patient, and all their parts, be in all things as they were; and there be no difference, except only in time, that is, that one action be former, the other later in time; it is manifest of itself, that the effects will be equal and like, as not differing in anything besides time. And as effects themselves proceed from their causes, so the diversity of them depends upon the diversity of their causes also.

9. All mutation is motion. This being true, it is necessary that mutation can be nothing else but motion of the parts of that body which is changed. For first, we do not say anything is changed, but that which appears to our senses otherwise than it appeared formerly. Secondly, both those appearances are effects produced in the sentient; and, therefore, if they be different, it is necessary, by the preceding article, that either some part of the agent, which was formerly at rest, is now moved, and so the mutation consists in this motion; or some part, which was formerly moved, is now otherwise moved, and so also the mutation consists in this new motion; or which, being formerly moved, is now at rest, which, as I have shown above, cannot come to pass without motion; and so again, mutation is motion; or lastly, it happens in some of these manners to the patient, or some of its parts; so that mutation, howsoever it be made, will consist in the motion of the parts, either of the body which is perceived, or of the sentient body, or of both. Mutation therefore is motion, namely, of the parts either of the agent or of

the patient; which was to be demonstrated. And to this it is consequent, that rest cannot be the cause of anything, nor can any action proceed from it; seeing neither motion nor mutation can be caused by it.

10. Contingent accidents. Accidents, in respect of other accidents which precede them, or are before them in time, and upon which they do not depend as upon their causes, are called *contingent* accidents; I say, in respect of those accidents by which they are not generated; for, in respect of their causes, all things come to pass with equal necessity; for otherwise they would have no causes at all; which, of things generated, is not intelligible.

Chapter 10

Of Power and Act

1. Power and Cause are the same thing. Correspondent to *cause* and *effect,* are POWER and ACT; nay, those and these are the same things; though, for divers considerations, they have divers names. For whensoever any agent has all those accidents which are necessarily requisite for the production of some effect in the patient, then we say that agent has *power* to produce that effect, if it be applied to a patient. But, as I have shown in the precedent chapter, those accidents constitute the efficient cause; and therefore the same accidents, which constitute the efficient cause, constitute also the *power* of the agent. Wherefore the *power of the agent* and the *efficient cause* are the same thing. But they are considered with this difference, that *cause* is so called in respect of the effect already produced, and power in respect of the same effect to be produced hereafter; so that *cause* respects the past, *power* the future time. Also, the *power of the agent* is that which is commonly called *active power.*

In like manner, whensoever any patient has all those accidents which it is requisite it should have, for the production of some effect in it, we say it is in the *power* of that patient to produce that effect, if it be applied to a fitting agent. But those accidents, as is defined in the precedent chapter, constitute the material cause; and therefore the *power of the patient,* commonly called *passive power,* and *material cause,* are the same thing; but with this different consideration, that in cause the past time, and in power the future, is respected. Wherefore the power of the agent and patient together, which may be called entire or *plenary power,* is the same thing with *entire cause;* for they both consist in the sum or aggregate of all the accidents, as well in the agent as in the patient, which are requisite for the production of the effect. Lastly, as the accident produced is, in respect of the cause, called an effect, so in respect of the power, it is called an *act*.

2. An act is produced at the same instant in which the power is plenary. As therefore the effect is produced in the same instant in which the cause is entire, so also every act that may be produced, is produced in the same instant in which the power is plenary. And as there can be no effect but from a sufficient and necessary cause, so also no act can be produced but by sufficient power, or that power by which it could not but be produced.

3. Active and passive power are parts only of plenary power. And as it is manifest, as I have shown, that the efficient and material causes are severally and by themselves parts only of an entire cause, and cannot produce any effect but by being joined together, so also power, active and passive, are parts only of plenary and entire power; nor, except they be joined, can any act proceed from them; and therefore these powers, as I said in the first article, are but conditional, namely, *the agent has power, if it be applied to a patient; and the patient has power, if it be applied to an agent;* otherwise neither of them have power, nor can the accidents, which are in them severally, be properly called powers; nor any action be said to be possible for the power of the agent alone or of the patient alone.

4. An act, when said to be possible. For that is an impossible act, for the production of which there is no power plenary. For seeing plenary power is that in which all things concur, which are requisite for the production of an act, if the power shall never be plenary, there will always be wanting some of those things, without which the act cannot be produced; wherefore that act shall never be produced; that is, that act is IMPOSSIBLE: and every act, which is not impossible, is POSSIBLE. Every act, therefore, which is possible, shall at some time be produced; for if it shall never be produced, then those things shall never concur which are requisite for the production of it; wherefore that act is *impossible*, by the definition; which is contrary to what was supposed.

5. An act necessary and contingent, what. A *necessary act* is that, the production whereof it is impossible to hinder; and

therefore every act, that shall be produced, shall necessarily be produced; for, that it shall not be produced, is impossible; because, as is already demonstrated, every possible act shall at some time be produced; nay, this proposition, *what shall be, shall be,* is as necessary a proposition as this, *a man is a man.*

But here, perhaps, some man may ask whether those future things, which are commonly called *contingents,* are necessary. I say, therefore, that generally all contingents have their necessary causes, as is shown in the preceding chapter; but are called contingents in respect of other events, upon which they do not depend; as the rain, which shall be tomorrow, shall be necessary, that is, from necessary causes; but we think and say it happens by chance, because we do not yet perceive the causes thereof, though they exist now; for men commonly call that *casual* or *contingent,* whereof they do not perceive the necessary cause; and in the same manner they used to speak of things past, when not knowing whether a thing be done or no, they say it is possible it never was done.

Wherefore, all propositions concerning future things, contingent or not contingent, as this, *it will rain tomorrow,* or this, *tomorrow the sun will rise,* are either necessarily true, or necessarily false; but we call them contingent, because we do not yet know whether they be true or false; whereas their verity depends not upon our knowledge, but upon the foregoing of their causes. But there are some, who though they confess this whole proposition, *tomorrow it will either rain, or not rain,* to be true, yet they will not acknowledge the parts of it, as, *tomorrow it will rain,* or, *tomorrow it will not rain,* to be either of them true by itself; because they say neither this nor that is true *determinately.* But what is this *determinately true,* but true upon our knowledge, or evidently true? And therefore they say no more but that it is not yet known whether it be true or no; but they say it more obscurely, and darken the evidence of the truth with the same words, with which they endeavor to hide their own ignorance.

6. Active power consists in motion. In the 9th article of the preceding chapter, I have shown that the efficient cause of all motion and mutation consists in the motion of the agent,

or agents; and in the first article of this chapter, that the power of the agent is the same thing with the efficient cause. From whence it may be understood, that all active power consists in motion also; and that power is not a certain accident, which differs from all acts, but is, indeed, an act, namely, motion, which is therefore called power, because another act shall be produced by it afterwards. For example, if of three bodies the first put forward the second, and this the third, the motion of the second, in respect of the first which produceth it, is the act of the second body; but, in respect of the third, it is the active power of the same second body.

7. *Cause, formal and final, what they are.* The writers of metaphysics reckon up two other causes besides the *efficient* and *material*, namely, the ESSENCE, which some call the *formal cause*, and the END, or *final cause*; both which are nevertheless efficient causes. For when it is said the essence of a thing is the cause thereof, *as to be rational is the cause of man*, it is not intelligible; for it is all one, as if it were said, *to be a man is the cause of man*; which is not well said. And yet the knowledge of the *essence* of anything, is the cause of the knowledge of the thing itself; for, if I first know that a thing is *rational*, I know from thence, that the same is *man*; but this is no other than an efficient cause. A *final cause* has no place but in such things as have sense and will; and this also I shall prove hereafter to be an efficient cause.

Chapter 11

Of Identity and Difference

1. *What it is for one thing to differ from another.* Hitherto I have spoken of body simply, and accidents common to all bodies, as *magnitude, motion, rest, action, passion, power, possible,* &c.; and I should now descend to those accidents by which one body is distinguished from another, but that it is first to be declared what it is to be *distinct* and *not distinct*, namely, what are the SAME and DIFFERENT; for this also is common to all bodies, that they may be distinguished and differenced from one another. Now, two bodies are said to *differ* from one another, when something may be said of one of them, which cannot be said of the other at the same time.

2. *To differ in number, magnitude, species, and genus, what.* And, first of all, it is manifest that no two bodies are the *same*; for seeing they are two, they are in two places at the same time; as that, which is the *same*, is at the same time in one and the same place. All bodies therefore differ from one another in *number,* namely, as one and another; so that the *same* and *different in number,* are names opposed to one another by contradiction.

In *magnitude* bodies differ when one is greater than another, as *a cubit long,* and *two cubits long,* of *two pound weight,* and of *three pound weight.* And to these, *equals* are opposed.

Bodies, which differ more than in magnitude, are called *unlike*; and those, which differ only in magnitude, *like.* Also, of unlike bodies, some are said to differ in the *species*, others in the *genus*; in the *species*, when their difference is perceived by one and the same sense, as *white* and *black*; and in the *genus*, when their difference is not perceived but by divers senses, as *white* and *hot*.

3. *What is relation, proportion, and relatives.* And the *likeness,* or *unlikeness, equality,* or *inequality* of one body to

another, is called their RELATION; and the bodies themselves
relatives or *correlatives; Aristotle* calls them τὰ πρὸς τί; the
first whereof is usually named the *antecedent*, and the second
the *consequent*; and the *relation* of the antecedent to the
consequent, according to magnitude, namely, the equality, the
excess or defect thereof, is called the PROPORTION of the antecedent to the consequent; so that *proportion* is nothing but
the equality or inequality of the magnitude of the antecedent
compared to the magnitude of the consequent by their difference only, or compared also with their difference. For example, the *proportion* of three to two consists only in this,
that three *exceeds* two by unity; and the proportion of two to
five in this, that two, compared with five, is *deficient* of it by
three, either simply, or compared with the numbers different;
and therefore in the proportion of unequals, the proportion
of the less to the greater, is called DEFECT; and that of the
greater to the less, EXCESS.

4. Proportionals, what. Besides, of unequals, some are
more, some less, and some equally unequal; so that there is
proportion of proportions, as well as of *magnitudes*; namely,
where two unequals have relation to two other unequals; as,
when the inequality which is between 2 and 3, is compared
with the inequality which is between 4 and 5. In which comparison there are always four magnitudes; or, which is all one,
if there be but three, the middlemost is twice numbered; and
if the proportion of the first to the second, be equal to the
proportion of the third to the fourth, then the four are said
to be *proportionals*; otherwise they are not proportionals.

5. The proportion of magnitudes to one another, wherein
it consists. The proportion of the antecedent to the consequent consists in their difference, not only simply taken, but
also as compared with one of the relatives; that is, either in
that part of the greater, by which it exceeds the less, or in
the remainder, after the less is taken out of the greater; as the
proportion of two to five consists in the three by which five
exceeds two, not in three simply only, but also as compared
with five or two. For though there be the same difference
between two and five, which is between nine and twelve,
namely three, yet there is not the same inequality; and there-

fore the proportion of two to five is not in all relation the same with that of nine to twelve, but only in that which is called arithmetical.

6. Relation is no new accident, but one of those that were in the relative, before the relation or comparison was made. Also the causes of accidents in correlatives are the cause of relation. But we must not so think of relation, as if it were an accident differing from all the other accidents of the relative; but one of them, namely, that by which the comparison is made. For example, the likeness of one *white* to another *white*, or its unlikeness to *black,* is the same accident with its *whiteness*; and *equality* and *inequality,* the same accident with the *magnitude* of the thing compared, though under another name: for that which is called *white* or *great,* when it is not compared with something else, the same when it is compared, is called *like* or *unlike, equal* or *unequal.* And from this it follows that the causes of the accidents, which are in relatives, are the causes also of *likeness, unlikeness, equality* and *inequality*; namely, that he, that makes two unequal bodies, makes also their inequality; and he, that makes a rule and an action, makes also, if the action be congruous to the rule, their congruity; if incongruous, their incongruity. And thus much concerning *comparison* of one body with another.

7. Of the beginning of individuation. But the same body may at different times be compared with itself. And from hence springs a great controversy among philosophers about the *beginning of individuation,* namely, in what sense it may be conceived that a body is at one time the same, at another time not the same it was formerly. For example, whether a man grown old be the same man he was whilst he was young, or another man; or whether a city be in different ages the same, or another city. Some place *individuity* in the unity of *matter*; others, in the unity of *form*; and one says it consists in the unity of the *aggregate of all the accidents together.* For *matter,* it is pleaded that a lump of wax, whether it be spherical or cubical, is the same wax, because the same matter. For *form,* that when a man is grown from an infant to be an old man, though his matter be changed, yet he is still the same numerical man; for that *identity,* which cannot be attributed

to the matter, ought probably to be ascribed to the form. For the *aggregate of accidents*, no instance can be made; but because, when any new accident is generated, a new name is commonly imposed on the thing, therefore he, that assigned this cause of *individuity*, thought the thing itself also was become another thing. According to the first opinion, he that sins, and he that is punished, should not be the same man, by reason of the perpetual flux and change of man's body; nor should the city, which makes laws in one age and abrogates them in another, be the same city; which were to confound all civil rights. According to the second opinion, two bodies existing both at once, would be one and the same numerical body. For if, for example, that ship of Theseus, concerning the difference whereof made by continual reparation in taking out the old planks and putting in new, the sophisters of Athens were wont to dispute, were, after all the planks were changed, the same numerical ship it was at the beginning; and if some man had kept the old planks as they were taken out, and by putting them afterwards together in the same order, had again made a ship of them, this, without doubt, had also been the same numerical ship with that which was at the beginning; and so there would have been two ships numerically the same, which is absurd. But, according to the third opinion, nothing would be the same it was; so that a man standing would not be the same he was sitting; nor the water, which is in the vessel, the same with that which is poured out of it. Wherefore the beginning of *individuation* is not always to be taken either from matter alone, or from form alone.

But we must consider by what name anything is called, when we inquire concerning the *identity* of it. For it is one thing to ask concerning Socrates, whether he be the same man, and another to ask whether he be the same body; for his body, when he is old, cannot be the same it was when he was an infant, by reason of the difference of magnitude; for one body has always one and the same magnitude; yet, nevertheless, he may be the same man. And therefore, whensoever the name, by which it is asked whether a thing be the same it was, is given it for the matter only, then, if the matter be the same, the thing also is *individually* the same; as the water, which was in the sea, is the same which is afterwards in the cloud; and any body is the same, whether the parts of it be put together, or dispersed; or whether it be congealed, or dissolved. Also, if the name be given for such form as is the beginning of motion, then, as long as that motion remains, it will be the same *individual* thing; as that man will be always the same, whose actions and thoughts proceed all from the same beginning of motion, namely, that which was in his generation; and that will be the same river which flows from one and the same fountain, whether the same water, or other water, or something else than water, flow from thence; and that the same city, whose acts proceed continually from the same institution, whether the men be the same or no. Lastly, if the name be given for some accident, then the *identity* of the thing will depend upon the matter; for, by the taking away and supplying of matter, the accidents that were, are destroyed, and other new ones are generated, which cannot be the same numerically; so that a ship, which signifies matter so figured, will be the same as long as the matter remains the same; but if no part of the matter be the same, then it is numerically another ship; and if part of the matter remain and part be changed, then the ship will be partly the same, and partly not the same.

Chapter 15

Of the Nature, Properties, and Divers Considerations of Motion and Endeavor

1. Repetition of some principles of the doctrine of motion formerly set down. The next things in order to be treated of are MOTION and MAGNITUDE, which are the most common accidents of all bodies. This place therefore most properly belongs to the elements of geometry. But because this part of philosophy, having been improved by the best wits of all ages, has afforded greater plenty of matter than can well be thrust together within the narrow limits of this discourse, I thought fit to admonish the reader, that before he proceed further, he take into his hands the works of Euclid, Archimedes, Apollonius, and other as well ancient as modern writers. For to what end is it, to do over again that which is already done? The little therefore that I shall say concerning geometry in some of the following chapters, shall be such only as is new, and conducing to natural philosophy.

I have already delivered some of the principles of this doctrine in the eighth and ninth chapters; which I shall briefly put together here, that the reader in going on may have their light nearer at hand.

First, therefore, in chap. 8 art. 10, *motion* is defined to be *the continual privation of one place, and acquisition of another*.

Secondly, it is there shown, that *whatsoever is moved is moved in time*.

*From *De Corpore* (Molesworth Ed. 1839, Vol. I of English Works), Chapter 15.

Thirdly, in the same chapter, art. 11, I have defined *rest to be when a body remains for some time in one place.*

Fourthly, it is there shown, that *whatsoever is moved is not in any determined place;* as also that the same *has been moved, is still moved, and will yet be moved;* so that in every part of that space, in which motion is made, we may consider three times, namely, the *past,* the *present,* and the *future time.*

Fifthly, in art. 15 of the same chapter, I have defined *velocity* or *swiftness to be motion considered as power, namely, that power by which a body moved may in a certain time transmit a certain length;* which also may more briefly be enunciated thus, *velocity is the quantity of motion determined by time and line.*

Sixthly, in the same chapter, art. 16, I have shown that *motion is the measure of time.*

Seventhly, in the same chapter, art. 17, I have defined motions to be equally swift, when in equal times equal lengths are transmitted by them.

Eighthly, in art. 18 of the same chapter, *motions* are defined to be *equal, when the swiftness of one moved body, computed in every part of its magnitude, is equal to the swiftness of another, computed also in every part of its magnitude.* From whence it is to be noted, that *motions equal to one another,* and *motions equally swift,* do not signify the same thing; for when two horses draw abreast, the motion of both is greater than the motion of either of them singly; but the swiftness of both together is but equal to that of either.

Ninthly, in art. 19 of the same chapter, I have shown, that *whatsoever is at rest will always be at rest, unless there be some other body besides it, which by getting into its place suffers it no longer to remain at rest.* And that *whatsoever is moved, will always be moved, unless there be some other body besides it, which hinders its motion.*

Tenthly, in chap. 9 art. 7, I have demonstrated, that *when any body is moved which was formerly at rest, the immediate efficient cause of that motion is in some other moved and contiguous body.*

Eleventhly, I have shown in the same place, that *whatsoever is moved, will always be moved in the same way, and with the same swiftness, if it be not hindered by some other moved and contiguous body.*

2. Other principles added to them. To which principles I shall here add those that follow. First, I define ENDEAVOR *to be motion made in less space and time than can be given; that is, less than can be determined or assigned by exposition or number; that is, motion made through the length of a point, and in an instant or point of time.* For the explaining of which definition it must be remembered, that by a point is not to be understood that which has no quantity, or which cannot by any means be divided; for there is no such thing in nature; but that, whose quantity is not at all considered, that is, whereof neither quantity nor any part is computed in demonstration; so that a point is not to be taken for an indivisible, but for an undivided thing; as also an instant is to be taken for an undivided, and not for an indivisible time.

In like manner, endeavor is to be conceived as motion; but so as that neither the quantity of the time in which, nor of the line in which it is made, may in demonstration be at all brought into comparison with the quantity of that time, or of that line of which it is a part. And yet, as a point may be compared with a point, so one endeavor may be compared with another endeavor, and one may be found to be greater or less than another. For if the vertical points of two angles be compared, they will be equal or unequal in the same proportion which the angles themselves have to one another. Or if a straight line cut many circumferences of concentric circles, the inequality of the points of intersection will be in the same proportion which the perimeters have to one another. And in the same manner, if two motions begin and end both together, their endeavors will be equal or unequal, according to the proportion of their velocities; as we see a bullet of lead descend with greater endeavor than a ball of wool.

Secondly, I define IMPETUS, *or quickness of motion, to be the swiftness or velocity of the body moved, but considered in the several points of that time in which it is moved. In which sense impetus is nothing else but the quantity or velocity of endeavor. But considered with the whole time, it is the whole velocity of the body moved taken together throughout all the time, and equal to the product of a line representing the time, multiplied into a line representing the arithmetically mean* impetus *or* quickness. Which arithmetical mean, what it is, is defined in the 29th article of chapter 13.

And because in equal times the ways that are passed are as the velocities, and the *impetus* is the velocity they go withal, reckoned in all the several points of the times, it followeth that during any time whatsoever, howsoever the *impetus* be increased or decreased, the length of the way passed over shall be increased or decreased in the same proportion; and the same line shall represent both the way of the body moved, and the several *impetus* or degrees of swiftness wherewith the way is passed over.

And if the body moved be not a point, but a straight line moved so as that every point thereof make a several straight line, the plane described by its motion, whether uniform, accelerated, or retarded, shall be greater or less, the time being the same, in the same proportion with that of the *impetus* reckoned in one motion to the *impetus* reckoned in the other. For the reason is the same in parallelograms and their sides.

For the same cause also, if the body moved be a plane, the solid described shall be still greater or less in the proportions of the several *impetus* or quicknesses reckoned through one line, to the several *impetus* reckoned through another.

This understood, let ABCD, (in figure 1, chap. 17) be a parallelogram; in which suppose the side AB to be moved parallelly to the opposite side CD, decreasing all the way till it vanish in the point C, and so describing the figure ABEFC; the point B, as AB decreaseth, will therefore describe the line BEFC; and suppose the time of this motion designed by the line CD; and in the same time CD, suppose the side AC to be moved parallel and uniformly to BD. From the point O taken at adventure in the line CD, draw OR parallel to BD, cutting the line BEFC in E, and the side AB in R. And again, from the point Q taken also at adventure in the line CD, draw QS parallel to BD, cutting the line BEFC in F, and the side AB in S; and draw EG and FH parallel to CD, cutting AC in G and H. Lastly, suppose the same construction done in all the points possible of the line BEFC. I say, that as the proportions of the swiftness wherewith QF, OE, DB, and all the rest supposed to be drawn parallel to DB and terminated in the line BEFC, are to the proportions of their several times designed by the several parallels HF, GE, AB, and all the rest supposed to be drawn parallel to the line of time CD and terminated in the line BEFC, the aggregate to the aggregate, so is the area or plane DBEFC to the area or plane ACFEB. For as AB decreasing continually by the line BEFC vanisheth in the time CD into the point C, so in the same time the line DC continually decreasing vanisheth by the same line CFEB into the point B; and the point D describeth in that decreasing motion the line DB equal to the line AC described by the point A in the decreasing motion of AB; and their swiftnesses are therefore equal. Again, because in the time GE the point O describeth the line OE, and in the same time the point S describeth the line SE, the line OE shall be to the line SE, as the swiftness wherewith OE is described to the swiftness wherewith SE is described. In like manner, because in the same time HF the point Q describeth the line QF, and the point R the line RF, it shall be as the swiftness by which QF is described to the swiftness by which RF is described, so the line itself QF to the line itself RF; and so in all the lines that can possibly be drawn parallel to BD in the points where they cut the line BEFC. But all the parallels to BD, as SE, RF, AC, and the rest that can possibly be drawn from the line AB to the line BEFC, make the area of the plane ABEFC; and all the parallels to the same BD, as QF, OE, DB and the rest drawn to the points where they cut the same line BEFC, make the area of the plane BEFCD. As therefore the aggregate of the swiftnesses wherewith the plane BEFCD is described, is to the aggregate of the swiftnesses wherewith the plane ACFEB is described, so is the plane itself BEFCD to the plane itself ACFEB. But the aggregate of the times represented by the parallels AB, GE, HF and the rest, maketh also the area ACFEB. And therefore, as the aggregate of all the lines QF, OE, DB and all the rest of the lines parallel to BD and terminated in the line BEFC, is to the aggregate of all the lines HF, GE, AB and all the rest of the lines parallel to CD and terminated in the same line BEFC; that is, as the aggregate of the lines of swiftness to the aggregate of the lines of time, or as the whole swiftness in the parallels to DB to the whole time in the parallels to CD, so is the plane BEFCD to the plane ACFEB. And the proportions of QF to FH, and of OE to EG, and of DB to BA, and so of all the rest taken together, are the proportions of the plane DBEFC to the plane ABEFC. But the lines QF, OE, DB and the rest are the lines that design the swiftness; and the lines HF, GE, AB and the rest are the lines that design the times of the motions; and therefore the proportion of the plane DBEFC to the plane ABEFC is the proportion of all the velocities taken together to all the times taken together. Wherefore, as the proportions of the swiftnesses, &c.; which was to be demonstrated.

The same holds also in the diminution of the circles, whereof the lines of time are the semidiameters, as may easily be conceived by imagining the whole plane ABCD turned round upon the axis BD; for the line BEFC will be everywhere in the superficies so made, and the lines HF, GE, AB, which are here parallelograms, will be there cylinders, the diameters of whose bases are the lines HF, GE, AB, &c. and the altitude a point, that is to say, a quantity less than any quantity that can possibly be named; and the lines QF, OE, DB, &c. small solids whose lengths and breadths are less than any quantity that can be named.

But this is to be noted, that unless the proportion of the sum of the swiftnesses to the proportion of the sum of the times be determined, the proportion of the figure DBEFC to the figure ABEFC cannot be determined.

Thirdly, I define RESISTANCE *to be the endeavor of one moved body either wholly or in part contrary to the endeavor of another moved body, which toucheth the same.* I say, wholly contrary, when the endeavor of two bodies proceeds in the same straight line from the opposite extremes, and contrary in part, when two bodies have their endeavor in two lines, which, proceeding from the extreme points of a straight line, meet without the same.

Fourthly, that I may define what it is to PRESS, I say, that *of two moved bodies one presses the other, when with its endeavor it makes either all or part of the other body to go out of its place.*

Fifthly, *a body, which is pressed and not wholly removed, is said to* RESTORE *itself, when, the pressing body being taken away, the parts which were moved do, by reason of the internal constitution of the pressed body, return every one into its own place.* And this we may observe in springs, in blown bladders, and in many other bodies, whose parts yield more or less to the endeavor which the pressing body makes at the first arrival; but afterwards, when the pressing body is removed, they do, by some force within them, *restore* themselves, and give their whole body the same figure it had before.

Sixthly, I define FORCE *to be the* impetus *or quickness of motion multiplied either into itself, or into the magnitude of the movent, by means whereof the said movent works more or less upon the body that resists it.*

3. Certain theorems concerning the nature of motion. Having premised thus much, I shall now demonstrate, first, that if a point moved come to touch another point which is at rest, how little soever the impetus or quickness of its motion be, it shall move that other point. For if by that impetus it do not at all move it out of its place, neither shall it move it with double the same impetus. For nothing doubled is still nothing; and for the same reason it shall never move it with that impetus, how many times soever it be multiplied, because nothing, however it be multiplied, will for ever be nothing. Wherefore, when a point is at rest, if it do not yield to the least impetus, it will yield to none; and consequently it will be impossible that that, which is at rest, should ever be moved.

Secondly, that when a point moved, how little soever the

impetus thereof be, falls upon a point of any body at rest, how hard soever that body be, it will at the first touch make it yield a little. For if it do not yield to the impetus which is in that point, neither will it yield to the impetus of never so many points, which have all their impetus severally equal to the impetus of that point. For seeing all those points together work equally, if any one of them have no effect, the aggregate of them all together shall have no effect as many times told as there are points in the whole body, that is, still no effect at all; and by consequent there would be some bodies so hard that it would be impossible to break them, that is, a finite hardness, or a finite force, would not yield to that which is infinite; which is absurd.

Coroll. It is therefore manifest, that rest does nothing at all, nor is of any efficacy; and that nothing but motion gives motion to such things as be at rest, and takes it from things moved.

Thirdly, that cessation in the movent does not cause cessation in that which was moved by it. For (by number 11 of art. 1 of this chapter) whatsoever is moved perseveres in the same way and with the same swiftness, as long as it is not hindered by something that is moved against it. Now it is manifest, that cessation is not contrary motion; and therefore it follows that the standing still of the movent does not make it necessary that the thing moved should also stand still.

Coroll. They are therefore deceived, that reckon the taking away of the impediment or resistance for one of the causes of motion.

4. Divers considerations of motions. Motion is brought into account for divers respects; first, as in a body *undivided,* that is, considered as a point; or, as in a *divided* body. In an undivided body, when we suppose the way, by which the motion is made, to be a line; and in a divided body, when we compute the motion of the several parts of that body, as of parts.

Secondly, from the diversity of the regulation of motion, it is in body, considered as undivided, sometimes *uniform* and sometimes *multiform, Uniform* is that by which equal lines are always transmitted in equal times; and *multiform*, when in one time more, in another time less space is transmitted. Again, of multiform motions, there are some in which the degrees of acceleration and retardation proceed in the same proportions, which the spaces transmitted have, whether duplicate, or triplicate, or by whatsoever number multiplied; and others in which it is otherwise.

Thirdly, from the number of the movents; that is, one motion is made by one movent only, and another by the concourse of many movents.

Fourthly, from the position of that line in which a body is moved, in respect of some other line; and from hence one motion is called *perpendicular*, another *oblique*, another *parallel*.

Fifthly, from the position of the movent in respect of the moved body; from whence one motion is *pulsion* or driving, another *traction* or drawing. *Pulsion*, when the movent makes the moved body go before it; and *traction*, when it makes it follow. Again, there are two sorts of *pulsion;* one, when the motions of the movent and moved body begin both together, which may be called *trusion* or *thrusting* and *vection;* the other, when the movent is first moved, and afterwards the moved body, which motion is called *percussion* or *stroke*.

Sixthly, motion is considered sometimes from the effect only which the movent works in the moved body, which is usually called *moment*. Now *moment is the excess of motion which the movent has above the motion or endeavor of the resisting body*.

Seventhly, it may be considered from the diversity of the *medium;* as one motion may be made in *vacuity* or *empty place;* another in a *fluid;* another in a *consistent medium*, that is, a *medium* whose parts are by some power so *consistent* and *cohering*, that no part of the same will yield to the movent, unless the whole yield also.

Eighthly, when a moved body is considered as having parts, there arises another distinction of motion into *simple* and *compound*. *Simple*, when all the several parts describe several equal lines; *compounded*, when the lines described are unequal.

5. The way by which the first endeavor of bodies moved tendeth. All endeavor tends towards that part, that is to say, in that way which is determined by the motion of the movent, if the movent be but one; or, if there be many movents, in that way which their concourse determines. For example, if a moved body have direct motion, its first endeavor will be in a straight line; if it have circular motion, its first endeavor will be in the circumference of a circle.

6. In motion, which is made by concourse, one of the movents ceasing, the endeavor is made by the way by which the rest tend. And whatsoever the line be, in which a body has its motion from the concourse of two movents, as soon as in any point thereof the force of one of the movents ceases, there immediately the former endeavor of that body will be changed into an endeavor in the line of the other movent.

Wherefore, when any body is carried on by the concourse of two winds, one of those winds ceasing, the endeavor and motion of that body will be in that line, in which it would have been carried by that wind alone which blows still. And in the describing of a circle, where that which is moved has its motion determined by a movent in a tangent, and by the radius which keeps it in a certain distance from the center, if the retention of the radius cease, that endeavor, which was in the circumference of the circle, will now be in the tangent, that is, in a straight line. For, seeing endeavor is computed in a less part of the circumference than can be given, that is, in a point, the way by which a body is moved in the circumference is compounded of innumerable straight lines, of which every one is less than can be given; which are therefore called points. Wherefore when any body, which is moved in the circumference of a circle, is freed from the retention of the radius, it will proceed in one of those straight lines, that is, in a tangent.

7. All endeavor is propagated in infinitum. All endeavor,

whether strong or weak, is propagated to infinite distance; for it is motion. If therefore the first endeavor of a body be made in space which is empty; it will always proceed with the same velocity; for it cannot be supposed that it can receive any resistance at all from empty space; and therefore, (by art. 7, chap. 9) it will always proceed in the same way and with the same swiftness. And if its endeavor be in space which is filled, yet, seeing endeavor is motion, that which stands next in its way shall be removed, and endeavor further, and again remove that which stands next, and so infinitely. Wherefore the propagation of endeavor, from one part of full space to another, proceeds infinitely. Besides, it reaches in any instant to any distance, how great soever. For in the same instant in which the first part of the full *medium* removes that which is next it, the second also removes that part which is next to it; and therefore all endeavor, whether it be in empty or in full space, proceeds not only to any distance, how great soever, but also in any time, how little soever, that is, in an instant. Nor makes it any matter, that endeavor, by proceeding, grows weaker and weaker, till at last it can no longer be perceived by sense; for motion may be insensible; and I do not here examine things by sense and experience, but by reason.

8. How much greater the velocity or magnitude is of a movent, so much the greater is the efficacy thereof upon any other body in its way. When two movents are of equal magnitude, the swifter of them works with greater force than the slower, upon a body that resists their motion. Also, if two movents have equal velocity, the greater of them works with more force than the less. For where the magnitude is equal, the movent of greater velocity makes the greater impression upon that body upon which it falls; and where the velocity is equal, the movent of greater magnitude falling upon the same point, or an equal part of another body, loses less of its velocity, because the resisting body works only upon that part of the movent which it touches, and therefore abates the impetus of that part only; whereas

in the mean time the parts, which are not touched, proceed, and retain their whole force, till they also come to be touched; and their force has some effect. Wherefore, for example, in batteries a longer than a shorter piece of timber of the same thickness and velocity, and a thicker than a slenderer piece of the same length and velocity, work a greater effect upon the wall.

PART 3

SENSE, ANIMAL MOTION, AND HUMAN BEHAVIOR

PHYSICS, OR THE PHENOMENA OF NATURE*

Chapter 25

Of Sense and Animal Motion

1. The connection of what hath been said with that which followeth. I have, in the first chapter, defined philosophy to be *knowledge of effects acquired by true ratiocination, from knowledge first had of their causes and generation; and of such causes or generations as may be, from former knowledge of their effects or appearances.* There are, therefore, two methods of philosophy; one, from the generation of things to their possible effects; and the other, from their effects or appearances to some possible generation of the same. In the former of these the truth of the first principles of our ratiocination, namely definitions, is made and constituted by ourselves, whilst we consent and agree about the appellations of things. And this part I have finished in the foregoing chapters; in which, if I am not deceived, I have affirmed nothing, saving the definitions themselves, which hath not good coherence with the definitions I have given; that is to say, which is not sufficiently demonstrated to all those, that agree with me in the use of words and appellations; for whose sake only I have written the same. I now enter upon the other part; which is the finding out by the appearances or effects of nature, which we know by sense, some ways and means by which they may be, I do not say they are, generated. The principles, therefore, upon which the following discourse depends, are not such as we ourselves make and pronounce in general terms, as definitions; but such, as being placed in the things themselves by the Author of Nature, are by us observed in them; and we make use of them in single and

*From *De Corpore* (Molesworth Ed. 1839, Vol. I of English Works), Chapter 25.

particular, not universal propositions. Nor do they impose upon us any necessity of constituting theorems; their use being only, though not without such general propositions as have been already demonstrated, to show us the possibility of some production or generation. Seeing, therefore, the science, which is here taught, hath its principles in the appearances of nature, and endeth in the attaining of some knowledge of natural causes, I have given to this part the title of PHYSICS, or the *Phenomena of Nature*. Now such things as appear, or are shown to us by nature, we call phenomena or appearances.

Of all the phenomena or appearances which are near us, the most admirable is apparition itself, τὸ φαίνεσθαι; namely, that some natural bodies have in themselves the patterns almost of all things, and others of none at all. So that if the appearances be the principles by which we know all other things, we must needs acknowledge sense to be the principle by which we know those principles, and that all the knowledge we have is derived from it. And as for the causes of sense, we cannot begin our search of them from any other phenomenon than that of sense itself. But you will say, by what sense shall we take notice of sense? I answer, by sense itself, namely, by the memory which for some time remains in us of things sensible, though they themselves pass away. For he that perceives that he hath perceived, remembers.

In the first place, therefore, the causes of our perception, that is, the causes of those ideas and phantasms which are perpetually generated within us whilst we make use of our senses, are to be inquired into; and in what manner their generation proceeds. To help which inquisition, we may observe first of all, that our phantasms or ideas are not always the same; but that new ones appear to us, and old ones vanish, according as we apply our organs of sense, now to one object, now to another. Wherefore they are generated, and perish. And from hence it is manifest, that they are some change or mutation in the sentient.

2. The investigation of the nature of sense, and the definition of sense. Now that all mutation or alteration is motion or endeavor (and endeavor also is motion) in the internal

parts of the thing that is altered, hath been proved (in art. 9, chap. 8) from this, that whilst even the least parts of any body remain in the same situation in respect of one another, it cannot be said that any alteration, unless perhaps that the whole body together hath been moved, hath happened to it; but that it both appeareth and is the same it appeared and was before. Sense, therefore, in the sentient, can be nothing else but motion in some of the internal parts of the sentient; and the parts so moved are parts of the organs of sense. For the parts of our body, by which we perceive any thing, are those we commonly call the organs of sense. And so we find what is the subject of our sense, namely, that in which are the phantasms; and partly also we have discovered the nature of sense, namely, that it is some internal motion in the sentient.

I have shown besides (in chap. 9, art. 7) that no motion is generated but by a body contiguous and moved: from whence it is manifest, that the immediate cause of sense or perception consists in this, that the first organ of sense is touched and pressed. For when the uttermost part of the organ is pressed, it no sooner yields, but the part next within it is pressed also; and, in this manner, the pressure or motion is propagated through all the parts of the organ to the innermost. And thus also the pressure of the uttermost part proceeds from the pressure of some more remote body, and so continually, till we come to that from which, as from its fountain, we derive the phantasm or idea that is made in us by our sense. And this, whatsoever it be, is that we commonly call *the object*. Sense, therefore, is some internal motion in the sentient, generated by some internal motion of the parts of the object, and propagated through all the media to the innermost part of the organ. By which words I have almost defined what sense is.

Moreover, I have shown (art. 2, chap. 15) that all resistance is endeavor opposite to another endeavor, that is to say, reaction. Seeing, therefore, there is in the whole organ, by reason of its own internal natural motion, some resistance or reaction against the motion which is propagated from the object to the innermost part of the organ, there is also in the same organ an endeavor opposite to the endeavor which proceeds from the object; so that when that endeavor inwards is the last action in the act of sense, then from the reaction, how little soever the duration of it be, a phantasm or idea hath its being, which, by reason that the endeavor is now outwards, doth always appear as something situate without the organ. So that now I shall give you the whole definition of sense, as it is drawn from the explication of the causes thereof and the order of its generation, thus: SENSE *is a phantasm, made by the reaction and endeavor outwards in the organ of sense, caused by an endeavor inwards from the object, remaining for some time more or less.*

3. The subject and object of sense. The *subject* of sense is is the *sentient* itself, namely, some living creature; and we speak more correctly, when we say a living creature seeth, than when we say the eye seeth. The object is the thing received; and it is more accurately said, that we see the sun, than that we see the light. For light and color, and heat and sound, and other qualities which are commonly called sensible, are not objects, but phantasms in the sentients. For a phantasm is the act of sense, and differs no otherwise from sense than *fieri*, that is, being a doing, differs from *factum esse*, that is, being done; which difference, in things that are done in an instant, is none at all; and a phantasm is made in an instant. For in all motion which proceeds by perpetual propagation, the first part being moved moves the second, the second the third, and so on to the last, and that to any distance, how great soever. And in what point of time the first or foremost part proceeded to the place of the second, which is thrust on, in the same point of time the last save one proceeded into the place of the last yielding part; which by reaction, in the same instant, if the reaction be strong enough, makes a phantasm; and a phantasm being made, perception is made together with it.

4. The organs of sense. The *organs* of sense, which are in the sentient, are such parts thereof, that if they be hurt, the very generation of phantasms is thereby destroyed, though all the rest of the parts remain entire. Now these parts in the most of living creatures are found to be certain spirits and

membranes, which, proceeding from the *pia mater*, involve the brain and all the nerves; also the brain itself, and the arteries which are in the brain; and such other parts, as being stirred, the heart also, which is the fountain of all sense, is stirred together with them. For whensoever the action of the object reacheth the body of the sentient, that action is by some nerve propagated to the brain; and if the nerve leading thither be so hurt or obstructed, that the motion can be propagated no further, no sense follows. Also if the motion be intercepted between the brain and the heart by the defect of the organ by which the action is propagated, there will be no perception of the object.

5. All bodies are not endued with sense. But though all sense, as I have said, be made by reaction, nevertheless it is not necessary that every thing that reacteth should have sense. I know there have been philosophers, and those learned men, who have maintained that all bodies are endued with sense. Nor do I see how they can be refuted, if the nature of sense be placed in reaction only. And, though by the reaction of bodies inanimate a phantasm might be made, it would nevertheless cease, as soon as ever the object were removed. For unless those bodies had organs, as living creatures have, fit for the retaining of such motion as is made in them, their sense would be such, as that they should never remember the same. And therefore this hath nothing to do with that sense which is the subject of my discourse. For by sense, we commonly understand the judgment we make of objects by their phantasms; namely, by comparing and distinguishing those phantasms; which we could never do, if that motion in the organ, by which the phantasm is made, did not remain there for some time, and make the same phantasm return. Wherefore sense, as I here understand it, and which is commonly so called, hath necessarily some memory adhering to it, by which former and later phantasms may be compared together, and distinguished from one another.

Sense, therefore, properly so called, must necessarily have in it a perpetual variety of phantasms, that they may be discerned one from another. For if we should suppose a man to be made with clear eyes, and all the rest of his organs of sight well disposed, but endued with no other sense; and that he should look only upon one thing, which is always of the same color and figure, without the least appearance of variety, he would seem to me, whatsoever others may say, to see, no more than I seem to myself to feel the bones of my own limbs by my organs of feeling; and yet those bones are always and on all sides touched by a most sensible membrane. I might perhaps say he were astonished, and looked upon it; but I should not say he saw it; it being almost all one for a man to be always sensible of one and the same thing, and not to be sensible at all of any thing.

6. But one phantasm at one and the same time. And yet such is the nature of sense, that it does not permit a man to discern many things at once. For seeing the nature of sense consists in motion; as long as the organs are employed about one object, they cannot be so moved by another at the same time, as to make by both their motions one sincere phantasm of each of them at once. And therefore two several phantasms will not be made by two objects working together, but only one phantasm compounded from the action of both.

Besides, as when we divide a body, we divide its place; and when we reckon many bodies, we must necessarily reckon as many places; and contrarily, as I have shown in the seventh chapter; so what number soever we say there be of times, we must understand the same number of motions also; and as oft as we count many motions, so oft we reckon many times. For though the object we look upon be of divers colors, yet with those divers colors it is but one varied object, and not variety of objects.

Moreover, whilst those organs which are common to all the senses, such as are those parts of every organ which proceed in men from the root of the nerves to the heart, are vehemently stirred by a strong action from some one object, they are, by reason of the contumacy which the motion, they have already, gives them against the reception of all other motion, made the less fit to receive any other impression from whatsoever other objects, to what sense soever those objects belong. And hence it is, that an earnest studying of one object, takes away the sense of all other objects for the present. For *study* is nothing else but a possession of the mind, that is to say, a vehement motion made by some one object in the organs of sense, which are stupid to all other motions as long as this lasteth; according to what was said by Terence, "*Populus studio stupidus in funambulo animum occuparat.*" For what is *stupor* but that which the Greeks call ἀναισθησία, that is, a cessation from the sense of other things? Wherefore at one and the same time, we cannot by sense perceive more than one single object; as in reading, we see the letters successively one by one, and not all together, though the whole page be presented to our eye; and though every several letter be distinctly written there, yet when we look upon the whole page at once, we read nothing.

From hence it is manifest, that every endeavor of the organ outwards, is not to be called sense, but that only, which at several times is by vehemence made stronger and more predominant than the rest; which deprives us of the sense of other phantasms, no otherwise than the sun deprives the rest of the stars of light, not by hindering their action, but by obscuring and hiding them with his excess of brightness.

7. Imagination, the remains of past sense; which also is memory. Of sleep. But the motion of the organ, by which a phantasm is made, is not commonly called sense, except the object be present. And the phantasm remaining after the object is removed or past by, is called *fancy*, and in Latin *imaginatio*; which word, because all phantasms are not images, doth not fully answer the signification of the word *fancy* in its general acceptation. Nevertheless I may use it safely enough, by understanding it for the Greek Φαντασία.

IMAGINATION therefore is nothing else but *sense decaying*, or *weakened*, by the absence of the object. But what may be the cause of this decay or weakening? Is the motion the weaker, because the object is taken away? If it were, then phantasms would always and necessarily be less clear in the imagination, than they are in sense; which is not true. For in dreams, which are the imaginations of those that sleep, they are no less clear than in sense itself. But the reason why in men waking the phantasms of things past are more obscure than those of things present, is this, that their organs being at the same time moved by other present objects, those phantasms are the less predominant. Whereas in sleep, the passages being shut up, external action doth not at all disturb or hinder internal motion.

If this be true, the next thing to be considered, will be, whether any cause may be found out, from the supposition whereof it will follow, that the passage is shut up from the external objects of sense to the internal organ. I suppose, therefore, that by the continual action of objects, to which a reaction of the organ, and more especially of the spirits, is necessarily consequent, the organ is wearied, that is, its parts are no longer moved by the spirits without some pain; and consequently the nerves being abandoned and grown slack, they retire to their fountain, which is the cavity either of the brain or of the heart; by which means the action which proceeded by the nerves is necessarily intercepted. For action upon a patient, that retires from it, makes but little impression at the first; and at last, when the nerves are by little and little slackened, none at all. And therefore there is no more reaction, that is, no more sense, till the organ being refreshed by rest, and by a supply of new spirits recovering strength and motion, the sentient awaketh. And thus it seems to be always, unless some other preternatural cause intervene; as heat in the internal parts from lassitude, or from some disease stirring the spirits and other parts of the organ in some extraordinary manner.

8. How phantasms succeed one another. Now it is not without cause, nor so casual a thing as many perhaps think it, that phantasms in this their great variety proceed from one another; and that the same phantasms sometimes bring into the mind other phantasms like themselves, and at other times extremely unlike. For in the motion of any continued body, one part follows another by cohesion; and therefore,

whilst we turn our eyes and other organs successively to many objects, the motion which was made by every one of them remaining, the phantasms are renewed as often as any one of those motions comes to be predominant above the rest; and they become predominant in the same order in which at any time formerly they were generated by sense. So that when by length of time very many phantasms have been generated within us by sense, then almost any thought may arise from any other thought; insomuch that it may seem to be a thing indifferent and casual, which thought shall follow which. But for the most part this is not so uncertain a thing to waking as to sleeping men. For the thought or phantasm of the desired end brings in all the phantasms, that are means conducing to that end, and that in order backwards from the last to the first, and again forwards from the beginning to the end. But this supposes both appetite, and judgment to discern what means conduce to the end, which is gotten by experience; and experience is store of phantasms, arising from the sense of very many things. For φαντάζεσθαι and *meminisse*, *fancy* and *memory*, differ only in this, that memory supposeth the time past, which fancy doth not. In memory, the phantasms we consider are as if they were worn out with time; but in our fancy we consider them as they are; which distinction is not of the things themselves, but of the considerations of the sentient. For there is in memory something like that which happens in looking upon things at a great distance; in which as the small parts of the object are not discerned, by reason of their remoteness; so in memory, many accidents and places and parts of things, which were formerly perceived by sense, are by length of time decayed and lost.

The perpetual arising of phantasms, both in sense and imagination, is that which we commonly call discourse of the mind, and is common to men with other living creatures. For he that thinketh, compareth the phantasms that pass, that is, taketh notice of their likeness or unlikeness to one another. And as he that observes readily the likenesses of things of different natures, or that are very remote from one another, is said to have a good fancy; so he is said to have a good judgment, that finds out the unlikenesses or differences of things that are like one another. Now this observation of differences is not perception made by a common organ of sense, distinct from sense or perception properly so called, but is memory of the differences of particular phantasms remaining for some time; as the distinction between hot and lucid, is nothing else but the memory both of a heating, and of an enlightening object.

9. Dreams, whence they proceed. The phantasms of men that sleep, are *dreams*. Concerning which we are taught by experience these five things. First, that for the most part there is neither order nor coherence in them. Secondly, that we dream of nothing but what is compounded and made up of the phantasms of sense past. Thirdly, that sometimes they proceed, as in those that are drowsy, from the interruption of their phantasms by little and little, broken and altered through sleepiness; and sometimes also they begin in the midst of sleep. Fourthly, that they are clearer than the imaginations of waking men, except such as are made by sense itself, to which they are equal in clearness. Fifthly, that when we dream, we admire neither the places nor the looks of the things that appear to us. Now from what hath been said, it is not hard to show what may be the causes of these phenomena. For as for the first, seeing all order and coherence proceeds from frequent looking back to the end, that is, from consultation; it must needs be, that seeing in sleep we lose all thought of the end, our phantasms succeed one another, not in that order which tends to any end, but as it happeneth, and in such manner, as objects present themselves to our eyes when we look indifferently upon all things before us, and see them, not because we would see them, but because we do not shut our eyes; for then they appear to us without any order at all. The second proceeds from this, that in the silence of sense there is no new motion from the objects, and therefore no new phantasm, unless we call that new, which is compounded of old ones, as a chimera, a golden mountain, and the like. As for the third, why a dream is

sometimes as it were the continuation of sense, made up of broken phantasms, as in men distempered with sickness, the reason is manifestly this, that in some of the organs sense remains, and in others it faileth. But how some phantasms may be revived, when all the exterior organs are benumbed with sleep, is not so easily shown. Nevertheless that, which hath already been said, contains the reason of this also. For whatsoever strikes the *pia mater*, reviveth some of those phantasms that are still in motion in the brain; and when any internal motion of the heart reacheth that membrane, then the predominant motion in the brain makes the phantasm. Now the motions of the heart are appetites and aversions, of which I shall presently speak further. And as appetites and aversions are generated by phantasms, so reciprocally phantasms are generated by appetites and aversions. For example, heat in the heart proceeds from anger and fighting; and again, from heat in the heart, whatsoever be the cause of it, is generated anger and the image of an enemy, in sleep. And as love and beauty stir up heat in certain organs; so heat in the same organs, from whatsoever it proceeds, often causeth desire and the image of an unresisting beauty. Lastly, cold doth in the same manner generate fear in those that sleep, and causeth them to dream of ghosts, and to have phantasms of horror and danger; as fear also causeth cold in those that wake. So reciprocal are the motions of the heart and brain. The fourth, namely, that the things we seem to see and feel in sleep, are as clear as in sense itself, proceeds from two causes; one, that having then no sense of things without us, that internal motion which makes the phantasm, in the absence of all other impressions, is predominant; and the other, that the parts of our phantasms which are decayed and worn out by time, are made up with other fictitious parts. To conclude, when we dream, we do not wonder at strange places and the appearances of things unknown to us, because admiration requires that the things appearing be new and unusual, which can happen to none but those that remember former appearances; whereas in sleep, all things appear as present.

But it is here to be observed, that certain dreams, especially such as some men have when they are between sleeping and waking, and such as happen to those that have no knowledge of the nature of dreams and are withal superstitious, were not heretofore nor are now accounted dreams. For the apparitions men thought they saw, and the voices they thought they heard in sleep, were not believed to be phantasms, but things subsisting of themselves, and objects without those that dreamed. For to some men, as well sleeping as waking, but especially to guilty men, and in the night, and in hallowed places, fear alone, helped a little with the stories of such apparitions, hath raised in their minds terrible phantasms, which have been and are still deceitfully received for things really true, under the names of *ghosts* and *incorporeal substances*.

10. Of the senses, their kinds, their organs and phantasms, proper and common. In most living creatures there are observed five kinds of senses, which are distinguished by their organs, and by their different kinds of phantasms; namely, *sight, hearing, smell, taste,* and *touch*; and these have their organs partly peculiar to each of them severally, and partly common to them all. The organ of sight is partly animate, and partly inanimate. The inanimate parts are the three humors; namely, the watery humor, which by the interposition of the membrane called uvea, the perforation whereof is called the apple of the eye, is contained on one side by the first concave superficies of the eye, and on the other side by the ciliary processes, and the coat of the crystalline humor; the crystalline, which, hanging in the midst between the ciliary processes, and being almost of spherical figure, and of a thick consistence, is enclosed on all sides with its own transparent coat; and the vitreous or glassy humor, which filleth all the rest of the cavity of the eye, and is somewhat thicker than the watery humor, but thinner than the crystalline. The animate part of the organ is, first, the membrane *choroeides*, which is a part of the *pia mater*, saving that it is covered with a coat derived from the marrow of the optic nerve, which is called the *retina*; and this *choroeides*, seeing it is part of the *pia mater*, is continued to

the beginning of the *medulla spinalis* within the skull, in which all the nerves which are within the head have their roots. Wherefore all the animal spirits that the nerves receive, enter into them there; for it is not imaginable that they can enter into them anywhere else. Seeing therefore sense is nothing else but the action of objects propagated to the furthest part of the organ; and seeing also that animal spirits are nothing but vital spirits purified by the heart, and carried from it by the arteries; it follows necessarily, that the action is derived from the heart by some of the arteries to the roots of the nerves which are in the head, whether those arteries be the *plexus retiformis*, or whether they be other arteries which are inserted into the substance of the brain. And, therefore, those arteries are the complement or the remaining part of the whole organ of sight. And this last part is a common organ to all the senses; whereas, that which reacheth from the eye to the roots of the nerves is proper only to sight. The proper organ of hearing is the tympanum of the ear and its own nerve; from which to the heart the organ is common. So the proper organs of smell and taste are nervous membranes, in the palate and tongue for the taste, and in the nostrils for the smell; and from the roots of those nerves to the heart all is common. Lastly, the proper organ of touch are nerves and membranes dispersed through the whole body; which membranes are derived from the root of the nerves. And all things else belonging alike to all the senses seem to be administered by the arteries, and not by the nerves.

The proper phantasm of sight is light; and under this name of light, color also, which is nothing but perturbed light, is comprehended. Wherefore the phantasm of a lucid body is light; and of a colored body, color. But the object of sight, properly so called, is neither light nor color, but the body itself which is lucid, or enlightened, or colored. For light and color, being phantasms of the sentient, cannot be accidents of the object. Which is manifest enough from this, that visible things appear oftentimes in places in which we know assuredly they are not, and that in different places they are of different colors, and may at one and the same time appear in divers places. Motion, rest, magnitude, and figure, are common both to the sight and touch; and the whole appearance together of figure, and light or color, is by the Greeks commonly called εἶδος, and εἴδωλον, and ἰδέα; and by the Latins, *species* and *imago*; all which names signify no more but appearance.

The phantasm, which is made by hearing, is sound; by smell, odor; by taste, savor; and by touch, hardness and softness, heat and cold, wetness, oiliness, and many more, which are easier to be distinguished by sense than words. Smoothness, roughness, rarity, and density, refer to figure, and are therefore common both to touch and sight. And as for the objects of hearing, smell, taste, and touch, they are not sound, odor, savor, hardness, &c., but the bodies themselves from which sound, odor, savor, hardness, &c. proceed; of the causes of which, and of the manner how they are produced, I shall speak hereafter.

But these phantasms, though they be effects in the sentient, as subject, produced by objects working upon the organs; yet there are also other effects besides these, produced by the same objects in the same organs; namely certain motions proceeding from sense, which are called *animal motions*. For seeing in all sense of external things there is mutual action and reaction, that is, two endeavors opposing one another, it is manifest that the motion of both of them together will be continued every way, especially to the confines of both the bodies. And when this happens in the internal organ, the endeavor outwards will proceed in a solid angle, which will be greater, and consequently the idea greater, than it would have been if the impression had been weaker.

11. The magnitude of images, how and by what it is determined. From hence the natural cause is manifest, first, why those things seem to be greater, which, *cæteris paribus*, are seen in a greater angle: secondly, why in a serene cold night, when the moon doth not shine, more of the fixed stars appear than at another time. For their action is less hindered by the serenity of the air, and not obscured by the greater

light of the moon, which is then absent; and the cold, making the air more pressing, helpeth or strengtheneth the action of the stars upon our eyes; in so much as stars may then be seen which are seen at no other time. And this may suffice to be said in general concerning sense made by the reaction of the organ. For, as for the place of the image, the deceptions of sight, and other things of which we have experience in ourselves by sense, seeing they depend for the most part upon the fabric itself of the eye of man, I shall speak of them then when I come to speak of man.

12. *Pleasure, pain, appetite, and aversion, what they are.* But there is another kind of sense, of which I will say something in this place, namely, the sense of pleasure and pain, proceeding not from the reaction of the heart outwards, but from continual action from the outermost part of the organ towards the heart. For the original of life being in the heart, that motion in the sentient, which is propagated to the heart, must necessarily make some alteration or diversion of vital motion, namely, by quickening or slackening, helping or hindering the same. Now when it helpeth, it is pleasure; and when it hindereth, it is pain, trouble, grief, &c. And as phantasms seem to be without, by reason of the endeavor outwards, so pleasure and pain, by reason of the endeavor of the organ inwards, seem to be within; namely, there where the first cause of the pleasure or pain is; as when the pain proceeds from a wound, we think the pain and the wound are both in the same place.

Now vital motion is the motion of the blood, perpetually circulating (as hath been shown from many infallible signs and marks by Doctor Harvey, the first observer of it) in the veins and arteries. Which motion, when it is hindered by some other motion made by the action of sensible objects, may be restored again either by bending or setting straight the parts of the body; which is done when the spirits are carried now into these, now into other nerves, till the pain, as far as is possible, be quite taken away. But if vital motion be helped by motion made by sense, then the parts of the organ will be disposed to guide the spirits in such manner as conduceth most to the preservation and augmentation of that motion, by the help of the nerves. And in animal motion this is the very first endeavor, and found even in the embryo; which while it is in the womb, moveth its limbs with voluntary motion, for the avoiding of whatsoever troubleth it, or for the pursuing of what pleaseth it. And this first endeavor, when it tends towards such things as are known by experience to be pleasant, is called *appetite*, that is, an approaching; and when it shuns what is troublesome, *aversion*, or flying from it. And little infants, at the beginning and as soon as they are born, have appetite to very few things, as also they avoid very few, by reason of their want of experience and memory; and therefore they have not so great a variety of animal motion as we see in those that are more grown. For it is not possible, without such knowledge as is derived from sense, that is, without experience and memory, to know what will prove pleasant or hurtful; only there is some place for conjecture from the looks or aspects of things. And hence it is, that though they do not know what may do them good or harm, yet sometimes they approach and sometimes retire from the same thing, as their doubt prompts them. But afterwards, by accustoming themselves by little and little, they come to know readily what is to be pursued and what to be avoided; and also to have a ready use of their nerves and other organs, in the pursuing and avoiding of good and bad. Wherefore appetite and aversion are the first endeavors of animal motion.

Consequent to this first endeavor, is the impulsion into the nerves and retraction again of animal spirits, of which it is necessary there be some receptacle or place near the original of the nerves; and this motion or endeavor is followed by a swelling and relaxation of the muscles; and lastly, these are followed by contraction and extension of the limbs, which is animal motion.

13. Deliberation and will, what. The considerations of appetites and aversions are divers. For seeing living creatures have sometimes appetite and sometimes aversion to the same thing, as they think it will either be for their good or their

hurt; while that vicissitude of appetites and aversions remains in them, they have that series of thoughts which is called *deliberation*; which lasteth as long as they have it in their power to obtain that which pleaseth, or to avoid that which displeaseth them. Appetite, therefore, and aversion are simply so called as long as they follow not deliberation. But if deliberation have gone before, then the last act of it, if it be appetite, is called *will*; if aversion, *unwillingness*. So that the same thing is called both will and appetite; but the consideration of them, namely, before and after deliberation, is divers. Nor is that which is done within a man whilst he willeth any thing, different from that which is done in other living creatures, whilst, deliberation having preceded, they have appetite.

Neither is the freedom of willing or not willing, greater in man, than in other living creatures. For where there is appetite, the entire cause of appetite hath preceded; and, consequently, the act of appetite could not choose but follow, that is, hath of necessity followed (as is shown in chapter 9, article 5). And therefore such a liberty as is free from necessity, is not to be found in the will either of men or beasts. But if by liberty we understand the faculty or power, not of willing, but of doing what they will, then certainly that liberty is to be allowed to both, and both may equally have it, whensoever it is to be had.

Again, when appetite and aversion do with celerity succeed one another, the whole series made by them hath its name sometimes from one, sometimes from the other. For the same deliberation, whilst it inclines sometimes to one, sometimes to the other, is from appetite called *hope*, and from aversion, *fear*. For where there is no hope, it is not to be called fear, but *hate*; and where no fear, not hope, but *desire*. To conclude, all the passions, called passions of the mind, consist of appetite and aversion, except pure pleasure and pain, which are a certain fruition of good or evil; as anger is aversion from some imminent evil, but such as is joined with appetite of avoiding that evil by force. But because the passions and perturbations of the mind are innumerable, and many of them not to be discerned in any creatures besides men; I will speak of them more at large in that section which is concerning *man*. As for those objects, if there be any such, which do not at all stir the mind, we are said to contemn them.

And thus much of sense in general. In the next place I shall speak of sensible objects.

FIRST PRINCIPLES OF SENSE
AND ANIMAL MOTION*

Section 1

1. That, whereto nothing is added, and from which nothing is taken, remains in the same state it was.

2. That which is no way touch'd by another, hath nothing added to nor taken from it. — *no action at a distance*

3. Agent is that which hath power to move.

4. Patient is that which hath power to be moved. — *passive potency*

5. Equal Agents are such as have equal power.

6. Equal Agents, equally distant from the Patient, move it equally.

7. Equal Agents, unequally distant from the Patient, move it unequally.

8. Unequal Agents, equally distant from the Patient, move it unequally.

9. Whatsoever moveth another, moveth it either by active power inherent in itself, or by motion received from another.

10. In Local Motion, the Action of the Agent, is the Local motion of the Patient.

11. An Agent produceth nothing in the Patient, but Motion, or some inherent form.

12. Necessary is that which cannot be otherwise.

13. A Necessary cause is that which cannot but produce the effect.

*This selection is Appendix 1 of *A Short Tract on First Principles* (*The Little Treatise*) as printed in F. Tonnies' edition of *The Elements of Law* (Cambridge University Press, 1928) pp. 152-167.

14. A Sufficient cause is that which hath all things requisite to produce the effect.

15. Substance is that which hath being not in another, so as it may be of itself, as Air, or Gold.

16. Accident is that which hath being in another, so as, without that other it could not be, as Color cannot be, but in somewhat colored.

Conclusions

1. Every thing is either Substance or Accident.

For, Every thing that hath a being in Nature, hath it either in another, or not in another: the one of these, is Substance (by 15 Prin.); the other, Accident (by 16 Prin.): therefore Everything that hath a being is either Substance or Accident.

2. No Accident can be without a Substance.

For seeing every Accident hath being in another (by 16 Prin.), if that other, in which it is, be an Accident, then must that also be in another (by 16 Prin.), and so forward, either *in infinitum*, which is absurd: or at last we must come to something that hath being not in another, which is Substance (by 15 Prin.).

3. The utmost Subject of Accident is Substance.

Let *A* be an Accident, and *B* the utmost Subject of it. I say, that *B* is a Substance. For if *B* be not a Substance, then (by 1 Concl.) it must be Accident, and so (by 16 Prin.) is in another, which other suppose to be *C*. Now if *A* be in *B*, and *B* in *C*, then is *A* also in *C*, as in an utter subject, and so *B* is not the utmost subject of *A*; which is against the Supposition.

4. No Accident can be Locally moved out of his Subject.

For seeing that which is moved must have being while it is moved; and no Accident can have being without that Subject in which it is (by 16 Prin.): it follows, that No Accident can be locally moved out of his own subject.

Corollary.—Hence it follows, that No Accident can be locally moved, unless his subject be moved with it, and that all Accidents that inhere in the subject, are moved with that subject, otherwise Accidents might have being without their subject (contrary to the 16 Prin.).

5. That which now resteth, cannot be moved, unless it be touched by some Agent. — *Inertia*

Suppose *A* to rest, I say it cannot be moved, unless some Agent touch it. For if *A* be no way touched by any agent, then is nothing added to, nor taken from it (by the 2 Prin.), and so *A* shall (by the 1 Prin.) remain in the same state it was, which is at rest.

6. Whatsoever is Agent or Patient, is Substance.

For seeing Active and passive power are inherent accidents (by the 16 Prin.)—because they have no being without those things, whose powers they are—and the utmost subject of those powers is the Agent and Patient: it follows (by the 3 Concl.) that the Agent and Patient are Substances.

7. Every Agent working produceth Motion in the Patient.

For (by the 3 Prin.) Agent is that which hath power to move. This power is either in Act, or not; if not, then the Agent is not working (contrary to the Supposition); if it be in Act, then the Patient is moved. For (by the 10 Prin.) the Action of the Agent is the Motion of the Patient.

8. The Agent that moveth by Active power originally in itself, applied to the Patient, shall always move it.

If *A* have power active of itself to move *B*, let that power be *C*; supposing then that *B* have passive power to be moved by *A*, if *A* move not *B*, either *A* hath not *C* (which is against the supposition), or *A* suspendeth *C*; if so, then *A* hath power to suspend *C*, which power let be *D*. Now if the power *D* be never suspended, then *C* is always suspended, and so *B* can never be moved by *A*; and if the power *D* be sometimes suspended, then hath *A* another power to suspend *D*, and so *in infinitum*, which is absurd.

9. Whatsoever once moveth another, and moveth it not still whensoever it toucheth it, when it moveth it, is itself also moved.

If *A* move *B* now, I say if *A* do not at all times it toucheth *B*, move *B*; when *A* moveth *B*, then shall *A* itself be moved. For seeing *A* moveth *B*, it moveth it either by active power in itself, or by motion from another (by the 9 Prin.); if *A* move *B* by active power of itself, then whensoever *A* toucheth *B* it shall move *B* (by the 8 Concl.), which is contrary to the supposition; and if *A* move *B* by motion from another, then *A* itself is moved.

10. Nothing can move itself.

Suppose (if it be possible) that *A* can move itself. This must be by active power in itself (else it moves not itself, but is moved by another); and seeing itself is always applied to itself, it shall (by the 8 Concl.) move itself always. Suppose then that *A* have power to be moved towards *B* then shall *A* move itself always towards *B*. Likewise suppose (as we may) that *A* hath power to be moved towards *C*; then shall *A* move itself always towards *C*; and so shall always move itself contrary ways, which is impossible. Or thus: Suppose *A* at rest, I say *A*, of itself, cannot move itself. For seeing nothing is added to nor taken from that which is itself, it shall (by the 1 Prin.) remain in the same state it was; and *A* being by supposition at rest, it shall rest always, and never be moved by itself.

$$B \quad A \quad C,$$

11. A Sufficient Cause is a Necessary cause.

That cause which cannot but produce the effect, is a Necessary cause (by the 13 Prin.), but a sufficient cause cannot but produce the effect, because it hath all things requisite to produce it (by the 14 Prin.). For if it produces it not, somewhat else is wanting to the production of it, and so the cause is not a sufficient cause, which is contrary to the supposition.

Corollary.—Hence appears that the definition of a Free Agent, to be that, which, all things requisite to work, being put, may work, or not work, implies a contradiction. No FREED

12. Every effect produced hath had a Necessary Cause.

For seeing every effect produced hath had a sufficient Cause (else it had not been produced), and every sufficient cause (by the 11 Concl.) is a Necessary cause; it follows that every effect produced hath had a Necessary cause.

13. Every effect to be produced shall be produced by a Necessary Cause.

For seeing no effect can be produced without a sufficient Cause, and every sufficient cause (by the 11 Concl.) is a Necessary cause; it follows, that every effect hereafter to be produced, shall be produced by a Necessary cause.

14. <u>Necessity hath no degrees.</u>

For that which is necessary is impossible to be otherwise (by the 12 Prin.), and that which is impossible is Non-Ens; and one Non-Ens cannot be more Non-Ens than another; therefore one Necessary cannot be more Necessary than another.

15. The Agent that hath active power inherent in itself, applied to several equal Patients, shall work on them equally.

Suppose *A* have active power inherent to move *B*, *C*, *D* equal patients, I say *A* shall work on them equally. For (by the 10 Concl.) *A*, being applied, cannot suspend his own power; therefore *A* shall work on *B*, *C*, *D*; and because the Agent is the same, and the Patients *B*, *C*, *D* equal, therefore (by the 6 Prin.) *A* shall work on them equally.

Section 2

1. Every agent that worketh on a distant Patient, toucheth it, either by the Medium, or by somewhat issuing from itself, which thing so issuing let be called <u>Species.</u>

Conclusions   <u>NO ACTION AT A DISTANCE.</u>

1. The Agent that worketh on a Patient at distance, worketh on it either by successive action on the parts of the corporal Medium, or by species.

For seeing the Agent cannot work on the Patient unless it touch it some way; and touch it the Agent cannot but by the Medium, successively wrought on, or by species (by the 1 Prin. Sect. 2) it follows that the Agent must work on the Patient distant, either successive, etc.

2. Agents at distance work not all on the Patient, by successive action on the parts of the Medium.

Suppose A to be the sun, and the superficies of some opacous body to be CDEFGHJ, I say

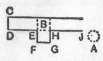

A shall not illuminate the superficies CD, or FG, by successive illumination of the air, which is the corporeal medium. For if it does, then every part of that air, shall have power to illuminate the next part to it in succession from A to CD, and by the same reason to FG. Therefore the square B, being part of that medium, hath power to illuminate the next part to it, both towards CD and towards FG; and likewise these parts illuminated to illuminate their next part, in succession from B to CD and FG. Therefore B illuminateth these parts either by active power inherent in itself, or by motion received from another (by 9 Prin. Sect. 1); if by active power inherent, then shall B illuminate CD and FG, after the same manner, as if A were in the place of *B* (because *B* hath in itself the power of *A*), though not in the same measure; and seeing the superficies *FG* is nearer to the Agent *B* than the superficies *CD*, *FG* shall be more strongly illuminated than *CD* (by the 7 Prin. Sect. 1), which is contrary to Experience. If by motion from another, then *CD* shall be illuminated by local motion of the parts of the air; and then, if a contrary Agent (as the wind) disturb that motion of the parts; or if a solid perspicuous medium (as Crystal) which is not easily moved, be interposed between *B* and *CD*, *CD* shall not at all, or very weakly be illuminated; both which are contrary to Experience. Therefore *A* illuminates not *CD* by successive illumination of the air, and therefore All Agents, at distance, work not by successive action on the parts of the Medium.

The same may be demonstrated in the multiplication of heat; by the former figure and likewise by reflection of visible species, and refraction of light through a burning-glass. Further, from the Experience of Magnetical virtue, and of Influence from the Moon on humid bodies, and generally from the stars on sublunary things, the same may be demonstrated in other species, besides heat, light, and other species visible.

3. Some Agents, at distance, work by Species.

For seeing all Agents at distance (by the 1 Concl. Sect. 2) work either by successive action on the parts of the Medium, or by species, and it is proved (by the 2 Concl. Sect. 2) that all Agents at distance work not by successive action on the parts of the Medium, it follows that some Agents work by species.

4. Species, the farther they go from the body whence they issue, the weaker they are.

Suppose the Agent *A* send out species to *DE*, I say the species in *DE* are weaker than the species in *BC*. For seeing there are no more species in *DE* than in *BC*, and in *DE* they are more diffused, and in *BC* more united; it follows that the species in *DE* are weaker than those in *BC*. By the same reason the species in

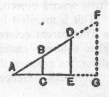

FG are weaker than the species in *DE*, and so forwards, the farther they go, still the weaker.

5. Agents send out their species continually.

For seeing the Agent hath power in itself to produce such species, and is always applied to the patient, which is somewhat in itself, it shall (by the 8 Concl. Sect. 1) produce and send out species continually.

6. Species proceed infinitely.

Suppose the point *A* be a particle of sand; I say that *A* sendeth out species *in infinitum*. For if not, let the species of *A* be finite in *B*. Seeing then the greater the object is, the farther it may be seen, if to *A* were added so many more particles of sand as would make a heap, represented by the circle *AC*, that heap would be seen farther off, as suppose in *D*. Visible species therefore proceed to *D*. But if no species come thither from *A*, no more shall there from any other particle of sand (because—by the 6 Prin. Sect. 1— Equal Agents work equally at equal distance), and so no species should come from *AC* to *D*, and consequently *AC* should not be seen in *D*, contrary to supposition. Species therefore do come from *A* to *D*; and by the same reason do proceed infinitely. *sounds like Zeno's Paradoxes*

If it be said that the species of *A* alone would go but to *B*, but being fortified by other species added, proceed farther: It appears that the species of *A* are not stronger than they were; because neither *A* nor any other particle is better discerned by addition, but only the whole heap is seen; which could not be, but by the beams of the parts, which if they existed not, could not move the sight; or if they were strengthened, would represent distinctly to the eye the several particles that send them out.

7. Species that come in one and the same straight line from several objects, are by the sense perceived as one.

This is manifest by Experience. For Light passing through a Transparent colored body (as through a glass of wine, or glass colored) casteth upon the superficies beyond that medium, the color of that wine or glass.

Corollary.—Hence it appears that color is Light diversified by the species of diverse bodies; which Species, as the bodies from which they come, are different.

8. Species are moved locally.

This is manifest, because the species proceed from the Agent to the Patient distant in Place (by Concl. 3, Sect. 2). Against this some Arguments are brought, which seem not to me to conclude that for which they are urged.

First this. Species pass not from the Agent to the distant Patient, in Time, but in an Instant. Therefore they are not moved locally. For suppose (say they) the sun in A send a beam to C; if that beam pass from A to C in time, then it shall pass a part of that line (to wit AB) in part of time; and the least part of that line in the least part of time. Likewise suppose some star of less force, to cast his beam from A to C; because that beam moves the whole line AC in Time, it shall move part of that line (to wit AB) in part of time, and the least part of that line in the least part of time; and so two Agents of unequal force shall move equal space, in equal time, which is absurd. Therefore the beams of the sun move not in time but in an Instant. *finite velocity of light*

But by this reason (if it were right) a Snaple might be demonstrated to move any space in an Instant. For if a snaple in A, move AC in time, it shall move AB in part of time, and the least part of AB in the least part of time. And Achilles shall do no more. Therefore a Snaple shall move as fast as Achilles.

The fault of this Argument lies in this, that it supposeth a least part in line and time, when there is no Minimum in either. Besides if it be absurd for two Agents of unequal force to move equal space in equal time (as indeed it is), it shall be much more absurd for two most unequal Agents to move the same space in an Instant, as will necessarily follow, if Light, etc., pass in an Instant; and all Instants are equal. Therefore the Species move not in an Instant.

Secondly this. If bodies continually send out so many substantial species, how can they subsist without supply? This indeed is hard to determine: but we may with probability

Remember Epicurus — infinite atoms constantly replenish the body as it gives off images.

imagine, that as Fiery bodies, which send out most Species, are manifestly and sensibly supplied with fuel: so other bodies, sending out fewer, may have a supply of Nutriment, by converting other bodies or Species adjacent, into themselves; though the way how this is done, as almost all the ways of Nature, be to us not so perceptible.

Thirdly this. Suppose a star in *D*, moving towards *E*, *F*. Let the eye be in *A*, and some opacous body, *BC*; it is manifest that the star *D* shall not be seen, till it be ascended to the point *E*, and seeing it touches that point *E* in an instant, and so moves continually towards *F*, if it send not out species from *E* to *A* in that instant, it cannot be seen that instant in *E*, but in some point higher towards *F*, and so shall not be seen in a straight line *ABE*, and in his right place, *E*, which seems against Experience. Therefore the beam comes from *E* to *A* in an instant.

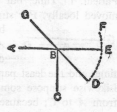

But neither doth this argument necessarily prove that which it seems to conclude. For seeing the star yet in *D* hath a beam passing by *B* to *G*, as *D* riseth towards *E*, by the same degrees shall *G* fall towards *A*, and so it shall touch *A* in an instant, as *D* toucheth *E*, though it move to *A* in time, as *D* in time moves to *E*. And though the beam *DG* continue not the same, and come to be the same in number with the beam *EBA*, yet by continual diffusion of the parts of that beam, as they ascend about *D*, a beam shall be maintained equivalent to it.

Besides, I know no reason to assure me, that visible objects in motion, are just in the same straight line, in which they appear to be. For when the species affects the eye, wherever the object be, it will seem to be in a straight line before the eye, though indeed it be not so, as in a looking glass, the object that is behind, seems to be before.

Wherefore, notwithstanding these, and the like objections, since motion from place to place, is local motion; and the Species have been demonstrated to proceed from the Agent to the Patient, distant in place, the former Conclusion remains still true, that Species are moved locally.

9. There is between Species Conveniency, and disconveniency, by which the Agents whence they issue, attrude and repel one the other.

This is manifest by Experience in things that attract or repeal one the other by Sympathy and Antipathy. For seeing they touch not one another, and motion of the Attraction or Repulsion is not wrought by alteration of the Medium (by the 2. Concl. Sect. 2.) it must be by Species; and seeing all Agents and Patients do not so move one the other, it follows that those which do so work, must work by somewhat proper to their Species, which is what we call Conveniency, or Disconveniency and the Greeks, Sympathy and Antipathy.

Corollary.—Hence may be collected the manner how the Lodestone attracts Steel. For the Species of the Lodestone meeting with the Species of the Steel in the medium, do so fortify their motion by Conveniency with them, that they issue out of the steel, with more speed and abundance than otherwise they would; and the body of that steel admitting but a determinate afflux, is drawn to follow after the Species, and so is moved to the Lodestone.

Proportionably to this the Motion of Repulsion is to be understood, in bodies that work by Antipathy; where the species of the one being weakened by the species of the other, as disconvenient with them, cannot issue out so fast, or in such measure, as the Nature of that body requires, and so that body is moved to retire back from the other.

Likewise it may be conceived, how one string of an Instrument being moved, and the Species of that string moved with it, working with the species of another string (that is either a unison or an eighth with it) by conveniency moveth the species of that other string, and consequently the string itself, whence they come.

10. Species are substances.

Primitive light and color etc. are Accidents; much more Derivative (by Primitive light is understood *Lux*, by derivative, *Lumen*), and seeing derivative light and color are not inherent in the Medium (by the 2 Concl. Sect. 2) their utmost subject must be the species; and consequently those species must be substance (by the 3 Concl. Sect. 1).

Corollary.—Hence it appears, that as Primitive light and color is to the lucid or colored body: so is derivative light and color to the species, and as the species are to the lucid or colored body: so is derivative light and color to primitive.

Section 3

1. Animal spirits are those spirits which are the Instruments of Sense and Motion.

2. By a Phantasma we understand the similitude or image of some external object, appearing to us after the external object is removed from the Sensorium; as in Dreams.

3. One Agent begetteth not the similitude of another Agent on the animal spirits, unless it be qualified with like power, by the other Agent.

4. One simply, as A', or Horse.

5. One by union of more Natures $-\overset{A}{\underset{B}{C}}-$, as A, Horse; B white; by union are C, one white horse.

6. One by comprehension of parts $|\overset{A}{\rule{0pt}{6pt}}\ \underset{\ }{|}\ \overset{B}{\rule{0pt}{6pt}}|$, as A, head; B, body; are one Man by Comprehension.

7. One partly by Union, partly by Comprehension is: First, when one is part of the other $|\overset{A}{\rule{0pt}{6pt}}\ \overset{B}{\underset{|}{\rule{0pt}{6pt}}}\ \overset{C}{\rule{0pt}{6pt}}|$, as AB and AC are one, partly by union, partly by Comprehension; because AB is one by union with part of AC, namely with AB; and one with part of AC by Comprehension, namely, with BC: as if AB be *Homo*, and AC, *Animal*, *Homo* and *Animal* are one by union from A to B, and one but by Comprehension only with BC. Secondly, when they have one common part $|\overset{A}{\rule{0pt}{6pt}}\ \overset{B}{\underset{|}{\rule{0pt}{6pt}}}\ \overset{C}{\underset{|}{\rule{0pt}{6pt}}}\ \overset{D}{\rule{0pt}{6pt}}|$ as AC and BD; where part of AC and part of BD are one by Union in BC and part of AC, that is AB; and part of BD, that is, CD, are one only by Comprehension.

8. Things that are one by union are one.

9. Parts of one by Comprehension are not one.

10. As objects are one by Union, or Comprehension, so are the Phantasmata that represent them: seeing these are but their similitudes.

Conclusions

1. The Animal Spirits are moved Locally.

N.B. Seeing the Animal Spirits move the body (by Prin. 1, Sect. 3) they must move it, either by power inherent in themselves, or by Motion received from another (by Prin. 9, Sect. 1). Not by power inherent in themselves, for then (by Concl. 8, Sect. 1) they should always move it, which is contrary to Experience. Therefore they move it by Motion received from another; and consequently they themselves are moved Locally.

2. The Animal Spirits are moved by the species of External objects, immediately or mediately.

Seeing the Animal Spirits are moved locally, by another (by Concl. 1, Sect. 3), and nothing can move them unless it touch them (by the 2 Prin. Sect. 1), and that which moveth them must be a Substance (by Prin. 6, Sect. 1), it follows that they cannot be moved by the will and Appetite; for these being faculties, are but Accidents. Of Substances nothing is present to touch them but the Species of objects, or the brain qualified by these Species with active power to produce the similitude of those objects whence they issue, or the soul. If the Species move the Spirits immediately, then is the Conclusion proved. If somewhat else move them immediately, that must be either the brain or the soul. If the brain, then the Species move the Spirits mediately by the brain, and so also the Conclusion is proved. If neither the Species nor the brain move the Spirits immediately, then must they be moved immediately by the Soul. If so, then the soul moveth them either by active power inherent in itself, or by motion received from another (by Prin. 9, Sect. 1). Not by active power in itself, for then, seeing it is always applied to them, it should always move them (by Concl. 8, Sect. 1), which is contrary to Experience, and if it move them by motion received from another, then is the soul locally moved itself, and that either by the mediation of the brain, or immediately by the Species, and consequently the Species move the Spirits mediately by the Soul. Therefore the

Spirits are locally moved by the Species immediately or mediately.

3. Light, Color, Heat, and other proper objects of sense, when they are perceived by sense, are nothing but the several Actions of External things upon the Animal Spirits, by several Organs, and when they are not actually perceived then they be power of the Agents to produce such actions.

For if Light and heat were qualities actually inherent in the Species, and not several manners of action, seeing the species enter, by all the organs to the spirits, heat should be seen and light felt, contrary to Experience.

4. A Phantasma is an Action of the brain on the Animal spirits by the power it receiveth from external sensible things.

A Phantasma must be produced by some Agent; but no Agent can produce the similitude of another, unless it be qualified by that other (by Prin. 3, Sect. 3), therefore it must be produced originally by the Species of that object, and that either immediately or mediately by the brain qualified with like power from the Species (by Concl. 2, Sect. 3). The Agent then being the External object, the Patient must be that, in the body, by which we have Sense; but the Animal Spirits are that by which we have Sense (by Prin. 1, Sect. 3), the Animal Spirits therefore are the Patient. And because the Phantasma is an effect of this Agent on that Patient, it must be either the Action of the Agent, or some quality inherent in the Patient (by Prin. 11, Sect. 1). Not a quality inherent, for seeing Color, Light, Heat, etc.; proper objects of sense are not qualities inherent, but Actions (by Concl. 3, Sect 3); much less can a Phantasma, which is but an image of these objects, be a quality inherent. A Phantasma therefore is the Action of the object. Not the Action of the Object itself immediately on the Spirits, for that is called Color, Light, heat, figure, etc., or by the name of their subjects, not a Phantasma; as when I see a man, I call it a man; and when the eyes are shut, or averted, a Phantasma. It must therefore be the Action of the brain on the animal spirits, etc.

Though it may be doubted how the brain can receive such power from the external object; yet it is no more, nor otherwise, than when steel, touched by the Lodestone, receiveth from it a Magnetical virtue, to work the same effects the Lodestone itself doeth.

5. The Act of Sense is Motion of the Animal Spirits, by the Species of the external object, supposed to be present.

The Species are Confessed to be Agents in the Act of Sense, and the Animal Spirits the patient (as in the Conclusion of Phantasma, Concl. 4, Sect. 3), and seeing the Agent produceth nothing in the Patient, but Motion, or some inherent quality (by Prin. 11, Sect. 1) and the Act of Sense, is an Accident belonging to the Patient that useth sense; it followeth that the Act of sense is either an inherent quality, or motion, or else the bare presence of the Agent. Not the bare presence of the Agent; for then, wherever the Species were present, there should be the Act of Sense (which is absurd). Nay, though the species be present in the very organ of sense (as the species of a friend in the eye), yet if the mind be otherwise bent, there shall not be actual sense of that friend, as is proved by Experience.

Again, actual sense cannot be an inherent quality; for that quality shall either remain after the Agent is removed, and so there may be actual sense, the object being not present (which is absurd), or if it vanish with the removal of the object, it cannot be removed without new Action. If it be removed, then either by the Action of the same object, or by the action of the brain formerly touched by that object. If by the brain, then, this quality being supposed to be actual sense, there shall be actual sense, though the object be absent (which is absurd), if it be not restored, but by new Action of the object, then all the while the object is absent, the Species not being present, and consequently no motion, and that quality, by supposition, now not existing, there will be no alteration in the patient, and then there can be no phantasma of the object till it come again to the sense, which is contrary to Experience. Therefore actual sense is a motion, etc.

Corollary.—Hence it appears that Sense (*sensus*) is a passive power of the Animal Spirits, to be moved by the species of an external object supposed to be present.

6. The Act of Understanding is a Motion of the Animal *N.B* Spirits, by the Action of the brain, qualified with the active-power of the external object.

We are said to understand a thing when we have the Phantasma or Apparition of it; but a Phantasma is the action of the brain qualified on the Animal Spirits (by Concl. 4, Sect. 3), and seeing the Action of the Agent is the Motion of the Patient (by Prin. 10, Sect. 1), the Act of understanding must be the motion of the Animal Spirits, etc.

Corollary.—Understanding (as a power) is a passive power in the Animal Spirits to be moved by the action of the brain qualified, etc.

7. Good is to every thing, that which hath active power to attract it locally.

Whatsoever is Good is desirable; and whatsoever is desirable is Good; and whatsoever is actually desired, supposeth actual sense or actual understanding; but actual sense and Understanding are local motions of the Animal Spirits (by Concls. 5 and 6, Sect. 3). Therefore whatsoever is actually desired, supposeth motion in the Animal Spirits, by the objects, immediately or mediately.

In this motion, that which is desired is either Agent or Patient (by the 5 and 6 Concl. Sect. 3). Therefore it is Agent; and because that which is desired is *Bonum*, therefore *Bonum* is the Agent; and because *Bonum* is desirable, therefore every *Bonum* may be Agent in this motion. Every *Bonum* therefore (by Prin. 3, Sect. 1) hath power to move; and because all motion is either to the Agent or from it, and that which is Good cannot be imagined to repel that, to which it is good, therefore Good hath power to attract, and because that which is desirable or good to one, may not be so to another, and so what attracts one, may not attract another; Good is to every thing that, which hath power to attract it. *N.B*

This definition agrees well with Aristotle, who defines Good to be that, to which all things are moved; which hath been metaphorically taken, but is properly true; as if we draw the object to us, whereas the object rather draws us to it by local motion.

Corollary—Malum, therefore to every thing is that which hath active power to repel it.

Goodness is the power of *Bonum*.

Badness is the power of *Malum*.

Corollary.—Hence also it appears that <u>*Pulchrum* is the species of Good</u>. For whatsoever is *Bonum* is *Pulchrum*, and whatsoever is *Pulchrum* is *Bonum;* but it is called *Bonum*, as it attracteth, and *Pulchrum*, as it pleaseth. *Bonum* supposeth absence of that which it attracteth, *Pulchrum* supposeth the Presence of that which it pleaseth. *Bonum* is the object of Desire, or Appetite; and *Pulchrum* is the object of Love.

Turpe is the Species of *Malum*.

Turpitudo and *Pulchritudo* are the powers of *Turpe* and *Pulchrum*.

8. The Act of Appetite is a Motion of the Animal Spirits towards the object that moveth them.

<u>The object is the Efficient cause, or Agent, of desire</u> (by Concl. 7, Sect. 3), and the Animal Spirits the Patient (by Concls. 5 and 6, Sect. 3). Appetite therefore is the Effect of the Agent, and because the Agent is desired as Good, Desire shall be the effect of Good. Good as Good produceth no effect but by the power Goodness, and consequently by the power attractive (Concl. 7, Sect. 3). But the effect of power attractive, as it is attractive, is Motion towards the Agent indued with that power: Therefore Appetite is a Motion of the Animal Spirits towards the object that moveth them.

Corollary.—Appetite, as a power, is a passive power in the Animal Spirits, to be moved towards the object that moveth them.

The Act, contrary to the Act of Appetite, with his power, are (by the same reason) a motion, or passive power in the Animal Spirits, to be moved from the object.

9. <u>Whatsoever is perceived by Sense or Understanding, is perceived as one in number.</u>

Suppose an Object BC were perceived by Sense (or Understanding), that is by the Animal Spirits, moved, in *A*, and let

B be Good, and C evil, and first of equal powers; I say they shall be perceived as one. For if they be perceived as two, then shall B, because perceived, move A; and because Good, move it directly towards B (by Concls. 5 and 7, Sect. 3). Likewise because C is perceived, it shall move A; and because evil, it shall move A directly from C; so shall A be moved directly to B, and directly from C, at once, which is impossible.

But if B be of greater force than C, then C shall not move A; because A is moved already by B, the stronger Agent; and consequently C shall not be perceived.

Corollary.—By the same reason it may be demonstrated, that whatsoever is desired, is desired as one. Seeing Appetite is also (by Concl. 8, Sect. 3) a Motion of the Animal Spirits, which in the former figure, are supposed to be A.

10. There are but two discerning faculties, in general, of the Soul; sense and understanding.

The Animal Spirits are not moved but by the Species, or by the brain qualified. The former of those motions is the Act of Sense (by Concl. 5, Sect. 3), the later, the Act of understanding (by Concl. 6, Sect. 3). Seeing then there are but two Acts, in general, belonging to the Soul, as it is discerning, there are also but two faculties whence they proceed.

HUMAN NATURE: OR THE FUNDAMENTAL ELEMENTS OF POLICY*
Thought and Experience†

Chapter 1

1. Introduction. The true and perspicuous explication of the elements of *laws natural and politic* (*which is my present scope*) dependeth upon the knowledge of what is *human nature,* what is *body politic,* and what it is we call a *law;* concerning which points, as the *writings* of men from antiquity downwards have still increased, so also have the *doubts* and *controversies* concerning the same: and seeing that true knowledge begetteth not doubt nor controversy, but knowledge, it is manifest from the present controversies, that they, which have *heretofore* written thereof, have not well understood their own subject.

2. *Harm* I can do none, though I err no less than they; for I shall leave men but as they are, in doubt and dispute: but, intending not to take any principle upon *trust,* but only to put men in mind of what they *know already,* or *may know* by their own experience, I hope to err the less; and when I do, it must proceed from too *hasty concluding,* which I will endeavor as much as I can to avoid.

3. On the other side, if *reasoning aright* win not *consent,* which may very easily happen, from them that being confident of their own knowledge weigh not what is said, the *fault* is not mine, but theirs; for as it is my part to *show* my reasons, so it is theirs to bring *attention.*

4. Man's nature is the sum of his natural faculties and powers, as the faculties of *nutrition, motion, generation, sense, reason,* &c. These powers we do unanimously call *natural,*

*From *Human Nature* (Molesworth Ed. 1839, Vol. IV of English Works), Chapters 1-13.

†Chapter numbers have been retained, but topical headings have been added for each corresponding discussion of that topic. —Ed.

and are contained in the definition of man, under these words, *animal* and *rational*.

5. According to the two principal parts of man, I divide his faculties into two sorts, faculties of the *body*, and faculties of the *mind*.

6. Since the minute and distinct anatomy of the powers of the *body* is nothing necessary to the present purpose, I will only sum them up in these three heads, power *nutritive*, power *motive*, and power *generative*.

7. Of the powers of the *mind* there be two sorts, *cognitive*, *imaginative*, or *conceptive* and *motive*; and first of *cognitive*.

For the understanding of what I mean by the power *cognitive*, we must remember and acknowledge that there be in our minds continually certain *images* or conceptions of the things without us, insomuch that if a man could be alive, and all the rest of the world annihilated, he should nevertheless retain the *image* thereof, and all those things which he had before seen or perceived in it; every one by his own experience knowing, that the *absence* or *destruction* of things once imagined doth not cause the *absence* or *destruction* of the *imagination* itself. This *imagery* and *representations* of the qualities of the thing without, is that we call our *conception*, *imagination*, *ideas*, *notice* or *knowledge* of them; and the *faculty* or power by which we are capable of such knowledge, is that I here call *cognitive power*, or *conceptive*, the power of knowing or conceiving.

Chapter 2

1. Having declared what I mean by the word *conception*, and others words equivalent thereunto, I come to the *conceptions* themselves, to show their *differences*, their *causes*, and the *manner of the production*, so far as is necessary for this place.

2. Definition of Sense. Originally all *conceptions* proceed from the *action of the thing itself*, whereof it is the conception: now when the action is *present*, the conception it produceth is also called *sense*; and the thing by whose action the same is produced, is called the *object of the sense*.

3. By our several *organs* we have several *conceptions* of several qualities in the objects; for by *sight* we have a conception or image composed of *color* and *figure*, which is all the notice and knowledge the object imparteth to us of its nature by the eye. By *hearing* we have a conception called *sound*, which is all the knowledge we have of the quality of the object from the ear. And so the rest of the senses are also conceptions of several qualities, or natures of their objects.

4. Four propositions concerning the nature of conceptions. Because the *image in vision* consisting of *color* and *shape* is the knowledge we have of the qualities of the object of that sense; it is no hard matter for a man to fall into this opinion, that the same *color* and *shape* are the *very qualities themselves*; and for the same cause, that *sound* and *noise* are the *qualities of the bell*, or of the air. And this opinion hath been so long received, that the *contrary* must needs appear a great paradox; and yet the introduction of *species visible* and *intelligible* (which is necessary for the maintenance of that opinion) passing to and fro from the *object*, is *worse* than any paradox, as being a plain impossibility. I shall therefore endeavor to make plain these points:

That the subject wherein color and image are inherent, is *not* the *object* or thing seen.

That there is nothing *without us* (really) which we call an *image* or color.

That the said image or color is but an *apparition* unto us of the *motion*, agitation, or alteration, which the *object* worketh in the *brain*, or spirits, or some internal substance of the head.

That as in *vision*, so also in conceptions that arise from the *other* senses, the subject of their *inherence* is not the *object*, but the *sentient*. *cf. P. 178 on species*

5. The first proved. Every man hath so much experience as to have seen the *sun* and the other visible objects by reflection in the *water* and *glasses;* and this alone is sufficient for this conclusion, that *color* and *image* may be there where the *thing seen* is *not*. But because it may be said that notwithstanding the *image* in the water be not in the object, but a thing merely *phantastical*, yet there may be *color* really in the thing itself: I will urge further this experience, that divers times men see directly the *same* object *double*, as *two candles* for *one*, which may happen from distemper, or otherwise without distemper if a man will, the organs being either in their right temper, or equally distempered; the *colors* and *figures* in two such images of the same thing *cannot be inherent* therein, because the thing seen cannot be in *two places*.

One of these images therefore is *not inherent* in the object: but seeing the organs of the sight are then in equal temper or distemper, the *one* of them is no more inherent than the *other;* and consequently *neither* of them both are in the object; which is the first proposition, mentioned in the precedent number.

6. The second proved. Secondly, that the image of any thing by *reflection* in a *glass* or *water* or the like, is *not* any thing *in* or *behind* the glass, or *in* or *under* the water, every man may grant to himself; which is the second proposition.

7. The third proved. For the third, we are to consider, first that upon every *great agitation* or *concussion* of the *brain* (as it happeneth from a stroke, especially if the stroke be upon the eye) whereby the optic nerve suffereth any great violence, there *appeareth* before the *eyes* a certain light, which light is *nothing without*, but an apparition only, all that

is real being the concussion or motion of the parts of that nerve; from which experience we may conclude, that *apparition of light is really nothing but motion* within. If therefore from *lucid bodies* there can be derived *motion*, so as to affect the optic nerve in such manner as is proper thereunto, there will follow an *image* of light somewhere in that line by which the motion was last derived to the eye; that is to say, in the object, if we look directly on it, and in the glass or water, when we look upon it in the line of reflection, which in effect is the third proposition; namely, that image and color is but an apparition to us of that motion, agitation, or alteration which the object worketh in the brain or spirits, or some *internal* substance in the head.

8. But that *from all lucid*, shining and illuminate bodies, there is a *motion produced* to the eye, and, through the eye, to the *optic* nerve, and so into the *brain*, by which that apparition of *light* or *color* is affected is not hard to prove. And first, it is evident that the *fire*, the only lucid body here upon earth, worketh by *motion* equally every way; insomuch as the motion thereof *stopped* or inclosed, it is presently *extinguished*, and no more fire. And further, that that motion, whereby the fire worketh, is *dilation*, and *contraction* of itself *alternately*, commonly called *scintillation* or glowing, is manifest also by experience. From such *motion* in the fire must needs arise a *rejection* or casting from itself of that part of the *medium* which is *contiguous* to it, whereby that part also rejecteth the *next*, and so successively one part beateth back another to the very *eye;* and in the same manner the *exterior* part of the eye presseth the *interior*, (the laws of refraction still observed). Now the interior coat of the eye is nothing else but a piece of the *optic* nerve; and therefore the motion is still continued thereby into the *brain*, and by *resistance* or reaction of the brain, is also a *rebound* into the optic nerve again; which we *not conceiving* as motion or rebound from *within*, do think it is *without*, and call it *light;* as hath been already shown by the experience of a stroke. We have no reason to doubt, that the fountain of light, the *sun*, worketh by any other ways than the *fire*, at least in this matter. And thus all *vision* hath its original from such *motion* as is here

described: for where there is no light, there is no sight; and therefore *color also must be the same thing with light,* as being the effect of the lucid bodies: their *difference* being only this, that when the light cometh *directly* from the fountain to the eye, or *indirectly* by reflection from *clean* and *polite* bodies, and such as have *not* any particular motion internal to alter it, we call it *light;* but when it cometh to the eye by reflection from *uneven, rough,* and coarse bodies, or such as are affected with internal motion of their own that may alter it, then we call it *color; color and light differing only in this, that the one is pure, and the other perturbed light.* By that which hath been said, not only the truth of the third proposition, but also the whole manner of producing light and color, is apparent.

9. The fourth proved. As color is not inherent in the object, but an effect thereof upon us, caused by such motion in the object, as hath been described: so *neither is sound in the thing we hear,* but in ourselves. One manifest sign thereof is, that as a man may *see,* so also he may *hear double* or *treble,* by multiplication of *echoes,* which echoes are sounds as well as the original; and *not* being in one and the *same place,* cannot be *inherent* in the body that maketh them. Nothing can make any thing which is not in itself: the *clapper* hath no *sound* in it, but *motion,* and maketh motion in the internal parts of the bell; so the *bell* hath motion, and not sound, that imparteth *motion* to the *air;* and the *air* hath motion, but not sound; the *air* imparteth motion by the *ear* and *nerve* unto the *brain;* and the brain hath motion but not sound; from the *brain,* it reboundeth back into the nerves *outward,* and thence it becometh an *apparition without,* which we call *sound.* And to proceed to the *rest* of the senses, *it is apparent* enough, that the *smell* and *taste of the same thing, are not the same to every man;* and therefore *are not in the thing smelled or tasted, but in the men.* So likewise the *heat* we feel from the fire is manifestly in *us,* and is quite *different* from the heat which is in the *fire:* for *our* heat is *pleasure* or *pain,* according as it is *great* or *moderate;* but in the *coal* there is no such thing. By this the fourth and last proposition is proved, *viz.* that as in vision, so also in conceptions that arise from

other senses, the subject of their inherence is not in the object, but in the sentient.

10. The main deception of sense. And from hence also it followeth, that *whatsoever accidents* or qualities our senses make us think there be in the *world*, they be *not* there, but are *seeming* and *apparitions* only: the things that really *are* in the world without us, are those *motions* by which these seemings are caused. And this is the *great deception of sense*, which also is to be by sense *corrected*: for as sense telleth me, when I see *directly*, that the color seemeth to be in the object; so also sense telleth me, when I see by *reflection*, that color is not in the object.

Chapter 3

1. Imagination defined. As standing water put into motion by the stroke of a *stone,* or blast of wind, doth *not presently* give over moving as soon as the wind ceaseth, or the stone settleth: so *neither* doth the *effect* cease which the *object* hath wrought upon the *brain,* so soon as ever by turning aside of the organs the *object ceaseth* to work; that is to say, though the *sense* be *past,* the *image* or *conception* remaineth; but more *obscure* while we are *awake,* because some *object* or other continually *plieth* and soliciteth our eyes, and ears, *keeping* the mind in a *stronger* motion, whereby the *weaker* doth not easily *appear.* And this obscure conception is that we call *phantasy,* or *imagination: imagination* being, to define it, *conception remaining, and by little and little decaying from and after the act of sense.*

2. Sleep and dreams defined. But when *present* sense is *not,* as in *sleep,* there the *images* remaining after sense, when there be many, as in dreams, are *not obscure,* but *strong* and *clear,* as in sense itself. The reason is, that which obscured and made the conceptions weak, namely sense, and present *operation* of the object, is *removed:* for sleep is the *privation of the act of sense,* (the power remaining) and *dreams* are the *imagination* of them that *sleep.*

3. Causes of dreams. The *causes* of dreams, if they be natural, are the *actions* or violence of the *inward* parts of a man upon his *brain,* by which the *passages* of sense by sleep *benumbed,* are *restored* to their motion. The signs by which this appeareth to be so, are the *differences* of dreams (old men commonly dream oftener, and have their dreams more painful than young) proceeding from the *different* accidents of man's body, as dreams of *lust,* as dreams of *anger,* according as the heart, or other parts within, work more or less upon the brain, by more or less *heat;* so also the descents of different *sorts of phlegm* maketh us a dream of different tastes of meats and drinks; and I believe there is a *reciprocation* of

motion from the brain to the vital parts, and back from the vital parts to the brain; whereby not only *imagination* begetteth *motion* in those parts; but also motion in those parts begetteth imagination like to that by which it was begotten. If this be true, and that *sad* imaginations nourish the *spleen*, then we see also a cause, why a strong *spleen* reciprocally causeth *fearful dreams*, and why the effects of *lasciviousness* may in a dream produce the image of some person that had *caused* them. Another sign that dreams are caused by the action of the inward parts, is the *disorder* and casual consequence of one conception or image to another: for when we are *waking*, the *antecedent* thought or conception introduceth, and is cause of the *consequent*, as the water followeth a man's finger upon a dry and level table; but in *dreams* there is commonly *no coherence*, and when there is, it is by chance, which must needs proceed from this, that the *brain* in dreams is *not restored* to its motion in every part alike; whereby it cometh to pass, that our thoughts appear like the stars between the flying clouds, not in the order which a man would choose to observe them, but as the uncertain flight of broken clouds permits.

4. Fiction defined. As when the *water*, or any liquid thing moved at once by *divers* movents, receiveth *one* motion compounded of them all; so also the *brain* or spirit therein, having been stirred by *divers* objects, composeth an imagination of *divers* conceptions that appeared single to the sense. As for example, the sense showeth at one time the figure of a *mountain*, and at another time the color of *gold;* but the imagination afterwards hath them both at once in a *golden mountain*. From the same cause it is, there appear unto us *castles* in the *air, chimeras*, and other monsters which are *not* in *rerum natura, but* have been conceived by the sense in pieces at several times. And this composition is that which we commonly call *fiction* of the mind.

5. Phantasms defined. There is yet another kind of imagination, which for *clearness contendeth* with *sense*, as well as a *dream;* and that is, when the *action* of sense hath been *long* or *vehement:* and the experience thereof is more frequent in the sense of seeing, than the rest. An example whereof is, the

image remaining before the *eye* after looking upon the *sun*. Also, those little images that appear before the eyes in the *dark* (whereof I think every man hath experience, but they most of all, who are *timorous* or superstitious) are examples of the same. And these, for distinction-sake, may be called *phantasms*.

6. Remembrance defined. By the *senses*, which are numbered according to the *organs* to be *five*, we take notice (as hath been said already) of the objects *without* us; and that *notice* is our *conception* thereof: but we take *notice* also some way or other *of our conceptions:* for when the conception of the same thing cometh *again*, we take notice that it is *again;* that is to say, that we have had the same conception *before;* which is as much as to imagine a thing *past;* which is impossible to the *sense*, which is only of things *present*. This therefore may be accounted a *sixth sense*, but *internal*, (not *external*, as the rest) and is commonly called *remembrance*.

7. Wherein remembrance consisteth. For the *manner* by which we take notice of a conception *past*, we are to remember, that in the *definition* of *imagination*, it is said to be a conception by *little* and *little decaying*, or growing more *obscure*. An *obscure* conception is that which representeth the *whole object* together, but *none* of the *smaller parts* by themselves; and as *more* or *fewer* parts be represented, so is the conception or representation said to be *more* or *less clear*. Seeing then the *conception*, which when it was *first* produced by sense, was *clear*, and represented the *parts* of the object *distinctly;* and when it cometh *again* is *obscure*, we find *missing* somewhat that we expected; by which we judge it *past* and *decayed*. For example, a man that is present in a foreign *city*, seeth not only *whole* streets, but can also distinguish particular *houses*, and *parts* of houses; but departed thence, he cannot distinguish them so particularly in his mind as he did, some *house* or turning escaping him; yet is this to *remember:* when *afterwards* there escape him *more* particulars, this is also to *remember*, but *not so* well. In process of time, the *image* of the city *returneth* but as a *mass* of building *only*, which is *almost* to have *forgotten* it. Seeing then remembrance is *more* or *less*, as we find more or less *obscurity*,

why may not we well think *remembrance* to be nothing else but the *missing of parts,* which every man expecteth should succeed after they have a conception of the whole? To see at a great distance of place, and to remember at a great distance of time, is to have like conceptions of the thing: for there wanteth distinction of parts in both; the one conception being weak by operation at distance, the other by decay.

8. Why in a dream a man never thinks he dreams. And from this that hath been said, there followeth, that a man can *never know* he *dreameth;* he *may* dream he *doubteth,* whether it be a dream or no: but the clearness of the imagination representeth every thing with as many parts as doth sense itself, and consequently, he can take notice of nothing but as present; whereas to think he dreameth, is to think those his conceptions, that is to say dreams, obscurer than they were in the sense: so that he must think them both as clear, and not as clear as sense; which is impossible.

9. Why few things seem strange in dreams. From the same ground it proceedeth, that men *wonder not* in their dreams at place and persons, as they would do waking: for waking, a man would think it strange to be in a place where he never was before, and remember nothing of how he came there; but in a dream, there cometh little of that kind into consideration. The *clearness* of conception in a dream, taketh away *distrust,* unless the *strangeness* be *excessive,* as to think himself fallen from on high without hurt, and then most commonly he *waketh.*

10. That a dream may be taken for reality and vision. Nor is it *impossible* for a man to be so far deceived, as when his dream is *past,* to think it real: for if he dream of such things as are ordinarily in his mind, and in such order as he useth to do waking, and withal that he laid him down to sleep in the place where he findeth himself when he awaketh; all which may happen: I know no κριτήριον, or mark by which he can discern whether it were a dream or not, and therefore do the less wonder to hear a man sometimes to tell his dream for a truth, or to take it for a vision.

Chapter 4

1. Discourse. The *succession* of conceptions in the mind, series or consequence of one after another, may be *casual* and incoherent, as in dreams for the most part; and it may be *orderly*, as when the former thought introduceth the latter; and this is discourse of the mind. But because the word discourse is commonly taken for the *coherence* and consequence of words, I will, to avoid equivocation, call it *discursion*.

2. The cause of coherence of thoughts. The *cause* of the *coherence* or consequence of one conception to another, is their first *coherence* or consequence at that *time* when they are produced by sense: as for example, from St. Andrew the mind runneth to St. Peter, because their names are read together; from St. Peter to a *stone*, for the same cause; from *stone* to *foundation*, because we see them together; and for the same cause, from foundation to *church*, and from church to *people*, and from people to *tumult*: and according to this example, the mind may run almost from anything to anything. But as in the *sense* the conception of cause and effect may succeed one another; so may they after sense in the *imagination:* and for the most part they do so; the *cause* whereof is the *appetite* of them, *who*, having a conception of the *end*, have next unto it a conception of the next *means* to that end: as, when a man, from a thought of *honor* to which he hath an appetite, cometh to the thought of *wisdom*, which is the next means thereunto; and from thence to the thought of *study*, which is the next means to wisdom.

3. Ranging. To omit that kind of discursion by which we proceed from anything to anything, there are of the *other* kind *divers* sorts: as first, in the *senses* there are certain coherences of conceptions, which we may call *ranging*; examples whereof are; a man casteth his *eye* upon the *ground*, to look about for some *small* thing lost; the *hounds* casting about at a fault in hunting; and the *ranging* of spaniels: and herein we take a beginning arbitrary.

4. Sagacity. Another sort of discursion is, when the *appetite* giveth a man his beginning, as in the example before, where honor to which a man hath appetite, maketh him think upon the next means of attaining it, and that again of the next, &c. And this the Latins call *sagacitas*, and we may call *hunting* or *tracing*, as dogs trace beasts by the smell, and men hunt them by their footsteps; or as men hunt after riches, place, or knowledge.

5. Reminiscence. There is yet another kind of discursion beginning with the appetite to *recover* something lost, proceeding from the *present backward*, from thought of the place where we *miss* at, to the thought of the place from whence we came *last*; and from the thought of that, to the thought of a place *before*, till we have in our mind some place, wherein we had the thing we miss: and this is called *reminiscence*.

6. Experience. The *remembrance* of succession of one thing to another, that is, of what was *antecedent*, and what *consequent*, and what *concomitant*, is called an *experiment;* whether the same be made by us *voluntarily*, as when a man putteth any thing into the fire, to see what effect the fire will produce upon it: or *not* made by us, as when we remember a fair morning after a red evening. To have had many *experiments*, is that we call *experience*, which is nothing else but *remembrance* of what antecedents have been followed by what consequents.

7. Expectation. No man can have in his mind a conception of the *future*, for the future is *not yet*: but of our conceptions of the *past*, we make a *future*; or rather, call *past*, *future* relatively. Thus after a man hath been accustomed to see like antecedents followed by like consequents, whensoever he seeth the like come to pass to any thing he had seen before, he looks there should follow it the same that followed then: as for example, because a man hath often seen offences followed by punishment, when he seeth an offence in present, he thinketh punishment to be consequent thereto; but consequent unto that which is present, men call future; and thus we make *remembrance* to be the *prevision* of things to come, or *expectation* or presumption of the future.

8. Conjecture. In the same manner, if a man seeth in present that which he hath seen before, he thinks that that which was antecedent to that which he saw before, is also antecedent to that he presently seeth: as for example, he that hath seen the ashes remain after the fire, and now again seeth ashes, concludeth again there hath been fire: and this is called again *conjecture* of the past, or presumption of the fact.

9. Signs. When a man hath *so often* observed like antecedents to be followed by like consequents, that *whensoever* he seeth the antecedent, he looketh again for the consequent; or when he seeth the consequent, maketh account there hath been the like antecedent; then he calleth both the antecedent and the consequent, *signs* one of another, as clouds are signs of rain to come, and rain of clouds past.

10. Prudence. This taking of signs by *experience*, is that wherein men do ordinarily think, the difference stands between man and man in *wisdom*, by which they commonly understand a man's whole ability or *power cognitive*; but this is an *error*: for the signs are but *conjectural*; and according as they have often or seldom failed, so their *assurance* is more or less; but *never full* and *evident*: for though a man have always seen the day and night to follow one another hitherto; yet can he not thence conclude they shall do so, or that they have done so eternally: *experience concludeth nothing universally.* If the signs hit twenty times for one missing, a man may lay a wager of twenty to one of the event; but may not conclude it for a truth. But by this it is plain, that they shall *conjecture best*, that have *most experience*, because they have most signs to conjecture by: which is the reason *old men* are *more prudent*, that is, conjecture better, *cæteris paribus*, than young: for, being old, they remember more; and experience is but remembrance. And *men* of *quick* imagination, *cæteris paribus*, are more *prudent* than those whose imaginations are slow: for they observe *more* in *less* time. Prudence is nothing but conjecture from experience, or taking of signs from experience warily, that is, that the experiments from which he taketh such signs be all remembered; for else the cases are not alike that seem so.

11. Caveats of concluding from experience. As in conjec-

ture concerning things past and future, it is prudence to conclude from experience, what is like to come to pass, or to have passed already; so it is an error to conclude from it, that *it is* so or so *called;* that is to say, we cannot from experience conclude, that any thing is to be called *just* or *unjust,* *true* or *false,* or any proposition *universal* whatsoever, except it be from remembrance of the use of names imposed arbitrarily by men: for example, to have heard a sentence given in the like case, the like sentence a thousand times is not enough to conclude that the sentence is just; though most men have no other means to conclude by: but it is *necessary,* for the drawing of such conclusions, to *trace* and *find out,* by many experiences, what men do mean by calling things just and unjust. Further, there is another *caveat* to be taken in concluding by experience, from the tenth section of the second chapter; that is, that we conclude such things to be without, that are within us.

Names and Knowledge

Chapter 5

1. Of marks. Seeing the *succession* of conceptions in the *mind* are caused, as hath been said before, by the succession they *had* one to another when they were produced by the *senses*, and that there is no conception that hath not been produced immediately before or after innumerable others, by the innumerable acts of sense; it must needs follow, that one *conception* followeth *not* another, according to our election, and the need we have of them, *but* as it *chanceth* us to hear or see such things as shall bring them to our mind. The experience we have hereof, is in such brute beasts, which, having the providence to hide the remains and superfluity of their meat, do nevertheless want the remembrance of the place where they hid it, and thereby make no benefit thereof in their hunger: but man, who in this point beginneth to rank himself somewhat above the nature of beasts, hath observed and remembered the cause of this defect, and to amend the same, hath imagined or devised to set up a visible or other sensible mark, the which, when he seeth it again, may bring to his mind the thought he had when he set it up. A *mark* therefore is a *sensible object* which a man erecteth voluntarily to himself, to the end to *remember* thereby somewhat past, when the same is objected to his sense again: as men that have passed by a rock at sea, set up some mark, thereby to remember their former danger, and avoid it.

2. Names or appellations. In the number of these *marks*, are those *human voices*, which we call the *names* or appellations of things sensible by the ear, by which we recall into our mind some conceptions of the things to which we gave those names or appellations; as the appellation *white* bringeth to remembrance the quality of such objects as produce that color or conception in us. A *name* or appellation therefore is the *voice* of a man *arbitrary*, imposed for a *mark* to bring into his mind some conception concerning the thing on which it is imposed.

3. Names positive and privative. Things named, are either the *objects* themselves, as a man; or the *conception* itself that we have of man, as shape and motion: or some privation, which is when we conceive that there is something which we conceive, not in him; as when we conceive he is not just, not finite, we give him the name of unjust, of infinite, which signify privation or defect; and to the privations themselves we give the names of injustice and infiniteness: so that here be *two sorts* of names; one of *things*, in which we conceive something; or of the conceptions themselves, which are called *positive*: the other of things wherein we conceive *privation* or defect, and those names are called *privative*.

4. Advantage of names maketh us capable of science. By the advantage of *names* it is that we are capable of *science*, which beasts, for want of them are not; nor man, without the use of them: for as a beast misseth not one or two out of many her young ones, for want of those names of order, one, two, and three, and which we call *number*; so neither would a man, without repeating orally or mentally the words of number, know how many pieces of money or other things lie before him.

5. Names universal and singular. Seeing there be *many* conceptions of *one* and the same thing, and for *every* conception we give it a *several* name; it followeth that for one and the same thing, we have many names or attributes; as to the same man we give the appellations of *just, valiant,* &c. for divers *virtues;* of *strong, comely,* &c., for divers *qualities* of the *body.* And again, because from divers things we receive like conceptions, many things must needs have the same appellation: as to all things we *see,* we give the same name of *visible*; and to all things we *see moveable,* we give the appellation of *moveable*: and those names we give to *many,* are called *universal* to them all; as the name of man to every particular of mankind: such appellation as we give to *one* only thing, we call *individual,* or singular; as Socrates, and other proper names: or, by circumlocution, he that writ the *Iliad,* for Homer.

6. Universals not in *rerum natura.* The universality of *one* *name* to many things, hath been the cause that men think the

things are themselves universal; and so seriously contend, that besides Peter and John, and all the rest of the men that are, have been, or shall be in the world, there is yet something else that we call *man*, and *man in general*, deceiving themselves, by taking the universal, or general appellation, for the thing it signifieth: for if one should desire the painter to make him the picture of a man, which is as much as to say, of a man in general; he meaneth no more, but that the painter should choose what man he pleaseth to draw, which must needs be some of them that are, or have been, or may be, none of which are *universal*. But when he would have him to draw the picture of the king, or any particular person, he limiteth the painter to that one person he chooseth. It is plain therefore, that there is *nothing universal* but *names*; which are therefore called *indefinite*; because we limit them not ourselves, but leave them to be applied by the hearer: whereas a singular name is limited and restrained to one of the many things it signifieth; as when we say, this man, pointing to him, or giving him his proper name, or by some such other way.

7. Equivocal names. The appellations that be *universal*, and common to many things, are *not* always given to all the *particulars*, (as they ought to be) for like conceptions, and like considerations in them all; which is the cause that many of them are *not* of *constant* signification, but bring into our mind other thoughts than those for which they were ordained, and these are called equivocal. As for example, the word faith signifieth the same with belief; sometimes it signifieth particularly that belief which maketh a Christian; and sometime it signifieth the keeping of a promise. Also all *metaphors* are by profession *equivocal*: and there is scarce any word that is not made *equivocal* by divers contextures of speech, or by diversity of pronunciation and gesture.

8. Understanding. This *equivocation* of names maketh it *difficult* to recover those conceptions for which the name was ordained; and that not only in the language of other men, wherein we are to consider the *drift*, and *occasion*, and *contexture* of the speech, as well as the *words* themselves; but also in our discourse, which being derived from the

custom and common use of speech, representeth unto us not our own conceptions. It is therefore a great ability in a man, out of the words, contexture, and other circumstances of language, to deliver himself from *equivocation*, and to find out the true meaning of what is said: and this is it we call *understanding*.

9. Affirmation, negation, proposition. Of two *appellations*, by the help of this little verb *is*, or something equivalent, we make an *affirmation* or *negation*, either of which in the Schools we call also a *proposition*, and consisteth of two appellations joined together by the said verb *is*: as for example, man is a living creature; or thus, man is not righteous: whereof the former is called an *affirmation*, because the appellation, living creature, is *positive*; the latter a *negative*, because not righteous is *privative*.

10. Truth, falsity. In *every proposition*, be it affirmative or negative, the latter appellation either comprehendeth the former, as in this proposition, charity is a virtue, the name of virtue comprehendeth the name of charity, and many other virtues beside; and then is the proposition said to be *true*, or *truth*: for, *truth*, and a *true proposition*, is all one. Or *else* the *latter* appellation comprehendeth *not* the former; as in this proposition, every man is just; the name of just comprehendeth not every man; for unjust is the name of the far greater part of men: and the proposition is said to be *false*, or falsity: *falsity* and a *false proposition* being also the same thing.

11. Ratiocination. In what manner of two propositions, whether *both* affirmative, or *one* affirmative, the *other* negative, is made a *syllogism*, I forbear to write. All this that hath been said of names or propositions, though *necessary*, is but *dry* discourse: and this place is not for the whole art of logic, which if I enter further into, I ought to pursue: besides, it is not needful; for there be few men which have not so much natural logic, as thereby to discern well enough, whether any conclusion I shall make in this discourse hereafter, be well or ill collected: only thus much I say in this place, that *making of syllogisms* is that we call *ratiocination* or *reasoning*.

12. According to reason, against reason. Now when a man *reasoneth* from *principles* that are *found* indubitable by experience, all deceptions of sense and equivocation of words avoided, the conclusion he maketh is said to be *according to right reason*: but when from his conclusion a man may, by good ratiocination, derive that which is *contradictory* to any evident truth whatsoever, then he is said to have concluded *against reason*: and such a conclusion is called *absurdity*.

13. Names causes of knowledge, so of error. As the *invention* of *names* hath been *necessary* for the drawing men *out of* ignorance, by calling to their remembrance the necessary *coherence* of one conception to another; so also hath it on the other side precipitated men into *error*: insomuch, that whereas by the benefit of *words* and ratiocination they exceed *brute beasts* in knowledge, and the commodities that accompany the same; so they exceed them also in *error*: for *true* and *false* are things not incident to beasts, because they adhere not to propositions and language; nor have they ratiocination, whereby to multiply one untruth by another, as men have.

14. Translation of the discourse of the mind into the discourse of the tongue, and of the errors thence proceeding. It is the *nature* almost of every *corporal* thing, being *often moved* in one and the same manner, to receive continually a *greater* and *greater easiness* and aptitude to the *same* motion, insomuch as in time the same becometh so *habitual*, that, to *beget* it, there needs no more than to *begin* it. The *passions* of man, as they are the beginning of *voluntary* motions; so are they the beginning of *speech*, which is the motion of the tongue. And men desiring to show others the knowledge, opinions, conceptions, and passions which are in themselves, and to that end having invented *language*, have by that means transferred all that *discursion* of their *mind* mentioned in the former chapter, by the *motion* of their *tongues*, into *discourse* of *words*: and *ratio* now is but *oratio*, for the most part, wherein custom hath so great a power, that the mind suggesteth only the first word; the rest follow *habitually*, and are not followed by the mind; as it is with beggars, when they say their *paternoster*, putting together such words, and in such

manner, as in their education they have learned from their nurses, from their companies, or from their teachers, having *no images* or *conceptions* in their mind, answering to the words they speak: and as they have learned themselves, so they teach posterity. Now, if we consider the power of those *deceptions* of the sense, mentioned chapter 2 section 10, and also how *unconstantly* names have been settled, and how subject they are to *equivocation*, and how *diversified* by *passion*, (scarce two men agreeing what is to be called good, and what evil; what liberality, what prodigality; what valor, what temerity) and how subject men are to paralogism or fallacy in reasoning, I may in a manner conclude, that it is impossible to *rectify* so many errors of any one man, as must needs proceed from those causes, without beginning *anew* from the very first grounds of all our knowledge and sense; and instead of books, reading over orderly one's own conceptions: in which meaning, I take *nosce teipsum* for a precept worthy the reputation it hath gotten.

Chapter 6

1. *Of the two kinds of knowledge.* There is a story some-where, of one that pretends to have been miraculously cured of blindness, wherewith he was born, by St. Alban or other Saints, at the town of St. Alban's; and that the Duke of Gloucester being there, to be satisfied of the truth of the miracle, asked the man, What color is this? who, by answer-ing, it was green, discovered himself, and was punished for a counterfeit: for though by his sight newly received he might distinguish between green, and red, and all other colors, as well as any that should interrogate him, yet he could not possibly know at first sight which of them was called green, or red, or by any other name. By this we may understand, there be *two kinds* of knowledge, whereof the *one* is noth-ing else but *sense*, or knowledge *original*, as I have said in the beginning of the second chapter, and *remembrance* of the same; the *other* is called *science* or knowledge of the *truth of propositions*, and how things are called, and is derived from *understanding*. Both of these sorts are but *experience*; the former being the experience of the effects of things that work upon us from *without*; and the latter experience men have from the proper use of *names* in language: and all experi-ence being, as I have said, but remembrance, all knowledge is remembrance: and of the *former*, the register we keep in books, is called *history*; but the registers of the *latter* are called the *sciences*.

2. *Truth and evidence necessary to knowledge.* There are *two things* necessarily implied in this word *knowledge;* the one is *truth*, the other *evidence*; for what is not truth, can never be known. For, let a man say he knoweth a thing never so well, if the same shall afterwards appear false, he is driven to confession, that it was not knowledge, but opinion. Like-wise, if the truth be not evident, though a man holdeth it, yet is his knowledge thereof no more than theirs who hold

the contrary: for if truth were enough to make it knowledge, all truth were known; which is not so.

3. Evidence defined. What *truth* is, hath been defined in the precedent chapter; what *evidence* is, I *now* set down: and it is the concomitance of a man's *conception* with the *words* that signify such conception in the act of ratiocination: for when a man reasoneth with his lips only, to which the mind suggesteth only the beginning, and followeth not the words of his mouth with the conceptions of his mind, out of custom of so speaking; though he begin his ratiocination with true propositions, and proceed with certain syllogisms, and thereby make always true conclusions; yet are not his conclusions *evident* to him, for want of the *concomitance of conception* with his words: for if the words alone were sufficient, a *parrot* might be taught as well to know truth, as to speak it. Evidence is to truth, as the sap to the tree, which, so far as it creepeth along with the body and branches, keepeth them alive; where it forsaketh them, they die: for this evidence, which is meaning with our words, is the life of truth.

4. Science defined. Knowledge thereof, which we call *science*, I define to be *evidence of truth*, from some beginning or principle of *sense:* for the truth of a proposition is never evident, until we conceive the meaning of the words or terms whereof it consisteth, which are always conceptions of the mind: nor can we remember those conceptions, without the thing that produced the same by our senses. The *first* principle of knowledge is, that we have such and such *conceptions*; the *second*, that we have thus and thus *named* the things whereof they are conceptions; the *third* is, that we have *joined* those *names* in such manner as to make true propositions; the *fourth* and last is, that we have *joined* those *propositions* in such manner as they be concluding, and the truth of the conclusion said to be known. And of these two kinds of knowledge, whereof the former is *experience of fact*, and the latter *evidence of truth*; as the *former*, if it be great, is called *prudence*; so the *latter*, if it be much, hath usually been called, both by ancient and modern writers, *sapience* or wisdom: and of this *latter*, *man* only is capable; of the *former*, *brute beasts* also participate.

5. Supposition defined. A proposition is said to be *supposed*, when, being *not evident*, it is nevertheless *admitted for a time*, to the end, that, joining to it other propositions, we may *conclude* something; and to *proceed* from conclusion to conclusion, for a *trial* whether the same will lead us into any *absurd* or impossible conclusion; which if it *do*, then we know such supposition to have been false.

6. Opinion defined. But if running through *many* conclusions, we come to *none* that are *absurd*, then we think the proposition *probable*; likewise we think probable whatsoever proposition we *admit* for truth by error of reasoning, or from trusting to other men: and all such propositions as are admitted by *trust* or error, we are not said to *know*, but to *think* them to be true; and the admittance of them is called *opinion*.

7. Belief defined. And particularly, when the opinion is admitted out of *trust* to *other* men, they are said to *believe* it; and their admittance of it is called *belief*, and sometimes *faith*.

8. Conscience defined. It is either *science* or *opinion* which we commonly mean by the word *conscience:* for men say that such and such a thing is true in or upon their conscience; which they *never* do, when they think it *doubtful*; and therefore they *know*, or *think* they know it to be true. But men, when they say things upon their conscience, are not therefore presumed certainly to know the truth of what they say; it remaineth then, that that word is used by them that have an *opinion, not* only of the *truth* of the thing, *but* also of their *knowledge* of it, to which the *truth* of the proposition is consequent. *Conscience* I therefore define to be *opinion of evidence*.

9. Belief, in some cases, no less from doubt than knowledge. *Belief*, which is the admitting of propositions upon *trust*, in many cases is no less free from *doubt*, than perfect and manifest *knowledge:* for as there is nothing whereof there is not some cause; so, when there is doubt, there must be some cause thereof conceived. Now there be many things which we receive from *report of others*, of which it is impossible to imagine any cause of *doubt:* for what can be opposed against the consent of all men, in things they can know, and have no cause to report otherwise than they are, such as is a great part of

our *histories*, unless a man would say that all the world had *conspired* to deceive him.

And thus much of *sense, imagination, discursion, ratiocination*, and *knowledge*, which are the acts of our *power cognitive*, or *conceptive*. That power of the *mind* which we call *motive*, differeth from the power *motive* of the *body*; for the power *motive* of the *body* is that by which it *moveth other* bodies, and we call *strength*: but the power motive of the *mind*, is that by which the mind giveth *animal motion* to that *body* wherein it existeth; the acts hereof are our *affections* and *passions*, of which I am to speak in general.

Chapter 7

1. Of delight, pain, love, hatred. In the eighth section of the second chapter is shown, *that conceptions* and *apparitions* are nothing *really*, but *motion* in some internal substance of the *head*; which motion *not stopping* there, but proceeding to the *heart*, of necessity must there either *help* or *hinder* the motion which is called *vital*; when it *helpeth*, it is called *delight, contentment*, or *pleasure*, which is nothing really but motion about the heart, as conception is nothing but motion in the head: and the *objects* that cause it are called *pleasant* or *delightful*, or by some name equivalent; the Latins have *jucundum, a juvando*, from helping; and the same delight, with reference to the object, is called *love:* but when such motion *weakeneth* or hindereth the vital motion, then it is called *pain*; and in relation to that which causeth it, hatred, which the Latins express sometimes by *odium*, and sometimes by *tædium*.

2. Appetite, aversion, fear. This motion, in which consisteth *pleasure* or *pain*, is also a *solicitation* or provocation either to draw *near* to the thing that pleaseth, or to *retire* from the thing that displeaseth; and this solicitation is the *endeavor* or internal beginning of *animal* motion, which when the object *delighteth*, is called *appetite*; when it *displeaseth*, it is called *aversion*, in respect of the displeasure *present*; but in respect of the displeasure *expected, fear*. So that *pleasure, love* and *appetite*, which is also called desire, are *divers names* for divers considerations of the *same thing*.

3. Good, evil, pulchritude, turpitude. Every man, for his own part, calleth that which *pleaseth*, and is delightful to himself, *good*; and that *evil* which *displeaseth* him: insomuch that while every man *differeth* from another in *constitution*, they differ also from one another concerning the common distinction of good and evil. Nor is there any such thing as absolute goodness, considered without relation: for even the goodness which we apprehend in God Almighty, is *his goodness to us*. And as we call *good* and *evil* the *things* that please and dis-

please; so call we *goodness* and *badness*, the *qualities* or powers whereby they do it: and the signs of that goodness are called by the Latins in one word *pulchritudo*, and the signs of evil, *turpitudo*; to which we have no words precisely answerable.

As all conceptions we have immediately by the *sense*, are, *delight*, or *pain*, or *appetite*, or *fear*; so are all the *imaginations* after sense. But as they are weaker imaginations, so are they also weaker pleasures, or weaker pain.

4. End, fruition. As *appetite* is the beginning of *animal* motion towards something that pleaseth us; so is the *attaining* thereof, the *end* of that motion, which we also call the *scope*, and aim, and final cause of the same: and when we attain that end, the delight we have thereby is called the *fruition*: so that *bonum* and *finis* are different names, but for different considerations of the same thing.

5. Profitable, use, vain. And of *ends*, some of them are called *propinqui*, that is, near at hand; others *remoti*, far off: but when the ends that be nearer attaining, be compared with those that be further off, they are called not ends, but *means*, and the *way* to those. But for an *utmost* end, in which the ancient *philosophers* have placed *felicity*, and disputed much concerning the way thereto, there is no such thing in this world, nor way to it, more than to Utopia: for while we live, we have desires, and desire presupposeth a further end. Those things which please us, as the way or *means* to a further end, we call *profitable*; and the *fruition* of them, *use*; and those things that profit not, *vain*.

6. Felicity. Seeing all *delight* is *appetite*, and presupposeth a *further* end, there can be *no contentment* but in *proceeding*: and therefore we are not to marvel, when we see, that as men attain to more riches, honor, or other power; so their appetite continually groweth more and more; and when they are come to the utmost degree of some kind of power, they pursue some other, as long as in any kind they think themselves behind any other: of those therefore that have attained to the highest degree of honor and riches, some have affected mastery in some art; as Nero in music and poetry, Commodus in the art of a gladiator; and such as affect not some such thing,

must find diversion and recreation of their thoughts in the contention either of play or business: and men justly complain of a great grief, that they know not what to do. *Felicity,* therefore, by which we mean continual delight, consisteth *not* in *having* prospered, but in *prospering.*

7. Good and evil mixed. There are few things in this world, but *either* have *mixture* of good and evil, *or* there is a chain of them so necessarily linked together, that the one cannot be taken without the other: as for example, the pleasures of sin, and the bitterness of punishment, are inseparable; as is also labor and honor, for the most part. Now when in the *whole chain,* the *greater part* is good, the *whole* is called *good;* and when the *evil* over-weigheth, the *whole* is called *evil.*

8. Sensual delight, and pain; joy and grief. There are two sorts of pleasure, whereof the *one* seemeth to affect the *corporeal* organ of the sense, and that I call *sensual;* the *greatest* part whereof, is that by which we are invited to give continuance to our *species;* and the *next,* by which a man is invited to meat, for the preservation of his *individual* person: the *other sort* of delight is not particular to any part of the body, and is called the delight of the *mind,* and is that which we call *joy.* Likewise of *pains,* some affect the *body,* and are therefore called the *pains* of the body; and some *not,* and those are called *grief.*

Chapter 8

1. *Wherein consist the pleasures of sense.* Having in the first section of the precedent chapter presupposed, that motion and *agitation of the brain* which we call conception, to be continued *to the heart*, and there to be called *passion*; I have therefore obliged myself, as far forth as I am able, to search out and declare *from what* conception *proceedeth* every one of those *passions* which we commonly take notice of: for, seeing the things that please and displease, are innumerable, and work innumerable ways, men have not taken notice but of a very few, which also are many of them without name.

2. And first, we are to consider, that of conceptions there are *three sorts*, whereof one is of that which is *present*, which is *sense*; another, of that which is *past*, which is *remembrance*; and the third, of that which is *future*, which we call *expectation*: all which have been manifestly declared in the second and third chapters; and every of these conceptions is *pleasure* or *pain present*. And first for the pleasures of the *body* which affect the sense of *touch* and *taste*, as far forth as they be *organical*, their conceptions are *sense*: so also is the pleasure of all *exonerations* of nature: all which passions I have before named, *sensual pleasures*; and their contrary, *sensual pains*: to which also may be added the pleasures and displeasures of *odors,* if any of them shall be found organical, which for the most part they are not, as appeareth by this experience which every man hath, that the same smells, when they seem to proceed from others, displease, though they proceed from ourselves; but when we think they proceed from ourselves, they displease not, though they come from others: the displeasure of this is a conception of hurt thereby from those odors, as being unwholesome, and is therefore a conception of evil to come, and not present. Concerning the delight of *hearing*, it is diverse, and the organ itself not affected thereby: *simple sounds* please by *equality*, as the sound of a bell or lute: insomuch as it seems, an equality continued by the percussion of

the object upon the ear, is pleasure; the contrary is called *harshness*, such as is grating, and some other sounds, which do not always affect the body, but only sometime, and that with a kind of horror beginning at the teeth. *Harmony*, or many sounds together agreeing, please by the same reason as the *unison*, which is the sound of equal strings equally stretched. Sounds that differ in any *height*, please by *inequality and equality alternate*, that is to say, the higher note striketh twice, for one stroke of the other, whereby they strike together every second time; as is well proved by Galileo, in the first dialogue concerning local motion: where he also showeth, that two sounds differing a *fifth*, delight the ear by an *equality* of striking *after two inequalities*; for the higher note striketh the ear thrice, while the other strikes but twice. In like manner he showeth wherein consisteth the pleasure of concord, and the displeasure of discord, in other difference of notes. There is yet *another* pleasure and displeasure of sounds, which consisteth in *consequence of one note after another, diversified* both by *accent* and *measure*; whereof that which pleaseth is called an *air*; but for what reason one succession in tone and measure is a more pleasing air than another, I confess I know not; but I conjecture the reason to be, for that some of them imitate and revive some passion which otherwise we take no notice of, and the other not; for *no air pleaseth but for a time*, no more doth imitation. Also the pleasures of the *eye* consist in a certain *equality* of *color*: for *light*, the most glorious of all colors, is made by *equal* operation of the object; whereas *color* is *perturbed*, that is to say, unequal light, as hath been said, chapter 2, section 8. And therefore colors, the more equality is in them, the more resplendent they are; and as *harmony* is pleasure to the *ear*, which consisteth of *divers sounds*; so perhaps may some mixture of *divers colors* be *harmony* to the *eye*, more than another mixture. There is yet another delight by the *ear*, which happeneth only to men of skill in music, which is of another nature, and not, as these, conception of the present, but rejoicing of their own skill; of which nature are the passions of which I am to speak next.

3. Of the imagination, or conception of power in man. Conception of the *future*, is but a *supposition* of the *same*, pro-

ceeding from *remembrance* of what is past; and we so far *conceive* that anything *will be hereafter*, as we *know* there is *something at the present* that hath power to produce it: and that anything hath power now to produce another thing hereafter, we cannot conceive, but by remembrance that it hath produced the like heretofore. Wherefore all conception of future, is conception of power able to produce something. Whosoever therefore expecteth pleasure to come, must conceive withal some power in himself by which the same may be attained. And because the passions, whereof I am to speak next, consist in conception of the future, that is to say, in conception of power past, and the act to come; before I go any further, I must in the next place speak somewhat concerning this power.

4. By this power I mean the same with the faculties of the *body, nutritive, generative, motive,* and of the *mind, knowledge*; and besides these, such *further* power as by them is acquired, *viz. riches, place* of authority, *friendship* or *favor,* and *good fortune; which* last is really nothing else but the favor of God Almighty. The *contraries* of these are *impotencies, infirmities,* or *defects* of the said powers respectively. And because the power of one man resisteth and hindereth the effects of the power of another, *power* simply is no more, but the *excess* of the power of one above that of another: for equal powers opposed, destroy one another; and such their opposition is called contention.

5. Honor, honorable, worth. The *signs* by which we know our own *power,* are those *actions* which proceed from the same; and the signs by which *other men* know it, are such *actions, gesture, countenance* and *speech,* as usually such powers produce: and the *acknowledgment* of power is called *honor*; and to honor a man inwardly, is to conceive or acknowledge that that man hath the odds or excess of that power above him with whom he contendeth or compareth himself. And honorable are those signs for which one man acknowledgeth power or excess above his concurrent in another: as for example, *beauty* of person, consisting in a lively aspect of the countenance, and other *signs* of *natural heat,* are honorable, being signs precedent of power *generative,* and

much issue; as also, general reputation among those of the other sex, because signs consequent of the same. And actions proceeding from *strength of body*, and open force, are honorable, as signs consequent of power *motive*, such as are victory in battle or duel; *a d'avoir tué son homme*. Also to adventure upon great exploits and danger, as being a sign consequent of opinion of our own strength, and that opinion a sign of the strength itself. And to teach or persuade are honorable, because they be signs of *knowledge*. And riches are honorable; as signs of the power that acquired them: and gifts, cost, and magnificence of houses, apparel, and the like, are honorable, as signs of riches. And *nobility* is honorable by reflection, as a sign of power in the ancestors: and *authority*, because a sign of the strength, wisdom, favor or riches by which it is attained. And *good fortune* or casual prosperity is honorable, because a sign of the favor of God, to whom is to be ascribed all that cometh to us by fortune, no less than that we attain unto by industry. And the contraries and defects of these signs are dishonorable; and according to the signs of honor and dishonor, so we estimate and make the value or worth of a man: for so much worth is every thing, as a man will give for the use of all it can do.

6. Signs of honor. The *signs* of *honor* are those by which we perceive that one man acknowledgeth the power and worth of another; such as these, to *praise*, to *magnify*, to *bless*, to call happy, to pray or supplicate to, to thank, to offer unto or present, to obey, to hearken unto with attention, to speak to with consideration, to approach unto in decent manner, to keep distance from, to give way to, and the like, which are the honor the inferior giveth to the superior.

But the *signs* of *honor* from the superior to the inferior, are such as these; to *praise* or prefer him before his concurrent, to hear more willingly, to speak to him more familiarly, to admit him nearer, to employ him rather, to ask his advice rather, to take his opinions, and to give him *any gifts rather than money*; or if money, so much as may *not* imply his *need* of a *little*: for need of a little is greater poverty than need of much. And this is enough for examples of the signs of honor and power.

7. Reverence. *Reverence* is the conception we have concerning another, that he hath the *power* to do unto us both *good* and *hurt*, but *not* the *will* to do us *hurt*.

8. Passions. In the pleasure men have, or displeasure from the signs of honor or dishonor done unto them, consisteth the nature of the passions, whereof we are to speak in the next chapter.

Chapter 9

1. *Glory aspiring, false glory, vain glory.* Glory, or internal gloriation or triumph of the mind, is the passion which proceedeth from the imagination or conception of our *own power* above the power of him that contendeth with us; the *signs* whereof, besides those in the countenance, and other gestures of the body which cannot be described, are, *ostentation* in words, and *insolency* in actions: and this passion, of them whom it displeaseth, is called *pride;* by them whom it pleaseth, it is termed a *just valuation* of himself. This imagination of our power or worth, may be from an assured and certain *experience* of our own actions; and then is that glory *just,* and well grounded, and begetteth an opinion of *increasing* the same by other actions to follow; in which consisteth the appetite which we call *aspiring,* or proceeding from one degree of power to another. The same passion may proceed *not* from any *conscience* of our own actions, but from fame and trust of *others,* whereby one may think well of himself, and yet be deceived; and this is *false glory,* and the aspiring consequent thereto procureth ill success. Further, the *fiction,* which is also imagination, of actions done by ourselves, which never were done, is *glorying;* but because it begetteth no appetite nor endeavor to any further attempt, it is merely *vain* and unprofitable; as when a man imagineth himself to do the actions whereof he readeth in some *romance,* or to be like unto some other man whose acts he admireth: and this is called *vain glory;* and is exemplified in the fable, by the fly sitting on the axletree, and saying to himself, What a dust do I make rise! The expression of *vain glory* is that wish, which some of the Schools mistaking for some appetite distinct from all the rest, have called *velleity,* making a new word, as they made a new passion which was not before. *Signs of vain glory* in the *gesture* are, *imitation* of others, counterfeiting and usurping the signs of virtue they have not, af-

fectation of fashions, captation of honor from their dreams, and other little stories of themselves, from their country, from their names, and from the like.

2. Humility and dejection. The passion *contrary to glory*, proceeding from apprehension of our own infirmity, is called *humility* by those by whom it is approved; by the rest, *dejection* and poorness: which conception may be well or ill grounded; if well, it produceth fear to attempt any thing rashly; if ill, it utterly cows a man, that he neither dares speak publicly, nor expect good success in any action.

3. Shame. It happeneth sometimes, that he that hath a *good* opinion of himself, and upon good ground, may nevertheless, by reason of the *frowardness* which that passion begetteth, discover in himself some *defect* or infirmity, the remembrance whereof dejecteth him; and this passion is called *shame;* by which being cooled and checked in his forwardness, he is more wary for the time to come. This passion, as it is a sign of *infirmity,* which is *dishonor;* so also it is a sign of *knowledge,* which is *honor.* The sign of it is *blushing,* which appeareth less in men conscious of their own defect, because they less betray the infirmities they acknowledge.

4. Courage. *Courage,* in a *large* signification, is the *absence* of *fear* in the presence of any evil whatsoever: but in a *strict* and more common meaning, it is *contempt* of *wounds* and *death,* when they oppose a man in the way to his end.

5. Anger. *Anger* or sudden courage is nothing but the *appetite* or desire of *overcoming present* opposition. It hath been defined commonly to be grief proceeding from an opinion of contempt; which is confuted by the often experience which we have of being moved to anger by things inanimate, and without sense, and consequently incapable of contemning us.

6. Revengefulness. *Revengefulness* is that passion which ariseth from an expectation or *imagination* of *making* him that hath *hurt* us, *find* his *own action hurtful* to himself, and to *acknowledge* the same; and this is the height of revenge: for though it be not hard, by returning evil for evil, to make

one's adversary displeased with his own fact; yet to make him acknowledge the same, is so difficult, that many a man had rather die than do it. Revenge aimeth not at the death, but at the captivity or subjection of an enemy; which was well expressed in the exclamation of Tiberius Cæsar, concerning one, that, to frustrate his revenge, had killed himself in prison; *Hath he escaped me?* To *kill,* is the aim of them that *hate,* to *rid* themselves out of fear: *revenge* aimeth at *triumph,* which over the dead is not.

7. Repentance. *Repentance* is the passion which proceedeth from *opinion* or knowledge that the *action* they have done is *out of the way* to the *end* they would attain: the effect whereof is, to pursue that way no longer, but, by the consideration of the end, to direct themselves into a better. The first motion therefore in this passion is *grief;* but the expectation or conception of returning again into the way, is *joy;* and consequently, the passion of *repentance* is compounded and allayed of both: but the *predominant* is *joy;* else were the whole grief, which cannot be, forasmuch as he that proceedeth towards the end, he conceiveth good, proceedeth with appetite; and appetite is joy, as hath been said, chapter 7, section 2.

8. Hope, despair, diffidence. *Hope* is *expectation* of *good* to come, as fear is the expectation of evil: but when there be causes, some that make us expect good, and some that make us expect evil, alternately working in our mind; if the causes that make us expect good, be greater than those that make us expect evil, the whole passion is hope; if contrarily, the whole is fear. Absolute *privation* of hope is *despair,* a degree whereof is *diffidence.*

9. Trust. *Trust* is a passion proceeding from the *belief of* him from whom we *expect* or *hope* for good, so *free* from *doubt* that upon the same we pursue no other way to attain the same good; as *distrust* or diffidence is *doubt* that maketh him endeavor to provide himself by other means. And that this is the meaning of the words trust and distrust, is manifest from this, that a man never provideth himself by a second way, but when he mistrusteth that the first will not hold.

10. Pity and hardness of heart. *Pity* is *imagination* or *fiction* of *future* calamity to *ourselves,* proceeding from the sense of *another* man's calamity. But when it lighteth on such as we think have not deserved the same, the compassion is greater, because then there appeareth more probability that the same may happen to us: for, the evil that happeneth to an innocent man, may happen to every man. But when we see a man suffer for great crimes, which we cannot easily think will fall upon ourselves, the pity is the less. And therefore men are apt to pity those whom they love: for, whom they love, they think worthy of good, and therefore not worthy of calamity. Thence it is also, that men pity the vices of some persons at the first sight only, out of love to their aspect. The contrary of pity is *hardness of heart,* proceeding either from *slowness* of imagination, or some extreme great *opinion* of their own *exemption* from the like calamity or from hatred of all or most men.

11. Indignation. *Indignation* is that *grief* which consisteth in the conception of *good success* happening to them whom they think *unworthy* thereof. Seeing therefore men think all those unworthy whom they hate, they think them not only unworthy of the good fortune they have, but also of their own virtues. And of all the passions of the mind, these two, indignation and pity, are most raised and increased by eloquence: for, the *aggravation* of *the calamity,* and *extenuation* of the *fault,* augmenteth *pity;* and the *extenuation* of the *worth* of the person, together with the magnifying of his success, which are the parts of an orator, are able to turn these two passions into *fury.*

12. Emulation and envy. *Emulation* is *grief* arising from seeing *one's self exceeded* or excelled by his *concurrent,* together with *hope* to *equal* or exceed him in time to come, by his own ability. But, *envy* is the same *grief* joined with *pleasure* conceived in the imagination of some *ill* fortune that may befall him.

13. Laughter. There is a passion that hath *no name;* but the sign of it is that distortion of the countenance which we

call *laughter,* which is always *joy:* but what joy, what we think, and wherein we triumph when we laugh, is not hitherto declared by any. That it consisteth in *wit,* or, as they call it, in the *jest,* experience *confuteth:* for men laugh at mischances and indecencies, wherein there lieth no wit nor jest at all. And forasmuch as the same thing is no more ridiculous when it groweth stale or usual, whatsoever it be that moveth laughter, it must be *new* and *unexpected.* Men laugh often, especially such as are greedy of applause from every thing they do well, at their *own* actions performed never so little beyond their own expectations; as also at their own *jests:* and in this case it is manifest, that the passion of laughter proceedeth from a *sudden conception* of some *ability* in himself that laugheth. Also men laugh at the *infirmities* of others, by comparison wherewith their own abilities are set off and illustrated. Also men laugh at *jests,* the *wit* whereof always consisteth in the elegant *discovering* and conveying to our minds some *absurdity* of *another:* and in this case also the passion of laughter proceedeth from the *sudden* imagination of our own odds and eminency: for what is else the recommending of ourselves to our own good opinion, by comparison with another man's infirmity or absurdity? For when a jest is broken upon ourselves, or friends of whose dishonor we participate, we never laugh thereat. I may therefore conclude, that the passion of laughter is nothing else but *sudden glory* arising from some sudden *conception* of some *eminency* in ourselves, by *comparison* with the *infirmity* of others, or with our own formerly: for men laugh at the follies of themselves past, when they come suddenly to remembrance, except they bring with them any present dishonor. It is no wonder therefore that men take heinously to be laughed at or derided, that is, triumphed over. Laughter *without offense,* must be at *absurdities* and infirmities *abstracted* from persons, and when all the company may laugh together: for laughing to one's-self putteth all the rest into jealousy and examination of themselves. Besides, it is vain glory, and an argument of little worth, to think the infirmity of another, sufficient matter for his triumph.

14. Weeping. The passion opposite hereunto, whose signs are another distortion of the face with tears, called *weeping,* is the *sudden falling out with* ourselves, or sudden conception of defect; and therefore *children* weep often; for seeing they think that every thing ought to be given them which they desire, of necessity every repulse must be a check of their expectation, and puts them in mind of their too much weakness to make themselves masters of all they look for. For the same cause *women* are more apt to weep than men, as being not only more accustomed to have their wills, but also to measure their powers by the power and love of others that protect them. Men are apt to weep that prosecute revenge, when the revenge is suddenly stopped or frustrated by the repentance of their adversary; and such are the tears of *reconciliation.* Also revengeful men are subject to this passion upon the beholding those men they pity, and suddenly remember they cannot help. Other weeping in men proceedeth for the most part from the same cause it proceedeth from in women and children.

15. Lust. The appetite which men call *lust,* and the fruition that appertaineth thereunto, is a *sensual* pleasure, but *not only* that; there is in it also a delight of the mind: for it consisteth of two appetites together, to *please,* and to *be pleased;* and the delight men take in delighting, is not sensual, but a pleasure or joy of the mind consisting in the imagination of the power they have so much to please. But the name *lust* is used where it is condemned; otherwise it is called by the general word *love:* for the passion is one and the same indefinite desire of different sex, as natural as hunger.

16. Love. Of *love,* by which is understood the joy man taketh in the fruition of any *present* good, hath been already spoken of in the first section, chapter 7 under which is contained the *love* men bear to one *another,* or pleasure they take in one another's company; and by which nature, men are said to be sociable. But there is another kind of love, which the Greeks call ῎Ερως, and is that which we mean, when we say that a man is in love: forasmuch as this passion

cannot be without diversity of sex, it cannot be denied but that it *participateth* of that indefinite *love* mentioned in the former section. But there is a great difference betwixt the desire of a man indefinite, and the same desire *limited ad hunc;* and this is that *love* which is the great theme of poets: but notwithstanding their praises, it must be defined by the word *need:* for it is a conception a man hath of his need of *that one person* desired. The cause of this passion is *not* always *nor* for the most part *beauty,* or other quality in the beloved, unless there be withal *hope* in the person that loveth: which may be gathered from this, that in great difference of persons, the *greater* have often fallen in love with the *meaner;* but not contrary. And from hence it is, that for the most part they have much better fortune in love, whose hopes are built upon something *in their person,* than those that trust to their *expressions* and *service;* and they that *care less,* than they that *care more*: which not perceiving, many men cast away their services, as one arrow after another, till, in the end, together with their hopes, they lose their wits.

17. Charity. There is yet another passion sometimes called *love,* but more properly *good will* or *charity.* There can be no greater argument to a man, of his own power, than to find himself able not only to accomplish his own desires, but also to assist other men in theirs: and this is that conception wherein consisteth *charity.* In which, first, is contained that *natural affection* of parents to their children, which the Greeks call Στοϱλή, as *also,* that affection wherewith men seek to *assist* those that adhere unto them. But the affection wherewith men many times bestow their benefits on *strangers,* is not to be called charity, but either *contract,* whereby they seek to purchase friendship; or *fear,* which maketh them to purchase peace. The opinion of Plato concerning honorable love, delivered according to his custom in the person of Socrates, in the dialogue intituled *Convivium,* is this, that a man full and pregnant with wisdom and other virtues, naturally seeketh out some beautiful person, of age and capacity to conceive, in whom he may, without sensual respects, engender and produce the like. And this is the *idea* of the then noted *love* of

Socrates wise and continent, to Alcibiades young and beautiful: in which, love is not the sought honor, but the issue of his knowledge; contrary to the common love, to which though issue sometimes follows, yet men seek not that, but to please, and to be pleased. It should be therefore this charity, or desire to assist and advance others. But why then should the wise seek the ignorant, or be more charitable to the beautiful than to others? There is something in it savoring of the use of that time: in which matter though Socrates be acknowledged for continent, yet the *continent* have the passion they *contain*, as *much* and more than they that *satiate* the appetite; which maketh me suspect this *platonic* love for merely sensual; but with an honorable pretense for the old to haunt the company of the young and beautiful.

18. Admiration and curiosity. Forasmuch as all *knowledge* beginneth from *experience*, therefore also *new experience* is the beginning of *new knowledge*, and the increase of experience the beginning of the increase of knowledge. Whatsoever therefore happeneth new to a man, giveth him matter of *hope* of *knowing* somewhat that he knew *not before*. And this hope and expectation of future knowledge from anything that happeneth new and strange, is that passion which we commonly call *admiration;* and the same considered as appetite, is called *curiosity,* which is appetite of knowledge. As in the discerning of faculties, *man leaveth* all community with *beasts* at the faculty of *imposing names;* so also doth he surmount their nature at this *passion* of *curiosity.* For when a beast seeth anything new and strange to him, he considereth it so far only as to discern whether it be likely to serve his turn, or hurt him, and accordingly approacheth nearer to it, or fleeth from it: whereas man, who in most events remembereth in what manner they were caused and begun, looketh for the cause and beginning of everything that ariseth new unto him. And from this passion of admiration and curiosity, have arisen not only the invention of names, but also supposition of such causes of all things as they thought might produce them. And from this beginning is derived all *philosophy;* as *astronomy* from the admiration of the course of heaven;

natural philosophy from the strange effects of the elements and other bodies. And from the degrees of curiosity, proceed also the degrees of knowledge amongst men: for, to a man in the chase of riches or authority, (which in respect of knowledge are but sensuality) it is a diversity of little pleasure, whether it be the motion of the sun or the earth that maketh the day, or to enter into other contemplations of any strange accident, otherwise than whether it conduce or not to the end he pursueth. Because *curiosity* is *delight,* therefore also *novelty* is so, but especially that novelty from which a man conceiveth an *opinion* true or false of *bettering* his own estate; for, in such case, they stand affected with the hope that all gamesters have while the cards are shuffling.

19. Of the passion of them that flock to see danger. Divers other passions there be, but they want names: whereof some nevertheless have been by most men observed: for example; from what passion proceedeth it, that men take *pleasure* to *behold* from the shore the *danger* of them that are at sea in a tempest, or in fight, or from a safe castle to behold two armies charge one another in the field? It is certainly, in the whole sum, *joy;* else men would never flock to such a spectacle. Nevertheless there is in it both *joy* and *grief:* for as there is novelty and remembrance of our own security present, which is *delight;* so there is also *pity,* which is grief; but the delight is so far predominant, that men usually are content in such a case to be spectators of the misery of their friends.

20. Of magnanimity and pusillanimity. *Magnanimity* is no more than *glory,* of the which I have spoken in the first section; but *glory well grounded* upon certain experience of a power sufficient to attain his end in open manner. And *pusillanimity* is the *doubt* of that. Whatsoever therefore is a sign of *vain glory,* the same is also a sign of *pusillanimity:* for sufficient power maketh glory a spur to one's end. To be *pleased* or *displeased* with *fame true* or *false,* is a *sign* of that same, because he that relieth on fame hath not his success in his own power. Likewise *art* and *fallacy* are signs of pusillanimity, because they depend not upon our own power, but the

ignorance of others. Also *proneness* to *anger*, because it argueth difficulty of proceeding. Also *ostentation* of *ancestors*, because all men are more inclined to make show of their own power when they have it, than of another's. To be at *enmity* and contention with *inferiors*, is a sign of the same, because it proceedeth from want of power to end the war. To *laugh* at others, because it is an affectation of glory from other men's infirmities, and not from any ability of their own. Also *irresolution*, which proceedeth from want of power enough to contemn the little difficulties that make deliberations hard.

21. A view of the passions represented in a race. The comparison of the life of man to a race, though it hold not in every part, yet it holdeth so well for this our purpose, that we may thereby both see and remember almost all the passions before mentioned. But this *race* we must suppose to have no other *goal*, nor other *garland*, but being foremost, and in it:

To endeavor, is *appetite*.
To be remiss, is *sensuality*.
To consider them behind, is *glory*.
To consider them before, is *humility*.
To lose ground with looking back, *vain glory*.
To be holden, *hatred*.
To turn back, *repentance*.
To be in breath, *hope*.
To be weary, *despair*.
To endeavor to overtake the next, *emulation*.
To supplant or overthrow, *envy*.
To resolve to break through a stop foreseen, *courage*.
To break through a sudden stop, *anger*.
To break through with ease, *magnanimity*.
To lose ground by little hindrances, *pusillanimity*.
To fall on the sudden, is disposition to *weep*.
To see another fall, is disposition to *laugh*.
To see one out-gone whom we would not, is *pity*.
To see one out-go whom we would not, is *indignation*.
To hold fast by another, is to *love*.

To carry him on that so holdeth, is *charity*.

To hurt one's-self for haste, is *shame*.

Continually to be out-gone, is *misery*.

Continually to out-go the next before, is *felicity*.

And to forsake the course, is to *die*.

Chapter 10

1. Having shown in the precedent chapters, that sense proceedeth from the action of external objects upon the *brain,* or some internal *substance* of the *head;* and that the *passions* proceed from the alteration there made, and continued to the *heart:* it is consequent in the next place, seeing the diversity of degrees in knowledge in divers men, to be greater than may be ascribed to the divers *tempers* of their brain, to declare *what other causes* may produce such *odds,* and excess of *capacity,* as we daily observe in one man above another. As for that difference which ariseth from *sickness,* and such accidental distempers, I omit the same, as impertinent to this place, and consider it only in such as have their *health,* and *organs* well disposed. If the difference were in the natural temper of the brain, I can imagine no reason why the same should not appear first and most of all in the senses, which being equal both in the wise and less wise, infer an equal temper in the common organ (namely the brain) of all the senses.

2. But we see by experience, that *joy* and *grief* proceed *not* in *all* men from the *same causes,* and that men differ very much in the constitution of the body; whereby, that which helpeth and furthereth *vital constitution* in one, and is therefore delightful, hindereth it and crosseth it in another, and therefore causeth grief. The *difference* therefore of *wits* hath its original *from* the *different passions,* and from the *ends* to which the appetite leadeth them.

3. And first, those men whose ends are *sensual* delight, and generally are addicted to *ease, food, onerations* and *exonerations* of the body, must needs be the *less* thereby delighted with those *imaginations* that *conduce not* to those ends, such as are imaginations of *honor* and *glory,* which, as I have said before, have respect to the future: for sensuality consisteth in the pleasure of the senses, which please only for the present, and take away the inclination to observe such things as conduce to honor, and consequently maketh men less

curious, and less ambitious, whereby they less consider the way either to knowledge or other power; in which two consisteth all the excellency of power cognitive. And this is it which men call *dullness*, and proceedeth from the appetite of sensual or bodily delight. And it may well be conjectured, that such passion hath its beginning from a *grossness* and *difficulty* of the *motion* of the *spirit* about the *heart*.

4. The contrary hereunto, is that *quick ranging* of mind described, chapter 4, section 3, which is joined with *curiosity* of comparing the things that come into the mind, one with another: in which comparison, a man delighteth himself either with finding unexpected *similitude* of things, otherwise much unlike, in which men place the excellency of *fancy*, and from whence proceed those grateful similies, metaphors, and other tropes, by which both *poets* and *orators* have it in their power to make things please or displease, and show well or ill to others, as they like themselves; or else in discerning suddenly *dissimilitude* in things that otherwise appear the same. And this virtue of the mind is that by which men attain to exact and perfect *knowledge;* and the pleasure thereof consisteth in continual instruction, and in distinction of places, persons, and seasons, and is commonly termed by the name of *judgment:* for, to judge is nothing else, but to distinguish or discern: and both *fancy* and *judgment* are commonly comprehended under the name of *wit*, which seemeth to be a tenuity and agility of spirits, contrary to that restiness of the spirits supposed in those that are dull.

5. There is another defect of the mind, which men call *levity*, which betrayeth also *mobility* in the spirits, but in excess. An example whereof is in them that in the midst of any serious discourse, have their minds diverted to every little jest or witty observation; which maketh them depart from their discourse by a parenthesis, and from that parenthesis by another, till at length they either lose themselves, or make their narration like a dream, or some studied nonsense. The passion from whence this proceedeth, is *curiosity*, but with *too much equality* and indifference: for when all things make equal impression and delight, they equally throng to be expressed.

6. The virtue opposite to this defect is *gravity*, or steadiness; in which the end being the great and master-delight, directeth and keepeth in the way thereto all other thoughts.

7. The *extremity* of dullness is that *natural folly* which may be called *stolidity:* but the extreme of *levity*, though it be natural folly distinct from the other, and obvious to every man's observation, I know *not* how to call it.

8. There is a fault of the mind called by the Greeks Ἀμαθία, which is *indocibility*, or *difficulty* of being taught; the which must needs arise from a *false opinion* that they *know already* the truth of that is called in question: for certainly men are not otherwise so unequal in capacity as the *evidence* is unequal between what is taught by the mathematicians, and what is commonly discoursed of in other books: and therefore if the minds of men were all of white paper, they would almost equally be disposed to acknowledge whatsoever should be in right method, and by right ratiocination delivered to them: but when men have once acquiesced in untrue opinions, and registered them as authentical records in their minds, it is no less impossible to speak intelligibly to such men, than to write legibly upon a paper already scribbled over. The immediate *cause* therefore of *indocibility*, is *prejudice;* and of prejudice, false opinion of our own knowledge.

9. Another, and a principal defect of the mind, is that which men call *madness*, which appeareth to be nothing else but some *imagination* of some such *predominancy* above the *rest*, that we have *no passion but from it;* and this conception is nothing else but excessive *vain glory*, or *vain dejection;* which is most probable by these examples following, which proceed in appearance every one of them from *pride*, or some *dejection* of mind. As first, we have had the example of one that preached in Cheapside from a cart there, instead of a pulpit, that he himself was Christ, which was *spiritual* pride or madness. We have had also divers examples of learned madness, in which men have manifestly been distracted upon any occasion that hath put them in remembrance of their own ability. Amongst the learned men, may be remembered, I think also, those that determine of the time of the world's end, and other such the points of

prophecy. And the gallant madness of Don Quixote is nothing else but an expression of such height of vain glory as reading of *romance* may produce in pusillanimous men. Also rage and madness of love, are but great indignations of them in whose brains is predominant contempt from their enemies, or their mistresses. And the *pride* taken in *form* and *behaviour,* hath made divers men run mad, and to be so accounted, under the name of fantastic.

10. And as these are the examples of extremities, so also are there examples too many of the degrees, which may therefore be well accounted follies; as it is a degree of the *first,* for a man, without certain evidence, to think himself to be *inspired,* or to have any other effect of God's holy spirit than other godly men have. Of the *second,* for a man continually to speak his mind in a *cento* of other men's Greek or Latin sentences. Of the *third,* much of the present gallantry in love and duel. Of *rage,* a degree is *malice;* and of *fantastic* madness, *affectation.*

11. As the former examples exhibit to us madness, and the degrees thereof, proceeding from the excess of self-opinion; so also there be other examples of madness, and the degrees thereof, proceeding from *too much vain fear* and *dejection;* as in those melancholy men that have imagined themselves brittle as glass, or have had some other like imagination: and degrees hereof are all those exorbitant and causeless fears, which we commonly observe in melancholy persons.

Chapter 11

1. Hitherto of the knowledge of things *natural*, and of the passions that arise naturally from them. Now forasmuch as we give names not only to things natural, but also to *supernatural;* and by all names we ought to have some meaning and conception: it followeth in the next place, to consider what thoughts and imaginations of the mind we have, when we take into our mouths the most blessed name of GOD, and the names of those *virtues* we attribute unto him; as also, what *image* cometh into the mind at hearing the name of *spirit*, or the name of *angel*, good or bad.

2. And forasmuch as God Almighty is *incomprehensible*, it followeth, that we can have *no* conception or *image* of the *Deity,* and consequently, all *his attributes* signify our *inability* and defect of power to *conceive* anything concerning his nature, and not any conception of the same, excepting only this, that *there is a God:* for the effects we acknowledge naturally, do include a power of their producing, before they were produced; and that power presupposeth something existent that hath such power: and the thing so existing with power to produce, if it were not eternal, must needs have been produced by somewhat before it, and that again by something else before that, till we come to an eternal, that is to say, the first power of all powers, and first cause of all causes: and this is it which all men conceive by the name of GOD, implying eternity, incomprehensibility, and omnipotency. And thus all that will consider, may know *that* God is, though not *what* he is: even a man that is born blind, though it be not possible for him to have any imagination what kind of thing fire is; yet he cannot but know that somewhat there is that men call fire, because it warmeth him.

3. And whereas we attribute to God Almighty, *seeing, hearing, speaking, knowing, loving,* and the like, by which names we understand something in *men* to whom we attribute them, we understand *nothing* by them in the nature

of God: for, as it is well reasoned, *Shall not the God that made the eye, see; and the ear, hear?* So it is also, if we say, shall God, which made the eye, not see without the eye; or that made the ear, not hear without the ear; or that made the brain, not know without the brain; or that made the heart, not love without the heart? The *attributes* therefore given unto the *Deity*, are such as *signify* either *our incapacity* or our *reverence:* our incapacity, when we say incomprehensible and infinite; our reverence, when we give him those names, which amongst us are the names of those things we most magnify and commend, as omnipotent, omniscient, just, merciful, &c. And when God Almighty giveth those names to himself in the Scriptures, it is but ἀνθρωποπαθῶς, that is to say, by descending to our manner of speaking; without which we are not capable of understanding him.

4. By the name of *spirit*, we understand a *body natural*, but of such *subtlety*, that it worketh not upon the senses; but that filleth up the place which the image of a visible body might fill up. Our conception therefore of spirit consisteth of *figure without color;* and in figure is understood dimension, and consequently, to conceive a spirit, is to conceive something that hath dimension. But *spirits supernatural* commonly signify some *substance without* dimension; which two words do flatly contradict one another: and therefore when we attribute the name of spirit unto God, we attribute it not as the name of anything we conceive, no more than we ascribe unto him sense and understanding; but as a signification of our reverence, we desire to abstract from him all corporal grossness.

5. Concerning other things, which some men call *spirits incorporeal*, and some *corporeal*, it is not *possible* by *natural* means only, to come to *knowledge* of so much, as that *there are such* things. We that are Christians *acknowledge* that there be angels good and evil, and that there are spirits, and that the soul of a man is a spirit, and that those spirits are immortal: *but,* to *know* it, that is to say, to have natural evidence of the same, it is *impossible:* for, all *evidence* is *conception,* as it is said, chap. 6 sect. 3, and all conception is imagi-

nation, and proceedeth from *sense,* chap. 3 sect. 1. And *spirits* we suppose to be those substances which work *not* upon the *sense,* and therefore not conceptible. But though the Scripture acknowledges spirits, yet doth it nowhere say, that they are incorporeal, meaning thereby, without dimension and quality; nor, I think, is that word incorporeal at all in the Bible; but it is said of the spirit, that it abideth in men; sometimes that it dwelleth in them, sometimes that it cometh on them, that it descendeth, and goeth, and cometh; and that spirits are angels, that is to say messengers: all which words do imply *locality;* and locality is *dimension;* and whatsoever hath dimension, is *body,* be it never so *subtle.* To me therefore it seemeth, that the Scripture favoreth them more, that hold angels and spirits corporeal, than them that hold the contrary. And it is a plain *contradiction* in natural discourse, to say of the soul of man, that it is *tota in toto, et tota in qualibet parte corporis,* grounded neither upon reason nor revelation, but proceeding from the ignorance of what those things are which are called *spectra,* images, that appear in the dark to children, and such as have strong fears, and other strange imaginations, as hath been said, chapter 3 sect. 5, where I call them phantasms: for, taking them to be things real, without us, like bodies, and seeing them to come and vanish so strangely as they do, unlike to bodies; what could they call them else, but *incorporeal bodies*? which is not a name, but an absurdity of speech.

6. It is true, that the heathens, and all nations of the world, have acknowledged that there be *spirits,* which for the most part they hold to be incorporeal; whereby it might be thought, that a man by natural reason, may arrive, without the Scriptures, to the knowledge of this, *that spirits are:* but the erroneous collection thereof by the heathens, may proceed, as I have said before, from the ignorance of the cause of ghosts and phantasms, and such other apparitions. And from thence had the Grecians their number of gods, their number of *dæmons* good or bad, and for every man his *genius;* which is not the acknowledging of this truth, *that spirits are;* but a false opinion concerning the force of imagination.

7. And seeing the *knowledge* we have of *spirits*, is *not natural* knowledge, but *faith* from supernatural revelation given to the holy writers of the Scriptures; it followeth, that of inspirations also, which is the operation of spirit in us, the knowledge which we have, must all proceed from Scripture. The *signs* there set down of *inspiration* are *miracles*, when they be great, and manifestly above the power of men to do by imposture: as for example, the inspiration of Elias was known by the miraculous burning of the sacrifice. But the *signs* to *distinguish* whether a *spirit* be *good* or *evil*, are the same by which we distinguish whether a man or a tree be good or evil, namely, *actions* and *fruit:* for there are *lying* spirits, wherewith men are inspired sometimes, as well as with *spirits* of *truth*. And we are commanded in Scripture, to judge of the spirits by their doctrine, and not of the doctrine by the spirits. For miracles, our Saviour (*Matth*. xxiv. 24) hath forbidden us to rule our faith by them. And Saint Paul saith, (*Gal*. i. 8): *Though an angel from heaven preach to you otherwise, &c. let him be accursed*. Where it is plain, that we are not to judge whether the doctrine be true or not, by the angel; but whether the angel say true or no, by the doctrine. So likewise, (I *Joh. iv.* 1): *Believe not every spirit: for false prophets are gone out into the world*. Verse 2: *Hereby shall ye know the spirit of God*. Verse 3: *Every spirit that confesseth not that Jesus Christ is come in the flesh, is not of God: and this is the spirit of Antichrist*. Verse 15: *Whosoever confesseth that Jesus is the Son of God, in him dwelleth God, and he in God*. The *knowledge* therefore we have of *good* and *evil* inspiration, cometh *not* by *vision* of an angel that may teach it, *nor* by a *miracle* that may seem to confirm it; *but* by *conformity* of doctrine with this article and fundamental point of Christian faith, which also Saint Paul (1 *Cor*. iii. 11) saith is the sole foundation, *That Jesus Christ is come in the flesh*.

8. But if *inspiration* be discerned by *this* point, and *this* point be acknowledged and believed upon the *authority* of the *Scriptures; how* (may some men ask) know we that the *Scripture deserveth* so great *authority*, which must be no less than that of the lively voice of God; that is, how do we

know the *Scriptures* to be the *word* of *God*? And first, it is manifest, that if by knowledge we understand science infallible and natural, as is defined, chap. 6 sect. 4, proceeding from sense, we cannot be said to know it, because it proceedeth not from the conceptions engendered by sense. And if we understand knowledge as supernatural, we cannot have it but by inspiration: and of that *inspiration* we cannot judge, but by the *doctrine*: it followeth, that we have not any way, natural or supernatural, of the *knowledge* thereof, which can properly be called *infallible science* and *evidence*. It remaineth, that the knowledge that we have that the Scriptures are the word of God, is only *faith*, which faith therefore is also by Saint Paul (*Heb*. xi. 1) defined to be *the evidence of things not seen*; that is to say, not otherwise evident but by faith: for, whatsoever either is evident by natural reason, or revelation supernatural, is not called faith; else should not faith cease, no more than charity, when we are in heaven; which is contrary to the doctrine of the Scripture. And, we are *not* said to *believe*, *but* to *know* those things that be *evident*.

9. Seeing then the acknowledgment of Scriptures to be the word of God, is not evidence, but faith, and faith (chapter 6 sect. 7) consisteth in the trust we have of other men, it appeareth plain, that the men so trusted, are the holy men of God's church succeeding one another from the time of those that saw the wondrous works of God Almighty in the flesh. Nor doth this imply that God is not the worker or efficient cause of faith, or that faith is begotten in man without the spirit of God: for, all those good opinions which we admit and believe, though they proceed from hearing, and hearing from teaching, both which are natural, yet they are the work of God: for, all the works of nature are his, and they are attributed to the Spirit of God: as for example, *Exod*. xxviii. 3: *Thou shalt speak unto all cunning men, whom I have filled with the* SPIRIT *of wisdom, that they may make Aaron's garments for his consecration, that he may serve me in the priest's office*. Faith therefore, wherewith we believe, is the work of the Spirit of God in that sense, by which the Spirit of God giveth to one man wisdom and

cunning in workmanship more than another; and by which he effecteth also in other points pertaining to our ordinary life, that one man believeth that, which, upon the same grounds, another doth not; and one man reverenceth the opinion, and obeyeth the commands of his superior, and others not.

10. And seeing our faith, that the Scriptures are the word of God, began from the confidence and trust we repose in the *church;* there can be no doubt but that their *interpretation* of the same Scriptures (when any doubt or controversy shall arise, by which this fundamental point, *that Jesus Christ is come in the flesh,* may be called in question) is *safer* for any man to trust to, than his *own,* whether *reasoning* or *spirit,* that is to say, his own *opinion.*

11. Now concerning men's *affections* to *Godward,* they are not the same always that are described in the chapter concerning passions. There, for to love, is to be delighted with the image or conception of the thing loved; but God is unconceivable: *to love God* therefore, in the Scripture, is to *obey his commandments,* and to *love one another.* Also to *trust God,* is different from our *trusting* one *another:* for, when a man trusteth a man, (chap. 9. sect. 9) he layeth aside his own endeavors: but if we do so in our trust to God Almighty, we disobey him; and how shall we trust to him whom we know we disobey? To *trust* to *God Almighty* therefore, is to *refer* to his *good pleasure* all that is *above our* own power to effect: and this is *all one* with *acknowledging one* only God, which is the first commandment. And to trust *in Christ,* is no more but to acknowledge him for God; which is the fundamental article of our Christian faith: and consequently, to trust, rely, or, as some express it, to cast and roll ourselves on Christ, is the same thing with the fundamental point of faith, namely, that *Jesus Christ is the son of the living God.*

12. To *honor* God internally in the heart, is the same thing with that we ordinarily call honor amongst men: for it is nothing but the *acknowledging* of his *power;* and the signs thereof, the same with the signs of the honor due to our superiors, mentioned chapter 8 section 6, viz. to

praise, to *magnify,* to *bless,* to pray to him, to thank him, to give oblations and sacrifices to him, to give attention to his word, to speak to him in prayer with consideration, to come into his presence with humble gesture, and in decent manner, and to adorn his worship with magnificence and cost: and these are natural signs of our honoring him internally: and therefore the contrary hereof, to neglect prayer, to speak to him *extempore,* to come to church slovenly, to adorn the place of his worship worse than our own houses, to take up his name in every idle discourse, are the manifest signs of contempt of the Divine Majesty. There be other signs which are arbitrary; as, to be uncovered, as we be here, to put off their shoes, as Moses at the fiery bush, and some other of that kind, which in their own nature are indifferent, till, to avoid indecency and discord, it be otherwise determined by common consent.

Chapter 12

1. It hath been declared already, how *external* objects cause *conceptions,* and conceptions, *appetite* and *fear,* which are the *first unperceived beginnings of our actions*: for *either* the actions immediately follow the first appetite, as when we do anything upon a sudden; *or else* to our first appetite there succeedeth some conception of evil to happen to us by such actions, which is fear, and which holdeth us from proceeding. And to that fear may succeed a new appetite, and to that appetite another fear alternately, till the action be either done, or some accident come between, to make it impossible; and so this alternate appetite and fear ceaseth. This *alternate succession of appetite and fear* during all the time the action is in our power to do or not to do, is that we call *deliberation*; which name hath been given it for that part of the definition wherein it is said that it lasteth so long as the action, whereof we deliberate, is in our power: for, so long we have liberty to do or not to do; and deliberation signifieth a taking away of our own liberty.

2. *Deliberation* therefore requireth in the action deliberated *two conditions*; one, that it be *future*; the other, that there be *hope* of doing it, or possibility of not doing it; for, *appetite* and *fear* are *expectations* of the future; and there is no expectation of good, without hope; or of evil, without possibility: of *necessaries* therefore there is *no deliberation*. In deliberation, the last appetite, as also the last fear, is called *will*, viz. the last appetite, will to do, or will to omit. It is all one therefore to say *will* and *last will*: for, though a man express his present inclination and appetite concerning the disposing of his goods, by words or writings; yet shall it not be counted his will, because he hath still liberty to dispose of them otherways: but when death taketh away that liberty, then it is his will.

3. *Voluntary* actions and omissions are such as have beginning in the *will*; all other are *involuntary*, or *mixed voluntary*;

237

involuntary, such as he doth by necessity of nature, as when he is pushed, or falleth, and thereby doth good or hurt to another: *mixed*, such as participate of both; as when a man is carried to prison, going is voluntary, to the prison, is involuntary: the example of him that throweth his goods out of a ship into the sea, to save his person, is of an action altogether voluntary: for, there is nothing therein involuntary, but the hardness of the choice, which is not his action, but the action of the winds: what he himself doth, is no more against his will, than to flee from danger is against the will of him that seeth no other means to preserve himself.

4. *Voluntary* also are the actions that proceed from sudden *anger*, or *other* sudden *appetite* in such men as can discern good or evil: for, in them the time precedent *is* to be judged deliberation: for then also he deliberateth in what cases it is good to strike, deride, or do any other action proceeding from anger or other such sudden passion.

5. *Appetite, fear, hope*, and the rest of the passions are *not* called *voluntary*; for they proceed *not from, but are the will*; and the will is not voluntary: for, a man can no more say he will will, than he will will will, and so make an infinite repetition of the word [*will*]; which is absurd, and insignificant.

6. Forasmuch as *will to do* is *appetite*, and *will to omit, fear*; the *cause* of *appetite* and *fear* is the *cause* also of our *will*: but the propounding of the benefits and of harms, that is to say, of reward and punishment, is the cause of our appetite, and of our fears, and therefore also of our wills, so far forth as we believe that such rewards and benefits as are propounded, shall arrive unto us; and consequently, our *wills* follow our *opinions*, as our *actions* follow our *wills*; in which sense they say truly, and properly, that say the world is governed by opinion.

7. When the wills of many concur to one and the same action and effect, this *concourse* of their *wills* is called *consent*; by which we must not understand one will of many men, for every man hath his several will, but many wills to the producing of one effect: but when the *wills* of two divers men *produce* such actions as are reciprocally *resistant* one to the

other, this is called *contention*; and, being upon the persons one of another, *battle*: whereas actions proceeding from *consent*, are mutual *aid*.

8. When many wills are involved or included in the will of one or more consenting, (which how it may be, shall be hereafter declared) then is that involving of many wills in one or more, called *union*.

9. In *deliberations* interrupted, as they may be by *diversion* of other business, or by *sleep*, the last *appetite* of such part of the deliberation is called *intention*, or *purpose*.

Chapter 13

1. Having spoken of the powers and acts of the mind, both cognitive and motive, considered in every man by *himself*, *without relation to others*; it will fall fitly into *this* chapter, to speak of the effects of the same power *one upon another*; which effects are also the signs, by which one taketh notice what another conceiveth and intendeth. Of these signs, *some* are such as *cannot* easily be *counterfeited*; as actions and gestures, especially if they be sudden, whereof I have mentioned some; (for example, look in chapter 9) with the several passions whereof they are signs: *others* there are which *may* be *counterfeited*; and those are *words* or *speech*; of the use and effects whereof, I am to speak in this place.

2. The first use of language, is the *expression* of our *conceptions*, that is, the begetting in one another the same conceptions that we have in ourselves; and this is called *teaching*; wherein, if the *conception* of him that teacheth continually accompany his words, *beginning* at something true in *experience*, then it begetteth the like evidence in the hearer that understandeth them, and maketh him to *know* something, which he is therefore said to *learn*: but if there be *not such evidence*, then such teaching is called *persuasion*, and begetteth no more in the hearer, than what is in the speaker's bare *opinion*. And the *signs* of two opinions contradictory one to another; namely, *affirmation* and *negation* of the same thing, is called *controversy*: but *both affirmations*, or both *negations, consent in opinion*.

3. The *infallible* sign of *teaching exactly*, and without error, is this, that *no man* hath *ever taught* the *contrary*: not that few, how few soever, if any; for commonly truth is on the side of a few, rather than of the multitude: but when in opinions and questions considered and discussed by many, it happeneth that not any one of the men that so discussed them differ from another, then it may be justly inferred, they know what they teach, and that otherwise they do not. And

this appears most manifestly to them that have considered the divers subjects wherein they have exercised their pens, and the divers ways in which they have proceeded, together with the diversity of the success thereof: for, those men who have taken in hand to consider nothing else but the comparison of *magnitudes, numbers, times,* and *motions,* and how their proportions are to one another, have thereby been the authors of all those excellencies by which we differ from such savage people as now inhabit divers places in America; and as have been the inhabitants heretofore of those countries where at this day arts and sciences do most flourish: for, from the studies of these men, have proceeded whatsoever cometh to us for ornament by *navigation,* and whatsoever we have beneficial to human society by the *division, distinction,* and *portraiting the face of the earth*; whatsoever also we have by the *account of times,* and *foresight of the course of heaven*; whatsoever by *measuring distances, planes,* and *solids* of all sorts; and whatsoever either *elegant* or *defensible* in *building*: all which supposed away, what do we differ from the wildest of the Indians? Yet to this day was it never heard of, that there was any *controversy* concerning any conclusion in this subject; the science whereof hath nevertheless been continually amplified and enriched by the conclusions of most difficult and profound speculation. The *reason* whereof is apparent to every man that looketh into their writings; for they proceed from most *low* and *humble* principles, evident even to the meanest capacity; going on *slowly,* and with most *scrupulous ratiocination*; viz. from the imposition of names, they infer the truth of their *first* propositions; and from two of the first, a *third*; and from any two of the three, a *fourth*; and so on, according to the steps of science, mentioned chapter 6 section 4. On the other side, those men who have written concerning the faculties, passions, and manners of men, that is to say, of *moral philosophy,* and of *policy, government,* and *laws,* whereof there be infinite volumes, have been so *far from removing doubt* and controversy in the questions they have handled, *that* they have very much *multiplied the same*: *nor* doth any man at this day so much as pretend to *know* more than hath been delivered two thousand years ago by

Aristotle: and yet every man thinks that in this subject he knoweth as much as any other; supposing there needeth thereunto no study but that accrueth unto them by natural wit; though they play, or employ their mind otherwise in the purchase of wealth or place. The reason whereof is no other, than that in their writings and discourses they take for principles those opinions which are already vulgarly received, whether true or false; being for the most part false. There is therefore a great deal of *difference* between *teaching* and *persuading*; the sign of *this* being *controversy*; the sign of the *former, no controversy.*

4. There be *two sorts* of men that commonly be called *learned*: one is that sort that proceedeth *evidently* from humble principles, as is described in the last section; and those men are called *mathematici*: *the other* are they that *take up* maxims from their *education*, and from the *authority* of men, or of custom, and *take the habitual discourse of the tongue for ratiocination*; and these are called *dogmatici*. Now seeing in the last section those we call *mathematici* are absolved of the crime of breeding controversy, and they that pretend not to learning cannot be accused, the fault lieth altogether in the *dogmatics*, that is to say, those that are imperfectly learned, and with passion press to have their opinions pass everywhere for truth, without any evident demonstration either from experience, or from places of Scripture of uncontroverted interpretation.

5. The expression of those conceptions which *cause* in us the *experience* of good while we deliberate, as also of those which cause our expectation of evil, is that which we call *counselling*, and is the internal deliberation of the mind concerning what we ourselves are to do or not to do. The *consequences* of our actions are our *counsellors*, by *alternate succession* in the mind. So in the counsel which a man taketh from *other* men, the *counsellors alternately* do *make appear the consequences* of the action, and do not any of them deliberate, but furnish among them all, him that is counselled with arguments whereupon to deliberate with himself.

6. Another use of speech is *expression* of *appetite, inten-*

tion, and *will;* as the appetite of knowledge by *interrogation;* appetite to have a thing done by another, as *request, prayer, petition:* expressions of our purpose or intention, as *promise,* which is the affirmation or negation of some action to be done in the future: *threatening,* which is the promise of evil; and *commanding,* which is that speech by which we signify to another our *appetite* or desire *to have* any *thing done,* or *left undone,* for reasons contained in the will itself: for it is not properly said, *Sic volo, sic jubeo,* without that other clause, *Stet pro ratione voluntas:* and when the command is a sufficient reason to move us to action, then is that command called a *law.*

7. Another use of speech is *instigation* and appeasing, by which we increase or diminish one another's passion: it is the same thing with *persuasion;* the difference not being real; for, the begetting of *opinion* and *passion* is the *same.* But whereas in *persuasion* we aim at *getting opinion from passion; here,* the end is, *to raise passion from opinion.* And as in raising an opinion from passion, any premises are good enough to enforce the desired conclusion; so, in raising passion from opinion, it is no matter whether the opinion be true or false, or the narration historical or fabulous; for, *not the truth,* but the *image,* maketh passion: and a tragedy, well acted, affecteth no less than a murder.

8. Though words be the *signs* we have of one another's *opinions* and intentions, because the *equivocation* of them is so *frequent according* to the *diversity of contexture,* and of the company wherewith they go, which, the presence of him that speaketh, our *sight* of his *actions,* and *conjecture* of his *intentions,* must help to discharge us of; it must therefore be *extremely hard* to find the *opinions* and meaning of those *men* that are *gone from us long ago,* and have left us no other signification thereof than their books, which cannot possibly be understood without *history,* to discover those aforementioned circumstances, and also without great prudence to *observe* them.

9. When it happeneth that a man signifieth unto two *contradictory* opinions, whereof the *one* is *clearly* and *directly signified,* and the *other* either *drawn* from that by *conse-*

quence, or not known to be contradictory to it; then, when he is not present to explicate himself better, we are to take the *former* for his opinion; for that is clearly signified to be his, and directly; whereas the other might proceed from error in the deduction, or ignorance of the repugnancy. The like also is to be held in two contradictory expressions of a man's intention and will, for the same reason.

10. Forasmuch as whosoever *speaketh* to another, intendeth thereby to *make* him *understand* what he saith, if he speak unto him either in a language which he that heareth understandeth not, or use any word in other sense than he believeth is the sense of him that heareth, he *intendeth also not* to make him understand what he saith; which is a *contradiction* of himself. It is therefore always to be supposed, that he which intendeth not to deceive, alloweth the private interpretation of his speech to him to whom it is addressed.

11. *Silence*, in him that *believeth* that the same shall be taken for *a sign of his intent, is* a sign thereof indeed: for, if he did not consent, the labor of speaking so much as to declare the same, is so little, as it is to be presumed he would have done it.

CONCLUSION

Thus have we considered the nature of man so far as was requisite for the finding out the first and most simple elements wherein the compositions of politic rules and laws are lastly resolved; which was my present purpose.

To the Lord Marquis of Newcastle*

RIGHT HONOURABLE,

I had once resolved to answer my Lord Bishop's objections to my book DE CIVE in the first place, as that which concerns me most; and afterwards to examine his Discourse of LIBERTY and NECESSITY, which, because I had never uttered my opinion of it, concerned me the less. But seeing it was your Lordship's and my Lord Bishop's desire that I should begin with the *latter*, I was contented so to do, and here I present and submit it to your Lordship's judgment.

And first I assure your Lordship I find in it no new argument neither from *Scripture* nor from *reason*, that I have not often heard before, which is as much as to say, I am not surprised.

The *preface* is a handsome one, but it appeareth even in that, that he hath mistaken the question. For whereas he says thus, *If I be free to write this Discourse, I have obtained the cause*: I deny that to be true, for it is enough to his freedom of writing, that he had not written it, unless he would himself. If he will obtain the cause, he must prove that before he writ it, it was not necessary he should prove it afterward. It may be his Lordship thinks it all one to say, *I was free* to write it, and, *It was not necessary* I should write it. But I think otherwise. For he is *free* to do a thing, that may do it if he have the will to do it, and may forbear, if he have the will to forbear. And yet if there be a *necessity* that he shall have the *will* to do it, the action is necessarily to follow: and if there be a *necessity* that he shall have the *will* to forbear, the forbearing also will be necessary. The question therefore is not, whether a man be a *free agent*, that is to say, whether he can write or forbear, speak or be silent, according to his *will;* but, whether the *will* to write, and the *will* to forbear, come upon him according to his *will*, or ac-

*From *Of Liberty and Necessity* (Molesworth Ed. 1839, Vol. IV of English Works) pp. 239-278.

cording to anything else in his own power. I acknowledge this *liberty*, that I *can* do if I *will*; but to say, I can *will* if I *will*, I take to be an absurd speech. Wherefore I cannot grant my Lord the cause upon his *preface*.

In the next place, he maketh certain distinctions of *liberty*, and says he meaneth not *liberty* from *sin*, nor from *servitude*, nor from *violence*; but, from *necessity, necessitation, inevitability*, and *determination to one*.

It had been better to *define* liberty, than thus to *distinguish*. For I understand never the more what he means by *liberty*; and though he say he means *liberty* from *necessitation*, yet I understand not how such a *liberty* can be, and it is a taking of the question without proof. For what is else the question between us, but whether *such* a liberty be possible or not?

There are in the same place other distinctions: as a liberty of *exercise only*, which he calls a *liberty of contradiction*, namely of doing not good, or evil *simply*, but of doing this or that good, or this or that evil *respectively*, and a *liberty of specification and exercise also*, which he calls a liberty of *contrariety*, namely a liberty not only to do good or evil, but also to do or not do this or that good or evil.

And with these *distinctions* his Lordship says he *clears the coast*, whereas in truth, he darkeneth his own meaning and the question, not only with the jargon of *exercise only, specification also, contradiction, contrariety*, but also with pretending distinction where none is: for how is it possible that the *liberty* of doing or not doing this or that good or evil, can consist, as he says it does in God and good angels, without a liberty of doing or not doing good or evil?

The next thing his Lordship does, after clearing of the coast, is the dividing of his forces, as he calls them, into *two* squadrons, *one* of places *of Scriptures*, the *other* of *reasons*, which allegory he useth, I suppose, because he addresseth the discourse to your Lordship, who is a military man. All that I have to say touching this, is, that I observe a great part of those his *forces* do look and *march* another way, and some of them *fight* amongst themselves.

And the first place of *Scripture*, taken from Numb. xxx. 13, is one of those that look another way; the words are, *If a wife make a vow, it is left to her husband's choice either to establish it or make it void.* For it proves no more but that the husband is a *free* and *voluntary agent*, but not that his *choice* therein is not *necessitated* or not *determined* to what he shall choose, by precedent *necessary* causes.

For if there come into the husband's mind greater good by establishing than abrogating such a vow, the establishing will follow necessarily; and if the evil that will follow in the husband's opinion outweigh the good, the contrary must needs follow: and yet in this following of one's *hopes* and *fears*, consisteth the nature of *election*. So that a man may both choose this, and cannot but choose this, and consequently *choosing* and *necessity* are joined together.

The second place of Scripture is Joshua, xxiv. 15. The third is 2 Sam. xxiv. 12, whereby it is clearly proved, that there is *election* in *man*, but not proved that such *election* was not *necessitated* by the *hopes*, and *fears*, and considerations of *good* and *bad* to follow, which depend not on the *will*, nor are subject to *election*. And therefore one answer serves all such places, if there were a thousand.

But his Lordship supposing, it seems, I might answer, as I have done, that *necessity* and *election* might stand together, and instance in the actions of *children*, *fools*, or *brute beasts*, whose *fancies*, I might say, are *necessitated* and *determined* to *one*; before these his proofs out of Scripture, desires to prevent that instance, and therefore says that the actions of *children*, *fools*, *madmen*, and *beasts*, are indeed *determined*, but that they proceed not from *election*, nor from *free*, but from *spontaneous agents*. As for example, that the *bee*, when it maketh honey, does it *spontaneously*; and when the *spider* makes his web, he does it *spontaneously*, but not by *election*.

Though I never meant to ground my answer upon the experience of what *children*, *fools*, *madmen*, and *beasts* do; yet that your Lordship may understand what can be meant by *spontaneous*, and how it differeth from *voluntary*, I will answer that *distinction*, and show that it *fighteth* against its fellow arguments.

Your Lordship therefore is to consider, that all *voluntary* actions, where the thing that induceth the *will* is not *fear*, are called also *spontaneous*, and said to be done by a man's *own* accord. As when a man giveth money voluntarily to another for merchandise, or out of affection, he is said to do it of his own accord, which in Latin is *sponte*, and therefore the action is *spontaneous*; though to give one's money willingly to a thief to avoid killing, or throw it into the sea to avoid drowning, where the motive is *fear*, be not called *spontaneous*. But every *spontaneous* action is not therefore *voluntary*, for *voluntary* presupposes some precedent *deliberation*, that is to say, some *consideration*, and *meditation*, of what is likely to *follow*, both upon the doing, and abstaining from the action deliberated of; whereas many actions are done of our *own* accord, and therefore *spontaneous*, for which nevertheless, as my Lord thinks, we never *consulted* nor *deliberated* in ourselves. As when making no question nor any the least doubt in the world, but the thing we are about is good, we *eat* and *walk*, or in anger *strike* or *revile*, which my Lord thinks *spontaneous*, but not *voluntary* nor *elective* actions, and with *such* kind of actions, he says *necessitation* may stand, but not with such as are *voluntary*, and proceed upon *election* and *deliberation*. Now if I make it appear to your Lordship, that those actions, which, he says, proceed from *spontaneity*, and which he ascribes to *children*, *fools*, *madmen*, and *beasts*, proceed from *election* and *deliberation*, and that actions *inconsiderate*, *rash*, and *spontaneous*, are ordinarily found in those, that are by themselves and many more thought as *wise*, or wiser than ordinarily men are, then my Lord Bishop's argument concludeth, that *necessity* and *election* may stand together, which is contrary to that which he intendeth by all the rest of his arguments to prove.

And first your Lordship's own experience furnishes you with proof enough, that *horses*, *dogs*, and other brute *beasts*, do *demur* oftentimes upon the way they are to take, the horse retiring from some strange figure that he sees, and coming on again to avoid the spur. And what else doth a man that *deliberateth*, but one while *proceed* toward action, another while *retire* from it, as the *hope* of greater *good* draws him, or the *fear* of greater evil *drives* him away.

A *child* may be so young as to do what it does without all *deliberation*, but that is but till it have the chance to be hurt by doing of somewhat, or till it be of age to understand the rod: for the actions, wherein he hath once had a check, shall be *deliberated* on the second time.

Fools and *madmen* manifestly *deliberate* no less than the the *wisest* men, though they make not so good a *choice*, the images of things being by disease altered

For *bees* and *spiders*, if my Lord Bishop had had so little to do as to be a spectator of their actions, he would have confessed not only *election*, but *art*, *prudence*, and *policy*, in them, very near equal to that of mankind. Of *bees*, Aristotle says, *their life is civil*.

Again, his Lordship is deceived, if he think any *spontaneous* action, after once being checked in it, differs from an action *voluntary* and *elective*: for even the setting of a man's foot, in the posture for *walking*, and the action of ordinary *eating*, was once *deliberated* of how and when it should be done, and though afterward it became *easy* and *habitual*, so as to be done without *forethought*; yet that does not hinder but that the act is *voluntary*, and proceedeth from *election*. So also are the *rashest* actions of *choleric* persons *voluntary* and upon *deliberation*: for who is there but very young children, that hath not *considered* when and how far he *ought*, or safely *may* strike or revile? Seeing then his Lordship agrees with me, that such actions are *necessitated*, and the *fancy* of those that do them *determined* to the action they do, it follows out of his Lordship's own doctrine, that the liberty of *election* does not take away the *necessity* of *electing* this or that *individual* thing. And thus one of his arguments fights against another.

The second argument from Scripture, consisteth in histories of men that did one thing, when if they would, they might have done another; the places are two: one is 1 Kings iii. 10, where the history says, God was pleased that Solomon, who might, if he would, have asked *riches*, or *revenge*, did nevertheless ask *wisdom* at God's hands: the other is the words of St. Peter to Ananias, Acts v. 4: *After it was sold, was it not in thine own power?*

To which the answer is the same with that I answered to the former places, that they prove there is *election*, but do not disprove the *necessity*, which I maintain, of what they so elect.

The fourth argument (for to the third and fifth I shall make but one answer) is to this effect; *If the decrees of God, or his foreknowledge, or the influence of the stars, or the concatenation of causes, or the physical or moral efficacy of causes, or the last dictate of the understanding, or whatsoever it be, do take away true liberty, then Adam before his fall had no true liberty. Quicquid ostendes mihi sic incredulus odi.*

That which I say *necessitateth and determinateth every action*, that his Lordship may no longer doubt of my meaning, *is the sum of all things, which being now existent, conduce and concur to the production of that action hereafter, whereof if any one thing now were wanting, the effect could not be produced.* This *concourse* of *causes*, whereof every one is *determined* to be such as it is by a like concourse of *former* causes, may well be called (in respect they were all set and ordered by the eternal cause of all things, God Almighty) the *decree* of God.

But that the *foreknowledge* of God should be a cause of any thing, cannot be truly said, seeing foreknowledge is knowledge, and knowledge depends on the existence of the things known, and not they on it.

The *influence of the stars* is but a small part of the whole cause, consisting of the concourse of all agents.

Nor does the *concourse of all causes* make one simple *chain* or concatenation, but an innumerable number of chains, joined together, not in all parts, but in the first link God Almighty; and consequently the whole cause of an event, doth not always depend on one single chain, but on many together.

Natural efficacy of *objects* does *determine voluntary* agents, and *necessitates* the *will*, and consequently the *action*; but for *moral* efficacy, I understand not what he means.

The last dictate of the judgment, concerning the good or bad, that may follow on any action, is not properly the *whole cause,* but the last part of it, and yet may be said to produce the effect *necessarily,* in such manner as the last feather may be said to break a horse's back, when there were so many laid on before as there wanted but that one to do it.

Now for his *argument,* that *if the concourse of all the causes necessitate the effect, that then it follows, Adam had no true liberty:* I deny the consequence; for I make not only the *effect,* but also the *election,* of that particular effect *necessary,* inasmuch as the will itself, and each propension of a man during his deliberation, is as much necessitated, and depends on a sufficient cause, as any thing else whatsoever. As for example, it is no more necessary that fire should burn, than that a man or other creature, whose limbs be moved by fancy, should have *election,* that is *liberty,* to do what he hath a fancy to do, though it be not in his *will* or *power* to *choose* his *fancy,* or choose his *election* and *will.*

This doctrine, because my Lord Bishop says he hates, I doubt had better been suppressed, as it should have been, if both your Lordship and he had not pressed me to an answer.

The arguments of greatest consequence, are the third and the fifth, and they fall both into one, namely: *If there be a necessity of all events, that it will follow, that praise and reprehension, and reward and punishment, are all vain and unjust; and that if God should openly forbid, and secretly necessitate the same action, punishing men for what they could not avoid, there would be no belief among them of heaven and hell.*

To oppose hereunto I must borrow an answer from St. Paul, Rom. ix. 20, 21. From the eleventh verse of the chapter to the eighteenth, is laid down the very same objection in these words: *When they,* meaning Esau and Jacob, *were yet unborn, and had done neither good nor evil, that the purpose of God according to election, not by works, but by him that calleth, might remain firm, it was said unto her* (viz. Rebecca) *that the elder should serve the younger, &c. What then shall we say? Is there injustice with God? God forbid. It is not therefore in him that willeth, nor in him that runneth, but in God that showeth mercy. For the Scripture saith to Pharaoh,*

*I have stirred thee up that I might show my power in thee,
and that my name might be set forth in all the earth. Therefore whom God willeth, he hath mercy on, and whom he
willeth he hardeneth.* Thus you see the case put by St. Paul, is
the same with that of my Lord Bishop, and the same objection in these words following:

*Thou wilt ask me then, why does God yet complain, for
who hath resisted his will?*

To this therefore the Apostle answers, not by denying it
was God's *will,* or that the decree of God concerning Esau
was not before he had sinned, or that Esau was not necessitated to do what he did; but thus: *Who art thou, O man, that
interrogatest God? Shall the work say to the workman, why
hast thou made me thus? Hath not the potter power over the
clay, of the same stuff to make one vessel to honour, another
to dishonour?* According therefore to this answer of St. Paul, I
answer my Lord's objection, and say; the *power* of God alone
without other helps is sufficient *justification* of any action he
doth. That which men make amongst themselves here by pacts
and covenants, and call by the name of justice, and according
whereunto men are accounted and termed rightly *just* or *unjust,* is not that by which God Almighty's actions are to be
measured or called just, no more than his counsels are to be
measured by human wisdom. That which he does, is made just
by his doing it; just, I say, in him, though not always just in
us.

For a man that shall command a thing openly, and plot
secretly the hindrance of the same, if he punish him that he so
commandeth, for not doing it, is unjust. So also, his counsels are therefore not in vain, because they be his, whether we
see the use of them or not. When God afflicted Job, he did
object no sin unto him, but justified his afflicting of him, by
telling him of his *power:* (Job xl. 9:) *Hast thou, saith God,
an arm like mine?* (Job xxviii. 4): *Where wert thou when I
laid the foundations of the earth?* and the like. So our Saviour,
(John ix. 3) concerning the man that was born blind, said, it
was not for his sin, or for his parents' sin, but that the power
of God might be shown in him. *Beasts* are subject to death

and torments, yet they cannot sin: it was God's will they should be so. *Power irresistible justifies all actions, really and properly*, in whomsoever it be found; less power does not, and because such power is in God only, he must needs be just in all actions, and we, that not comprehending his counsels, call him to the bar, commit injustice in it.

I am not ignorant of the usual reply to his answer, by distinguishing between *will* and *permission*, as that God Almighty does indeed sometimes *permit* sins, and that he also foreknoweth that the sin he permitteth, shall be committed, but does not *will* it, nor *necessitate* it.

I know also they distinguish the action from the sin of the action, saying, that God Almighty does indeed cause the *action*, whatsoever action it be, but not the *sinfulness* or *irregularity* of it, that is, the *discordance* between the *action* and the *law*. Such distinctions as these dazzle my understanding; I find no difference between the *will* to have a thing done, and the *permission* to do it, when he that permitteth can hinder it, and knows that it will be done unless he hinder it. Nor find I any difference between an *action* and the *sin* of that action; as for example, between the killing of Uriah, and the sin of David in killing Uriah, nor when *one* is *cause* both of the *action* and of the *law*, how *another* can be cause of the *disagreement* between them, no more than how one man making a longer and a shorter garment, another can make the inequality that is between them. This I know; God cannot sin, because his doing a thing makes it just, and consequently, no sin; as also because whatsoever can sin, is subject to another's law, which God is not. And therefore it is blasphemy to say, God can sin; but to say, that God can so order the world, as a sin may be necessarily caused thereby in a man, I do not see how it is any dishonor to him. Howsoever, if such or other *distinctions* can make it clear, that St. Paul did not think Esau's or Pharaoh's actions proceeded from the *will* and *purpose* of God, or that proceeding from his will, could not therefore without injustice be blamed or punished, I will, as soon as I understand them, turn unto my Lord's opinion: for I now hold nothing in all this question betwixt us, but what seemeth to me, not obscurely, but most expressly said in this place by St. Paul. And thus much in answer to his places of Scripture.

To the Arguments from Reason

Of the arguments from *reason*, the first is that which his Lordship saith is drawn from Zeno's beating of his man, which is therefore called *argumentum baculinum*, that is to say, a wooden argument. The story is this; Zeno held, that all actions were necessary; his man therefore being for some fault beaten, excused himself upon the necessity of it: to avoid this excuse, his master pleaded likewise the necessity of beating him. So that not he that maintained, but he that derided the necessity, was beaten, contrary to that his Lordship would infer. And the argument was rather withdrawn than drawn from the story.

The second argument is taken from certain inconveniences which his Lordship thinks would follow such an opinion. It is true that ill use might be made of it, and therefore your Lordship and my Lord Bishop ought, at my request, to keep private what I say here of it. But the inconveniences are indeed none, and what use soever be made of truth, yet truth is truth, and now the question is not, what is fit to be preached, but, what is true.

The first inconvenience he says, is this; *That the laws, which prohibit any action, will be unjust.*

2. *That all consultations are vain.*

3. *That admonitions to men of understanding, are of no more use, than to children, fools, and madmen.*

4. *That, praise, dispraise, reward and punishment, are in vain.*

5, 6. *That counsels, acts, arms, books, instruments, study, tutors, medicines, are in vain.*

To which arguments his Lordship expecting I should answer, by saying, the ignorance of the event were enough to make us use the means, adds, as it were a reply to my answer foreseen, these words: *Alas! how should our not knowing the event be a sufficient motive to make us use the means?*

Wherein his Lordship says right, but my answer is not that which he expecteth: I answer,

First, that the *necessity* of an *action* doth not make the *laws*, that prohibit it, *unjust*. To let pass, that not the *necessity*, but the *will* to break the *law*, maketh the action *unjust*, because the *law* regardeth the *will*, and no other precedent causes of action. And to let pass, that no *law* can possibly be *unjust*, inasmuch as every man maketh, by his consent, the law he is bound to keep, and which consequently must be just, unless a man can be unjust to himself. I say, what *necessary* cause soever precede an *action*, yet if the action be *forbidden*, he that doth it *willingly* may justly be punished. For instance, suppose the law on pain of death prohibit stealing, and that there be a man, who by the strength of temptation is *necessitated* to steal, and is thereupon put to death, does not this punishment deter others from theft? Is it not a cause that others steal not? Doth it not frame and make their wills to justice?

To make the *law*, is therefore to make a *cause* of *justice*, and to *necessitate* justice; and consequently, it is no injustice to make such a law.

The intention of the *law* is not to grieve the *delinquent*, for that which is past, and not to be undone; but to make him and others *just*, that else would not be so, and respecteth not the evil act *past*, but the *good to come*; insomuch as without the good intention for the future, no past act of a delinquent could justify his killing in the sight of God. But you will say, how is it just to kill one man to amend another, if what were done were *necessary*? To this I answer, that men are justly killed, not for that their *actions* are not *necessitated*, but because they are *noxious*, and they are spared and preserved whose actions are not noxious. For where there is no law, there no killing nor anything else can be unjust; and by the right of nature, we destroy, without being unjust, all that is noxious, both beasts and men; and for beasts we kill them justly, when we do it in order to our own preservation, and yet my Lord himself confesseth, that their actions, as being only *spontaneous*, and not *free*, are all *necessitated* and determined to that one thing they shall do. For men, when we make societies or commonwealths, we lay not down our right to kill, excepting in certain cases, as murder, theft or other offensive action; so that the right, which the *commonwealth* hath to put a man to death for crimes, is not created by the *law*, but remains from the first right of *nature*, which every man hath to preserve himself; for that the law doth not take the right away in the case of criminals, who were by the law excepted. Men are not therefore put to death, or punished, for that their theft proceedeth from *election*; but because it was *noxious* and contrary to men's preservation, and the punishment conducing to the preservation of the rest, inasmuch as to punish those that do voluntary hurt, and none else, frameth and maketh men's *wills* such as men would have them. And thus it is plain, that from the *necessity* of a *voluntary* action, cannot be inferred the *injustice* of the *law* that forbiddeth it, or the magistrate that punisheth it.

Secondly, I deny that it maketh *consultations* to be in *vain*; it is the *consultation* that *causeth* a man, and *necessitateth* him to *choose* to do one thing rather than another: so that unless a man say that that cause is in vain which necessitateth the effect, he cannot infer the superfluousness of consultation out of the necessity of the election proceeding from it. But it seemeth his Lordship reasons thus: If I must do this rather that that, I shall do this rather than that, though I consult not at all; which is a false proposition and a false consequence, and no better than this: If I shall live till to-morrow, I shall live till to-morrow, though I run myself through with a sword to-day. If there be a *necessity* that an action shall be done, or that any effect shall be brought to pass, it does not therefore follow, that there is nothing necessarily requisite as a means to bring it to pass; and therefore when it is determined, that one thing shall be chosen before another, it is determined also for what *cause* it shall so be chosen, which cause, for the most part, is *deliberation* or *consultation*, and therefore consultation is not in vain, and indeed the less in vain by how much the election is more necessitated, if *more* and *less* had any place in *necessity*.

The same answer is to be given to the third supposed inconvenience, namely, that *admonitions* are in *vain*; for the admonitions are parts of consultation, the admonitor being a counsellor for the time to him that is admonished.

The fourth pretended inconvenience is, that *praise*, *dispraise*, *reward*, and *punishment* will be in *vain*. To which I answer, that for *praise* and *dispraise*, they depend not at all on the *necessity* of the action praised or dispraised. For what is it else to *praise*, but to say a thing is good? Good, I say, for me, or for somebody else, or for the state and commonwealth? And what is it to say an action is good, but to say it is as I would wish? or as another would have it, or according to the will of the state? that is to say, according to the law. Does my Lord think that no action can please me, or him, or the commonwealth, that should proceed from *necessity*? Things may be therefore *necessary*, and yet *praise-worthy*, as also *necessary*, and yet *dispraised*, and neither of them both in vain, because *praise* and *dispraise*, and likewise *reward* and *punishment*, do by example make and conform the will to good and evil. It was a very great praise in my opinion, that Velleius Paterculus (Lib. II. 35) gives Cato, where he says that he was good by *nature, et quia aliter esse non potuit*.

To the fifth and sixth inconveniences, that *counsels*, *arts*, *arms*, *instruments*, *books*, *study*, *medicines*, and the like, would be *superfluous*, the same answer serves as to the former, that is to say, that this consequence, *if the effect shall necessarily come to pass, then it shall come to pass without its causes*, is a false one, and those things named counsels, arts, arms, &c. are the causes of these effects.

His Lordship's *third* argument consisteth in other *inconveniences*, which he saith will follow, namely, *impiety* and *negligence* of religious duties, as repentance, and *zeal* to God's service, &c.

To which I answer as to the rest, that they follow not. I must confess, if we consider the greatest part of mankind, not as they should be, but as they are, that is, as men, whom either the study of acquiring wealth, or preferment, or whom the appetite of sensual delights, or the impatience of meditating, or the rash embracing of wrong principles, have made unapt to discuss the truth of things: I must, I say, confess that the dispute of this question will rather hurt than help their piety; and therefore if his Lordship had not desired this answer, I should not have written it, nor do I write it but in hopes your Lordship and his will keep it private. Nevertheless in very truth, the *necessity* of events does not of itself draw with it any *impiety* at all. For *piety* consisteth only in *two* things; one, that we honor God in our hearts, which is, that we think as highly of his *power* as we can, for to honor anything is nothing else but to think it to be of great power; the other is, that we signify that honor and esteem by your words and actions, which is called *cultus*, or *worship of God*. He therefore that thinketh that all things proceed from God's *eternal will*, and consequently are *necessary*, does he not think God *omnipotent*? Does he not esteem of his *power* as highly as is possible? which is to honor God as much as may be in his heart. Again, he that thinketh so, is he not more apt by *external* acts and words to acknowledge it, than he that thinketh otherwise? yet is this external acknowledgment the same thing which we call *worship*. So that this opinion fortifies *piety* in both kinds, external and internal; therefore is far from destroying it. And for *repentance*, which is nothing else but a glad returning into the right way, after the grief of being out of the way; though the cause that made him go astray were necessary, yet there is no reason why he should not grieve; and, again though the cause why he returned into the way were necessary, there remained still the causes of joy. So that the *necessity* of the actions taketh away neither of those parts of *repentance*, grief for the error, and joy for returning.

And for *prayer*, whereas he saith that the *necessity* of things destroy *prayer*, I deny it; for though *prayer* be none of the *causes* that *move* God's *will*, his will being unchangeable, yet since we find in God's word, he will not give his blessings but to those that ask, the motive of prayer is the same. *Prayer* is the gift of God no less than the *blessing*, and the prayer is decreed together in the same decree wherein the blessing is decreed. It is manifest that *thanksgiving* is no cause of the blessing past, and that which is past is sure and necessary, yet even amongst men thanks is in use as an acknowledgment of the benefit past, though we should expect no new benefit for our gratitude. And prayer to God Almighty is but thanksgiving for God's blessings in general, and though it precede the particular thing we ask, yet it is not a cause or means of it, but a signification that we expect nothing but from God, in such manner, as he, not as we, will; and our Savior by word of mouth bids us pray, *thy will*, not our will, *be done*, and by example teaches us the same; for he prayed thus, *Father if it be thy will, let this cup pass*, &c. The end of prayer, as of thanksgiving, is not to *move* but to *honor* God Almighty, in acknowledging that what we ask can be effected by him only.

The fourth argument from reason is this: the order, beauty, and perfection of the world requireth that in the universe should be agents of all sorts; some necessary, some free, some contingent. He that shall make all things necessary, or all things free, or all things contingent, doth overthrow the beauty and perfection of the world.

In which argument I observe, first a *contradiction;* for seeing he that *maketh* anything, in that he maketh it, maketh it to be *necessary;* it followeth that he that maketh all things, maketh all things necessarily to be: as if a workman make a garment, the garment must necessarily be; so if God make every thing, every thing must necessarily be. Perhaps the beauty of the world requireth, though we know it not, that some agents should work without deliberation (which his lordship calls *necessary* agents) and some agents with deliberation (and those both he and I call *free* agents) and that some agents should work, and we not know how (and their effects we both call *contingents*); but this hinders not but that he that electeth may have his *election* necessarily determined to *one* by *former* causes, and that which is *contingent,* and imputed to fortune, be nevertheless *necessary* and depend on *precedent* necessary causes. For by *contingent,* men do not mean that which hath *no* cause, but that which hath not for cause anything that we perceive; as for example, when a traveller meets with a shower, the journey had a cause, and the rain had a cause sufficient to produce it; but because the journey caused not the rain, nor the rain the journey, we say they were contingent one to another. And thus you see that though there be three sorts of events *necessary, contingent,* and *free,* yet they may be *all* necessary without destruction of the beauty or perfection of the universe.

To the first argument from reason, which is, *That if liberty be taken away, the nature and formal reason of sin is taken away;* I answer by denying the consequence: the nature of sin consisteth in this, that the *action* done proceed from our *will* and be against the *law.* A judge in judging whether it be sin or no, which is done against the law, looks at no higher cause of the action, than the will of the doer. Now when I say the action was *necessary,* I do not say it was done *against* the will of the doer, but *with* his will, and *necessarily,* because man's will, that is every volition or act of the will and purpose of man had a *sufficient,* and therefore a *necessary* cause, and consequently every *voluntary* action was *necessitated.* An action therefore may be *voluntary* and a *sin,* and nevertheless be *necessary;* and because God may afflict by a right derived from his *omnipotence,* though sin were not, and because the example of punishment on voluntary sinners, is the cause that produceth justice, and maketh sin less frequent, for God to punish such sinners, as I have said before, is no injustice. And thus you have my answer to his Lordship's objections both out of Scripture, and from reason.

Certain Distinctions, Which His Lordship Supposing Might Be Brought to Evade His Arguments, Are by Him Removed

He says a man may perhaps answer, that the *necessity* of things held by him, is not a *stoical* necessity, but a *Christian* necessity, &c. But this distinction I have not used, nor indeed ever heard before, nor could I think any man could make *stoical* and *Christian* two kinds of *necessity*, though they may be two kinds of *doctrine*. Nor have I drawn my answer to his Lordship's arguments from the authority of any sect, but from the nature of the things themselves.

But here I must take notice of certain words of his Lordship's in this place, as making against his own tenet. *Where all the causes*, saith he, *being joined together, and subordinate one to another, do make but one total cause, if any one cause, much more the first, in the whole series or subordination of causes, be necessary, it determines the rest, and without doubt maketh the effect necessary*. For that which I call the *necessary* cause of any effect, is the *joining* together of all causes subordinate to the first, into one total cause. *If any of these*, saith he, *especially the first, produce its effect necessarily, then all the rest* are determined. Now it is manifest, that the first cause is a necessary cause of all the effects that are next and immediate to it, and therefore by his Lordship's own reason all effects are necessary.

Nor is that distinction of necessary in respect of the *first cause*, and necessary in respect of *second causes*, mine; it does, as his Lordship well notes, imply a contradiction. But the distinction of *free* into *free from compulsion*, and *free from necessitation*, I acknowledge. For to be *free from compulsion* is to do a thing so as *terror* be not the cause of his *will* to do it; for a man is then only said to be compelled, when fear makes him willing to it: as when a man willingly throws his goods into the sea to save himself, or submits to his enemy for fear of being killed. Thus all men that do anything for *love*, or *revenge*, or *lust*, are *free from compulsion*, and yet their actions may be as necessary as those that are done by compulsion; for sometimes other passions work as forcibly as fear. But *free from necessitation*, I say, no man can be, and it is that which his Lordship undertook to disprove.

This *distinction*, his Lordship says, uses to be *fortified* by two reasons, but they are not mine. The first he says, is, that it is granted by all divines, that a *hypothetical necessity*, or necessity upon supposition, may stand with liberty. That you may understand this, I will give you an example of *hypothetical necessity*. If *I shall live, I shall eat*. This is a *hypothetical necessity*. Indeed it is a necessary proposition, that is to say, it is necessary that that proposition should be true whensoever uttered, but it is not the necessity of the thing, nor is it therefore necessary that the man should live, nor that the man should eat. I do not use to *fortify* my distinctions with such reasons; let his Lordship confute them how he will, it contents me; but I would have your Lordship take notice hereby, how easy and plain a thing, but withal false, with the grave usage of such terms as *hypothetical necessity*, and *necessity* upon *supposition*, and such like terms of Schoolmen, may be obscured and made to seem *profound learning*.

The second reason that may confirm the distinction of *free from compulsion*, and *free from necessitation*, he says is, that God and good angels do good necessarily, and yet are more free than we. This reason, though I had no need of, yet I think it so far forth good, as it is true that God and good angels do good necessarily, and yet are free; but because I find not in the articles of our faith, nor in the decrees of our church, set down in what manner I am to conceive God and good angels to work by necessity, or in what sense they work *freely*, I suspend my sentence in that point, and am content that there be a *freedom from compulsion*, and yet no *freedom from necessitation*, as hath been proved, in that a man may be necessitated to some action without threats and without fear of danger. But how my Lord can avoid the consisting together of *freedom* and *necessity*, supposing God and good angels are freer than men, and yet do good necessarily, that we must examine: *I confess*, saith he, *that God and good angels are more free than we, that is, intensively in degree of freedom, not extensively in the latitude of the object, according to a liberty of exercise not of specification.*

Again, we have here two distinctions that are no distinctions, but made to seem so by terms invented by I know not whom to cover ignorance, and blind the understanding of the reader: for it cannot be conceived that there is any liberty greater, than for a man to do what he will. One heat may be more intensive than another, but not one liberty than another; he that can do what he will, hath all liberty possible, and he that cannot, hath none at all. Also *liberty*, as his Lordship says the Schools call it, of *exercise*, which is as I have said before, a liberty to do or not to do, cannot be without a *liberty*, which they call, of *specification*, that is to say, a liberty to do, or not to do this or that in particular. For how can a man conceive he hath liberty to do anything, that hath not liberty to do this, or that, or somewhat in particular? If a man be forbidden in Lent to eat this, and that, and every other particular kind of flesh, how can he be understood to have a liberty to eat flesh, more than he that hath no licence at all? You may by this again see the vanity of distinctions used in the *Schools*, and I do not doubt but that the imposing of them, by authority of *doctors* in the *Church*, hath been a great cause that men have laboured, though by sedition and evil courses, to shake them off; for nothing is more apt to beget hatred, than the tyrannizing over men's reason and understanding, especially when it is done, not by the Scriptures, but by the pretense of learning, and more judgment than that of other men.

In the next place his Lordship bringeth two arguments against distinguishing between *free from compulsion* and *free from necessitation*.

The first is, that *election* is opposite not only to *coaction* or *compulsion*, but also *necessitation* or determination to one. This is it he was to prove from the beginning, and therefore bringeth no new argument to prove it; and to those brought formerly, I have already answered. And in this place I deny again, that election is opposite to either; for when a man is compelled, for example, to subject himself to an enemy or to die, he hath still election left him, and a deliberation to bethink which of the two he can better endure. And he that is led to prison by force, hath election, and may deliberate whether he will be hauled and trained on the ground, or make use of his own feet: likewise when there is no *compulsion*, but the strength of *temptation* to do an evil action, being greater than the motives to *abstain*, it necessarily determines him to the doing of it; yet he deliberates while sometimes the motives to do, sometimes the motives to forbear, are working on him, and consequently he *electeth* which he will. But commonly when we see and know the strength that moves us, we acknowledge *necessity;* but when we see not, or mark not the force that moves us, we then think there is none, and that it is not *causes* but *liberty* that produceth the action. Hence it is that they think he does not choose this, that of necessity chooses it; but they might as well say, fire doth not burn, because it burns of necessity.

The second argument is not so much an argument as a distinction, to show in what sense it may be said that *voluntary* actions are *necessitated*, and in what sense not. And therefore his Lordship allegeth, as from the authority of the *Schools*, and that which rippeth up the bottom of the *question*, that there is a double act of the *will*. The one, he says, is *actus imperatus*, an act done at the command of the will, by some inferior faculty of the soul; as to open or shut one's eyes; and this act may be compelled: the other, he says, is *actus elicitus*, an act allured or drawn forth by allurement out of the will, as to *will*, to *choose*, to *elect*; this he says cannot be compelled. Wherein, letting pass that metaphorical speech of attributing command and subjection to the faculties of the soul, as if they made a commonwealth or family within themselves, and could speak one to another, which is very improper in searching the truth of a question, you may observe, first, that to compel a *voluntary* act, is nothing else but to will it; for it is all one to say, my will commands the shutting of my eyes, or the doing of any other action; and to say, I have the will to shut my eyes: so that *actus imperatus*, here, might as easily have been said in English a *voluntary action*, but that they that invented the term, understood not anything it signified.

Secondly, you may observe, that *actus elicitus*, is exemplified by these words, to *will*, to *elect*, to *choose*, which are all one, and so to will is here made an act of the will; and indeed as the will is a faculty or power in a man's soul, so to will is an act of it according to that power; but as it is absurdly said, that to dance is an act allured or drawn by fair means out of the ability to dance; so is it also to say, that to will is an act allured or drawn out of the power to will, which power is commonly called the will. Howsoever it be, the sum of his Lordship's distinction is, that a *voluntary* act may be done by *compulsion,* that is to say, by foul means, but to will that, or any act, cannot be but by allurement, or fair means. Now seeing fair means, allurements, and enticements, produce the action which they do produce, as *necessarily* as foul means and threatening; it follows, that to *will* may be made as *necessary* as anything that is done by *compulsion.* So that distinction of *actus imperatus* and *actus elicitus* are but words, and of no effect against necessity.

His Lordship in the rest of his discourse, reckoneth up the opinion of certain professions of men, touching the causes wherein the necessity of things, which they maintain, consisteth. And first he saith, the *astrologer* deriveth his *necessity* from the *stars;* secondly, that the *physician* attributeth it to the *temper* of the body. For my part, I am not of their opinion, because, neither the stars alone, nor the temperature of the patient alone, is able to produce any effect, without the concurrence of all other agents. For there is hardly any one action, how casual soever it seem, to the causing whereof concur not whatsoever is *in rerum naturâ,* which because it is a great paradox, and depends on many antecedent speculations, I do not press in this place. Thirdly, he disputeth against the opinion of them that say, *external objects* presented to men of such and such temperatures, do make their actions *necessary;* and says, the power such objections have over us, proceeds from our own fault: but that is nothing to the purpose, if such fault of ours proceedeth from causes not in our own power, and therefore that opinion may hold true for all that answer.

Further he says, *prayer, fasting,* &c. may alter our *habits;* it is true, but when they do so, they are *causes* of the contrary *habit,* and make it *necessary,* as the former habit had been necessary, if *prayer, fasting,* &c. had not been. Besides, we are not moved or disposed to prayer or any other action, but by outward objects, as pious company, godly preachers, or something equivalent. Fourthly, he says a resolved mind is not easily surprised, as the mind of Ulysses, who when others wept, alone wept not; and of the philosopher, that abstained from striking, because he found himself angry; and of him that poured out the water when he was thirsty, and the like. Such things I confess have, or may have been done, and do prove only that it was not necessary for Ulysses then to weep, nor for that philosopher to strike, nor for that other man to drink; but it does not prove that it was not necessary for Ulysses then to abstain, as he did, from weeping, nor for the philosopher to abstain, as he did, from striking, nor for the other man to forbear drinking, and yet that was the thing his Lordship ought to have proved. Lastly his Lordship confesses, that the *dispositions* of objects may be *dangerous* to *liberty,* but cannot be *destructive.* To which I answer, it is impossible: for *liberty* is never in any other danger than to be lost; and if it cannot be lost, which he confesses, I may infer, it can be in no danger at all.

The fourth opinion his Lordship rejecteth, is of them that make the will necessarily to follow the last dictate of the understanding; but it seems his Lordship understands that tenet in another sense than I do; for he speaketh as if they that held it, did suppose men must dispute the sequel of every action they do, great and small, to the least grain; which is a thing his Lordship, with reason, thinks untrue. But I understand it to signify, that the *will* follows the *last* opinion or *judgment* immediately preceding the *action,* concerning whether it be good to do it or not, whether he have weighed it long before, or not at all, and that I take to be the meaning of them that hold it. As for example, when a man strikes, his will to strike follows necessarily that thought he had of the sequel of his stroke, immediately before the lifting up of his hand. Now if it be understood in that sense, the *last* dictate of the understanding does *necessitate* the *action,* though not as the whole cause, yet as the last cause, as the last feather necessitates the breaking of a horse's back, when there are so many laid on before, as there needed but the addition of one to make the weight sufficient.

That which his Lordship allegeth against this, is first, out of a poet, who in the person of Medea says,

> "Video meliora, proboque,
> Deteriora sequor."

But that saying, as pretty as it is, is not true; for though Medea saw many reasons to forbear killing her children, yet the last dictate of her judgment was, that the present revenge on her husband outweighed them all, and thereupon the wicked action *necessarily* followed. Then the story of the Roman, who of two competitors, said, one had the better reason, but the other must have the office. This also maketh against his Lordship, for the last dictate of his judgment that had the bestowing of the office, was this, that it was better to take a great bribe, than reward a great merit.

Thirdly, he objects that things nearer the sense, move more powerfully than reason; what followeth thence but this, the sense of the present good is commonly more immediate to the action, than the foresight of the evil consequence to come? Fourthly, whereas his Lordship says, that do what a man can, he shall sorrow more for the death of his son than for the sin of his soul, makes nothing to the last dictate of the understanding; but it argues plainly, that sorrow for sin is not *voluntary*, and by consequence, that *repentance* proceedeth from causes.

The last part of this discourse containeth his Lordship's opinions about reconciling *liberty* with the *prescience* and *decrees* of God, otherwise than some *divines* have done, against whom, he says, he had formerly written a treatise, out of which he repeateth only two things: one is, *That we ought not to desert a certain truth, for not being able to comprehend the certain manner of it.* And I say the same, as for example, that his Lordship ought not to desert this certain truth, *that there are certain and* necessary causes *which make every man to* will *what he willeth, though he do not* yet conceive in what manner the *will* of man is *caused.* And yet I think the manner of it is not very hard to conceive, seeing we see daily, that *praise, dispraise, reward,* and *punishment, good* and *evil,* sequels of men's *actions* retained in *memory,* do frame and make us to the *election* of whatsoever it be that we elect, and that the memory of such things proceeds from the *senses,* and *sense* from the operation of the objects of sense, which are external to us, and governed only by God Almighty; and by consequence all *actions,* even of *free* and *voluntary* agents are necessary.

The other thing that he repeateth, is, that the best way to reconcile *contingence* and *liberty* with *prescience* and the *decrees* of God, is to subject future *contingencies* to the *aspect of God.* The same is also my opinion, but contrary to what his Lordship all this while labored to prove. For hitherto he held *liberty* and *necessity,* that is to say, *liberty* and the *decrees* of God, irreconcilable, unless the *aspect of God,* which word appeareth now the first time in this discourse, signify somewhat else besides *God's will* and *decree,* which I cannot understand. But he adds that we must subject them, according to that *presentiality* which they have in eternity, which he says cannot be done by them that conceive *eternity* to be an *everlasting succession,* but only by them that conceive it as an *indivisible point.* To which I answer, that as soon as I can conceive *eternity* to be an *indivisible point,* or anything but an *everlasting succession,* I will renounce all that I have written on this subject. I know St. Thomas Aquinas calls *eternity, nunc stans,* an *ever-abiding now;* which is easy enough to say, but though I fain would, yet I could never conceive it: they that can, are more happy than I. But in the mean time his Lordship alloweth all men to be of my opinion, save only those that can conceive in their minds a *nunc stans,* which I think are none. I understand as little how it can be true his Lordship says, that God is not *just,* but *justice* itself; not *wise,* but *wisdom* itself; not *eternal,* but *eternity* itself, nor how he concludes thence, that *eternity* is a *point indivisble,* and not a *succession,* nor in what sense it can be said, that an *infinite point,* and wherein is no *succession,* can comprehend all *time,* though time be *successive.* These phrases I find not in the Scripture: I wonder therefore what was the design of the Schoolmen to bring them up, unless they thought a man could not be a true Christian unless his understanding be first strangled with such hard sayings. And thus much for answer to his Lordship's discourse, wherein I think not only his *squadrons of arguments,* but also his *reserve of distinctions,* are defeated. And now your Lordship shall have my doctrine concerning the same question, with my *reasons* for it, positively, and as briefly as I can, without any terms of *art,* in plain English.

My Opinion About Liberty and Necessity

First I conceive, that when it cometh into a man's mind to do or not to do some certain action, if he have no time to *deliberate,* the doing it or abstaining *necessarily* follow the *present* thought he hath of the *good* or *evil* consequence thereof to himself. As for example, in sudden *anger,* the *action* shall follow the thought of *revenge;* in sudden *fear,* the thought of *escape.* Also when a man hath time to *deliberate,* but deliberates not, because never anything appeared that could make him doubt of the consequence, the *action* follows his opinion of the *goodness* or *harm* of it. These actions I call VOLUNTARY, my Lord, if I understand him aright that calls them SPONTANEOUS. I call them *voluntary,* because those actions that follow immediately the *last* appetite, are *voluntary,* and here where is one only appetite, that one is the last. Besides, I see it is reasonable to punish a *rash* action, which could not be justly done by man to man, unless the same were *voluntary.* For no *action* of a man can be said to be without *deliberation,* though never so sudden, because it is supposed he had time to *deliberate* all the precedent time of his life, whether he should do that kind of action or not. And hence it is, that he that killeth in a sudden passion of *anger,* shall nevertheless be justly put to *death,* because all the time, wherein he was able to consider whether to kill were good or evil, shall be held for one continual *deliberation,* and consequently the killing shall be judged to proceed from *election*.

Secondly, I conceive when a man *deliberates* whether he shall do a thing or not do it, that he does nothing else but consider whether it be better for himself to do it or not to do it. And to *consider* an action, is to imagine the *consequences* of it, both *good* and *evil*. From whence is to be inferred, that *deliberation* is nothing else but *alternate* imagination of the *good* and *evil* sequels of an *action*, or, which is the same thing, alternate *hope* and *fear*, or alternate *appetite* to do or quit the action of which he *deliberateth*.

Thirdly, I conceive that in all *deliberations*, that is to say, in all alternate *succession* of contrary *appetites*, the last is that which we call the WILL, and is immediately next before the doing of the action, or next before the doing of it become impossible. All other *appetites* to do, and to quit, that come upon a man during his deliberations, are called *intentions* and *inclinations*, but not *wills*, there being but one *will*, which also in this case may be called the *last will*, though the *intentions* change often.

Fourthly, I conceive that those *actions*, which a man is said to do upon *deliberation*, are said to be *voluntary*, and done upon *choice* and *election*, so that *voluntary* action, and action proceeding from *election* is the same thing; and that of a *voluntary agent*, it is all one to say, he is *free*, and to say, he hath not made an end of *deliberating*.

Fifthly, I conceive *liberty* to be rightly defined in this manner: *Liberty is the absence of all the impediments to action that are not contained in the nature and intrinsical quality of the agent.* As for example, the water is said to descend *freely*, or to have *liberty* to descend by the channel of the river, because there is no impediment that way, but not across, because the banks are impediments. And though the water cannot ascend, yet men never say it wants the *liberty* to ascend, but the *faculty* or *power*, because the impediment is in the nature of the water, and intrinsical. So also we say, he that is tied, wants the *liberty* to go, because the impediment is not in him, but in his bands; whereas we say not so of him that is sick or lame, because the impediment is in himself.

Sixthly, I conceive that nothing taketh beginning from *itself*, but from the *action* of some other immediate *agent* without itself. And that therefore, when first a man hath an *appetite* or *will* to something, to which immediately before he had no appetite nor will, the *cause* of his *will*, is not the *will* itself, but *something* else not in his own disposing. So that whereas it is out of controversy, that of *voluntary* actions the *will* is the *necessary* cause, and by this which is said, the *will* is also *caused* by other things whereof it disposeth not, it followeth, that *voluntary* actions have all of them *necessary* causes, and therefore are *necessitated*. *Cf. P. 166 # 11-12*

Seventhly, I hold that to be a *sufficient cause*, to which nothing is wanting that is needful to the producing of the *effect*. The same also is a *necessary* cause. For if it be possible that a *sufficient* cause shall not bring forth the *effect*, then there wanteth somewhat which was needful to the producing of it, and so the *cause* was not *sufficient*; but if it be impossible that a *sufficient* cause should not produce the *effect*, then is a *sufficient* cause a *necessary* cause, for that is said to produce an effect *necessarily* that cannot but produce it. Hence it is manifest, that whatsoever is produced, is produced *necessarily*; for whatsoever is produced hath had a *sufficient* cause to produce it, or else it had not been; and therefore also *voluntary* actions are *necessitated*.

Lastly, that ordinary *definition* of a *free agent*, namely, *that a free agent is that, which, when all things are present which are needful to produce the* effect, *can nevertheless not produce it*, implies a contradiction, and is nonsense; being as much as to say, the cause may be *sufficient*, that is to say, *necessary*, and yet the effect shall not follow.

My Reasons

For the first five points, wherein it is explicated I, what *spontaneity* is; II, what *deliberation* is; III, what *will*, *propension*, and *appetite* are; IV, what a *free agent* is: V, what *liberty* is; there can no other proof be offered but every man's own experience, by reflection on himself, and remembering what he useth in his mind, that is, what he himself meaneth when he saith an action is *spontaneous*, a man *deliberates*; such is his *will*, that *agent* or that *action* is *free*. Now he that reflecteth so on himself, cannot but be satisfied, that *deliberation is the consideration of the good and evil sequels of an action to come*; that by *spontaneity* is meant *inconsiderate action*, or else nothing is meant by it; that *will* is the *last act of our deliberation*; that a *free agent* is he *that can do if he will*, and *forbear if he will*; and that *liberty* is *the absence of external impediments*. But to those that out of custom speak not what they conceive, but what they hear, and are not able, or will not take the pains to consider what they think when they hear such words, no argument can be sufficient, because *experience* and *matter of fact* are not verified by other men's arguments, but by every man's own *sense* and *memory*. For example, how can it be proved that to *love* a thing and to think it *good* is all one, to a man that doth not mark his own meaning by those words? Or how can it be proved that *eternity* is not *nunc stans* to a man that says those words by custom, and never considers how he can conceive the thing in his mind?

Also the sixth point, that a man cannot imagine anything to begin *without a cause*, can no other way be made known, but by trying how he can imagine it; but if he try, he shall find as much reason, if there be no cause of the thing, to conceive it should begin at one time as another, that he hath equal reason to think it should begin at all times, which is impossible, and therefore he must think there was some special cause why it began then, rather than sooner or later; or else that it began never, but was *eternal*.

For the seventh point, which is, that all *events* have *necessary* causes, it is there proved, in that they have *sufficient* causes. Further let us in this place also suppose any event never so casual, as the throwing, for example, *ames ace* upon a pair of dice, and see, if it must not have been *necessary* before it was thrown. For seeing it was thrown, it had a *beginning*, and consequently a *sufficient* cause to produce it, consisting partly in the *dice*, partly in outward things, as the posture of the parts of the *hand*, the measure of *force* applied by the caster, the posture of the parts of the *table*, and the like. In sum, there was nothing wanting which was necessarily requisite to the producing of that particular cast, and consequently the cast was necessarily thrown; for if it had not been thrown, there had wanted somewhat requisite to the throwing of it, and so the cause had not been *sufficient*. In the like manner it may be proved that every other accident, how *contingent* soever it seem, or how *voluntary* soever it be, is produced *necessarily*, which is that that my Lord Bishop disputes against. The same may be proved also in this manner. Let the case be put, for example, of the weather. *It is necessary that to-morrow it shall rain or not rain.* If therefore it be not *necessary* it shall rain, it is *necessary* it shall not rain, otherwise there is no necessity that the proposition, *it shall rain or not rain,* should be true. I know there be some that say, it may necessarily be true that one of the two shall come to pass, but not, singly that it shall rain, or that it shall not rain, which is as much to say, *one* of them is *necessary*, yet neither of them is *necessary*; and therefore to seem to avoid that absurdity, they make a distinction, that neither of them is true *determinate,* but *indeterminate*; which distinction either signifies no more but this, one of them is true, but we know not which, and so the necessity remains, though we know it not; or if the meaning of the distinction be not that, it hath no meaning, and they might as well have said, one of them is true *Titirice,* but neither of them, *Tu patulice.*

The last thing, in which also consisteth the whole controversy, namely that there is no such thing as an agent, *which when all things requisite to action are present, can nevertheless forbear to produce it*; or, which is all one, that there is no such thing as *freedom from necessity*, is easily inferred from that which hath been before alleged. For if it be an *agent*, it can *work*; and if it *work*, there is nothing wanting of what is requisite to produce the *action*, and consequently the cause of the action is *sufficient*; and if *sufficient*, then also *necessary*, as hath been proved before.

And thus you see how the *inconveniences*, which his Lordship objecteth must follow upon the holding of *necessity*, are avoided, and the *necessity* itself *demonstratively* proved. To which I could add, if I thought it good logic, the *inconvenience* of denying *necessity*, as that it destroyeth both the *decrees* and the *prescience* of God Almighty; for whatsoever God hath *purposed* to bring to pass by *man*, as an instrument, or foreseeth shall come to pass; a man, if he have *liberty*, such as his Lordship affirmeth, from *necessitation*, might frustrate, and make not to come to pass, and God should either not *foreknow* it, and not *decree* it, or he should *foreknow* such things shall be, as shall never be, and *decree* that which shall never *come to pass*.

This is all that hath come into my mind touching this question since I last considered it. And I humbly beseech your Lordship to communicate it only to my Lord Bishop. And so praying God to prosper your Lordship in all your designs, I take leave, and am,

My most noble and most obliging Lord,

Your most humble servant,

Rouen; *Aug.* 20, 1652.*   THOMAS HOBBES.

* In the first edition of 1654 this date is 1646.

PART 4

CITIZENS AND THE LAW

DE CORPORE POLITICO*—PART THE FIRST
Laws of Nature

Chapter 1

1. *Men by nature equal.* In a former treatise of human nature already printed, hath been set forth the whole nature of man, consisting in the powers natural of his body and mind, and may all be comprehended in these four, *strength of body, experience, reason,* and *passion.*

2. In this, it will be expedient to consider in what estate of security this our nature hath placed us, and what probability it hath left us, of continuing and preserving ourselves against the violence of one another. And first, if we consider how little odds there is of strength or knowledge, between men of mature age, and with how great facility he that is the weaker in strength or in wit, or in both, may utterly destroy the power of the stronger; since there needeth but little force to the taking away of a man's life, we may conclude, that men considered in mere nature, ought to admit amongst themselves equality; and that he that claimeth no more, may be esteemed moderate.

3. *By vain glory indisposed to allow equality with themselves, to others.* On the other side, considering the great difference there is in men, from the diversity of their passions, how some are vainly glorious, and hope for precedency and superiority above their fellows, not only when they are equal in power, but also when they are inferior; we must needs acknowledge that it must necessarily follow, that those men who are moderate, and look for no more but equality of nature, shall be obnoxious to the force of others, that will attempt to subdue them. And from hence shall proceed a general diffidence in mankind, and mutual fear one of another.

4. *Apt to provoke another by comparisons.* Further,

*From *De Corpore Politico* (Molesworth Ed. 1839, Vol. IV of English Works), Part I, Chapters 1-6; Part II, Chapters 1-10. On addition of topical headings, see note, p. 182.

since men by natural passion are divers ways offensive one to another, every man thinking well of himself, and hating to see the same in others, they must needs provoke one another by words, and other signs of contempt and hatred, which are incident to all comparison, till at last they must determine the pre-eminence by strength and force of body.

5. Apt to encroach one upon another. Moreover, considering that many men's appetites carry them to one and the same end; which end sometimes can neither be enjoyed in common, nor divided, it followeth, that the stronger must enjoy it alone, and that it be decided by battle who is the stronger. And thus the greatest part of men, upon no assurance of odds, do nevertheless, through vanity, or comparison, or appetite, provoke the rest, that otherwise would be contented with equality.

6. Right defined. And forasmuch as necessity of nature maketh men to will and desire bonum sibi, that which is good for themselves, and to avoid that which is hurtful; but most of all, the terrible enemy of nature, death, from whom we expect both the loss of all power, and also the greatest of bodily pains in the losing; it is not against reason, that a man doth all he can to preserve his own body and limbs both from death and pain. And that which is not against reason, men call right, or jus, or blameless liberty of using our own natural power and ability. It is therefore a right of nature, that every man may preserve his own life and limbs, with all the power he hath.

7. Right to the end, implieth right to the means. And because where a man hath right to the end, and the end cannot be attained without the means, that is, without such things as are necessary to the end, it is consequent that it is not against reason, and therefore right, for a man to use all means, and do whatsoever action is necessary for the preservation of his body.

8. Every man his own judge by nature. Also, every man by right of nature, is judge himself of the necessity of the means, and of the greatness of the danger. For if it be against reason, that I be judge of mine own danger myself,

N.B

"The terrible enemy of nature - death"
compare w Epicurus - "Death is nothing to us"

then it is reason, that another man be judge thereof. But the same reason that maketh another man judge of those things that concern me, maketh me also judge of that that concerneth him. And therefore I have reason to judge of his sentence, whether it be for my benefit, or not.

9. *Every man's strength and knowledge for his own use.* As a man's judgment in right of nature is to be employed for his own benefit, so also the strength, knowledge, and art, of every man is then rightly employed, when he useth it for himself; else must not a man have right to preserve himself.

10. *Every man by nature hath right to all things.* Every man by nature hath right to all things, that is to say, to do whatsoever he listeth to whom he listeth, to possess, use, and enjoy all things he will and can. For seeing all things he willeth, must therefore be good unto him in his own judgment, because he willeth them, and may tend to his preservation some time or other, or he may judge so, and we have made him judge thereof, section 8, it followeth, that all things may rightly also be done by him. And for this cause it is rightly said, *Natura dedit omnia omnibus*, that Nature hath given all things to all men; insomuch, that *jus* and *utile*, right and profit, is the same thing. But that right of all men to all things, is in effect no better than if no man had right to any thing. For there is little use and benefit of the right a man hath, when another as strong, or stronger than himself, hath right to the same.

11. *War and peace defined.* Seeing then to the offensiveness of man's nature one to another, there is added a right of every man to every thing, whereby one man invadeth with right, and another man with right resisteth, and men live thereby in perpetual diffidence, and study how to preoccupate each other; the estate of men in this natural liberty, is the estate of war. For *war* is nothing else but that time wherein the will and contention of contending by force, is either by words or actions sufficiently declared; and the time which is not war, is *peace*.

12. *Men by nature in the state of war.* The estate of hostility and war being such, as thereby nature itself is destroyed,

and men kill one another, (as we know also that it is, both by the experience of savage nations that live at this day, and by the histories of our ancestors the old inhabitants of Germany, and other now civil countries, where we find the people few, and short lived, and without the ornaments and comforts of life, which by peace and society are usually invented and procured) he therefore that desireth to live in such an estate as is the estate of liberty and right of all to all, contradicteth himself. For every man by natural necessity desireth his own good, to which this estate is contrary, wherein we suppose contention between men by nature equal, and able to destroy one another.

13. In manifest inequality might is right. Seeing this right of protecting ourselves by our own discretion and force, proceedeth from danger, and that danger from the equality between men's forces, much more reason is there, that a man prevent such equality before the danger cometh, and before the necessity of battle. A man therefore that hath another man in his power to rule or govern, to do good to, or harm, hath right, by the advantage of this his present power, to take caution at his pleasure, for his security against that other in time to come. He therefore that hath already subdued his adversary, or gotten into his power any other, that either by infancy, or weakness, is unable to resist him, by right of nature may take the best caution, that such infant, or such feeble and subdued person can give him, of being ruled and governed by him for the time to come. For seeing we intend always our own safety and preservation, we manifestly contradict that our intention, if we willingly dismiss such a one, and suffer him at once to gather strength and be our enemy. Out of which may also be collected, that irresistible might, in the state of nature, is right.

14. Reason dictateth peace. But since it is supposed by the equality of strength, and other natural faculties of men, that no man is of might sufficient, to assure himself for any long time, of preserving himself thereby, whilst be remaineth in the state of hostility and war; reason therefore dictateth to every man for his own good, to seek after peace, as far

forth as there is hope to attain the same; and strengthen himself with all the help he can procure, for his own defense against those, from whom such peace cannot be obtained; and to do all those things which necessarily conduce thereunto.

Chapter 2

1. **The law of nature consisteth not in consent of men, but in reason.** What it is we call the law of nature, is not agreed upon by those, that have hitherto written. For the most part, such writers as have occasion to affirm, that anything is against the law of nature, do allege no more than this, that it is against the consent of all nations, or the wisest and most civil nations. But it is not agreed upon, who shall judge which nations are the wisest. Others make that against the law of nature, which is contrary to the consent of all mankind; which definition cannot be allowed, because then no man could offend against the law of nature; for the nature of every man is contained under the nature of mankind. But forasmuch as all men are carried away by the violence of their passion, and by evil customs do those things which are commonly said to be against the law of nature; it is not the consent of passions, or consent in some error gotten by custom, that makes the law of nature. Reason is no less of the nature of man than passion, and is the same in all men, because all men agree in the will to be directed and governed in the way to that which they desire to attain, namely, their own good, which is the work of reason: there can therefore be no other law of nature than reason, nor no other precepts of *natural law*, than those which declare unto us the ways of peace, where the same may be obtained, and of defense where it may not.

2. **That every man divest himself of the right he hath to all things, is one precept of nature.** One precept of the law of nature therefore is this, *that every man divest himself of the right he hath to all things by nature.* For when divers men having right not only to all things else, but to one another's persons, if they use the same, there ariseth thereby invasion on the one part, and resistance on the other, which is *war*, and therefore contrary to the law of nature, the sum whereof consisteth in making peace.

3. *What it is to relinquish and transfer one's right.* When N.B.
a man divesteth and putteth from himself his right, he
either simply relinquisheth it, or transferreth the same to
another man. To *relinquish* it, is by sufficient signs to declare, that it is his will no more to do that action, which of
right he might have done before. To *transfer* right to another,
is by sufficient signs to declare to that other accepting thereof,
that it is his will not to resist, or hinder him, according to
that right he had thereto before he transferred it. For seeing
that by nature every man hath right to every thing, it is impossible for a man to transfer unto another any right that he
had not before. And therefore all that a man doth in transferring of right, is no more but a declaring of the will, to
suffer him, to whom he hath so transferred his right, to make
benefit of the same, without molestation. As for example,
when a man giveth his lands or goods to another, he taketh
from himself the right to enter into, and make use of the said
lands or goods, or otherwise to hinder him of the use of what
he hath given.

4. *The will to transfer, and the will to accept, both necessary to the passing away of right.* In transferring of right, two
things therefore are required: one on the part of him that
transferreth, which is a sufficient signification of his will
therein; the other, on the part of him to whom it is transferred, which is a sufficient signification of his acceptation
thereof. Either of these failing, the right remaineth where
it was: nor is it to be supposed, that he which giveth his
right to one that accepteth it not, doth thereby simply relinquish it, and transfer it to whomsoever will receive it: inasmuch as the cause of transferring the same to one, rather
than to another, is in the one, rather than in the rest.

5. *Right not transferred by words* de futuro *only.* When
there appear no other signs that a man hath relinquished, or
transferred his right, but only words, it behoveth that the
same be done in words, that signify the present time, or the
time past, and not only the time to come. For he that saith
of the time to come, as for example, to-morrow I will give,
declareth evidently, that he hath not yet given. The right,
therefore, remaineth in him today, and so continues, till he

have given actually. But he that saith, I give, presently, or have given to another anything, to have and enjoy the same to-morrow, or any other time further, hath now actually transferred the said right, which otherwise he should have had at the time that the other is to enjoy it.

6. Words *de futuro*, together with other signs of the will, may transfer right. But because words alone are not a sufficient declaration of the mind, as hath been shown chapter 13 section 8, words spoken *de futuro*, when the will of him that speaketh them may be gathered by other signs, may be taken very often as if they were meant *de præsenti*: for when it appeareth, that he that giveth, would have his words so understood by him to whom he giveth, as if he did actually transfer his right, then he must needs be understood to will all that is necessary to the same.

7. Free gift defined. When a man transferreth any right of his to another, without consideration of reciprocal benefit, past, present, or to come, this is called *free gift*. And in free gift, no other words can be binding, but those which are *de præsenti*, or *de præterito*: for being *de futuro* only, they transfer nothing, nor can they be understood, as if they proceeded from the will of the giver; because being a free gift, it carrieth with it no obligation greater than that which is enforced by the words. For he that promiseth to give, without any other consideration but his own affection, so long as he hath not given, deliberateth still, according as the causes of his affections continue, or diminish; and he that deliberateth, hath not yet willed, because the will is the last act of his deliberation. He that promiseth therefore, is not thereby a *donor*, but *doson*; which name was given to that Antiochus, that promised often, but seldom gave.

8. Contract, and the sorts of it. When a man transferreth his right upon consideration of reciprocal benefit, this is not free gift, but mutual *donation*, and is called *contract*. And in all contracts, either both parties presently perform, and put each other into a certainty and assurance of enjoying what they contract for, as when men buy or sell, or barter; or one party performeth presently, and the other promiseth, as when one selleth upon trust; or else neither party performeth pres-

ently, but trust one other. And it is impossible there should be any kind of contract besides these three. For either both the contractors trust, or neither; or else one trusteth, and the other not.

9. Covenant defined. In all contracts where there is trust, the promise of him that is trusted, is called a *covenant*. And this, though it be a promise, and of the time to come, yet it doth transfer the right, when that time cometh, no less than an actual donation. For it is a manifest sign, that he which did perform, understood it was the will of him that was trusted, to perform also. Promises therefore, upon consideration of reciprocal benefit, are covenants and signs of the will, or last act of deliberation, whereby the liberty of performing, or not performing, is taken away, and consequently are obligatory. For where liberty ceaseth, there beginneth obligation.

10. Contract of mutual trust, is of no validity in the estate of hostility. Nevertheless, in contracts that consist of such mutual trust, as that nothing be by either party performed for the present, when the contract is between such as are not compellable, he that performeth first, considering the disposition of men to take advantage of every thing for their benefit, doth but betray himself thereby to the covetousness, or other passion of him with whom he contracteth. And therefore such covenants are of none effect. For there is no reason why the one should perform first, if the other be likely not to perform afterward. And whether he be likely or not, he that doubteth, shall be judge himself, as hath been said chap. 1 sect. 8, as long as they remain in the estate and liberty of nature. But when there shall be such power coercive over both the parties, as shall deprive them of their private judgments in this point, then may such covenants be effectual, seeing he that performeth first shall have no reasonable cause to doubt of the performance of the other, that may be compelled thereunto.

11. No covenant of men but with one another. And forasmuch as in all covenants, and contracts, and donations, the acceptance of him to whom the right is transferred, is necessary to the essence of those covenants, donations, &c., it is

impossible to make a covenant or donation to any, that by nature, or absence, are unable, or if able, do not actually declare their acceptation of the same. First of all, therefore, it is impossible for any man to make a covenant with God Almighty, further than it hath pleased him to declare who shall receive and accept of the said covenant in his name. Also it is impossible to make covenant with those living creatures of whose wills we have no sufficient sign, for want of common language.

12. *Covenant how dissolved.* A covenant to do any action at a certain time and place, is then dissolved by the covenanter, when that time cometh, either by the performance, or by the violation. For a covenant is void that is once impossible. But a covenant not to do, without time limited, which is as much as to say, a covenant never to do, is dissolved by the covenanter then only, when he violateth it, or dieth. And generally, all covenants are dischargeable by the covenantee, to whose benefit, and by whose right, he that maketh the covenant is obliged. This right therefore of the covenantee relinquished, is a release of the covenant. And universally, for the same reason, all obligations are determinable at the will of the obliger.

13. *Covenant extorted by fear, in the law of nature valid.* It is a question often moved, whether such covenants oblige, as are extorted from men by fear. As for example, whether if a man for fear of death, hath promised to give a thief a hundred pounds the next day, and not discover him; whether such covenant be obligatory, or not. And though in some cases such covenant may be void, yet it is not therefore void because extorted by fear. For there appeareth no reason, why that which we do upon fear, should be less firm than that which we do for covetousness. For both the one and the other maketh the action <u>voluntary</u>. And if no covenant should be good, that proceedeth from fear of death, no condition of peace between enemies, nor any laws, could be of force, which are all consented to from that fear. For who would lose the liberty that nature hath given him, of governing himself by his own will and power, if they feared not death in

the retaining of it? What prisoner in war might be trusted to seek his ransom, and ought not rather to be killed, if he were not tied by the grant of his life, to perform his promise? But after the introduction of policy and laws, the case may alter; for if by the law the performance of such a covenant be forbidden, then he that promiseth anything to a thief, not only may, but must refuse to perform it. But if the law forbid not the performance, but leave it to the will of the promiser, then is the performance still lawful: and the covenant of things lawful is obligatory, even towards a thief.

14. Covenant contrary to former covenant, void. He that giveth, promiseth or covenanteth to one, and after, giveth, promiseth, or covenanteth the same to another, maketh void the latter act. For it is impossible for a man to transfer that right which he himself hath not; and that right he hath not, which he himself hath before transferred.

15. An oath defined. An *oath* is a clause annexed to a promise, containing a renunciation of God's mercy by him that promiseth, in case he perform not as far as is lawful and possible for him to do. And this appeareth by the words which make the essence of the oath, *so help me God*. So also was it amongst the heathen. And the form of the Romans was, *Thou Jupiter kill him that breaketh, as I kill this beast.* The intention therefore of an oath being to provoke vengeance upon the *breakers* of covenant; it is to no purpose to swear by men, be they never so great, because their punishment by divers accidents may be avoided, whether they will, or no, but God's punishment not. Though it were a custom of many nations, to swear by the life of their princes; yet those princes being ambitious of divine honor, give sufficient testimony, that they believed, nothing ought to be sworn by, but the Deity.

16. Oath to be administered to every man in his own religion. And seeing men cannot be afraid of the power they believe not, and an oath is to no purpose, without fear of him they swear by, it is necessary that he that sweareth, do it in that form which himself admitteth in his own religion, and not in that form which he useth, that putteth him to the oath. For though all men may know by nature, that there

is an Almighty power, nevertheless they believe not, that they swear by him in any other form or name, than what their own, which they think the true, religion teacheth them.

17. Oath addeth not to the obligation. And by the definition of an oath, it appeareth that it addeth not a greater obligation to perform the covenant sworn, than the covenant carrieth in itself, but it putteth a man into a greater danger, and of greater punishment.

18. Covenants bind but to endeavor. Covenants and oaths are *de voluntariis*, that is, *de possibilibus*. Nor can the covenantee understand the covenanter to promise *impossibles;* for they fall not under deliberation: and consequently, (by chap. 13. sect. 10 of the Treatise of Human Nature, which maketh the covenantee interpreter) no covenant is understood to bind further, than to our best endeavor, either in performance of the thing promised, or in something equivalent.

1. That men stand to their covenants. It is a common saying that nature maketh nothing in vain. And it is most certain, that as the truth of a conclusion, is no more but the truth of the premises that make it; so the force of the command, or law of nature, is no more than the force of the reasons inducing thereunto. Therefore the law of nature mentioned in the former chapter, section 2, namely, *That every man should divest himself of the right*, &c. were utterly vain, and of none effect, if this also were not a law of the same nature, *That every man is obliged to stand to, and perform, those covenants he maketh.* For what benefit is it to a man, that any thing be promised, or given unto him, if he that giveth, or promiseth, performeth not, or retaineth still the right of taking back what he hath given?

2. Injury defined. The breach or violation of covenant, is that which men call *injury*, consisting in some action or omission, which is therefore called *unjust*. For it is action or omission, without *jus*, or right, which was transferred or relinquished before. There is a great similitude between that we call *injury*, or *injustice* in the actions and conversations of men in the world, and that which is called *absurd* in the arguments and disputations of the Schools. For as he, which is driven to contradict an assertion by him before maintained, is said to be reduced to an absurdity; so he that through passion doth, or omitteth that which before by covenant he promised to do, or not to omit, is said to commit injustice; and there is in every breach of covenant a contradiction properly so called. For he that covenanteth, willeth to do, or omit, in the time to come. And he that doth any action, willeth it in that present, which is part of the future time contained in the covenant. And therefore he that violateth a covenant, willeth the doing and the not doing of the same thing, at the same time, which is a plain contradiction. And so *injury* is an *absurdity* of conversation, as absurdity is a kind of injustice in disputation.

289

3. That injury is done only to the covenantee. In all violation of covenant, (to whosoever accrueth the damage) the injury is done only to him to whom the covenant was made. For example, if a man covenant to obey his master, and the master command him to give money to a third, which he promiseth to do, and doth not, though this be to the damage of the third, yet the injury is done to the master only. For he could violate no covenant with him, with whom none was made, and therefore doth him no injury. For injury consisteth in violation of covenant by the definition thereof.

4. The signification of those names, just and unjust. The names of *just*, *unjust*, *justice*, *injustice*, are equivocal, and signfy diversly. For justice and injustice, when they be attributed to actions, signify the same thing with *no injury*, and *injury*, and denominate the action *just*, or *unjust*, but not the man so. For they denominate him *guilty*, or *not guilty*. But when justice or injustice, are attributed to men, they signify *proneness*, and affection and inclination of nature, that is to say, passions of the mind, apt to produce just and unjust actions. So that when a man is said to be just, or unjust; not the action, but the passion and aptitude, to do such actions, is considered. And therefore a just man may have committed an unjust act; and an unjust man may have done justly, not only one, but most of his actions. For there is an *oderunt peccare* in the unjust, as well as in the just, but from different causes. For the unjust man who abstaineth from injuries for fear of punishment, declareth plainly, that the justice of his actions dependeth upon civil constitution, from whence punishments proceed, which would otherwise in the estate of nature be unjust, according to the fountain from whence they spring. This distinction therefore of *justice*, and *injustice*, ought to be remembered, that when injustice is taken for guilty, the action is unjust, but not therefore the man; and when justice is taken for *guiltlessness*, the actions are just, and yet not always the man. Likewise when justice and injustice are taken for habits of the mind, the man may be just, or unjust, and yet not all his actions so.

5. Justice not rightly divided into commutative, and distributive. Concerning the justice of actions, the same is usually

divided into two kinds, whereof men call the one *commutative*, and the other *distributive*; and are said to consist, the one in proportion *arithmetical*; the other in *geometrical*: and *commutative* justice, they place in permutation, as buying, selling, and bartering; *distributive*, in giving to every man according to their deserts. Which distinction is not well made, inasmuch as injury, which is the injustice of action, consisteth not in the inequality of the things changed, or distributed, but in the inequality that men, contrary to nature and reason, assume unto themselves above their fellows. Of which inequality, shall be spoken hereafter. And for *commutative* justice placed in buying and selling, though the thing bought be unequal to the price given for it, yet forasmuch as both the buyer and the seller are made judges of the value, and are thereby both satisfied, there can be no injury done on either side, neither party having trusted, or covenanted with the other. And for *distributive* justice, which consisteth in the distribution of our own benefits, seeing a thing is therefore said to be our own, because we may dispose of it at our own pleasure, it can be no injury to any man, though our liberality be farther extended towards another, than towards him; unless we be thereto obliged by covenant: and then the injustice consisteth in the violation of that covenant, and not in the inequality of distribution.

6. It is a law of nature, that he that is trusted, turn not that trust to the damage of him that trusteth. It happeneth many times that man benefitteth, or contributeth, to the power of another, without any covenant, but only upon confidence and trust of obtaining the grace and favor of that other, whereby he may procure a greater, or no less benefit, and assistance to himself. For by necessity of nature, every man doth in all his voluntary actions intend some good unto himself. In this case it is a law of nature, *That no man suffer him, that thus trusteth to his charity, or good affection towards him, to be in the worse estate for his trusting.* For if he shall so do, men will not dare to confer mutually to each other's defense, nor put themselves into each other's mercy upon any terms whatsoever, but rather abide the utmost and worst event of hostility; by which general diffidence, men will not only be enforced to

war, but also afraid to come so much within the danger of one another, as to make any overture of peace. But this is to be understood of those only, that confer their benefits (as I have said) upon trust only, and not for triumph or ostentation. For as when they do it upon trust, the end they aimed at, namely to be well used, is the reward; so also when they do it for ostentation, they have the reward in themselves.

7. Ingratitude defined. But seeing in this case there passeth no covenant, the breach of this law of nature is not to be called *injury*. It hath another name, to wit, *ingratitude*.

8. It is a law of nature, to endeavor to accommodate one another. It is also a law of nature, *That every man do help and endeavor to accommodate each other as far as may be, without danger of their persons, and loss of their means, to maintain and defend themselves.* For seeing the causes of war and desolation proceed from those passions, by which we strive to accommodate ourselves, and to leave others as far as we can behind us, it followeth, that that passion by which we strive mutually to accommodate each other, must be the cause of peace. And this passion is that charity defined chapter 9 section 17.

9. And that man forgive, upon caution for the future. And in this precept of nature, is included and comprehended also this, *That a man forgive and pardon him that hath done him wrong, upon his repentance and caution for the future.* For *pardon* is peace granted to him, that, having provoked to war, demandeth it. It is not therefore charity, but fear, when a man giveth peace to him that repenteth not, nor giveth caution for maintaining thereof in the time to come. For he that repenteth not, remaineth with the affection of an enemy; as also doth he that refuseth to give caution, and consequently, is presumed not to seek after peace, but advantage. And therefore to forgive him is not commanded in this law of nature, nor is charity, but may sometime be prudence. Otherwise, not to pardon upon repentance and caution, considering men cannot abstain from provoking one another, is never to give *peace*. And that is against the general definition of the law of nature.

10. And that revenge ought to respect the future only. And seeing the law of nature commandeth pardon, when there is repentance and caution for the future, it followeth, that the same law ordaineth, *That no revenge be taken upon the consideration only of the offense past, but of the benefit to come;* that is to say, that all revenge ought to tend to amendment, either of the person offending, or of others, by the example of his punishment; which is sufficiently apparent, in that the law of nature commandeth pardon, where the future time is secured. The same is also apparent by this, that revenge when it considereth the offense past, is nothing else, but present triumph and glory, and directeth to no end: and what is directed to no end, is therefore unprofitable; and consequently the triumph of revenge, is vain glory: and whatsoever is vain, is against reason; and to hurt one another without reason, is contrary to that, which by supposition is every man's benefit, namely peace; and what is contrary to peace, is contrary to the law of nature.

11. That reproach and contempt declared is against the law of nature. And because all signs which we show to one another of hatred and contempt, provoke in the highest degree to quarrel and battle, (inasmuch as life itself, with the condition of enduring scorn, is not esteemed worth the enjoying, much less peace) it must necessarily be implied as a law of nature, *That no man reproach, revile, deride, or any otherwise declare his hatred, contempt, or disesteem of any other.* But this law is very little practiced. For what is more ordinary than reproaches of those that are rich, towards them that are not? or of those that sit in place of judicature, towards those that are accused at the bar? although to grieve them in that manner, be no part of the punishment for their crime, nor contained in their office. But use hath prevailed, that what was lawful in the lord towards the servant whom he maintaineth, is also practiced as lawful in the more mighty towards the less; though they contribute nothing towards their maintenance.

12. That indifference of commerce is of the law of nature. It is also a law of nature, *That one man allow commerce*

and traffic indifferently to one another. For he that alloweth that to one man, which he denieth to another, declareth his hatred to him, to whom he denieth. And to declare hatred is war. And upon this title was grounded the great war between the Athenians and the Peloponnesians. For would the Athenians have condescended to suffer the Megareans, their neighbors, to traffic in their ports and markets, that war had not begun.

13. That messengers employed to procure or maintain peace, ought to be safe by the law of nature. And this also is a law of nature, *That all messengers of peace, and such as are employed to procure and maintain amity between man and man, may safely come and go.* For seeing peace is the general law of nature, the means thereto, such as are these men, must in the same law be comprehended.

Chapter 4

1. A law of nature, that every man acknowledge other for his equal. The question, which is the better man, is determinable only in the estate of government and policy, though it be mistaken for a question of nature, not only by ignorant men, that think one man's blood better than another's by nature, but also by him, whose opinions are at this day, and in these parts, of greater authority than any other human writings. For he putteth so much difference between the powers of men by nature, that he doubteth not to set down, as the ground of all his politics, that some men are by nature worthy to govern, and others by nature ought to serve. Which foundation hath not only weakened the whole frame of his politics, but hath also given men color and pretenses, whereby to disturb and hinder the peace of one another. For though there were such a difference of nature, that master and servant were not by consent of men, but by inherent virtue; yet who hath that eminency of virtue, above others, and who is so stupid, as not to govern himself, shall never be agreed upon amongst men, who do every one naturally think himself, as able, at the least, to govern another, as another to govern him. And when there was any contention between the finer and the courser wits, (as there hath been often in times of sedition and civil war) for the most part, these latter carried away the victory; and as long as men arrogate to themselves more honor than they give to others, it cannot be imagined, how they can possibly live in peace: and consequently we are to suppose, that for peace sake, nature hath ordained this law, *That every man acknowledge other for his equal.* And the breach of this law, is that we call *pride.*

2. Another, that men allow *æqualia æqualibus.* As it was necessary that a man should not retain his right to every thing, so also was it, that he should retain his right to some things; to his own body, for example, the right of defending, whereof he could not transfer; to the use of fire, water, free

air, and place to live in, and to all things necessary for life. Nor doth the law of nature command any divesting of other rights, than of those only which cannot be retained without the loss of peace. Seeing then many rights are retained, when we enter into peace one with another, reason and the law of nature dictateth, *Whatsoever right any man requireth to retain, he allow every other man to retain the same.* For he that doth not so, alloweth not the equality mentioned in the former section. For there is no acknowledgment of worth, without attribution of the equality of benefit and respect. And this allowance of *æqualia æqualibus,* is the same thing with the allowing of *proportionalia proportionalibus.* For when a man alloweth to every man alike, the allowance he maketh, will be in the same proportion, in which are the numbers of men to whom they are made. And this is it men mean by *distributive justice,* and is properly termed *equity.* The breach of the law is that which the Greeks call Πλεονεξία, which is commonly rendered *covetousness,* but seemeth to be more precisely expressed by the word *encroaching.*

3. Another, that those things which cannot be divided, be used in common. If there pass no other covenant, the law of nature is, *That such things as cannot be divided, be used in common, proportionably to the numbers of them that are to use the same, or without limitation, when the quantity thereof sufficeth.* For first supposing the thing to be used in common, not sufficient for them that are to use it without limitation, if a few shall make more use thereof than the rest, that equality is not observed, which is required in the second section. And this is to be understood, as all the rest of the laws of nature, without any other covenant antecedent: for a man may have given away his right of common, and so the case be altered.

4. Another, that things indivisible and incommunicable, be divided by lot. In those things which neither can be divided, nor used in common, the rule of nature must needs be one of these, *lot,* or *alternate* use; for besides these two ways, there can no other equality be imagined; and for alternate use, he that beginneth, hath the advantage; and to reduce that advantage to equality, there is no other way but lot, in things, therefore indivisible and incommunicable, it is the law of

nature, *That the use be alternate, or the advantage given away by lot;* because there is no other way of equality. And equality is the law of nature.

5. Natural lot, primogeniture, and first possession. There be two sorts of lots; one arbitrary, made by men, and commonly known by the names of *lot, chance, hazard,* and the like; and there is *natural lot,* such as is *primogeniture,* which is no more but the chance, or lot, of being first born, which it seemeth they considered, that call inheritance by the name of κληρονομία, which signifieth *distribution* by lot. Secondly, *prima occupatio,* first seizing, or finding of a thing, whereof no man made use before, which for the most part also is merely *chance.*

6. That men submit to arbitration. Although men agree upon these laws of nature, and endeavor to observe the same; yet considering the passions of men, that make it difficult to understand by what actions, and circumstances of actions, those laws are broken, there must needs arise many great controversies about the interpretation thereof, by which the peace must needs be dissolved, and men return again to their former estate of hostility. For the taking away of which controversies, it is necessary that there be some common *arbitrator* and *judge,* to whose sentence both the parties in the controversies ought to stand. And therefore it is a law of nature, *That in every controversy, the parties thereto ought mutually to agree upon an arbitrator, whom they both trust; and mutually to covenant to stand to the sentence he shall give therein.* For where every man is his own *judge,* there properly is no judge at all; as where every man carveth out his own right, it hath the same effect, as if there were no right at all: and where is no judge, there is no end of controversy: and therefore the right of hostility remaineth.

7. Of an arbitrator. An *arbitrator* therefore, or he that is judge, is trusted by the parties to any controversy, to determine the same by the declaration of his own judgment therein. Out of which followeth first, that the judge ought not to be concerned in the controversy he endeth; for in that case he is a party, and ought by the same reason to be judged by another. Secondly, that he maketh no covenant with either of

the parties, to pronounce sentence for the one, more than for the other. Nor doth he covenant so much, as that his sentence shall be just; for that were to make the parties judges of the sentence, whereby the controversy would remain still undecided. Nevertheless for the trust reposed in him, and for the equality which the law of nature requireth him to consider in the parties, he violateth that law, if for favor, or hatred to either party, he give other sentence than he thinketh right. And thirdly, that no man ought to make himself judge in any controversy between others, unless they consent and agree thereto.

8. That no man press his counsel upon any man against his will. It is also the law of nature, *That no man obtrude or* *press his advice or counsel to any man, that declareth himself unwilling to hear the same.* For seeing a man taketh counsel concerning what is good or hurt of himself only, and not of his counsellor, and that counsel is a voluntary action, and therefore tendeth also to the good of the counsellor, there may be often just cause to suspect the counsellor: and though there be none, yet seeing counsel unwillingly heard, is a needless offense to him that is not willing to hear it, and offenses tend all to the breach of peace, it is therefore against the law of nature to obtrude it.

9. How to know suddenly what is the law of nature. A man that shall see these laws of nature set down and inferred with so many words, and so much ado, may think there is yet much more difficulty and subtlety required to acknowledge and do according to the said laws in every sudden occasion, when a man hath but a little time to consider. And while we consider man in most passions, as of *anger, ambition, covetousness, vain glory*, and the like, that tend to the excluding of natural equality, it is true. But without these passions, there is an easy rule to know upon a sudden, whether the action I be to do, be against the law of nature, or not. And it is but this: *That a man imagine himself in the place of the party with whom he hath to do, and reciprocally him in his.* Which is no more but a changing, as it were, of the scales. For every man's passion weigheth heavy in his own scale, but not in the scale of his neighbor. And this rule is very well known and

expressed in this old dictate, *Quod tibi fieri non vis, alteri ne feceris.*

10. That the law of nature taketh place after security from others to observe the same. These laws of nature, the sum whereof consisteth in forbidding us to be our own judges, and our own carvers, and in commanding us to accommodate one another, in case they should be observed by some, and not by others, would make the observers but a prey to them that should neglect them, leaving the good both without defense against the wicked, and also with a charge to assist them: which is against the scope of the said laws, that are made only for the protection and defense of them that keep them. Reason therefore, and the law of nature over and above all these particular laws, doth dictate this law in general, *That those particular laws be so far observed, as they subject us not to any incommodity, that in our own judgments may arise, by the neglect thereof in those towards whom we observe them;* and consequently requireth no more but the desire and constant intention to endeavor and be ready to observe them, unless there be cause to the contrary in other men's refusal to observe them towards us. The force therefore of the law of nature, is not *in foro externo,* till there be security for men to obey it, but is always *in foro interno,* wherein the action of obedience being unsafe, the will and readiness to perform, is taken for the performance.

11. The right of nature not to be taken away by custom, nor the law of nature abrogated by any act. Amongst the laws of nature, customs and prescriptions are not numbered. For whatsoever action is against reason, though it be reiterated never so often, or that there be never so many precedents thereof, is still against reason, and therefore not a law of nature, but contrary to it. But consent and covenant may so alter the cases, which in the law of nature may be put, by changing the circumstances, that that which was reason before, may afterwards be against it; and yet is reason still the law. For though every man be bound to allow equality to another, yet if that other shall see cause to renounce the same, and make himself inferior, then, if from thenceforth he consider him as inferior, he breaketh not thereby that law of

Here is the great danger to [the] civil state; man is still left as judge of his place in society — even Hobbes can't avoid it.

nature that commandeth to allow equality. In sum, *a man's own consent may abridge him of the liberty which the law of nature leaveth him, but custom not;* nor can either of them abrogate either these, or any other law of nature.

12. Why the dictates of nature are called laws. And forasmuch as law, to speak properly, is a command, and these dictates, as they proceed from nature, are not commands, they are not therefore called laws, in respect of nature, but in respect of the author of nature, God Almighty.

13. Whatsoever is against conscience in a man, that is his own judge, is against the law of nature. And seeing the laws of nature concern the conscience, not he only breaketh them that doth any action contrary, but also he whose action is conformable to them, in case he think it contrary. For though the action chance to be right, yet in his judgment he despiseth the law.

14. Of *malum pœnæ, malum culpæ;* virtue and vice. Every man by natural passion, calleth that good which pleaseth him for the present, or so far forth as he can foresee; and in like manner, that which displeaseth him, evil. And therefore he that foreseeth the whole way to his preservation, which is the end that every one by nature aimeth at, must also call it good, and the contrary evil. And this is that good and evil, which not every man in passion calleth so, but all men by reason. And therefore the fulfilling of all these laws is good in reason, and the breaking of them evil. And so also the habit, or disposition, or intention to fulfil them good; and the neglect of them evil. And from hence cometh that distinction of *malum pœnæ*, and *malum culpæ;* for *malum pœnæ* is any pain or molestation of the mind whatsoever; but *malum culpæ* is that action which is contrary to reason and the law of nature: as also the habit of doing according to these and other laws of nature, that tend to our preservation, is that we call *virtue;* and the habit of doing the contrary, *vice.* As for example, justice is that habit by which we stand to covenants, injustice the contrary vice; equity that habit by which we allow equality of nature, arrogancy the contrary vice; gratitude the habit whereby we requite the benefit and trust of others, ingratitude the contrary vice; temperance the habit by

which we abstain from all things that tend to our destruction, intemperance the contrary vice; prudence, the same with virtue in general. As for the common opinion, that virtue consisteth in mediocrity, and vice in extremes, I see no ground for it, nor can find any such mediocrity. Courage may be virtue, when the daring is extreme, if the cause be good, and extreme fear no vice when the danger is extreme. To give a man more than his due, is no injustice, though it be to give him less: and in gifts it is not the sum that maketh liberality, but the reason. And so in all other virtues and vices. I know that this doctrine of mediocrity is Aristotle's, but his opinions concerning virtue and vice, are no other than those, which were received then, and are still by the generality of men unstudied, and therefore not very likely to be accurate.

15. Aptitude to society, fulfilleth the law of nature. The sum of virtue is to be sociable with them that will be sociable, and formidable to them that will not. And the same is the sum of the law of nature: for in being sociable, the law of nature taketh place by way of peace and society; and to be formidable, is the law of nature in war, where to be feared is a protection a man hath from his own power: and as the former consisteth in actions of equity and justice, the latter consisteth in actions of honor. And equity, justice, and honor, contain all virtues whatsoever.

Chapter 5

1. **Confirmation out of Scripture, &c.** The laws mentioned in the former chapters, as they are called the laws of nature, for that they are the dictates of natural reason, and also moral laws, because they concern the manners and conversation of men, one towards another; so are they also divine laws in respect of the author thereof, God Almighty; and ought therefore to agree, or at least, not to be repugnant to the word of God revealed in Holy Scripture. In this chapter therefore, I shall produce such places of Scripture, as appear to be most consonant to the said laws.

2. And first, the word of God seemeth to place the divine law in reason, by all such texts as ascribe the same to the heart and understanding; as Psalm xl. 8: *Thy law is in my heart.* Heb. viii. 10: *After those days, saith the Lord, I will put my laws in their mind:* and Heb. x. 16, the same. Psalm xxxvii. 31, speaking of the righteous man, he saith, *The law of God is in his heart.* Psalm xix. 7, 8: *The law of God is perfect, converting the soul. It giveth wisdom to the simple, and light unto the eyes.* Jer. xxxi. 33: *I will put my law in their inward parts, and write it in their hearts.* And (John i.) the lawgiver himself, God Almighty, is called by the name of Λόγος, which is also called (verse 4) *The light of men;* and (verse 9) *The light which lighteth every man, which cometh into the world.* All which are descriptions of natural reason.

3. And that the law divine, for so much as is moral, are those precepts which tend to peace, seemeth to be much confirmed by such places of Scripture as these: Rom. iii. 17, righteousness which is the fulfilling of the law, is called *The way of peace.* And Psalm lxxxv. 10: *Righteousness and peace shall kiss each other.* And Matth. v. 9: *Blessed are the peacemakers.* And Heb. vii. 2, *Melchisedec king of Salem* is interpreted *king of righteousness,* and *king of peace.* And (verse 21) our Saviour Christ is said to be *a priest for ever after the order of Melchisedec:* out of which may be inferred, that the

doctrine of our Saviour Christ annexeth the fulfilling of the law to peace.

4. That the law of nature is unalterable, is intimated by this, that the priesthood of Melchisedec is everlasting; and by the words of our Saviour, (Matth. v. 18): *Heaven and earth shall pass away, but one jot or tittle of the law shall not pass till all things be fulfilled.*

5. That men ought to stand to their convenants, is taught Psalm xv, where the question being asked (verse 1), *Lord who shall dwell in thy tabernacle, &c.* It is answered (verse 4), *He that sweareth to his own hindrance, and yet changeth not.* And that men ought to be gratified, where no covenant passeth, Deut. xxv. 4: *Thou shalt not muzzle the ox that treadeth out the corn,* which St. Paul (1 Cor. ix. 9) interpreteth not of oxen but of men.

6. That men content themselves with equality, as it is the foundation of natural law, so also is it of the second table, of the divine law, Matth. xxii. 39, 40: *Thou shalt love thy neighbor as thyself. On these two laws depend the whole law and the prophets;* which is not so to be understood, as that a man should study so much his neighbor's profit as his own, or that he should divide his goods amongst his neighbors; but that he should esteem his neighbor worthy all rights and privileges that himself enjoyeth; and attribute unto him, whatsoever he looketh should be attributed unto himself: which is no more, but that he should be humble, meek, and content with equality.

7. And that in distributing of right amongst equals, that distribution is to be made according to the proportions of the numbers, which is the giving of *æqualia æqualibus, et proportionalia proportionalibus;* we have Numb. xxvi. 53, 54, the commandment of God to Moses: *Thou shalt divide the land according to the number of names; to many thou shalt give more, to few thou shalt give less, to every one according to his number.* That decision by lot is a means of peace, Prov. xviii. 18: *The lot causeth contention to cease, and maketh partition among the mighty.*

8. That the accommodation and forgiveness of one another, which have before been put for laws of nature, are also

law divine, there is no question. For they are the essence of charity, which is the scope of the whole law. That we ought not to reproach, or reprehend one another, is the doctrine of our Saviour, Matth. vii. 1: *Judge not, that ye be not judged:* (verse 3): *Why seest thou the mote that is in thy brother's eye, and seest not the beam that is in thine own eye?* Also the law that forbiddeth us to press our counsel upon others further than they admit, is a divine law. For after our charity and desire to rectify one another is rejected, to press it further, is to reprehend him, and condemn him, which is forbidden in the text last recited; as also Rom. xiv. 12, 13: *Every one of us shall give account of himself to God. Let us not therefore judge one another any more, but use your judgment rather in this, that no man put an occasion to fall, or a stumbling block before his brother.*

9. Further, the rule of men concerning the law of nature, *Quod tibi fieri non vis, alteri ne feceris,* is confirmed by the like, Matth. vii. 12: *Whatsoever therefore you would have men do unto you, that do you unto them: for this is the law and the prophets.* And Rom. ii. 1: *In that thou judgest another, thou condemnest thyself,* &c.

10. It is also manifest by the Scriptures, that these laws concern only the tribunal of our conscience; and that the actions contrary to them, shall be no further punished by God Almighty, than as they proceed from negligence, or contempt. And first, that these laws are made to the conscience, appeareth, Matth. v. 20: *For I say unto you, except your righteousness exceed the righteousness of the Scribes and Pharisees, ye shall not enter into the kingdom of heaven.* Now the Pharisees were the most exact amongst the Jews in the external performance; they therefore must want the sincerity of conscience; else could not our Saviour have required a greater righteousness than theirs. For the same reason our Saviour Christ saith (Luke, xviii. 14). *The publican departed from the temple justified, rather than the Pharisee.* And Christ saith, (Matth. xi. 30): *My yoke is easy, and my burthen light;* which proceedeth from this, that Christ required no more than our best endeavor. And Rom. xiv. 23: *He that doubteth, is condemned, if he eat.* And in innumerable places both

in the Old and New Testament, God Almighty declareth, that he taketh the will for the deed, both in good and evil actions. By all which it plainly appears, that the divine law is dictated to the conscience. On the other side it is no less plain, that how many and heinous actions soever a man commit through infirmity, he shall nevertheless, whensoever he shall condemn the same in his own conscience, be freed from the punishments that to such actions otherwise belong. For, *At what time soever a sinner doth repent him of his sins from the bottom of his heart, I will put all his iniquities out of my remembrance, saith the Lord.*

11. Concerning revenge, which by the law of nature ought not to aim, as I have said chapter 3 section 10, at present delight, but future profit, there is some difficulty made, as if the same accorded not with the law divine, by such as object the continuance of punishment after the day of judgment, when there shall be no place, neither for amendment, nor for example. This objection had been of some force, if such punishment had been ordained after all sins were past; but considering the punishment was instituted before sin, it serveth to the benefit of mankind, because it keepeth men in peaceable and virtuous conversation by the terror. And therefore such revenge was directed to the future only.

12. Finally, there is no law of natural reason, that can be against the law divine: for God Almighty hath given reason to a man to be a light unto him. And I hope it is no impiety to think, that God Almighty will require a strict account thereof, at the day of judgment, as of the instructions which we were to follow in our peregrination here, notwithstanding the opposition and affronts of supernaturalists nowadays, to rational and moral conversation.

Chapter 6

1. **That men, notwithstanding these laws, are still in the state of war, till they have security one against another.** In chapter 12. section 16, of the *Treatise of Human Nature*, it hath been shown, that the opinions men have of the rewards and punishments which are to follow their actions, are the causes that make and govern the will to those actions. In this estate of man therefore, wherein all men are equal, and every man allowed to be his own judge, the fears they have one of another are equal, and every man's hopes consist in his own sleight and strength: and consequently when any man by his natural passion, is provoked to break these laws of nature, there is no security in any other man of his own defense but *anticipation*. And for this cause, every man's right, howsoever he be inclined to peace, of doing whatsoever seemeth good in his own eyes, remaineth with him still, as the necessary means of his preservation. And therefore till there be security amongst men for the keeping of the law of nature one towards another, men are still in the estate of war, and nothing is unlawful to any man that tendeth to his own safety or commodity: and this safety and commodity consisteth in the mutual aid and help of one another, whereby also followeth the mutual fear of one another.

2. **The law of nature in war, is nothing but honor.** It is a proverbial saying, *inter arma silent leges*. There is a little therefore to be said concerning the laws that men are to observe one towards another in time of war, wherein every man's being and well-being is the rule of his actions. Yet thus much the law of nature commandeth in war, that men satiate not the cruelty of their present passions, whereby in their own conscience they foresee no benefit to come. For that betrayeth not a necessity, but a disposition of the mind to war, which is against the law of nature. And in old time we read, that rapine was a trade of life, wherein nevertheless many of them that used it, did not only spare the lives of those they invaded,

but left them also such things, as were necessary to preserve that life which they had given them; as namely their oxen and instruments for tillage, though they carried away all their other cattle and substance. And as the rapine itself was warranted in the law of nature, by the want of security otherwise to maintain themselves, so the exercise of cruelty was forbidden by the same law of nature, unless fear suggested anything to the contrary. For nothing but fear can justify the taking away of another's life. And because fear can hardly be made manifest, but by some action dishonorable, that betrayeth the conscience of one's own weakness, all men, in whom the passion of courage or magnanimity hath been predominant, have abstained from cruelty; insomuch, that though there be in war no law, the breach whereof is injury, yet there are in war those laws, the breach whereof is dishonor. In one word, therefore, the only law of actions in war, is *honor;* and the right of war, *providence.*

3. No security without the concord of many. And seeing natural aid is necessary for defense, as mutual fear is necessary for peace, we are to consider how great aids are required for such defense, and for the causing of such mutual fear, as men may not easily adventure on one another. And first, it is evident, that the mutual aid of two or three men is of very little security. For the odds on the other side, of a man or two, giveth sufficient encouragement to an assaut. And therefore before men have sufficient security in the help of one another, their number must be so great, that the odds of a few which the enemy may have, be no certain and sensible advantage.

4. That concord of many cannot be maintained without power to keep them all in awe. And supposing how great a number soever of men assembled together for their mutual defense, yet shall not the effect follow, unless they all direct their actions to one and the same end; which direction to one and the same end is that which, chap. 12. sect. 7, is called *consent.* This *consent,* or concord, amongst so many men, though it may be made by the fear of a present invader, or by the hope of a present conquest, or booty, and endure as long as that action endureth, nevertheless, by the diversity of

judgments and passions in so many men contending naturally for honor and advantage one above another, it is impossible, not only that their consent to aid each other against an enemy, but also that the peace should last between themselves, without some mutual and common fear to rule them.

5. *The cause why concord remaineth in a multitude of some irrational creatures, and not of men.* But contrary hereunto may be objected, the experience we have of certain living creatures irrational, that nevertheless continually live in such good order and government for their common benefit, and are so free from sedition and war amongst themselves, that for peace, profit, and defense, nothing more can be imaginable. And the experience we have in this, is in that little creature the bee, which is therefore reckoned amongst *animalia politica.* Why therefore may not men, that foresee the benefit of concord, continually maintain the same without compulsion, as well as they? To which I answer, that amongst other living creatures, there is no question of precedence in their own species, nor strife about honor, or acknowledgment of one another's wisdom, as there is amongst men, from whence arise envy and hatred of one towards another, and from thence sedition and war. Secondly, those living creatures aim every one at peace and food common to them all; men aim at dominion, superiority, and private wealth, which are distinct in every man, and breed contention. Thirdly, those living creatures that are without reason, have not learning enough to espy, or to think they espy, any defect in the government; and therefore are contented therewith. But in a multitude of men, there are always some that think themselves wiser than the rest, and strive to alter what they think amiss, and divers of them strive to alter divers ways, and that causeth war. Fourthly, they want speech, and are therefore unable to instigate one another to faction, which men want not. Fifthly, they have no conception of right and wrong, but only of pleasure and pain, and therefore also no censure of one another, nor of their commander, as long as they are themselves at ease; whereas men that make themselves judges of right and wrong, are then least at quiet, when they are most at ease. Lastly, natural concord, such as is amongst those

creatures, is the work of God by the way of nature; but concord amongst men is artificial, and by way of covenant. And therefore no wonder, if such irrational creatures as govern themselves in multitude, do it much more firmly than mankind, that do it by arbitrary institution.

6. That union is necessary for the maintaining of concord. It remaineth therefore still, that consent, by which I understand the concurrence of many men's wills to one action, is not sufficient security for their common peace, without the erection of some common power, by the fear whereof they may be compelled both to keep the peace amongst themselves, and to join their strengths together, against a common enemy. And that this may be done, there is no way imaginable, but only union, which is defined, chapter 12, section 8, to be the involving, or including the wills of many in the will of one man, or in the will of the greatest part of any one number of men, that is to say, in the will of one man, or of one *council*. For a council is nothing else but an *assembly* of men deliberating concerning something common to them all.

7. How union is made. The making of union consisteth in this, that every man by covenant oblige himself to some one and the same man, or to some one and the same council, by them all named and determined, to do those actions, which the said man or council shall command them to do, and to do no action, which he or they shall forbid, or command them not to do. And further, in case it be a council, whose commands they covenant to obey, that then also they covenant, that every man shall hold that for the command of the whole council, which is the command of the greater part of those men, whereof such council consisteth. And though the will of man being not voluntary, but the beginning of voluntary actions, is not subject to deliberation and covenant; yet when a man covenanteth to subject his will to the command of another, he obligeth himself to this, that he resign his strength and means to him, whom he covenanteth to obey. And hereby he that is to command, may by the use of all their means and strength, be able by the terror thereof, to frame the will of them all to unity and concord, amongst themselves.

8. Body politic defined. This union so made, is that which men call nowadays, *a body politic*, or civil society; and the Greeks call it πόλις, that is to say, a city, which may be defined to be a multitude of men, united as one person, by a common power, for their common peace, defense, and benefit.

N.B.

9. Corporation defined. And as this union into a city or body politic, is instituted with common power over all the particular persons, or members thereof, to the common good of them all; so also may there be amongst a multitude of those members instituted, a subordinate union of certain men, for certain common actions to be done by those men for some common benefit of theirs, or of the whole city; as for subordinate government, for counsel, for trade, and the like. And these subordinate bodies politic are usually called *corporations;* and their power such over the particulars of their own society, as the whole city, whereof they are members, have allowed them.

10. Sovereign and subject defined. In all cities, or bodies politic not subordinate, but independent, that one man, or one council, to whom the particular members have given that common power, is called their *sovereign,* and his power, the sovereign power; which consisteth in the power and the strength, that every of the members have transferred to him from themselves by covenant. And because it is impossible for any man really to transfer his own strength to another, or for that other to receive it; it is to be understood, that to transfer a man's power and strength, is no more but to lay by, or relinquish his own right of resisting him to whom he so transferreth it. And every member of the body politic, is called a *subject,* to wit, to the *sovereign.*

11. Two sorts of bodies politic, patrimonial and commonwealth. The cause in general, which moveth a man to become subject to another, is (as I have said already) the fear of not otherwise preserving himself. And a man may subject himself to him that invadeth, or may invade him, for fear of him; or men may join amongst themselves, to subject themselves to such as they shall agree upon for fear of others. And when many men subject themselves the former way, there ariseth thence a body politic, as it were naturally. From whence

proceedeth *dominion, paternal* and *despotic*. And when they subject themselves the other way, by mutual agreement amongst many, the body politic they make, is for the most part, called a *commonwealth*, in distinction from the former, though the name be the general name for them both. And I shall speak in the first place of commonwealth, and afterwards of bodies politic, patrimonial, and despotical.

THE SECOND PART
The Nature of the Body Politic

Chapter 1

1. Introduction. That *Treatise of Human Nature,* which was formerly printed, hath been wholly spent in the consideration of the natural power, and the natural estate of man, namely, of his cognition and passions in the first eleven chapters, and how from thence proceed his actions; in the twelfth, how men know one another's minds: in the last, in what estate men's passions set them. In the first, second, third, fourth, and fifth chapters of the former Part of this Treatise is showed, what estate they are directed unto by the dictates of reason, that is to say, what be the principal articles of the law of nature. And lastly, how a multitude of persons natural, are united by covenants into one person civil, or body politic. In this part therefore shall be considered, the nature of a body politic, and the laws thereof, otherwise called civil laws. And whereas it hath been said in the last chapter, and last section of the former part, that there be two ways of erecting a body politic; one by arbitrary institution of many men assembled together, which is like a creation out of nothing by human wit; the other by compulsion, which is as it were a generation thereof out of natural force; I shall first speak of such erection of a body politic, as proceedeth from the assembly and consent of a multitude.

2. A multitude before their union, &c. Having in this place to consider, a multitude of men about to unite themselves into a body politic, for their security, both against one another, and against common enemies, and that by covenants; the knowledge of what covenants they must needs make, dependeth on the knowledge of the persons, and the knowledge of their end. First, for their persons they are many, and (as yet) not one; nor can any action done in a multitude of people met together, be attributed to the multitude, or truly called the action of the multitude, unless every

man's hand, and every man's will, (not so much as one excepted) have concurred thereto. For multitude, though in their persons they run together, yet they concur not always in their designs. For even at that time when men are in tumult, though they agree a number of them to one mischief, and a number of them to another; yet, in the whole, they are amongst themselves in the state of hostility, and not of peace; like the seditious Jews besieged in Jerusalem, that could join against their enemies, and fight amongst themselves. Whensoever therefore any man saith, that a number of men hath done any act, it is to be understood, that every particular man in that number hath consented thereunto, and not the greatest part only. Secondly, though thus assembled with intention to unite themselves, they are yet in that estate in which every man hath right to everything, and consequently, as hath been said, chapter 1. section 10, in an estate of enjoying nothing. And therefore *meum* and *tuum* hath no place amongst them.

3. Express consent of every particular, &c. The first thing therefore they are to do, is expressly every man to consent to something, by which they may come near to their ends, which can be nothing else imaginable, but this, that they allow the wills of the major part of their whole number, or the wills of the major part of some certain number of men by them determined and named; or lastly, the will of some one man, to involve and be taken for the wills of every man. And this done, they are united, and a *body politic*. And if the major part of their whole number be supposed to involve the wills of all the particulars, then are they said to be a *democracy*, that is to say, a government wherein the whole number, or so many of them as please, being assembled together, are the sovereign, and every particular man a subject. If the major part of a certain number of men named or distinguished from the rest, be supposed to involve the wills of every one of the particulars, then are they said to be an *oligarchy*, or *aristocracy*, which two words signify the same thing, together with the divers passions of those that use them. For when the men that be in that office please, they are called an aristocracy, or otherwise an oligarchy, wherein those, the major part of which declare the wills of the whole multitude being assembled, are

the sovereign, and every man severally a subject. Lastly,
their consent be such, that the will of one man, whom the
name, shall stand for the wills of them all, then is their go
ernment or union called a *monarchy*, and that one man
sovereign, and every of the rest a subject.

4. Democratical, aristocratical, and monarchical union ma
be instituted for ever. And those several sorts of unions, go
ernments, and subjections of man's will, may be understoo
to be made, either absolutely, that is to say, for all futur
time, or for a time limited only. But forasmuch as we spea
here of a body politic, instituted for the perpetual benefit an
defense of them that make it; which therefore men desir
should last forever, I will omit to speak of those that be tem
porary, and consider of those that be forever.

5. *Without security no private right relinquished.* The en
for which one man giveth up, and relinquisheth to another, c
others, the right of protecting and defending himself by his ow
power, is the security which he expecteth thereby, of protec
tion and defense from those to whom he doth so relinquish i
and a man may then account himself in the estate of security
when he can foresee no violence to be done unto him, from
which the doer may not be deterred by the power of tha
sovereign, to whom they have every one subjected themselves
and without that security, there is no reason for a man t
deprive himself of his own advantages, and make himself
prey to others. And therefore when there is not such a sovei
eign power erected, as may afford this security, it is to be u
derstood, that every man's right of doing whatsoever seeme
good in his own eyes, remaineth still with him; and contrar
wise, where any subject hath right by his own judgment an
discretion, to make use of his force, it is to be understood
that every man hath the like, and consequently, that there i
no commonwealth at all established. How far therefore in th
making of a commonwealth, man subjecteth his will to th
power of others, must appear from the end, namely, security
For whatsoever is necessary to be by convenant transferre
for the attaining thereof, so much is transferred, or else ever
man is in his natural liberty to secure himself.

6. *Covenants of government without power of coercior*

re no security. Covenants agreed upon by every man assembled for the making of a commonwealth, and put in writing without erecting of a power of coercion, are no reasonable security for any of them that so covenant, nor are to be called laws, and leave men still in the estate of nature and hostility. For seeing the wills of most men are governed only by fear, and where there is no power of coercion, there is no fear, the wills of most men will follow their passions of covetousness, lust, anger, and the like, to the breaking of those covenants, whereby the rest, also, who otherwise would keep them, are set at liberty, and have no law, but from themselves.

7. Power coercive, &c. This power of coercion, as hath been said, chap. 2. sect. 3, of the former part, consisteth in the transferring of every man's right of resistance against him, to whom he hath transferred the power of coercion. It followeth therefore, that no man in any commonwealth whatsoever, hath right to resist him, or them, to whom they have transferred this power coercive, or (as men use to call it) the sword of justice, supposing the not-resistance possible. For, Part I chapter 2. sect. 18, covenants bind but to the utmost of our endeavor.

8. The sword of war, &c. And forasmuch as they who are amongst themselves in security, by the means of this sword of justice, that keeps them all in awe, are nevertheless in danger of enemies from without, if there be not some means found, to unite their strengths and natural forces, in the resistance of such enemies, their peace amongst themselves is but in vain. And therefore it is to be understood as a covenant of every member to contribute their several forces for the defense of the whole, whereby to make one power as sufficient, as is possible for their defense. Now seeing that every man hath already transferred the use of his strength to him, or them, that have the sword of justice, it followeth, that the power of defense, that is to say, the sword of war, be in the same hands wherein is the sword of justice; and consequently those two swords are but one, and that inseparably and essentially annexed to the sovereign power.

9. Decision in all debates, &c. annexed to the sword. Moreover, seeing to have the right of the sword, is nothing

else but to have the use thereof depending only on th
judgment and discretion of him or them that have it, it follow
eth, that the power of indenture in all controversies, wherei
the sword of justice is to be used; and in all deliberations co
cerning war, wherein the use of that sword is required, th
right of resolving and determining what is to be done, belon
to the same sovereign.

10. Laws civil, &c. Further, considering it is no less, b
much more necessary to prevent violence and rapine, tha
to punish the same when it is committed, and all violenc
proceedeth from controversies that arise between men co
cerning *meum* and *tuum*, right and wrong, good and bad, an
the like, which men use every one to measure by their ow
judgments, it belongeth also to the judgment of the same sove
eign power, to set forth and make known the common measur
by which every man is to know what is his, and wh
another's; what is good, and what bad, and what he ought t
do, and what not, and to command the same to be observe
And these measures of the actions of the subjects are thos
which men call *laws politic,* or civil: the making whereo
must of right belong to him that hath the power of the swor
by which men are compelled to observe them; for otherwis
they should be made in vain.

11. Appointment of magistrates, &c. Furthermore, seeing
is impossible that any one man that hath such sovereig
power, can be able, in person, to hear and determine all co
troversies, to be present at all deliberations concerning co
mon good, and to execute and perform all those commo
actions that belong thereunto, whereby there will be necessit
of magistrates and ministers of public affairs; it is consequen
that the appointment, nomination, and limitation of the sam
be understood, as an inseparable part of the same sovereignt
to which the sum of all judicature, and execution, hath bee
already annexed.

12. Sovereign power includeth impunity. And forasmuch
as the right to use the forces of every particular member,
transferred from themselves, to their sovereign, a man w
easily fall upon this conclusion of himself, that to sovereig
power, whatsoever it doth, there belongeth impunity.

13. A supposed commonwealth where laws are made first, and the commonwealth after. The sum of these rights of sovereignty; namely, the absolute use of the sword in peace and war, the making and abrogating of laws, *supreme judicature, and decision,* in all debates judicial and deliberative, the nomination of all magistrates and ministers, with other rights contained in the same, make the sovereign power no less absolute in the commonwealth, than before commonwealth every man was absolute in himself, to do, or not to do, what he thought good; which men, that have not had the experience of that miserable estate, to which men are reduced by long war, think so hard a condition, that they cannot easily acknowledge such covenants, and subjection on their parts, as are here set down, to have been ever necessary to their peace. And therefore some have imagined, that a commonwealth may be constituted in such manner, as the sovereign power may be so limited, and moderated, as they shall think fit themselves. For example: they suppose a multitude of men to have agreed upon certain articles, which they presently call laws, declaring how they will be governed, and that done, to agree further upon some man, or number of men, to see the same articles performed, and put in execution; and to enable him, or them, thereunto, they allot unto them a provision limited, as of certain lands, taxes, penalties, and the like, than which, if mispent, they shall have no more, without a new consent of the same men that allowed the former. And thus they think they have made a commonwealth, in which it is unlawful for any private man to make use of his own sword for his security; wherein they deceive themselves.

14. The same refelled. For first, if to the revenue, it did necessarily follow, that there might be forces raised and procured at the will of him that hath such revenue; yet since the revenue is limited, so must also the forces: but limited forces against the power of an enemy, which we cannot limit, are insufficient. Whensoever therefore there happeneth an invasion greater than those forces are able to resist, and there be no other right to levy more, then is every man, by necessity of nature, allowed to make the best provision he can for himself; and thus is the private sword, and the estate of war again

reduced. But seeing revenue, without the right of commanding men, is of no use, neither in peace, nor war, it is necessary to be supposed, that he that hath the administration of those articles, which are in the former section supposed, must have also right to make use of the strengths of particular men. And what reason soever giveth him that right over any one, giveth him the same over all. And then is his right absolute. For he that hath right to all their forces, hath right to dispose of the same. Again, supposing those limited forces and revenue either by the necessary, or negligent use of them, to fail, and that for a supply, the same multitude be again to be assembled, who shall have power to assemble them, that is to compel them to come together? If he that demandeth the supply hath that right, to wit, the right to compel them all, then is his sovereignty absolute; if not, then is every particular man at liberty to come or not; to frame a new commonwealth, or not; and so the right of the private sword returneth. But suppose them willingly, and of their own accord, assembled to consider of this supply, if now it be still in their choice, whether they shall give it, or not, it is also in their choice, whether the commonwealth shall stand or not. And therefore there lieth not upon any of them any civil obligation that may hinder them from using force, in case they think it tend to their defense. This device therefore of them that will make civil law first, and then a civil body afterwards, (as if policy made a body politic, and not a body politic made policy) is of no effect.

15. *Mixed forms of government supposed in sovereignty.* Others, to avoid the hard condition, as they take it, of absolute subjection, which, in hatred thereto, they also call slavery, have devised a government, as they think, mixed of the three sorts of sovereignty. As for example: they suppose the power of making laws, given to some great assembly democratical, the power of judicature to some other assembly, and the administration of the laws to a third, or to some one man; and this policy they call mixed monarchy, or mixed aristocracy, or mixed democracy, according as any of these three sorts do most visibly predominate. And in this estate of government, they think the use of the private sword excluded.

16. That refelled. And supposing it were so, how were this condition, which they call *slavery*, eased thereby. For in this estate they would have no man allowed, either to be his own judge, or own carver, or to make any laws unto himself; and as long as these three agree, they are as absolutely subject to them, as is a child to the father, or a slave to the master, in the state of nature. The ease therefore of this subjection, must consist in the disagreement of those amongst whom they have distributed the rights of sovereign power. But the same disagreement is war. The division therefore of the sovereignty, either worketh no effect to the taking away of simple subjection, or introduceth war, wherein the private sword hath place again. But the truth is, as hath been already showed in the seventh, eighth, ninth, tenth, eleventh, and twelfth precedent sections, the sovereignty is indivisible. And that seeming mixture of several kinds of government, is not mixture of the things themselves, but confusion in our understandings, that cannot find out readily to whom we have subjected ourselves.

17. Mixed government, &c. But though the sovereignty be not mixed, but be always either simple democracy, or simple aristocracy, or pure monarchy, nevertheless in the administration thereof, all those sorts of government may have place subordinate. For suppose the sovereign power be democracy, as it was sometimes in Rome, yet at the same time they may have a council aristocratical, such as was the senate; and at the same time they may have a subordinate monarch, such as was their dictator, who had, for a time, the exercise of the whole sovereignty, and such as are all generals in war. So also in monarchy there may be a council aristocratical of men, chosen by the monarch; or democratical of men, chosen by the consent, the monarch permitting, of all the particular men of the commonwealth. And this mixture is it that imposeth, as if it were the mixture of sovereignty. As if a man should think, because the great council of Venice doth nothing ordinarily but choose magistrates, ministers of state, captains, and governors of towns, ambassadors, counsellors, and the like, that therefore their part of the sovereignty is only choosing of magistrates; and that the making of war, and peace, and laws, were not theirs, but the part of such counsellors as they ap-

pointed thereto: whereas it is the part of *these* to do it bu
subordinately, the supreme authority thereof being in the grea
council that choose them.

18. Reason and experience to prove absolute sovereignty
somewhere in all commonwealths. And as reason teacheth us
that a man, considered out of subjection to laws, and out o
all covenants obligatory to others, is free to do and undo, ani
deliberate as long as he listeth, every member being obedien
to the will of the whole man, that liberty being nothing els
but his natural power, without which he is no better than ai
inanimate creature, not able to help himself; so also it teach
eth us, that a body politic, of what kind soever, not subject ti
another, nor obliged by covenants, ought to be free, and in ai
actions to be assisted by the members, every one in their place
or at least, not resisted by them. For otherwise, the power o
a body politic, the essence whereof is the not-resistance of th
members, is none, nor a body politic of any benefit. And th
same is confirmed by the use of all nations and common
wealths, wherein that man or council, which is virtually th
whole, hath any absolute power over every particular mem
ber; or what nation or commonwealth is there, that hath no
power and right to constitute a general in their wars? But th
power of a general is absolute; and consequently there wa
absolute power in the commonwealth, from whom it was de
rived. For no person, natural or civil, can transfer unto anothe
more power than himself hath.

19. Some principal, &c. marks of sovereignty. In every
commonwealth, where particular men are deprived of thei
right to protect themselves, there resideth an absolute sover
eignty, as I have already showed. But in what man, or in wha
assembly of men the same is placed, is not so manifest, a
not to need some marks, whereby it may be discerned. An
first, it is an infallible mark of absolute sovereignty in a man
or in an assembly of men, if there be no right in any othe
person, natural or civil, to punish that man, or to dissolv
that assembly. For he that cannot of right be punished, canno
of right be resisted; and he that cannot of right be resisted
hath coercive power over all the rest, and thereby can fram
and govern their actions at his pleasure, which is absolut

sovereignty. Contrariwise, he that in a commonwealth is punishable by any, or that assembly that is dissolvable, is not sovereign. For a greater power is always required to punish and dissolve, than theirs who are punished or dissolved; and that power cannot be called sovereign, than which there is a greater. Secondly, that man or assembly, that by their own right not derived from the present right of any other, may make laws, or abrogate them at his or their pleasure, have the sovereignty absolute. For seeing the laws they make, are supposed to be made by right, the members of the commonwealth, to whom they are made, are obliged to obey them, and consequently not resist the execution of them; which notresistance, maketh the power absolute of him that ordaineth them. It is likewise a mark of this sovereignty, to have the right original of appointing magistrates, judges, counsellors, and ministers of state. For without that power, no act of sovereignty, or government, can be performed. Lastly, and generally, whosoever by his own authority independent, can do any act, which another of the same commonwealth may not, must needs be understood to have the sovereign power. For by nature men have equal right. This inequality therefore must proceed from the power of the commonwealth. He therefore that doth any act lawfully by his own authority, which another may not, doth it by the power of the commonwealth in himself, which is absolute sovereignty.

Chapter 2

1. Democracy preceedeth all other, &c. Having spoken in general concerning instituted policy in the former chapter, I come in this, to speak of the sorts thereof in special, how every of them is instituted. The first in order of time of these three sorts, is democracy; and it must be so of necessity, because an aristocracy and a monarchy, require nomination of persons agreed upon, which agreement in a great multitude of men, must consist in the consent of the major part; and where the votes of the major part involve the votes of the rest, there is actually a democracy.

2. The sovereign people covenanteth not with the subjects. In the making of a democracy, there passeth no covenant between the sovereign, and any subject. For while the democracy is a making, there is no sovereign with whom to contract. For it cannot be imagined, that the multitude should contract with itself, or with any one man, or number of men, parcel of itself, to make itself sovereign; nor that a multitude, considered as one aggregate, can give itself anything which before it had not. Seeing then that sovereignty democratical is not conferred by the covenant of any multitude, which supposeth union and sovereignty already made, it resteth, that the same be conferred by the particular covenants of every several man; that is to say, every man with every man, for and in consideration of the benefit of his own peace and defense, covenanteth to stand to and obey whatsoever the major part of their whole number, or the major part of such a number of them, as shall be pleased to assemble at a certain time and place, shall determine and command. And this is that which giveth being to a democracy, wherein the sovereign assembly was called of the Greeks, by the name of *Demus,* that it, the people, from whence cometh democracy. So that, where to the supreme and independent court, every man may come that will, and give his vote, there the sovereign is called the people.

3. The sovereign, &c. cannot, &c. do injury, &c. Out of this that hath been said, may readily be drawn, that whatsoever the people doth to any one particular member or subject of the commonwealth, the same by him ought not to be styled injury. For first, injury, by the definition, Part I chap. 3. sect. 2, is breach of covenant; but covenants, as hath been said in the precedent section, there passed none from the people to any private man; and consequently it, to wit, the people, can do him no injury. Secondly, how unjust soever the action be, that this sovereign *demus* shall do, is done by the will of every particular man subject to him, who are therefore guilty of the same. If therefore they style it *injury*, they but accuse themselves. And it is against reason for the same man, both to do and complain; implying this contradiction, that whereas he first ratified the people's acts in general, he now disalloweth the same of them in particular. It is therefore said truly, *volenti non fit injuria*. Nevertheless nothing doth hinder, but that divers actions done by the people, may be unjust before God Almighty, as breaches of the laws of nature.

4. The faults of the sovereign people, &c. And when it happeneth, that the people by plurality of voices, decree or command anything contrary to the law of God or nature, though the decree and command be the act of every man, not only present in the assembly, but also absent from it; yet is not the injustice of the decree, the injustice of every particular man, but only of those men, by whose express suffrages, the decree or command was passed. For a body politic, as it is a fictitious body, so are the faculties and will thereof fictitious also. But to make a particular man unjust, which consisteth of a body and soul natural, there is required a natural and very will.

5. Democracy, &c., an aristocracy of orators. In all democracies, though the right of sovereignty be in the assembly, which is virtually the whole body; yet the use thereof is always in one, or a few particular men. For in such great assemblies, as those must be, whereinto every man may enter at his pleasure, there is no means any ways to deliberate and give counsel what to do, but by long and set orations, where-

by to every man there is more or less hope given, to incline and sway the assembly to their own ends. In a multitude of speakers therefore, where always either one is eminent alone, or a few being equal amongst themselves, are eminent above the rest, that one or few must of necessity sway the whole. Insomuch, that a democracy, in effect, is no more than an aristocracy of orators, interrupted sometimes with the temporary monarchy of one orator.

6. Aristocracy how made. And seeing a democracy is by institution, the beginning both of artistocracy and monarchy, we are to consider next, how aristocracy is derived from it. When the particular members of the commonwealth growing weary of attendance at public courts, as dwelling far off, or being attentive to their private businesses, and withal, displeased with the government of the people, assemble themselves to make an aristocracy, there is no more required to the making thereof but putting to the question one by one, the names of such men as it shall consist of, and assenting to their election; and by plurality of vote, to transfer that power, which before the people had, to the number of men so named and chosen.

7. The body of the *optimates* not properly said to injure the subjects. And from this manner of erecting an aristocracy, it is manifest, that the few, or *optimates*, have entered into no covenant with any of the particular members of the commonwealth, whereof they are sovereign; and consequently cannot do any thing to any private man, that can be called *injury* to him, howsoever their act be wicked before Almighty God, according to that which hath been said before, section 3. Further, it is impossible, that the people, as one body politic, should covenant with the aristocracy or *optimates*, on whom they intend to transfer their sovereignty. For no sooner is the aristocracy erected, but the democracy is annihilated, and the covenants made unto them void.

8. The election of the *optimates*, &c. In all aristocracies, the admission of such, as are from time to time to have vote in the sovereign assembly, dependeth on the will and decree of the present *optimates*. For they being the sovereign, have the nomination, by the eleventh section of the former chap-

ter, of all magistrates, ministers, and counsellors of state whatsoever, and may therefore choose either to make them elective, or hereditary, at their pleasure.

9. An elective king, &c. Out of the same democracy, the institution of a political monarch proceedeth in the same manner, as did the the institution of the aristocracy, to wit, by a decree of the sovereign people, to pass the sovereignty to one man named and approved by plurality of suffrage. And if this sovereignty be truly and indeed transferred, the estate or commonwealth is an absolute monarchy, wherein the monarch is at liberty, to dispose as well of the succession, as of the possession, and not an elective kingdom. For suppose a decree be made first in this manner, that such a one shall have the sovereignty for his life, and that afterward they will choose anew. In this case, the power of the people is dissolved, or not; if dissolved, then after the death of him that is chosen, there is no man bound to stand to the decrees of them that shall, as private men, run together to make a new election; and consequently, if there be any man, who by the advantage of the reign of him that is dead, hath strength enough to hold the multitude in peace and obedience, he may lawfully, or rather is by the law of nature obliged so to do: if this power of the people were not dissolved at the choosing of their king for life, then is the people sovereign still, and the king a minister thereof only, but so, as to put the whole sovereignty in execution; a great minister, but no otherwise for his time, than a dictator was in Rome. In this case, at the death of him that was chosen, they that meet for a new election, have no new, but their old authority for the same. For they were the sovereign all the time, as appeareth by the acts of those elective kings, that have procured from the people, that their children might succeed them. For it is to be understood, when a man receiveth any thing from the authority of the people, he receiveth it not from the people his subjects, but from the people his sovereign. And further, though in the election of a king for his life, the people grant him the exercise of their sovereignty for that time; yet if they see cause, they may recall the same before the time. As a prince that conferreth an office for life, may nevertheless,

upon suspicion of abuse thereof, recall it at his pleasure; inasmuch as offices that require labor and care, are understood to pass from him that giveth them, as *onera, burthens,* to them that have them; the recalling whereof are therefore not *injury,* but *favor.* Nevertheless, if in making an elective king, with intention to reserve the sovereignty, they reserve not a power at certain known and determined times and places to assemble themselves, the reservation of their sovereignty is of no effect, inasmuch as no man is bound to stand to the decrees and determinations of those that assemble themselves without the sovereign authority.

10. A conditional king, etc. In the former section is showed, that elective kings that exercise their sovereignty for a time, which determines with their life, either are subjects, or not sovereigns; and that it is, when the people in election of them, reserve unto themselves the right of assembling at certain times and places limited and made known; or else absolute sovereigns, to dispose of the succession at their pleasure, and that is, when the people in their election have declared no time nor place of their meeting, or have left it to the power of the elected king, to assemble and dissolve them at such times, as he himself shall think good. There is another kind of limitation of time, to him that shall be elected to use the sovereign power, which whether it hath been practiced anywhere, or not, I know not, but it may be imagined, and hath been objected against the rigor of sovereign power; and it is this, that the people transfer their sovereignty upon conditions. As for example, for so long as he shall observe such and such laws, as they then prescribe him. And here as before in elected kings, the question is to be made, whether in the electing of such a sovereign, they reserved to themselves a right of assembling at times and places limited and known, or not; if not, then is the sovereignty of the people dissolved, and they have neither power to judge of the breach of the conditions given him, nor to command any forces for the deposing of him, whom on that condition they had set up, but are in the estate of war amongst themselves, as they were before they made themselves a democracy: and consequently, if he that is elected by the advantage of the possession he

hath of the public means, be able to compel them to unity and obedience, he hath not only the right of nature to warrant him, but the law of nature to oblige him thereunto. But if in electing him, they reserved to themselves a right of assembling, and appointed certain times and places to that purpose, then are they sovereign still, and may call their conditional king to account at their pleasure, and deprive him of his government, if they judge he deserve it, either by breach of the conditions set him, or otherwise. For the sovereign power can by no covenant with a subject be bound to continue him in the charge he undergoeth by their command, as a burden imposed not particularly for his good, but for the good of the sovereign people.

11. The word people equivocal. The controversies that arise concerning the right of the people, proceed from the equivocation of the word. For the word people hath a double signification. In one sense it signifieth only a number of men, distinguished by the place of their habitation; as the *people* of England, or the *people* of France, which is no more, but the multitude of those particular persons that inhabit those regions, without consideration of any contracts or covenants amongst them, by which any one of them is obliged to the rest. In another sense, it signifieth a person civil, that is to say, either one man, or one council, in the will whereof, is included and involved the will of every one in particular. As for example, in this latter sense, the lower house of parliament is all the commons, as long as they sit there with authority and right thereto; but after they be dissolved, though they remain, they be no more the people, nor the commons, but only the aggregate, or multitude of the particular men there sitting, how well soever they agree, or concur, in opinions amongst themselves; whereupon, they that do not distinguish between these two significations, do usually attribute such rights to a dissolved multitude, as belong only to the people virtually contained in the body of the commonwealth or sovereignty. And when a great number of their own authority flock together in any nation, they usually give them the name of the whole nation. In which sense they say the people rebelleth, or the people demandeth, when it is no

more than a dissolved multitude, of which though any one man may be said to demand or have right to something, yet the heap, or multitude, cannot be said to demand or have right to anything. For where every man hath his right distinct, there is nothing left for the multitude to have right unto: and when the particulars say, this is mine, this is thine, and this is his, and have shared all amongst them, there can be nothing whereof the multitude can say, this is mine; nor are they one body, as behoveth them to be, that demand anything under the name of mine, or his: and when they say ours, every man is understood to pretend in several, and not the multitude. On the other side, when the multitude is united into a body politic, and thereby are a people in the other signification, and their wills virtually in the sovereign, there the rights and demands of the particulars do cease; and he or they that have the sovereign power, doth for them all, demand, and vindicate under the name of his, that which before they called in the plural, theirs.

12. *Obedience discharged by release, &c.* We have seen how particular men enter into subjection, by transferring their rights; it followeth to consider, how such subjection may be discharged. And first, if he or they that have the sovereign power, shall relinquish the same voluntarily, there is no doubt, but every man is again at liberty to obey, or not. Likewise, if he or they retaining the sovereignty over the rest, do nevertheless exempt some one or more, from their subjection, every man so exempted, is discharged. For he or they to whom any man is obliged, hath the power to release him.

13. *How such releases are to be understood.* And here it is to be understood, that when he or they that have the sovereign power, give such exemption, or privilege, to a subject, as is not separable from the sovereignty, and nevertheless directly retaineth the sovereign power, not knowing the consequence of the privilege they grant, the person or persons exempted or privileged, are not thereby released. For in contradictory significations of the will (*Human Nature*, chap. 13. sect. 9), that which is directly signified, is to be under-

stood for the will, before that which is drawn from it by consequence.

14. Obedience discharged by exile. Also exile perpetual, is a release of subjection, forasmuch, as being out of the protection of the sovereignty that expelled him, he hath no means of subsisting but from himself. Now every man may lawfully defend himself, that hath no other defense; else there had been no necessity that any man should enter into voluntary subjection, as they do in commonwealths.

15. By conquest. Likewise a man is released of his subjection by conquest. For when it cometh to pass, that the power of a commonwealth is overthrown, and any particular man thereby lying under the sword of his enemy, yieldeth himself captive, he is thereby bound to serve him that taketh him, and consequently discharged of his obligation to the former. For no man can serve two masters.

16. By ignorance of the right of succession. Lastly, ignorance of the succession dischargeth obedience. For no man can be understood to be obliged to obey he knoweth not whom.

Chapter 3

1. *Titles to dominion; master and servant, &c.* Having set forth in the two preceding chapters, the nature of a commonwealth *institutive* by the consent of many men together, I come now to speak of dominion, or a body politic by acquisition, which is commonly called a *patrimonial* kingdom. But before I enter thereinto, it is necessary to make known upon what title one man may acquire right, that is to say, property or dominion, over the person of another. For when one man hath dominion over another, there is a little kingdom. And to be a king by acquisition, is nothing else, but to have acquired a right or dominion over many.

2. Considering men therefore again in the state of nature, without covenants or subjection one to another, as if they were but even now all at once created male and female, there be three titles only, by which one man may have right and dominion over another; whereof two may take place presently, and those are, voluntary offer of subjection, and yielding by compulsion: the third is to take place, upon the supposition of children begotten amongst them. Concerning the first of these three titles, it is handled before in the two last chapters. For from thence cometh the right of sovereigns over their subjects in a commonwealth institutive. Concerning the second title, which is when a man submitteth to an assailant for fear of death, thereby accrueth a right of dominion. For where every man, as it happeneth in this case, hath right to all things, there needs no more for the making of the said right effectual, but a covenant from him that is overcome, not to resist him that overcometh. And thus cometh the victor to have right of absolute dominion over the conquered. By which there is presently constituted a little body politic, which consisteth of two persons, the one sovereign, which is called the *master*, or lord; the other subject, which is called the *servant*. And when a man hath acquired right over a number of servants so considerable, as they cannot by their neighbors be securely invaded, this body politic is a kingdom despotical.

3. Chains and other, &c., bonds, &c., slave defined. And it is to be understood, that when a servant taken in the wars, is kept bound in natural bonds, as chains, and the like, or in prison, there hath passed no covenant from the servant to his master. For those natural bonds have no need of strengthening by the verbal bonds of covenant, and they show that the servant is not trusted But covenant, (Part I chapter 2 section 9), supposeth trust. There remaineth therefore in the servant thus kept bound, or in prison, a right of delivering himself, if he can, by what means soever. This kind of servant is that which ordinarily and without passion, is called a *slave*. The Romans had no such distinct name, but comprehended all under the name of *servus;* whereof such as they loved and durst trust, were suffered to go at liberty, and admitted to places of office, both near to their persons, and in their affairs abroad; the rest were kept chained, or otherwise restrained with natural impediments to their resistance. And as it was amongst the Romans, so it was amongst other nations, the former sort having no other bond but a supposed covenant, without which the master had no reason to trust them; the latter being without covenant, and no otherwise tied to obedience, but by chains, or other like forcible custody.

4. Servants have no property against their lord, &c. A master therefore is to be supposed to have no less right over those, whose bodies he leaveth at liberty, than over those he keepeth in bonds and imprisonment, and hath absolute dominion over both, and may say of his servant, that he is his, as he may of any other thing. And whatsoever the servant had, and might call his, is now the master's; for he that disposeth of the person, disposeth of all the person could dispose of: insomuch, as though there be *meum* and *tuum* amongst servants distinct from one another by the dispensation, and for the benefit of their master; yet there is no *meum* and *tuum* belonging to any of them against the master himself, whom they are not to resist, but to obey all his commands as law.

5. The master hath right to alienate his servant. And seeing both the servant and all that is committed to him, is the

property of the master, and every man may dispose of his own, and transfer the same at his pleasure, the master may therefore alienate his dominion over them, or give the same by his last will to whom he list.

6. The servant of the servant, &c. And if it happen, that the master himself by captivity or voluntary subjection, become servant to another, then is that other master *paramount;* and those servants of him that becometh servant, are no further obliged, than their master paramount shall think good; forasmuch as he disposing of the master subordinate, disposeth of all he hath, and consequently of his servants, so that the restriction of absolute power in masters, proceedeth not from the law of nature, but from the political law of him that is their master supreme or sovereign.

7. How servitude is discharged. Servants immediate to the supreme master, are discharged of their servitude, or subjection, in the same manner that subjects are released of their allegiance in a commonwealth institutive. As first, by release. For he that captiveth, which is done by accepting what the captive transferreth to him, setteth again at liberty, by transferring back the same. And this kind of release is called *manumission.* Secondly, by exile. For that is no more but manumission given to a servant, not in the way of benefit, but punishment. Thirdly, by a new captivity, where the servant having done his endeavor to defend himself, hath thereby performed his covenant to his former master, and for the safety of his life, entering into new covenant with the conqueror, is bound to do his best endeavor to keep that likewise. Fourthly, ignorance of who is successor to his deceased master, dischargeth him of obedience: for no covenant holdeth longer than a man knoweth to whom he is to perform it. And lastly, that servant that is no longer trusted, but committed to his chains and custody, is thereby discharged of the obligation *in foro interno,* and therefore if he can get loose, may lawfully go his way.

8. The middle lord, &c. But servants subordinate, though manumitted by their immediate lord, are not thereby discharged of their subjection to their lord paramount. For the immediate master hath no property in them, having trans-

ferred his right before to another, namely, to his own and supreme master. Nor if the chief lord should manumit his immediate servant, doth he thereby release his servants of their obligation to him that is so manumitted. For by this manumission, he recovereth again the absolute dominion he had over them before. For after a release, which is the discharge of a covenant, the right standeth as it did before the covenant was made.

9. *The title of man, &c., over beasts.* This right of conquest, as it maketh one man master over another, so also maketh it a man to be master of the irrational creatures. For if a man in the state of nature be in hostility with men, and thereby have lawful title to subdue or kill, according as his own conscience and discretion shall suggest unto him for his safety and benefit, much more may he do the same to beasts; that is to say, save and preserve for his own service, according to his discretion, such as are of nature apt to obey, and commodious for use; and to kill and destroy, with perpetual war, all other, as fierce, and noisome to him. And this dominion is therefore of the law of nature, and not of the divine law positive. For if there had been no such right before the revealing of God's will in the Scripture, then should no man, to whom the Scripture hath not come, have right to make use of those his creatures, either for his food or sustenance. And it were a hard condition of mankind, that a fierce and savage beast should with more right kill a man, than a man a beast.

Chapter 4

1. The dominion over the child, &c. Of three ways by which a man becometh subject to another, mentioned section 2, chapter the last, namely, voluntary offer, captivity and birth, the former two have been spoken of, under the name of subjects, and servants. In the next place, we are to set down the third way of subjection, under the name of children, and by what title one man cometh to have propriety in a child, that proceedeth from the common generation of two; to wit, of male and female. And considering men again dissolved from all covenants one with another, and that (Part I chap. 4. sect. 2) every man by the law of nature, hath right or propriety to his own body, the child ought rather to be the propriety of the mother, of whose body it is part, till the time of separation, than of the father. For the understanding therefore of the right that a man or woman hath to his or their child, two things are to be considered; first, what title the mother, or any other, originally hath, to a child new born: secondly, how the father, or any other man, pretendeth by the mother.

2. Pre-eminence of sex giveth not the child to the father, rather than to the mother. For the first, they that have written of this subject, have made generation to be a title of dominion over persons, as well as the consent of the persons themselves. And because generation giveth title to two, namely, father and mother, whereas dominion is indivisible, they therefore ascribe dominion over the child to the father only, *ob præstantiam sexûs;* but they show not, neither can I find out by what coherence, either generation inferreth dominion, or advantage of so much strength, which, for the most part, a man hath more than a woman, should generally and universally entitle the father to a propriety in the child, and take it away from the mother.

3. The title of the father or mother, &c. The title to dominion over a child, proceedeth not from the generation, but

from the preservation of it; and therefore in the estate of nature, the mother, in whose power it is to save or destroy it, hath right thereto by that power, according to that which hath been said, Part I chapter 1 sect. 13. And if the mother shall think fit to abandon, or expose her child to death, whatsoever man or woman shall find the child so exposed, shall have the same right which the mother had before; and for this same reason, namely, for the power not of generating, but preserving. And though the child thus preserved, do in time acquire strength, whereby he might pretend equality with him or her that hath preserved him, yet shall that pretense be thought unreasonable, both because his strength was the gift of him, against whom he pretendeth, and also because it is to be presumed, that he which giveth sustenance to another, whereby to strengthen him, hath received a promise of obedience in consideration thereof. For else it would be wisdom in men, rather to let their children perish, while they are infants, than to live in their danger or subjection, when they are grown.

4. The child of a woman servant, &c. For the pretenses which a man may have to dominion over a child by the right of the mother, they be of divers kinds. One by the absolute subjection of the mother; another, by some particular covenant from her, which is less than a covenant of such subjection. By absolute subjection, the master of the mother, hath right to her child, according to section 6, chapter 3, whether he be the father thereof, or not. And thus the children of the servant are the goods of the master *in perpetuum*.

5. The right to the child given from the mother, &c. Of covenants that amount not to subjection between a man and woman, there be some which are made for a time: they are covenants of cohabitation, or else of copulation only. And in this latter case, the children pass by covenants particular. And thus in the copulation of the Amazons with their neighbors, the fathers by covenant had the male children only, the mothers retaining the females.

6. The child of the concubine, &c. And covenants of cohabitation are either for society of bed, or for society of all things; if for society of bed only, then is the woman called

a *concubine*. And here also the child shall be his or hers, as they shall agree particularly by covenant. For although for the most part, a concubine is supposed to yield up the right of her children to the father, yet doth not concubinate enforce so much.

7. The child of the husband and the wife, &c. But if the covenants of cohabitation be for society of all things, it is necessary that but one of them govern and dispose of all that is common to them both; without which, as hath been often said before, society cannot last. And therefore the man, to whom for the most part the woman yieldeth the government, hath for the most part, also, the sole right and dominion over the children. And the man is called the husband, and the woman the wife. But because sometimes the government may belong to the wife only, sometimes also the dominion over the children shall be in her only. As in the case of a sovereign queen, there is no reason that her marriage should take from her the dominion over her children.

8. The father, or he or she that bringeth up the child, have absolute power over him. Children therefore, whether they be brought up and preserved by the father, or by the mother, or by whomsoever, are in most absolute subjection to him or her, that so bringeth them up, or preserveth them. And they may alienate them, that is, assign his or her dominion, by selling, or giving, in adoption or servitude to others; or may pawn them for hostages, kill them for rebellion, or sacrifice them for peace, by the law of nature, when he or she, in his or her conscience, think it to be necessary.

9. Freedom in subjects, what it is. The subjection of them who institute a commonwealth amongst themselves, is no less absolute, than the subjection of servants. And therein they are in equal estate. But the hope of those is greater than the hope of these. For he that subjecteth himself uncompelled, thinketh there is reason he should be better used, than he that doth it upon compulsion; and coming in freely, calleth himself, though in subjection, a *freeman;* whereby it appeareth, that liberty is not any exemption from subjection and obedience to the sovereign power, but a state of better hope than theirs, that have been subjected by force and conquest.

And this was the reason, that the name which signifieth children in the Latin tongue, is *liberi*, which also signifieth *freemen*. And yet in Rome, nothing at that time was so obnoxious to the power of others, as children in the family of their fathers. For both the state had power over their life without consent of their fathers, and the father might kill his son by his own authority, without any warrant from the state. Freedom therefore in commonwealths is nothing but the honor of equality of favor with other subjects, and servitude the estate of the rest. A freeman therefore may expect employments of honor, rather than a servant. And this is all that can be understood by the liberty of the subject. For in all other senses, liberty is the state of him that is not subject.

10. A great family is a patrimonial kingdom. Now when a father that hath children, hath servants also, the children, not by the right of the child, but by the natural indulgence of the parents, are such freemen. And the whole, consisting of the father or mother, or both, and of the children, and of the servants, is called a *family*, wherein the father or mother of the family is sovereign of the same, and the rest, both children and servants equally, subjects. The same family, if it grow by multiplication of children, either by generation, or adoption; or of servants, either by generation, conquest, or voluntary submission, to be so great and numerous, as in probability it may protect itself, then is that family called a *patrimonial kingdom*, or monarchy by acquisition, wherein the sovereignty is in one man, as it is in a monarch made by *political institution*. So that whatsoever rights be in the one, the same also be in the other. And therefore I shall no more speak of them as distinct, but of monarchy in general.

11. Succession of the sovereign power, &c. Having showed by what right the several sorts of commonwealths, democracy, aristocracy, and monarchy, are erected, it followeth, to show by what right they are continued. The right by which they are continued, is called the right of succession to the sovereign power; whereof there is nothing to be said in a democracy, because the sovereign dieth not, as long as there be subjects alive: nor in an aristocracy, because it cannot

easily fall out, that the *optimates* should every one fail at
once; and if it should so fall out, there is no question, but
the commonwealth is thereby dissolved. It is therefore in a
monarchy only, that there can happen a question concerning
the succession. And first, forasmuch as a monarch, which is
absolute sovereign, hath the dominion in his own right, he
may dispose thereof at his own will. If therefore by his last
will, he shall name his successor, the right passeth by that
will.

12. Though the successor be not declared, yet there is
always one to be presumed. Nor if the monarch die without
any will concerning the succession declared, it is not therefore to be presumed, it was his will, his subjects, which are
to him as his children and servants, should return again to
the state of anarchy, that is, to war and hostility. For that
were expressly against the law of nature, which commandeth
to procure peace, and to maintain the same. It is therefore
to be conjectured with reason, that it was his intention to
bequeath them peace, that is to say, a power coercive, whereby to keep them from sedition amongst themselves; and
rather in the form of a monarchy, than any other government; forasmuch as he, by the exercise thereof in his own
person, hath declared, that he approveth the same.

13. The children preferred to the succession, &c. Further,
it is to be supposed, his intention was, that his own children
should be preferred in the succession, when nothing to the
contrary is expressly declared, before any other. For men
naturally seek their own honor, and that consisteth in the
honor of their children after them.

14. The males before the females. Again, seeing every
monarch is supposed to desire to continue the government
in his successors, as long as he may; and that generally men
are endued with greater parts of wisdom and courage, by
which all monarchies are kept from dissolution, than women
are; it is to be presumed, where no express will is extant
to the contrary, he preferreth his male children before the
female. Not but that women may govern, and have in divers
ages and places governed wisely, but are not so apt thereto
in general, as men.

15. The eldest before the rest of the brothers. Because the sovereign power is indivisible, it cannot be supposed, that he intended the same should be divided, but that it should descend entirely upon one of them, which is to be presumed, should be the eldest, assigned thereto by the lot of nature, because he appointed no other lot for the decision thereof. Besides, what difference of ability soever there may be amongst the brethren, the odds shall be adjudged to the elder, because no subject hath authority otherwise to judge thereof.

16. The brother next to the children. And for want of issue in the possessor, the brother shall be presumed successor. For by the judgment of nature, next in blood is next in love; and next in love is next to preferment.

17. The succession of the possessor, &c. And as the succession followeth the first monarch, so also it followeth him or her that is in possession; and consequently, the children of him in possession, shall be preferred before the children of his father, or predecessor.

Chapter 5

1. The utility of the commonwealth, &c. Having set forth the nature of a Body Politic, and the three sorts thereof, democracy, aristocracy, and monarchy; in this chapter shall be declared, the *conveniences,* and *inconveniences,* that arise from the same, both in general, and of the said several sorts in particular. And first, seeing a body politic is erected only for the ruling and governing of particular men, the benefit and damage thereof, consisteth in the benefit or damage of being ruled. The benefit is that for which a body politic was instituted, namely, the peace and preservation of every particular man, than which it is not possible there can be a greater, as hath been touched before, Part I chapter 1. section 12. And this benefit extendeth equally both to the *sovereign,* and to the *subjects.* For he or they that have the sovereign power, have but the defense of their persons, by the assistance of the particulars; and every particular man hath his defense by their union in the sovereign. As for other benefits, which pertain not to their safety and sufficiency, but to their well and delightful being, such as are superfluous riches, they so belong to the sovereign, as they must also be in the subject; and so to the subject, as they must also be in the sovereign. For the riches and treasure of the sovereign, is the dominion he hath over the riches of his subjects. If therefore the sovereign provide not so as that particular men may have means, both to preserve themselves, and also to preserve the public; the common or sovereign treasure can be none. And on the other side, if it were not for a common and public treasure belonging to the sovereign power, men's private riches would sooner serve to put them into confusion and war, than to secure and maintain them. Insomuch, as the profit of the sovereign and subject goeth always together. That distinction therefore of government, that there is one government for the good of him that governeth, and another for the good of them that be governed;

whereof the former is *despotical,* that is lordly; the other, a government of *freemen,* is not right. No more is the opinion of them that hold it to be no city, which consisteth of a master and his servants. They might as well say, it were no city, that consisted in a father and his own issue, how numerous soever they were. For to a master that hath no children, the servants have in them all those respects, for which men love their children. For they are his strength and his honor. And his power is no greater over them, than over his children.

2. The loss of liberty, &c. The inconvenience arising from government in general to him that governeth, consisteth partly in the continual care and trouble about the business of other men, that are his subjects; and partly, in the danger of his person. For the head always is that part, not only where the care resideth, but also against which the stroke of an enemy most commonly is directed. To balance this incommodity, the sovereignty, together with the necessity of this care and danger, comprehendeth so much honor, riches, and means, whereby to delight the mind, as no private man's wealth can attain unto. The inconveniences of government in general to a subject are none at all, if well considered, but in appearance. There be two things that may trouble his mind, or two general grievances; the one is, loss of liberty; the other, the uncertainty of *meum* and *tuum.* For the first, it consisteth in this, that a subject may no more govern his own actions according to his own discretion and judgment, or, which is all one, conscience, as the present occasions from time to time shall dictate to him; but must be tied to do according to that will only, which once for all he had long ago laid up, and involved in the wills of the major part of an assembly, or in the will of some one man. But this is really no inconvenience. For, as it hath been showed before, it is the only means, by which we have any possibility of preserving ourselves. For if every man were allowed this liberty of following his conscience, in such difference of consciences, they would not live together in peace an hour. But it appeareth a great inconvenience to every man in particular, to be debarred of this liberty, because every one apart considereth it as in himself, and not as in the rest; by which means, liberty ap-

peareth in the likeness of rule and government over others. For where one man is at liberty, and the rest bound, there that one hath government; which honor, he that understandeth not so much, demanding by the name simply of liberty, thinketh it a great grievance and injury to be denied it. For the second grievance concerning *meum* and *tuum*, it is also none, but in appearance only; it consisteth in this, that the sovereign power taketh from him that which he used to enjoy, knowing no other propriety, but use and custom. But without such sovereign power, the right of men is not propriety to anything, but a community, no better than to have no right at all, as hath been showed, Part I chapter 1, section 10. Propriety therefore being derived from the sovereign power, is not to be pretended against the same, especially, when by it every subject hath his propriety against every other subject, which when sovereignty ceaseth, he hath not, because in that case they return to war amongst themselves. Those levies therefore which are made upon men's estates, by the sovereign authority, are no more but the price of that peace and defense which the sovereignty maintaineth for them. If this were not so, no money nor forces for the wars, nor any other public occasion, could justly be levied in the world. For neither king, nor democracy, nor aristocracy, nor the estates of any land, could do it, if the sovereignty could not. For in all those cases, it is levied by virtue of the sovereignty. Nay more, by the three estates here, the land of one man may be transferred to another, without crime of him from whom it was taken, and without pretense of public benefit, as hath been done; and this without injury, because done by the sovereign power. For the power whereby it is done, is no less than sovereign, and cannot be greater. Therefore this grievance for *meum* and *tuum* is not real, unless more be exacted than is necessary; but it seemeth a grievance, because to them that either know not the right of sovereignty, or to whom that right belongeth, it seemeth an injury; and injury, how little soever the damage, is always grievous, as putting us in mind of our disability to help ourselves, and into envy of the power to do us wrong.

3. *Monarchy approved by, &c.* Having spoken of the in-

conveniences of the subject, by government in general, let us consider the same in the three several sorts thereof, namely, *democracy, aristocracy* and *monarchy;* whereof the two former are in effect but one. For, as I have showed before, democracy is but the government of a few orators. The comparison therefore will be between monarchy and aristocracy: and to omit that the world, as it was created, so also it is governed by one God Almighty; and that all the ancients have preferred monarchy before other governments, both in opinion, because they feigned a monarchical government amongst their gods, and also by their custom; for that in the most ancient times all people were so governed: and that paternal government, which is monarchy, was instituted in the beginning from the creation; and that other governments have proceeded from the dissolution thereof, caused by the rebellious nature of mankind, and be but pieces of broken monarchies cemented by human wit, I will insist only on this comparison, upon the inconveniences that may happen to the subjects in consequence to each of these governments.

4. Monarchy less subject to passion, &c. And first, it seemeth inconvenient there should be committed so great a power to one man, as that it might be lawful to no other man or men to resist the same; and some think it inconvenient *eo nomine,* because he hath the power. But this reason we may not by any means admit, for it maketh it inconvenient to be ruled by Almighty God, who without question hath more power over every man, than can be conferred upon any monarch. This inconvenience therefore must be derived not from the power, but from the affections and passions which reign in every one, as well monarch as subject, by which the monarch may be swayed to use that power amiss: and because an aristocracy consisteth of men, if the passions of many men be more violent when they are assembled together, than the passions of one man alone, it will follow, that the inconvenience arising from passions will be greater in an *aristocracy,* than a *monarchy.* But there is no doubt, when things are debated in great assemblies, but every man delivering his opinion at large without interruption, endeavoreth to make whatsoever he is to set forth for good, better; and what h

would have apprehended as evil, worse, as much as is possible, to the end his counsel may take place; which counsel also is never without aim at his own benefit, or honor; every man's end being some good to himself. Now this cannot be done without working on the passions of the rest. And thus the passions of these that are singly moderate, are altogether vehement; even as a great many coals, though but warm asunder, being put together, inflame one another.

5. *Subjects in monarchy, &c.* Another inconvenience of monarchy, is this, that the monarch, besides the riches necessary for the defense of the commonwealth, may take so much more from the subjects, as may enrich his children, kindred and favorites, to what degree he pleaseth; which though it be indeed an inconvenience, if he should so do, yet is the same both greater in an aristocracy, and also more likely to come to pass, for there not one only, but many have children, kindred, and friends to raise. And in that point they are as twenty monarchs for one, and likely to set forward one another's designs mutually, to the oppression of all the rest. The same also happeneth in a democracy, if they all do agree; otherwise they bring a worse inconvenience; to wit, sedition.

6. Another inconvenience of monarchy, is the power of dispensing with the execution of justice, whereby the family and friends of the monarch, may, with impunity, commit outrages upon the people, or oppress them with extortion. But in aristocracies, not only one, but many have power of taking men out of the hands of justice, and no man is willing his kindred or friends should be punished according to their demerits. And therefore they understand amongst themselves without further speaking, as a tacit convenant, *hodie mihi, cras tibi.*

7. *Laws in monarchy less changeable, &c.* Another inconvenience of monarchy, is the power of altering laws. Concerning which, it is necessary that such a power be, that laws may be altered, according as men's manners change, or as the conjuncture of all circumstances within and without the commonwealth shall require; the change of law being then inconvenient, when it proceedeth from the change, not of the occasion, but of the minds of him or them, by whose authority

he laws are made. Now it is manifest enough of itself, that he mind of one man is not so variable in that point, as are he decrees of an assembly. For not only they have all their natural changes, but the change of any one man may be nough, with eloquence and reputation, or by solicitation and action, to make that law to-day, which another by the very same means, shall abrogate to-morrow.

8. Monarchies less subject to dissolution. Lastly, the greatest inconvenience that can happen to a commonwealth, is the aptitude to dissolve into civil war; and to this are monarchies much less subject, than any other governments. For where the union, or band of a commonwealth, is one man, here is no distraction; whereas in assemblies, those that are of different opinions, and give different counsel, are apt to fall out amongst themselves, and to cross the designs of the commonwealth for one another's sake: and when they cannot have the honor of making good their own devices, they yet seek the honor to make the counsels of their adversaries prove vain. And in this contention, when the opposite factions happen to be anything equal in strength, they presently fall to war. Wherein necessity teacheth both sides, that an absolute monarch, to wit, a general, is necessary both for their defense against one another, and also for the peace of each faction within itself. But this aptitude to dissolution, is to be understood for an inconvenience in such aristocracies only where the affairs of state are debated in great and numerous assemblies, as they were anciently in Athens, and in Rome; and not in such as do nothing else in great assemblies, but choose magistrates and counsellors, and commit the handling of state affairs to a few; such as is the aristocracy of Venice at this day. For these are no more apt to dissolve from this occasion, than monarchies, the counsel of state being both in the one and the other alike.

Concerning a Theological Difficulty

Chapter 6

1. A difficulty concerning absolute subjection to man, arising from our absolute subjection to God Almighty, propounded. Having showed, that in all commonwealths whatsoever, the necessity of peace and government requireth, that there be existent some power, either in one man, or in one assembly of men, by the name of the power sovereign, which it is not lawful for any member of the same commonwealth to disobey; there occurreth now a difficulty, which, if it be not removed, maketh it unlawful for a man to put himself under the command of such absolute sovereignty as is required thereto. And the difficulty is this; we have amongst us the Word of God for the rule of our actions: now if we shall subject ourselves to men also, obliging ourselves to do such actions as shall be by them commanded, when the commands of God and man shall differ, we are to obey God, rather than man; and consequently, the covenant of general obedience to man is unlawful.

2. That this difficulty is only amongst those Christians that deny the interpretation of Scripture to depend upon the sovereign authority of the commonwealth. This difficulty hath not been of very great antiquity in the world. There was no such *dilemma* amongst the Jews; for their civil law, and divine law, was one and the same law of Moses; the interpreters whereof were the priests, whose power was subordinate to the power of the king; as was the power of Aaron, to the power of Moses. Nor is it a controversy that was ever taken notice of amongst the Grecians, Romans, or other Gentiles: for amongst these their several civil laws were the rules whereby not only righteousness and virtue, but also religion, and the external worship of God, was ordered and approved; that being esteemed the true worship of God, which was κατὰ τὸ νόμιμα, according to the laws civil. Also those Christians that dwell under the temporal dominion of the bishop of Rome,

re free from this question; for that they allow unto him, their sovereign, to interpret the Scriptures, which are the law of God, as he in his own judgment shall think right. This difficulty therefore remaineth amongst, and troubleth those Christians only, to whom it is allowed, to take for the sense of the Scripture, that which they make thereof, either by their own private interpretation, or by the interpretation of such as are not called thereunto by public authority; they that follow their own interpretation continually, demanding liberty of conscience; and those that follow the interpretation of others not ordained thereunto by the sovereign of the commonwealth, requiring a power in matters of religion either above the power civil, or at least not depending on it.

3. That human laws are not made to govern the consciences of men, but their words & actions. To take away this scruple of conscience, concerning obedience to human laws, amongst those that interpret to themselves the word of God in the Holy Scriptures, I propound to their consideration, first, that no human law is intended to oblige the conscience of a man, unless it break out into action, either of the tongue, or other part of the body. The law made thereupon would be of none effect, because no man is able to discern, but by word or other action whether such law be kept or broken. Nor did the apostles themselves pretend dominion over men's consciences, concerning the faith they preached, but only persuasion and instruction. And therefore St. Paul saith (2 Cor. i. 24), writing to the Corinthians, concerning their controversies, that he and the rest of the apostles had no dominion over their faith, but were helpers of their joy.

4. Places of Scripture to prove obedience due from Christians to their sovereign in all things. And for the actions of men which proceed from their consciences, the regulating of which actions is the only means of peace, if they might not stand with justice, it were impossible that justice towards God, and peace amongst men, should stand together in that religion that teacheth us, that *justice and peace shall kiss each other*, and in which we have so many precepts of absolute obedience to human authority; as Matth. xxiii. 2, 3, we have this precept:

The Scribes and Pharisees sit in Moses' seat; all therefore whatsoever they bid you observe, that observe and do. And yet were the Scribes and Pharisees not priests, but men of temporal authority. Again Luke xi. 17: *Every kingdom divided against itself shall be desolate;* and is not that kingdom divided against itself, where the actions of every one shall be ruled by his private opinion, or conscience, and yet those actions such as give occasion of offense and breach of peace? Again Rom. xiii. 5: *Wherefore you must be subject, not because of wrath only, but also for conscience sake.* Titus iii. 1: *Put them in remembrance, that they be subject to principalities and powers.* 1 Peter ii. 13, 14: *Submit yourselves unto all manner of ordinance of man, for the Lord's sake, whether it be unto the king, as unto the superior, or unto governors, as unto them that are sent by him for the punishment of evil doers.* Jude, verse 8: *These dreamers also that defile the flesh, and despise government, and speak evil of them that are in authority.* And forasmuch as all subjects in commonwealths are in the nature of children and servants, that which is a command to them, is a command to all subjects. But to these St. Paul saith (Colos. iii. 20, 22): *Children, obey your parents in all things; servants, be obedient to your masters according to the flesh in all things.* And verse 23: *Do it heartily as to the Lord.* These places considered, it seemeth strange to me, that any man in a Christian commonwealth, should have any occasion to deny his obedience to public authority, upon this ground, that *it is better to obey God than man.* For though St. Peter and the apostles did so answer the council of the Jews, that forbade them to preach Christ, there appeareth no reason that Christians should allege the same against their Christian governors, that command them to preach Christ. To reconcile this seeming contradiction of simple obedience to God, and simple obedience to man, we are to consider a Christian subject, as under a Christian sovereign, or under an infidel.

5. A distinction propounded between a fundamental point of faith and a superstructure. And under a Christian sovereign we are to consider, what actions we are forbidden by God

Almighty to obey them in, and what not. The actions we are forbidden to obey them in, are such only, as imply a denial of that faith which is necessary to our salvation: for otherwise there can be no pretense of disobedience; for why should a man incur the danger of a temporal death, by displeasing of his superior, if it were not for fear of eternal death hereafter? It must therefore be inquired, what those propositions and articles be, the belief whereof our Saviour or his apostles have declared to be such, as without believing them, a man cannot be saved; and then all other points, that are now controverted, and made distinction of sects, Papists, Lutherans, Calvinists, Arminians, &c. (as in old time, the like made Paulists, Apollonians, and Cephasians), must needs be such, as a man needeth not for the holding thereof, deny obedience to his superiors. And for the points of faith necessary to salvation, I shall call them *fundamental*, and every other point a *superstruction*.

6. An explication of the points of faith, that be fundamental. And without all controversy, there is not any more necessary point to be believed for man's salvation than this, that *Jesus is the Messiah*, that is, *the Christ*; which proposition is explicated in sundry sorts, but still the same in effect; as, that *he is God's anointed;* for that is signified by the word Christ: that *he was the true and lawful king of Israel, the son of David, the Saviour of the world, the redeemer of Israel, the salvation of God, he that should come into the world, the son of God*, and, which I desire by the way to have noted, against the now sect of Arians, *the begotten Son of God*, Acts ii. 13; Heb. v. 5: *The only begotten Son of God*, John i. 14, 18; John iii. 16, 18; 1 John iv. 9: *That he was God*, John i. 1; John xx. 28: *That the fulness of the Godhead dwelt in him bodily*, Coloss. ii. 9: Moreover, *the Holy One, the Holy One of God, the forgiver of sins, that he is risen from the dead.* These are explications, and parts of that general article, that *Jesus is the Christ*. This point therefore, and all the explications thereof are fundamental: as also all such as be evidently inferred from thence; as, BELIEF IN GOD THE FATHER: John xii. 44: *He that believeth in me, believeth not in me, but in him*

that sent me; 1 John ii. 23: *He that denieth the Son, hath not the Father:* BELIEF IN GOD THE HOLY GHOST, of whom Christ saith, John xiv. 26: *But the Comforter, which is the Holy Ghost, whom the Father will send in my name:* and John xv. 26: *But when the Comforter shall come, whom I will send unto you from the Father, even the Spirit of truth:* BELIEF OF THE SCRIPTURES, by which we believe those points and of the immortality of the soul, without which we cannot believe he is a Saviour.

7. That the belief of those fundamental points, is all that is required to salvation, as of faith. And as these are the fundamental points of faith necessary to salvation; so also are they only necessary as matter of faith, and only essential to the calling of a Christian; as may appear by many evident places of Holy Scripture: John v. 39: *Search the Scriptures, for in them ye think ye have eternal life, and they are they which testify of me.* Now, forasmuch as by the *Scripture,* is meant there the Old Testament (the New being then not written), the belief of that which was written concerning our Saviour in the Old Testament, was sufficient belief for the obtaining of eternal life: but in the Old Testament, there is nothing revealed concerning Christ, but that he is the Messiah, and such things as belong to the fundamental points thereupon depending. And therefore those *fundamental* points are sufficient to salvation as of faith. And John vi. 28, 29: *Then said they unto him, What shall we do, that we might work the works of God? Jesus answered and said unto them, This is the work of God, that ye believe in him, whom he hath sent.* So that the point to be believed is, *That Jesus Christ came forth from God, and he which believeth it, worketh the works of God.* John xi. 26, 27: *Whosoever liveth and believeth in me, shall never die. Believest thou this? She said unto him, Yea, Lord, I believe that thou art the Christ, the Son of God, which should come into the world.* Hence followeth, *He that believeth this, shall never die.* John xx. 31: *But these things are written, that ye might believe, that Jesus is the Christ, the Son of God; and that believing, ye might have life through his name.* By which appeareth, that this *fundamental* point is all that is required,

as of faith to our salvation. 1 John iv. 2: *Every spirit that confesseth that Jesus Christ is come in the flesh, is of God:* 1 John v. 1: *Whosoever believeth that Jesus is the Christ, is born of God;* and (verse 5) *Who is he that overcometh the world, but he that believeth, that Jesus is the Son of God:* and verse 13: *These things have I written unto you that believe in the name of the Son of God, that ye may know that ye have eternal life.* Acts, viii. 36, 37: *The eunuch said, Here is water, what doth hinder me to be baptized? And Philip said unto him, If thou believest with all thy heart, thou mayest. He answered and said, I believe that Jesus Christ is the Son of God.* This point therefore was sufficient for the reception of man into baptism, that is to say, to Christianity. And Acts, xvi. 29-31: *The keeper of the prison fell down before Paul and Silas, and said, Sirs, what shall I do to be saved? And they said, Believe in the Lord Jesus Christ.* And the sermon of St. Peter, upon the day of Pentecost, was nothing else but an explication, that *Jesus was the Christ. And when they had heard him, they asked him, What shall we do? He said unto them,* (Acts, ii. 38): *Amend your lives, and be baptized every one of you in the name of Jesus Christ for the remission of sins.* Rom. x. 9: *If thou shalt confess with thy mouth the Lord Jesus, and shalt believe in thy heart, that God raised him up from the dead, thou shalt be saved.* To these places may be added, that wheresoever our Saviour Christ doth approve the faith of any man, the proposition believed, if the same be to be collected out of the text, is always some of these fundamental points before mentioned, or something equivalent: as the faith of the centurion (Matth. viii. 8): *Speak the word only, and my servant shall be healed;* believing he was omnipotent: the faith of the woman, which had an issue of blood, (Matth. ix. 21): *If I may but touch the hem of his garment;* implying, he was the Messiah: the faith required of the blind men, (Matth. ix. 28): *Believe you that I am able to do this?* the faith of the Canaanitish woman, (Matth. xv. 22), that he was the *Son of David,* implying the same. And so it is in every one of those places, none excepted, where our Saviour commendeth any man's faith, which because they are too many to insert here, I omit, and refer them to his inquisition that is not otherwise satisfied. And as there is no other faith required, so there was no other preaching: for the prophets of the Old Testament preached no other; and John the Baptist preached only the approach of the kingdom of heaven, that is to say, of the kingdom of Christ. The same was the commission of the apostles (Matth. x. 7): *Go preach, saying, The kingdom of heaven is at hand.* And Paul preaching amongst the Jews, (Acts, xviii. 5), did but testify unto the Jews, that *Jesus was the Christ.* And the heathens took notice of Christians no otherwise, but by this name, that they believed *Jesus to be a king,* crying out, (Acts, xvii. 6, 7): *These are they that have subverted the state of the world, and here they are, whom Jason hath received. And these all do against the decrees of Cæsar, saying, that there is another king, one Jesus.* And this was the sum of the predictions, the sum of the confessions of them that believed, as well men as devils. This was the title of his cross, *Jesus of Nazareth, king of the Jews;* this the occasion of the crown of thorns, sceptre of reed, and a man to carry his cross; this was the subject of the *Hosannas;* and this was the title, by which our Saviour, commanding to take another man's goods, bade them say, *The Lord hath need;* and by this title he purged the temple of the profane market kept there. Nor did the apostles themselves believe any more than that *Jesus was the Messiah,* nor understand so much; for they understood the Messiah to be no more than a temporal king, till after our Saviour's resurrection. Furthermore, this point, that *Christ is the Messiah,* is particularly set forth for *fundamental* by that word, or some other equivalent thereunto in divers places. Upon the confession of Peter (Matth. xvi. 16): *Thou are the Christ, the son of the living God,* our Saviour (verse 18) saith, *Upon this rock will I build my church.* This point therefore is the whole foundation of Christ's church. St. Paul saith, (Rom. xv. 20) *I so enforced myself to preach the Gospel, not where Christ was named, lest I should have built upon another man's foundation.* St. Paul, (1 Cor. iii. 10) when he had reprehended the Corinthians for their sects, and curious doctrines and questions, he distinguisheth between *fundamental* points, and *superstruction;* and saith, *I have laid the foundation, and another buildeth thereupon; but let every man take heed how he buildeth upon it. For other foundation can no man lay than that which is laid, which is Jesus Christ.* Coloss. ii. 6, 7: *As you have received Christ Jesus the Lord, so walk in him, rooted and builded in him, and stablished in the faith.*

8. That other points not fundamental are not necessary to salvation as matters of faith; and that no more is required by way of faith to the salvation of one man than to the salvation of another. Having showed this proposition, *Jesus is the Christ,* to be the only fundamental and necessary point of faith, I shall set down a few places more, to show, that other points, though they may be true, are not so necessary to be believed, as that a man may not be saved, though he believe them not. And first, if a man could not be saved without assent of the heart to the truth of all controversies, which are now in agitation concerning religion, I cannot see, how any man living can be saved; so full of subtilty, and curious knowledge it is to be so great a divine. Why therefore should a man think that our Saviour, who (Matth. xi. 30), saith, that his *yoke is easy,* should require a matter of that difficulty? or how are little children said to believe, (Matth. xviii. 6); or how could the good thief be thought sufficiently catechised upon the cross? or St. Paul so perfect a Christian presently upon his conversion; and though there may be more obedience required in him that hath the fundamental points explicated unto him, than in him that hath received the same but implicitly; yet there is no more faith required for salvation in one man, than other. For if it be true, that *Whosoever shall confess with his mouth the Lord Jesus, and believe in his heart, that God raised him from the dead, shall be saved;* as it is, Rom. x. 9, and that *Whosoever believeth that Jesus is the Christ, is born of God;* the belief of that point is sufficient for the salvation of any man whosoever he be, forasmuch as concerneth faith. And seeing he that believeth not that *Jesus is the Christ,* whatsoever he believe else, cannot be saved; it

followeth, that there is no more required of the salvation of one man, than another, in matter of faith.

9. That superstructions are not points of the faith necessary to a Christian. About these points fundamental, there is little controversy amongst Christians, though otherwise of different sects amongst themselves. And therefore the controversies of religion, are altogether about points unnecessary to salvation; whereof some are doctrines raised by human ratiocination, from the points *fundamental*. As for example; such doctrines as concern the manner of the real presence, wherein are mingled tenets of faith concerning the omnipotency and divinity of Christ, with the tenets of Aristotle and the Peripatetics concerning substance and accidents, species, hypostasis, and the subsistence and migration of accidents from place to place; words some of them without meaning, and nothing but the canting of Grecian sophisters. And these doctrines are condemned expressly, Col. ii. 8, where after St. Paul had exhorted them to *be rooted and builded in Christ*, he giveth them this further caveat: *Beware lest there be any man that spoil you through philosophy and vain deceits, through the traditions of men, according to the rudiments of the world.* And such are such doctrines, as are raised out of such places of the Scriptures, as concern not the foundation, by men's natural reason; as about the concatenation of causes, and the manner of God's predestination; which are also mingled with philosophy: as if it were possible for men that know not in what manner God seeth, heareth, or speaketh, to know nevertheless the manner how he intendeth, and predestinateth. A man therefore ought not to examine by reason any point, or draw any consequence out of Scripture by reason, concerning the nature of God Almighty, of which reason is not capable. And therefore St. Paul, (Rom. xii. 3) giveth a good rule, *That no man presume to understand above that which is meet to understand, but that he understand according to sobriety:* which they do not, who presume out of Scripture, by their own interpretation, to raise any doctrine to the understanding, concerning those things which are incomprehensible. And this whole controversy concerning the pre-

destination of God, and the free-will of man, is not peculiar to Christian men. For we have huge volumes of this subject, under the name of *fate* and *contingency*, disputed between the Epicureans and the Stoics, and consequently it is not matter of faith, but of philosophy: and so are also all the questions concerning any other point, but the foundation before named; and God receiveth a man, which part of the question soever he holdeth. It was a controversy in St. Paul's time, whether a Christian Gentile might eat freely of any thing which the Christian Jews did not; and the Jew condemned the Gentile that he did eat, to whom St. Paul saith, (Rom. xiv. 3): *Let not him that eateth not, judge him that eateth; for God hath received him.* And verse 6, in the question concerning the observing of holy days, wherein the Gentiles and Jews differed, he saith unto them, *He that observeth the day, observeth it to the Lord; and he that observeth not the day, observeth it not to the Lord.* And they who strive concerning such questions, and divide themselves into sects, are not therefore to be accounted zealous of the faith, their strife being but carnal, which is confirmed by St. Paul (1 Cor. iii. 4): *When one saith, I am of Paul, and another, I am of Appollos, are ye not carnal?* For they are not questions of faith, but of wit, wherein, carnally, men are inclined to seek the mastery one of another. For nothing is truly a point of faith, but that *Jesus is the Christ;* as St. Paul testifieth, (1 Cor. ii. 2): *For I esteemed not the knowledge of any thing amongst you, save Jesus Christ, and him crucified.* And 1 Tim. vi. 20, 21: *O Timotheus, keep that which is committed unto thee, and avoid profane and vain babblings, and opposition of science falsely so called, which while some profess, they have erred concerning the faith.* 2 Tim. ii. 16: *Shun profane and vain babblings, &c.* Verse 17, 18: *Of which sort is Hymenæus and Philetus, which as concerning the truth, have erred, saying, that the resurrection is past already.* Whereby St. Paul showed, that the raising of questions by human ratiocination, though it be from the fundamental points themselves, is not only not necessary, but most dangerous to the faith of a Christian. Out of all these places, I draw only this conclusion in general, that neither the points now in controversy amongst Christians of different sects, or in any point that ever shall be in controversy, excepting only those that are contained in this article, *Jesus is the Christ*, are necessary to salvation, as of faith; though in matter of obedience, a man may be bound not to oppose the same.

10. How faith and justice concur to salvation. Although to the obtaining of salvation, there be required no more, as hath been already declared, out of the Holy Scriptures, as matter of faith, but the belief of those fundamental articles before set forth; nevertheless, there are required other things, as matter of obedience. For, as it is not enough in temporal kingdoms, to avoid the punishment which kings may inflict, to acknowledge the right and title of the king, without obedience also to his laws: so also it is not enough, to acknowledge our Saviour Christ to be the king of heaven, in which consisteth Christian faith, unless also we endeavor to obey his laws, which are the laws of the kingdom of heaven, in which consisteth Christian obedience. And forasmuch as the laws of the kingdom of heaven, are the laws of nature, as hath been showed, Part I chapter 5, not only faith, but also the observation of the law of nature, (which is that for which a man is called just or righteous, in that sense, in which justice is taken not for the absence of guilt, but for the endeavor and constant will to do that which is just) not only faith, but this justice, which also from the effect thereof, is called repentance, and sometimes works, is necessary to salvation. So that faith and justice do both concur thereto; and in the several acceptation of this word (justification) are properly said both of them to justify; and the want of either of them is properly said to condemn. For not only he that resisteth a king upon doubt of his title, but also he that doth it upon the inordinateness of his passions, deserveth punishment. And when faith and works are separated, not only the faith is called dead without works, but also works are called dead works without faith. And therefore St. James, (chapter ii. 17), saith, *Even so the faith, if it have no works, is dead in itself;* and verse 26: *For as the body without the spirit is dead, even so*

faith without works is dead. And St. Paul, (Heb. vi. 1), calleth works without faith, *dead works,* where he saith, *Not laying again the foundation of repentance from dead works.* And by these dead works, is understood not the obedience and justice of the inward man, but the *opus operatum,* or external action, proceeding from fear of punishment, or from vainglory, and desire to be honored of men: and these may be separated from faith, and conduce no way to a man's justification. And for that cause, St. Paul, (Rom. iv.) excludeth the righteousness of the law, from having part in the justification of a sinner. For by the law of Moses, which is applied to men's actions, and requireth the absence of guilt, all men living are liable to damnation; and therefore no man is justified by works, but by faith only. But if works be taken for the endeavor to do them, that is, if the will be taken for the deed, or internal for external righteousness, then do works contribute to salvation. And then taketh place that of St. James, (chap. ii. 24): *Ye see then, how that of works a man is justified, and not of faith only.* And both of these are joined to salvation, as in St. Mark i. 15: *Repent and believe the gospel.* And Luke xviii. 18-22, when a certain ruler asked our Saviour, what he ought to do to inherit eternal life, he propounded to him the keeping of the commandments; which when the ruler said he had kept, he propounded to him the faith, *Sell all that thou hast, and follow me.* And John iii. 36: *He that believeth in the Son, hath everlasting life.* And *He that obeyeth not the Son, shall not see life.* Where he manifestly joineth obedience and faith together. And Rom. i. 17: *The just shall live by faith;* not every one, but *the just.* For also *the devils believe and tremble.* But though both faith and justice (meaning still by justice, not absence of guilt, but the good intentions of the mind, which is called righteousness by God, that taketh the will for the deed) be both of them said to justify, yet are their parts in the act of justification to be distinguished. For justice is said to justify, not because it absolveth, but because it denominates him just, and setteth him in an estate, or capacity of salvation, whensoever he shall have faith. But faith is said to justify, that is, to absolve, because by it a just man is absolved of, and forgiven his unjust actions. And thus are reconciled the places of St. Paul and St. James, that *Faith only justifieth*, and *a man is not justified by faith only*; and showed how faith and repentance must concur to salvation.

11. That in Christian commonwealths, obedience to God and man stand well together. These things considered, it will easily appear, that under the sovereign power of a Christian commonwealth, there is no danger of damnation from simple obedience to human laws; for in that the sovereign alloweth Christianity, no man is compelled to renounce that faith, which is enough for his salvation, that is to say, the fundamental points. And for other points, seeing they are not necessary to salvation, if we conform our actions to the laws, we do not only what we are allowed, but also what we are commanded by the law of nature, which is the moral law taught by our Saviour himself. And it is part of that obedience which must concur to our salvation.

12. This tenet, whatsoever is against the conscience is sin, interpreted. And though it be true, whatsoever a man doth against his conscience, is sin; yet the obedience in these cases, is neither sin, nor against the conscience. For the conscience being nothing else but a man's settled judgment and opinion, when he hath once transferred his right of judging to another, that which shall be commanded, is no less his judgment, than the judgment of that other. So that in obedience to laws, a man doth still according to his own conscience, but not his private conscience. And whatsoever is done contrary to private conscience, is then a sin, when the laws have left him to his own liberty, and never else. And then whatsoever a man doth, not only believing it is ill done, but doubting whether it be ill or not, is done ill, in case he may lawfully omit the doing.

13. That all men do confess the necessity of submitting of controversies to some human authority. And as it hath been proved, that a man must submit his opinions in matter of controversy to the authority of the commonwealth; so also is the same confessed by the practice of every one of them that otherwise deny it. For who is there differing in opinion from another, and thinking himself to be in the right, and the other

in the wrong, that would not think it reasonable, if he be of the same opinion that the whole state alloweth, that the other should submit his opinion also thereunto; or that would not be content, if not that one or a few men, yet all the divines of a whole nation, or at least an assembly of all those he liketh, should have the power to determine all the controversies of religion? or, who is there that would not be content, to submit his opinions, either to the pope, or to a general council, or to a provincial council, or to a presbytery of his own nation? And yet in all these cases he submitteth himself to no greater than human authority. Nor can a man be said to submit himself to Holy Scripture, that doth not submit himself to some or other for the interpretation thereof. Or, why should there be any church government at all instituted, if the Scripture itself could do the office of a judge in controversies of faith? But the truth is apparent, by continual experience, that men seek not only liberty of conscience, but of their actions; nor that only, but a further liberty of persuading others to their opinions; nor that only, for every man desireth, that the sovereign authority should admit no other opinions to be maintained, but such as he himself holdeth.

14. That Christians under an infidel are discharged of the injustice of disobeying him, in that which concerneth the faith necessary to salvation, by not resisting. The difficulty therefore of obeying both God and man in a Christian commonwealth is none: all the difficulty resteth in this point, whether he that hath received the faith of Christ, having before subjected himself to the authority of an infidel, be discharged of his obedience thereby, or not, in matters of religion. In which case it seemeth reasonable to think, that since all covenants of obedience are entered into for the preservation of a man's life, if a man be content without resistance to lay down his life, rather than obey the commands of an infidel, in so hard a case he hath sufficiently discharged himself thereof. For no covenant bindeth further than to endeavor; and if a man cannot assure himself to perform a just duty, when thereby he is assured of present death, much less can it be expected that

a man should perform that, for which he believeth in his heart he shall be damned eternally. And thus much concerning the scruple of conscience, that may arise concerning obedience to human laws, in them that interpret the law of God to themselves. It remaineth, to remove the same scruple from them, that submit their controversies to others not ordained thereunto by the sovereign authority. And this I refer to the chapter following.

Magistrates in the Kingdom of Christ

Chapter 7

1. The question propounded, who are the magistrates in the kingdom of Christ. In the former chapter have been removed those difficulties opposing our obedience to human authority, which arise from misunderstanding of our Saviour's title and laws: in the former whereof, namely, his title, consisteth our faith; and in the latter, our justice. Now they who differ not amongst themselves concerning his title and laws, may nevertheless have different opinions concerning his magistrates, and the authority he hath given them. And this is the cause, why many Christians have denied obedience to their princes, pretending that our Saviour Christ hath not given this magistracy to them, but to others. As for example: some say, to the pope universally; some, to a synod aristocratical; some, to a synod democratical in every several commonwealth; and the magistrates of Christ being they by whom he speaketh, the question is, whether he speak unto us by the pope, or by convocations of bishops and ministers, or by them that have the sovereign power in every commonwealth.

2. The question exemplified, in the controversies between Moses and Aaron, and between Moses and Corah. This controversy was the cause of those two mutinies, that happened against Moses in the wilderness. The first by Aaron and his sister Miriam, who took upon them to censure Moses, for marrying an Ethiopian woman. And the state of the question between them and Moses, they set forth (Numb. xii. 2) in these words: *What hath the Lord spoken but only by Moses? hath he not spoken also by us? And the Lord heard this,* &c., and punished the same in Miriam, forgiving Aaron upon his repentance. And this is the case of all them that set up the priesthood against the sovereignty. The other was of Corah, Dathan, and Abiram, who with two hundred and fifty captains gathered themselves together against Moses, and against Aaron. The state of their controversy was this, whether God were not with the multitude, as well as with Moses, and every

man as holy as he. For (Numb. xvi. 3) thus they say, *You take too much upon you, seeing all the congregation is holy; every one of them, and the Lord is amongst them: wherefore then lift ye yourselves above the congregation of the Lord?* And this is the case of them that set up their private consciences, and unite themselves to take the government of religion out of the hands of him or them, that have the sovereign power of the commonwealth: which how well it pleaseth God, may appear by the hideous punishment of Corah and his accomplices.

3. Amongst the Jews, the power temporal and spiritual in the same hand. In the government therefore of Moses there was no power, neither civil, nor spiritual, that was not derived from him. Nor in the state of Israel under kings, was there any earthly power, by which those kings were compellable to any thing, or any subject allowed to resist them in any case whatsoever. For though the prophets by extraordinary calling, did often admonish and threaten them, yet they had no authority over them. And therefore amongst the Jews, the power spiritual and temporal, was always in the same hand.

4. Parallel of the twelve princes of Israel, and the twelve apostles. Our Saviour Christ, as he was the rightful king of the Jews in particular, as well as king of the kingdom of Heaven, in the ordaining of magistrates, received that form of policy which was used by Moses. According to the number of the children of Jacob, Moses took unto him by the appointment of God (Numb. i. 4) twelve men, every one of the chief of their tribe, which were to assist him in the muster of Israel. And these twelve, verse 44, are called the *princes of Israel, twelve men, every one for the house of their fathers;* which are said also (Numb. vii. 2), *to be heads over the houses of their fathers, and princes of the tribes, and over them that were numbered.* And these were every one equal amongst themselves. In like manner our Saviour took unto him twelve apostles, to be next unto him in authority, of whom he saith (Matth. xix. 28), *When the Son of Man shall sit in the throne of his majesty, ye which follow me in the regeneration, shall sit also upon twelve thrones, and judge the twelve tribes of Israel.* And concerning the equality of the

twelve apostles amongst themselves, our Saviour saith (Matth. xx. 25), *Ye know that the Lords of the Gentiles have domination over them*, &c. Verse 26: *But it shall not be so amongst you; but whosoever will be greatest among you, let him be your servant*. And Matth. xxiii. 11: *He that is greatest among you, let him be your servant*. And a little before, verse 8, *Be not called Rabbi; for one is your doctor, Christ, and all ye are brethren*. And Acts i. in choosing of Matthias to be an apostle, though St. Peter used the part of a *prolocutor*, yet did no man take upon him the authority of election, but referred the same to lot.

5. Parallel of the seventy elders and seventy disciples. Again, Moses had the command of God, Numb. xi. 16: *Gather to me seventy men of the elders of Israel, whom thou knowest that they are the elders of the people, and governors over them, and bring them unto the tabernacle*, &c. And Moses, verse 24, did accordingly. And these were chosen to help Moses in bearing the burthen of the government, as appeareth, verse 17 of the same chapter. And as the twelve princes of the tribes were according to the number of Jacob's children; so were the seventy elders according to the number of the persons that went down with Jacob into Egypt. In like manner our Saviour in his kingdom of Heaven, the church, out of the whole number of those that believed in him, ordained seventy persons, which peculiarly were called the seventy disciples, to whom he gave power to preach the Gospel and baptize.

6. The hierarchy of the church in our Saviour's time, consisted in the twelve, and in the seventy. In our Saviour's time therefore, the hierarchy of the church consisted, besides himself that was the head, of twelve apostles, who were equal amongst themselves, but ordained over others, as were the twelve heads of the tribes, and seventy disciples, who had every one of them power to baptize and teach, and help to govern the whole flock.

7. Why Christ ordained no priests for sacrifices, as Moses did. And whereas in the commonwealth instituted by Moses, there was not only a high-priest for the present, but also a succession and order of priests; it may be demanded, why our

Saviour Christ did not ordain the like? To which may be answered, that the high-priesthood, forasmuch as concerneth the authority thereof, was in the person of Christ, as he was Christ, that is king. So also was it in Moses, Aaron having the ministerial part only. For notwithstanding that Aaron was the high-priest, yet the consecration of him belonged (Exod. xxix. 1) to Moses. All the utensils of sacrifice, and other holy things, were ordered by Moses; and in sum, the whole Levitical law was delivered by God by the hand of Moses, who was to Aaron a God, and Aaron to him a mouth. And for the ministerial part, there could no high-priest be ordained but himself; for seeing our Saviour was himself the sacrifice, who but himself could offer him up? And for the celebration of that sacrifice for ever after, our Saviour annexed the priesthood to those whom he had appointed to govern in the church.

8. The hierarchy of the church, in the apostles' time, apostles, bishops, and priests. After the ascension of our Saviour, the apostles dispersed themselves for the spreading of the Gospel, and continually as they converted any number of men, in any city or region, to the faith, they chose out such as they thought fittest, to direct them in matter of conversation and life, according to Christ's law, and to explicate unto them, that mystery of Christ come in the flesh, that is to say, to unfold unto them at large the office of the Messiah. And of those elders, some were subordinate to others, according as the apostles, who ordained them, thought meet. So St. Paul gave power unto Titus, to ordain elders in Crete, and to redress things that were amiss. So that Titus was both an elder, and ordained elders (Tit. i. 5): *For this cause I left thee in Crete, that thou shouldest continue to redress the things that remain, and ordain elders in every city;* where the word is καταστήσῃς, that is constitute; whereby it appeareth, that in the apostles' times, one elder had authority over another, to ordain and rule them. For 1 Tim. v. 19, Timothy an elder, is made judge of accusations against other elders. And Acts xiv. 23, the disciples are said to ordain elders, for all the congregations of the cities they had preached in. And though the word there be χειροτονήσαντες, yet it signifieth not election by

holding up of hands, but simply and absolutely ordination. For the ordinary choosing of magistrates amongst the Grecians, which were all either popularly governed, or else by *oligarchy*, being performed by holding up of hands, made that word be taken simply, for an election or ordination, howsoever made. And thus in the primitive church, the hierarchy of the church, was apostles, elders that governed other elders, and elders that ruled not, but their office was to preach, to administer the sacraments, to offer up prayers and thanksgiving in the name of the people. But at that time there appeared no distinction between the names of bishop and elder. But immediately after the apostles' time, the word bishop was taken to signify such an elder as had the government of elders, and other elders were called by the name of priests, which signifieth the same that elder doth. And thus the government of bishops hath a divine pattern in the twelve rulers, and seventy elders of Israel, in the twelve apostles and seventy disciples of our Saviour, in the ruling elders, and not ruling elders, in the time of the apostles.

9. The preaching of the gospel was not commanding, but persuading. And thus much of the magistrates over Christ's flock in the primitive church. For the office of a minister, or ministress, was to be subject to the flock, and to serve them in those things which appertain to their temporal business. The next thing to be considered is the authority which our Saviour gave them, either over those whom they had converted, or those whom they were about to convert. And for these latter, which as yet were without the church, the authority which our Saviour gave to his apostles was no more but this, to preach unto them that Jesus was the Christ, and to explicate the same in all points, that concern the kingdom of heaven, and to persuade men to embrace our Saviour's doctrine, but by no means to compel any man to be subject to them: for seeing the laws of the kingdom of heaven, as hath been showed, Part I, chap. 5. sect. 10, are dictated to the conscience only, which is not subject to compulsion and constraint, it was not congruent to the style of the King of Heaven to constrain men to submit their actions to him, but to advise them only; nor for him that professeth the sum of his law to be love, to extort any

duty from us with fear of temporal punishment. And therefore as the mighty men in the world, that hold others in subjection by force, are called in Scripture by the name of hunters; so our Saviour calleth those whom he appointed to draw the world unto him, by subduing their affections, *fishers*. And therefore he saith to Peter and Andrew, (Matth. iv. 19): *Follow me, and I will make ye fishers of men.* And Luke x. 3: *Behold,* saith Christ, *I send ye forth as lambs amongst wolves.* And it were to no end to give them the right of compelling, without strengthening the same with greater power than of *lambs* amongst *wolves.* Moreover, Matth. x, where our Saviour giveth a commission to his apostles, to go forth and convert the nations to the faith, he giveth them no authority of *coercion* and punishment, but only saith, (verse 14, 15) *Whosoever shall not receive you, nor hear your words, when ye depart out of that house, or that city, shake off the dust of your feet. It shall be easier for the land of Sodom and Gomorrah in the day of judgment, than for that city.* Whereby it is manifest, that all that the apostles could do by their authority, was no more than to renounce communion with them, and leave their punishment to God Almighty, in the day of judgment. Likewise the comparisons of the kingdom of heaven to the seed, Matth. xiii. 3, and to the leaven, Matth. xiii. 33, doth intimate unto us that the increase thereof ought to proceed from internal operation of God's word preached, and not from any law or compulsion of them that preach it. Moreover our Saviour himself saith (John xviii. 36), *That his kingdom is not of this world;* and consequently his magistrates derive not from him any authority of punishing men in this world. And therefore also, Matth. xxvi. 52, after St. Peter had drawn his sword in his defense, our Saviour saith, *Put up thy sword into his place. For all that take the sword, shall perish by the sword.* And, verse 54, *How then shall the Scriptures be fulfilled, which say, that it must be so?* showing out of the Scriptures, that the kingdom of Christ was not to be defended by the sword.

10. Excommunication. Sovereigns immediate rulers ecclesiastical under Christ. But concerning the authority of the apostles or bishops over those who were already converted

and within the church, there be that think it greater than over them without. For some have said, (Bellarmin. *Lib. de Rom. Pont.* cap. 29), *Though the law of Christ deprive no prince of his dominion, and Paul did rightly appeal unto Cæsar, whilst kings were infidels and out of the church; yet when they became Christians, and of their own accord underwent the laws of the gospel, presently as sheep to a shepherd, and as members to the head, they became subject to the prelate of the ecclesiastical hierarchy.* Which, whether it be true or not, is to be considered by that light which we have from the Holy Scripture, concerning the power of our Saviour and his apostles, over such as they had converted. But our Saviour, as he imitated the commonwealth of the Jews in his magistrates, the twelve and the seventy; so did he also in the censure of the church, which was *excommunication;* but amongst the Jews, the church did put the excommunicated persons from the congregation, which they might do by their power temporal; but our Saviour and his apostles, who took upon them no such power, could not forbid the excommunicated person to enter into any place and congregation, into which he was permitted to enter, by the prince, or sovereign of the place. For that had been to deprive the sovereign of his authority. And therefore the excommunication of a person subject to an earthly power, was but a declaration of the church, which did excommunicate, that the person so excommunicated was to be reputed still as an infidel, but not to be driven by their authority, out of any company, he might otherwise lawfully come into. And this is it our Saviour saith (Matth. xviii. 17): *If he refuse to hear the church, let him be unto thee as an heathen man and a publican.* So that the whole effect of excommunicating a Christian prince, is no more than he or they that so excommunicate him depart and banish themselves out of his dominion. Nor can they thereupon discharge any of his subjects of their obedience to him; for that were to deprive him of his dominion; which they may not do, for being out of the church. It is confessed by them that make this objection, and proved in the former section, that our Saviour gave no authority to his apostles to be judges over them. And therefore in no case can the sovereign power of a commonwealth be subject to any authority ecclesiastical, besides that of Christ himself. And though he be informed concerning the kingdom of heaven, and subject himself thereto at the persuasions of persons ecclesiastical, yet is he not thereby subject to their government and rule. For if it were by their authority he took that yoke upon him, and not by their persuasion, then by the same authority he might cast it off. But this is unlawful. For if all the churches in the world should renounce the Christian faith, yet is not this sufficient authority for any of the members to do the same. It is manifest therefore, that they who have sovereign power, are immediate rulers of the church under Christ, and all other but subordinate to them. If that were not, but kings should command one thing upon pain of death, and priests another, upon pain of damnation, it would be impossible that peace and religion should stand together.

11. That no man hath any just pretense of religion against obedience to commonwealth. God speaketh to man by his vicegerents. And therefore there is no just cause for any man to withdraw his obedience from the sovereign state, upon pretense that Christ hath ordained any state ecclesiastical above it. And though kings take not upon them the ministerial priesthood, yet are they not so merely laic, as not to have sacerdotal jurisdiction. To conclude this chapter, since God speaketh not in these days to any man by his private interpretation of the Scriptures, nor by the interpretation of any power above, or not depending on the sovereign power of every commonwealth, it remaineth, that he speaketh by his vice-gods, or lieutenants here on earth, that is to say, by sovereign kings, or such as have sovereign authority as well as they.

Further Reflections on the Body Politic: Destruction of the Body Politic

Chapter 8

1. The things that dispose to rebellion, discontent, pretense and hope of success. Hitherto of the causes why, and the manner how, men have made commonwealth. In this chapter I shall show briefly by what causes, and in what manner, they be again destroyed; not meaning to say anything concerning the dissolution of a commonwealth, from foreign invasions, which is as it were the violent death thereof. I shall speak only of sedition, which is also the death of the commonwealth, but like to that which happeneth to a man from sickness and distemper. To dispose men to sedition, three things concur. The first is discontent; for as long as a man thinketh himself well, and that the present government standeth not in his way to hinder his proceeding from well to better, it is impossible for him to desire the change thereof. The second is pretense of right; for though a man be discontent, yet if in his own opinion there be no just cause of stirring against, or resisting the government established, nor any pretense to justify his resistance, and to procure aid, he will never show it. The third is hope of success; for it were madness to attempt without hope, when to fail, is to die the death of a traitor. Without these three, discontent, pretense, and hope, there can be no rebellion: and when the same are all together, there wanteth nothing thereto, but a man of credit to set up the standard, and to blow the trumpet.

2. Discontent that disposeth to sedition, consisteth partly in fear of want, or punishment: And as for discontent, it is of two sorts: for it consisteth either in bodily pain present or expected, or else in trouble of the mind; which is the general division of pleasure and pain, *Human Nature*, chap. 7 sect. 9. The presence of bodily pain disposeth not to sedition; the fear of it doth. As for example; when a great multitude, or heap of people, have concurred to a crime worthy of death, they join together, and take arms to defend themselves for fear thereof. So also the fear of want, or in present want, the

369

fear of arrests and imprisonment dispose to sedition. An
therefore great exactions, though the right thereof be acknowl
edged, have caused great seditions. As in the time of Henr
VII the seditions of the Cornish men, that refused to pay
subsidy, and, under the conduct of the Lord Audley, gave th
King battle upon Blackheath; and that of the northern people
who in the same king's time, for demanding a subsidy grante
in parliament, murdered the Earl of Northumberland in hi
house.

3. Partly in ambition. Thirdly, the other sort of discontent
which troubleth the mind of them who otherwise live at ease
without fear of want, or danger of violence, ariseth only fron
a sense of their want of that Power, and that honor and testi
mony thereof, which they think is due unto them. For all jo
and grief of mind consisting (as hath been said, *Huma
Nature*, chap. 9 sect. 21) in a contention for precedence t
them with whom they compare themselves; such men mus
needs take it ill, and be grieved with the state, as find them
selves postposed to those in honor, whom they think the
excel in virtue and ability to govern. And this is it for whic.
they think themselves regarded but as slaves. Now seeing free
dom cannot stand together with subjection, liberty in a com
monwealth is nothing but government and rule, which becaus
it cannot be divided, men must expect in common; and tha
can be no where but in the popular state, or democracy. An
Aristotle saith well, (lib. VI. cap. 2 of his *Politics*), *Th
ground or intention of a democracy, is liberty*. Which he con
firmeth in these words: *For men ordinarily say this, that n
man can partake of liberty, but only in a popular common
wealth*. Whosoever therefore in a monarchical estate, wher
the sovereign power is absolutely in one man, claimeth liberty
claimeth (if the hardest construction should be made thereof
either to have the sovereignty in his turn, or to be colleagu
with him that hath it, or to have the monarchy changed int
a democracy. But if the same be construed, with pardon o
that unskilful expression, according to the intention of hir
that claimeth, then doth he thereby claim no more but this
that the sovereign should take notice of his ability and deserv
ing, and put him into employment and place of subordinat

government, rather than others that deserve less. And as one claimeth, so doth another, every man esteeming his own desert greatest. Amongst all those that pretend to, or are ambitious of such honor, a few only can be served, unless it be in a *democracy;* the rest therefore must be discontent. And so much of the first thing that disposeth to rebellion, namely, discontent, consisting in fear and ambition.

4. Six heads of pretenses to rebellion. The second thing that disposeth to rebellion, is *pretense of right.* And that is when men have an opinion, or pretend to have an opinion, that in certain cases they may lawfully resist him or them that have the sovereign power, or deprive him or them of the means to execute the same. Of which pretenses, there be six special cases. One is, when the command is against their conscience, and they believe it is unlawful for a subject at the command of the sovereign power to do any action, which he thinketh in his own conscience not lawful for him to do, or to omit any action, which he thinketh not lawful for him to omit. Another is, when the command is against the laws, and they think the sovereign power in such sort obliged to his own laws, as the subject is; and that when he performeth not his duty, they may resist his power. A third is, when they receive commands from some man or men, and a *supersedeas* to the same from others, and think the authority is equal, as if the sovereign power were divided. A fourth is, when they are commanded to contribute their persons or money to the public service, and think they have a propriety in the same distinct from the dominion of the sovereign power; and that therefore they are not bound to contribute their goods and persons, no more than every man shall of himself think fit. A fifth, when the commands seem hurtful to the people; and they think, every one of them, that the opinion and sense of the people, is the same with the opinion of himself, and those that consent with him; calling by the name of people, any multitude of his own faction. The sixth is, when the commands are grievous; and they account him that commandeth grievous things a tyrant; and tyrannicide, that is, the killing of a tyrant, not only lawful, but also laudable.

5. The first of them, that men ought to do nothing against conscience, confuted. All these opinions are maintained in the books of the *dogmatics,* and divers of them taught in public chairs, and nevertheless are most incompatible with peace and government, and contradictory to the necessary and demonstrable rules of the same. And for the first, namely that a man may lawfully do or omit any thing against his conscience, and from whence arise all seditions concerning religion and ecclesiastical government, it hath been plainly declared in the two last chapters, that such opinion is erroneous. For those two chapters have been wholly spent, to prove, that Christian religion not only forbiddeth not, but also commandeth, that in every commonwealth, every subject should in all things to the uttermost of his power obey the commands of him or them that is the sovereign thereof, that a man in so obeying, doth according to his conscience and judgment, as having deposited his judgment in all controversies in the hands of the sovereign power; and that this error proceedeth from the ignorance of what and by whom God Almighty speaketh.

6. The second, that sovereigns are subject to their own laws, confuted. As for the second opinion, which is this, that the sovereign is in such sort obliged to his own laws, as the subject is; the contrary thereof hath been showed, Part I chapter 1 sections 7-12, by which it appeareth, that the sovereign power is not to be resisted; that it carrieth the sword both of war and justice; that it hath the right of deciding all controversies, both judicial and deliberative; that it hath the making of all the laws civil; that it appointeth magistrates and public ministers, and that it implieth a universal impunity. How then can he or they be said to be subject to the law which they may abrogate at their pleasure, or break without fear of punishment? And this error seemeth to proceed from this, that men ordinarily understand not aright, what is meant by this word law, confounding law and covenant, as if they signify the same thing. But law implieth a command; covenant is but a promise. And not every command is a law, but only (*Human Nature,* chap. 13 sect. 6) when the command is the reason we have of doing the action commanded. And

then only is the reason of our actions in the command, when the omitting is therefore hurtful, because the action was commanded, not because it was hurtful of itself; and doing contrary to a command, were not at all hurtful, if there were not a right in him that commandeth to punish him that so doth. He or they that have all punishments in their own disposing, cannot be so commanded, as to receive hurt for disobeying, and consequently no command can be a law unto them. It is an error therefore to think, that the power which is virtually the whole power of the commonwealth, and which in whomsoever it resideth, is usually called supreme or sovereign, can be subject to any law but that of God Almighty.

7. The third, that the sovereignty is divisible, confuted. The third opinion, *that the sovereign power may be divided,* is no less an error than the former, as hath been proved, Part II chapter 1 sect. 15. And if there were a commonwealth, wherein the rights of sovereignty were divided, we must confess with Bodin, Lib. II. chap. I. *De Republica,* that they are not rightly to be called commonwealths, but the corruption of commonwealths. For if one part should have power to make the laws for all, they would by their laws at their pleasure, forbid others, to make peace or war, to levy taxes, or to yield fealty and homage without their leave; and they that had the right to make peace and war, and command the *militia,* would forbid the making of other laws, than what themselves liked. And though monarchies stand long, wherein the right of sovereignty hath seemed so divided, because monarchy of itself is a durable kind of government, yet monarchs have been thereby divers times thrust out of their possession. But the truth is, that the right of sovereignty is such, as he or they that have it, cannot, though they would, give away any part thereof, and retain the rest. As for example; if we should suppose the people of Rome to have had the absolute sovereignty of the Roman state, and to have chosen them a council by the name of the senate, and that to this senate they had given the supreme power of making laws, reserving nevertheless to themselves, in direct and express terms, the whole right and title of the sovereignty; which may easily happen amongst them that see not the inseparable con-

nection between the sovereign power, and the power of making laws: I say, this grant of the people to the senate is of no effect, and the power of making laws is in the people still. For the senate understanding it to be the will and intention of the people, to retain the sovereignty, ought not to take that for granted, which was contradictory thereto, and passed by error. For (*Human Nature*, chap. 13 sect. 9) in contradictory promises, that which is directly promised, is preferred before that which is opposite thereunto by consequence; because the consequence of a thing is not always obscured, as is the thing itself. The error concerning mixed government hath proceeded from want of understanding of what is meant by this word *body politic*, and how it signifieth not the concord, but the union of many men. And though in the chapters of subordinate corporations, a corporation being declared to be one person in law, yet the same hath not been taken notice of in the body of a commonwealth or city, nor have any of those innumerable writers of politics, observed any such union.

8. *The fourth, that subjects have a propriety distinct from the dominion of the sovereign, confuted.* The fourth opinion, to wit, that subjects have their *meum, tuum,* and *suum,* in property, not only by virtue of the sovereign power over them all, distinct from one another, but also against the sovereign himself, by which they would pretend to contribute nothing to the public, but what they please, hath been already confuted, by proving the absoluteness of the sovereignty, and more particularly, Part II chapter 5 sect. 2; and ariseth from this, that they understand not ordinarily that before the institution of sovereign power, *meum* and *tuum,* implied no propriety, but a community, where every man had right to every thing, and was in state of war with every man.

9. *The fifth, that the people is a person distinct from the sovereign, confuted.* The fifth opinion, *That the people is a distinct body from him or them that have the sovereignty over them,* is an error already confuted, Part II chap. 2 sect. 11, where it is showed, that when men say, *the people rebelleth,* it is to be understood of those particular persons only, and not of the whole nation. And when the people claimeth any thing otherwise than by the voice of the sovereign power,

it is not the claim of the people, but only of those particular men, that claim in their own persons; and this error ariseth from the equivocation of the word *people*.

10. The sixth, that tyrannicide is lawful, confuted. Lastly, for the opinion, *that tyrannicide is lawful*, meaning by a tyrant any man in whom resideth the right of sovereignty, is no less false and pernicious to human society, than frequent in the writings of those moral philosophers, Seneca and others, so greatly esteemed amongst us. For when a man hath the right of sovereignty, he cannot justly be punished, as hath been often showed already, and therefore much less deposed, or put to death. And howsoever he might deserve punishment, yet punishment is unjust without judgment preceding, and judgment unjust without power of judicature, which a subject hath not over a sovereign. But this doctrine proceedeth from the Schools of Greece, and from those that writ in the Roman state, in which not only the name of a tyrant, but of a king, was hateful.

11. Four heads of hope of success in rebellion. Besides *discontent*, to the disposing of a man to rebellion, and *pretense*, there is required, in the third place, *hope of success*, which consisteth in four points: I. That the discontented have mutual intelligence; II. That they have sufficient number; III. That they have arms; IV. That they agree upon a head. For these four must concur to the making of one body of rebellion, in which intelligence is the life, number the limbs, arms the strength, and a head the unity, by which they are directed to one and the same action.

12. Two things necessary to an author of rebellion, much eloquence, and little wisdom. The authors of rebellion, that is, the men that breed these dispositions to rebel in others, of necessity must have in them these three qualities: I. To be discontented themselves; II. To be men of mean judgment and capacity; and, III. To be eloquent men, or good orators. And as for their discontent, from whence it may proceed, hath been already declared. And for the second and third, I am to show now, first, how they may stand together; for it seemeth a contradiction, to place small judgment and great eloquence, or, as they call it, powerful speaking, in the same

man: and then in what manner they concur, to dispose othe
men to sedition.

13. That the authors of rebellion necessarily, are to b
men of little wisdom. It was noted by Sallust, that in Catiline
who was author of the greatest sedition that ever was i
Rome, there was *Eloquentiæ satis, sapientiæ parum; eloquenc
sufficient,* but *little wisdom.* And perhaps this was said c
Catiline, as he was Catiline: but it was true of him as a
author of sedition. For the conjunction of these two qualitie
made him not Catiline, but seditious. And that it may b
understood, how want of *wisdom,* and store of *eloquence*
may stand together, we are to consider, what it is we ca
wisdom, and what eloquence. And therefore I shall her
again remember some things, that have been said already
Human Nature, chap. 5, 6. It is manifest that wisdor
consisteth in knowledge. Now of knowledge there are tw
kinds; whereof the one is the remembrance of such thing
as we have conceived by our senses, and of the order in whic
they follow one another. And this *knowledge* is calle
experience; and the wisdom that proceedeth from it, is th
ability to conjecture by the present, of what is past, and t
come, which men call *prudence.* This being so, it is manifes
presently, that the author of sedition, whosoever he be, mus
not be prudent. For if he consider and take his experience
aright, concerning the success which they have had, wh
have been the movers and authors of sedition, either in thi
or any other state, he shall find, that for one man that hat
thereby advanced himself to honor, twenty have come t
a reproachful end. The other kind of knowledge, is th
remembrance of the names or appellations of things, an
how every thing is called, which is, in matters of commo
conversation, a remembrance of pacts and covenants of me
made amongst themselves, concerning how to be understoo
of one another. And this kind of knowledge is generall
called science, and the conclusions thereof truth. But whe
men remember not how things are named, by general agree
ment, but either mistake and misname things, or name the
aright by chance, they are not said to have science, b
opinion, and the conclusions thence proceeding, are u

certain, and for the most part erroneous. Now that science in particular, from which proceed the true and evident conclusions of what is right and wrong, and what is good and hurtful to the being, and well-being of mankind, the Latins call *sapientia*, and we by the general name of wisdom. For generally, not he that hath skill in geometry, or any other science speculative, but only he that understandeth what conduceth to the good and government of the people, is called a wise man. Now that no author of sedition can be wise in this acceptation of the word, is sufficiently proved, in that it hath been already demonstrated, that no pretense of sedition can be right or just. And therefore the authors of sedition must be ignorant of the right of state, that is to say, unwise. It remaineth therefore, that they be such, as name things, not according to their true and generally agreed upon names, but call right and wrong, good and bad, according to their passions, or according to the authorities of such as they admire, as Aristotle, Cicero, Seneca, and others of like authority, who have given the names of right and wrong, as their passions have dictated; or have followed the authority of other men, as we do theirs. It is required therefore in an author of sedition, that he think right, that which is wrong; and profitable, that which is pernicious; and consequently that there be in him *sapientiæ parum*, little wisdom.

14. That the same are necessarily eloquent. Eloquence is nothing else but the power of winning belief of what we say. And to that end we must have aid from the passions of the hearer. Now to demonstration and teaching of the truth, there are required long deductions, and great attention, which is unpleasant to the hearer. Therefore they which seek not truth, but belief, must take another way, and not only derive what they would have to be believed, from somewhat believed already, but also, by aggravations and extenuations, make good and bad, right and wrong, appear great or less, according as shall serve their turns. And such is the power of eloquence, as many times a man is made to believe thereby, that he sensibly feeleth smart and damage, when he feeleth none, and to enter into rage and indignation, without any other cause, than what is in the words and passion of the

speaker. This considered, together with the business that he hath to do, who is the author of rebellion, namely, to make men believe that their rebellion is just, their discontents grounded upon great injuries, and their hopes great; there needeth no more to prove, there can be no author of rebellion, that is not an eloquent and powerful speaker, and withal, as hath been said before, a man of little wisdom. For the faculty of speaking powerfully, consisteth in a habit gotten of putting together passionate words, and applying them to the present passions of the hearer.

15. In what manner they concur to their common effects. Seeing then eloquence and want of discretion concur to the stirring of rebellion, it may be demanded, what part each of these acteth therein? The daughters of Pelias, king of Thessaly, desiring to restore their old decrepit father to the vigor of his youth, by the counsel of Medea, chopped him in pieces, and set him a boiling with I know not what herbs in a cauldron, but could not revive him again. So when eloquence and want of judgment go together, want of judgment, like the daughters of Pelias, consenteth, through eloquence, which is as the witchcraft of Medea, to cut the commonwealth in pieces, upon pretense or hope of reformation, which when things are in combustion, they are not able to effect.

Chapter 9

1. The law over sovereigns *salus populi*. Having hitherto set forth how a body politic is made, and how it may be destroyed, this place requireth to say something concerning the preservation of the same, not purposing to enter into the particulars of the art of government, but to sum up the general heads, wherein such art is to be employed, and in which consisteth the duty of him or them that have the sovereign power. For the duty of a sovereign consisteth in the good government of the people. And although the acts of sovereign power be no injuries to the subjects who have consented to the same by their implicit wills, yet when they tend to the hurt of the people in general, they be breaches of the law of nature, and of the divine law; and consequently, the contrary acts are the duties of sovereigns, and required at their hands to the utmost of their endeavor, by God Almighty, under the pain of eternal death. And as the art and duty of sovereigns consist in the same acts, so also doth their profit. For the end of art, is profit; and governing to the profit of the subjects, is governing to the profit of the sovereign, as hath been showed Part 2 chapter 5 section 1. And these three: 1. The law over them that have sovereign power: 2. Their duty: 3. Their profit: are one and the same thing contained in this sentence, *Salus populi suprema lex.* By which must be understood, not the mere preservation of their lives, but generally their benefit and good. So that this is the general law for sovereigns, *That they procure, to the uttermost of their endeavor, the good of the people.*

2. That sovereigns ought to establish the religion they hold for best. And forasmuch as eternal is better than temporal good, it is evident, that they who are in sovereign authority, are by the law of nature obliged to further the establishing of all such doctrines and rule, and the commanding of all such actions, as in their conscience they believe to be the true way thereunto. For unless they do so, it cannot be said truly, that they have done the uttermost of their endeavor.

3. That to forbid unnatural copulation, promiscuous use of women, &c. is the law of nature. For the temporal good of the people, it consisteth in four points: I. Multitude: 2. Commodity of living: 3. Peace amongst themselves: 4. Defense against foreign power. Concerning multitude, it is the duty of them that are in sovereign authority, to increase the people, in as much as they are governors of mankind under God Almighty, who having created but one man, and one woman, declared, that it was his will they should be multiplied and increased afterwards. And seeing this is to be done by ordinances concerning copulation, they are by the law of nature bound to make such ordinances concerning the same, as may tend to the increase of mankind. And hence it cometh, that in them who have sovereign authority, not to forbid such copulations as are against the use of nature; not to forbid the promiscuous use of women, not to forbid one woman to have many husbands, not to forbid marriages within certain degrees of kindred and affinity, are against the law of nature. For though it be not evident, that a private man living under the law of natural reason only, doth break the same, by doing any of the things aforesaid; yet it is manifestly apparent, that being so prejudicial as they are to the improvement of mankind, that not to forbid the same, is against the law of natural reason in him, that hath taken into his hands any portion of mankind to improve.

4. That to leave man as much liberty as may be, &c. is the duty of a sovereign by the law of nature. The commodity of living consisteth in liberty and wealth. By liberty, I mean, that there be no prohibition without necessity of any thing to any man, which was lawful to him in the law of nature; that is to say, that there be no restraint of natural liberty, but what is necessary for the good of the commonwealth, and that wellmeaning men may not fall into the danger of laws, as into snares, before they be aware. It appertaineth also to this liberty, that a man may have commodious passage from place to place, and not be imprisoned or confined with the difficulty of ways, and want of means for transportation of things necessary. And for the wealth of people, it consisteth in three things, the well ordering of trade, procuring of labor, and forbidding

the superfluous consuming of food and apparel. All those therefore that are in sovereign authority, and have taken upon them the government of people, are bound by the law of nature to make ordinances consisting in the points afore named, as being contrary to the law of nature, unnecessarily, either for one's own fancy, to enthral, or tie men so, as they cannot move without danger; or to suffer them whose maintenance is our benefit, to want anything necessary for them, by our negligence.

5. *Meum* and *tuum*, to be set out to the subjects, distinct from one another, &c. a duty of sovereigns by the law of nature. For maintaining of peace at home, there be so many things necessarily to be considered, and taken order in, as there be several causes concurring to sedition. And first, it is necessary to set out to every subject, his propriety, and distinct lands and goods, upon which he may exercise and have the benefit of his own industry, and without which men would fall out amongst themselves, as did the herdsmen of Abraham and Lot, every man encroaching and usurping as much of the common benefit as he can, which tendeth to quarrel and sedition. Secondly, to divide the burdens and charges of the commonwealth proportionably. Now there is a *proportionably* to every man's ability, and there is a *proportionably* to his benefit by commonwealth: and this latter is it, which is according to the law of nature. For the burdens of the commonwealth being the price that we pay for the benefit thereof, they ought to be measured thereby. And there is no reason, when two men equally enjoying, by the benefit of the commonwealth, their peace and liberty, to use their industry to get their livings, whereof one spareth, and layeth up somewhat, the other spendeth all he gets, why they should not equally contribute to the common charge. That seemeth therefore to be the most equal way of dividing the burden of public charge, when every man shall contribute according to what he spendeth, and not according to what he gets. And this is then done, when men pay the commonwealth's part in the payments they make for their own provision. And this seemeth not only most equal, but also least sensible, and least to trouble the mind of them that pay it. For there is nothing so aggravateth the grief of

parting with money to the public, as to think they are overrated, and that their neighbors whom they envy, do thereupon insult over them, and this disposeth them to resistance, and, after that such resistance hath produced a mischief, to rebellion.

6. *An extraordinary power for judging the abuses of magistrates, necessary, &c.* Another thing necessary for the maintaining of peace, is the due execution of justice, which consisteth principally in the right performance of their duties, which are the magistrates, ordained for the same by and under the authority of the sovereign power, which being private men in respect of the sovereign, and consequently such as may have private ends, whereby they may be corrupted with gifts, or intercession of friends, ought to be kept in awe by an higher power, lest people, grieved by their injustice, should take upon them to make their own revenges, to the disturbance of the common peace; which can by no way be avoided in the principal and immediate magistrates, without the judicature of the sovereign himself, or some extraordinary power delegated by him. It is therefore necessary, that there be a power extraordinary, as there shall be occasion from time to time, for the syndication of judges and other magistrates, that shall abuse their authority, to the wrong and discontent of the people; and a free and open way for the presenting of grievances to him or them that have the sovereign authority.

7. *The suppressing of popularity, &c. necessary, &c.* Besides these considerations, by which are prevented the discontents that arise from oppression, there ought to be some means for the keeping under of those, that are disposed to rebellion by ambition; which consist principally in the constancy of him that hath the sovereign power, who ought therefore constantly to grace and encourage such, as being able to serve the commonwealth, do nevertheless contain themselves within the bounds of modesty, without repining at the authority of such as are employed, and without aggravating the errors, which, as men, they may commit, especially when they suffer not in their own particular; and constantly to show displeasure, and dislike of the contrary. And not only so, but also to ordain severe punishments for such, as shall by repre-

hension of public actions, affect popularity and applause amongst the multitude, by which they may be enabled to have a faction in the commonwealth at their devotion.

8. *The instruction of youth, &c. necessary, &c.* Another thing necessary, is the rooting out of the consciences of men, all those opinions which seem to justify and give pretense of right to rebellious actions; such as are the opinions, that a man can do nothing lawfully against his private conscience; that they who have the sovereignty, are subject to the civil laws; that there is any authority of subjects, whose negative may hinder the affirmative of the sovereign power; that any subject hath a propriety distinct from the dominion of the commonwealth; that there is a body of the people without him or them that have the sovereign power; and that any lawful sovereign may be resisted under the name of a tyrant; which opinions are they, which, Part II chap. 8. sect. 5–10, have been declared to dispose men to rebellion. And because opinions which are gotten by education, and in length of time, are made habitual, cannot be taken away by force, and upon the sudden; they must therefore be taken away also by time and education. And seeing the said opinions have proceeded from private and public teaching, and those teachers have received them from grounds and principles, which they have learned in the Universities, from the doctrine of Aristotle, and others, who have delivered nothing concerning morality and policy demonstratively; but being passionately addicted to popular government, have insinuated their opinions by eloquent sophistry. There is no doubt, if the true doctrine concerning the law of nature, and the properties of a body politic, and the nature of law in general, were perspicuously set down and taught in the Universities, but that young men, who come thither void of prejudice, and whose minds are as white paper, capable of any instruction, would more easily receive the same, and afterward teach it to the people, both in books and otherwise, than now they do the contrary.

9. *Avoiding of unnecessary war, a necessary duty of the sovereign, &c.* The last thing contained in that supreme law, *salus populi*, is their defense; and consisteth partly in the obedience and unity of the subjects, of which hath been already

spoken, and in which consisteth the means of levying soldiers, and of having money, arms, ships, and fortified places in readiness for defense; and partly, in the avoiding of unnecessary wars. For such commonwealth, or such monarchs, as affect war for itself, that is to say, out of ambition, or of vain-glory, or that make account to revenge every little injury, or disgrace done by their neighbors, if they ruin not themselves, their fortune must be better than they have reason to expect.

Chapter 10

1. *All expressions, &c. concerning future actions, are either covenant, counsel, or command.* Thus far concerning the Nature of Man, and the constitution and properties of a Body Politic. There remaineth only for the last chapter, to speak of the nature and sorts of law. And first it is manifest, that all laws are declarations of the mind, concerning some action future to be done, or omitted. And all declarations and expressions of the mind concerning future actions and omissions, are either *promissive,* as *I will do, or not do; or provisive,* as for example, *If this be done or not done, this will follow;* or *imperative,* as *Do this, or do it not.* In the first sort of these expressions, consisteth the nature of a covenant; in the second, consisteth counsel; in the third, command.

2. *The difference between a law and a covenant.* It is evident when a man doth, or forbeareth to do any action, if he be moved thereto by this only consideration, that the same is good or evil in itself; and that there be no reason why the will or pleasure of another, should be of any weight in his deliberation, that then neither to do nor omit the action deliberated, is any breach of law. And consequently, whatsoever is a law to a man, respecteth the will of another, and the declaration thereof. But a covenant is a declaration of a man's own will. And therefore a law and a covenant differ: and though they be both obligatory, and a law obligeth no otherwise than by virtue of some covenant made by him who is subject thereunto, yet they oblige by several sorts of promises. For a covenant obligeth by promise of an action, or omission especially named and limited; but a law bindeth by a promise of obedience in general, whereby the action to be done, or left undone, is referred to the determination of him, to whom the covenant is made. So that the difference between a covenant, and a law, standeth thus: in simple covenant, the action to be done, or not done, is first limited and made known, and then followeth the promise to do or not do;

but in a law, the obligation to do or not to do, precedeth, and the declaration what is to be done, or not done, followeth after.

3. The command of him whose command is law in one thing, is law in every thing. And from this may be deduced, that which to some may seem a *paradox, That the command of him, whose command is a law in one thing, is a law in every thing.* For seeing a man is obliged to obedience before what he is to do be known, he is obliged to obey in general, that is to say, in every thing.

4. The difference between law and counsel. That the counsel of a man is no law to him that is counselled, and that he who alloweth another to give him counsel, doth not thereby oblige himself to follow the same, is manifest enough. And yet men usually call counselling, by the name of governing; not that they are not able to distinguish between them, but because they envy many times those men that are called to counsel, and are therefore angry with them that they are counselled. But if to counsellors there should be given a right to have their counsel followed, then are they no more counsellors, but masters of them whom they counsel; and their counsels no more counsels, but laws. For the difference between a law and a counsel being no more but this, that in counsel the expression is, *Do, because it is best;* in a law, *Do, because I have a right to compel you;* or *Do, because I say, do;* when counsel should give the reason of the action it adviseth to, because the reason thereof itself is no more counsel, but a law.

5. The difference between *jus & lex.* The names *lex* and *jus,* that is to say, law and right, are often confounded, and yet scarce are there any two words of more contrary signification. For right is that liberty which law leaveth us, and laws those restraints by which we agree mutually to abridge one another's liberty. Law and right therefore are no less different than restraint and liberty, which are contrary; and whatsoever a man doth, that liveth in a commonwealth *jure,* he doth it *jure civili, jure naturæ,* and *jure divino.* For whatsoever is against any of these laws, cannot be said to be *jure.* For the civil law cannot make that to be done *jure,* which is

against the law *divine*, or of *nature*. And therefore whatsoever any subject doth, if it be not contrary to the civil law, and whatsoever a sovereign doth, if it be not against the law of nature, he doth it *jure divino*, by *divine right*. But to say, *lege divinâ*, by *divine law*, is another thing. For the laws of God and nature allowing greater liberty than is allowed by the law civil; for subordinate laws do still bind more than superior laws, the essence of law being not to loose, but to bind, a man may be commanded that by a law civil, which is not commanded by the law of nature, nor by the law divine. So that of things done *lege*, that is to say, by command of the law, there is some place for a distinction between *lege divinâ*, and *lege civili*. As when a man giveth an alms, or helpeth him that is in need, he doth it not *lege civili*, but *lege divinâ*, by the divine law, the precept whereof is charity. But for things that are done *jure*, nothing can be said to be done *jure divino*, that is not also *jure civili*, unless it be done by them that having sovereign power, are not subject to the civil law.

6. The division of laws, &c. The differences of laws, are according to the differences, either of the authors and lawmakers, or of the promulgation, or of those that are subject to them. From the difference of the authors, or lawmakers, cometh the division of law into *divine, natural,* and *civil*. From the difference of promulgation, proceedeth the division of laws into *written* and *unwritten*. And from the difference of the persons to whom the law appertaineth, it proceedeth, that some laws are called simply laws, and some penal. As for example, *thou shalt not steal*, is simply a law; but this, *he that stealeth an ox, shall restore four-fold*, is a penal, or as others call it, a judicial law. Now in those laws, which are simply laws, the commandment is addressed to every man; but in penal laws the commandment is addressed to the magistrate, who is only guilty of the breach of it, when the penalties ordained, are not inflicted; to the rest appertaineth nothing, but to take notice of their danger.

7. That the divine moral law, and the law of nature, is the same. As for the first division of law into *divine, natural,* and *civil*, the first two branches are one and the same law. For

the law of nature, which is also the moral law, is the law of the author of nature, God Almighty; and the law of God taught by our Saviour Christ, is the moral law. For the sum of God's law is, *Thou shalt love God above all, and thy neighbor as thyself;* and the same is the sum of the law of nature, as hath been showed, Part I chap. 5. And although the doctrine of our Saviour be of three parts, *moral, theological,* and *ecclesiastical;* the former part only, which is the moral, is of the nature of a law universal; the latter part is a branch of the law civil; and the theological, which containeth those articles concerning the divinity and kingdom of our Saviour, without which there is no salvation, is not delivered in the nature of laws, but of counsel and direction, how to avoid the punishment, which by the violation of the moral law, men are subject to. For it is not infidelity that condemneth, though it be faith that saveth, but the breach of the law and commandments of God, written first in man's heart, and afterwards in tables, and delivered to the Jews by the hands of Moses.

8. That the civil laws are the common measure of right and wrong, &c. In the state of nature, where every man is his own judge, and differeth from other concerning the names and appellations of things, and from those differences arise quarrels and breach of peace, it was necessary there should be a common measure of all things, that might fall in controversy. As for example; of what is to be called right, what good, what virtue, what much, what little, what *meum* and *tuum,* what a pound, what a quart, &c. For in these things private judgments may differ, and beget controversy. This common measure, some say, is *right reason:* with whom I should consent, if there were any such thing to be found or known in *rerum naturâ.* But commonly they that call for *right reason* to decide any controversy, do mean their own. But this is certain, seeing *right reason* is not existent, the reason of some man or men must supply the place thereof; and that man or men, is he or they, that have the sovereign power, as hath been already proved; and consequently the civil laws are to all subjects the measures of their actions, whereby to determine, whether they be right or wrong, profitable or

unprofitable, virtuous or vicious; and by them the use and definition of all names not agreed upon, and tending to controversy, shall be established. As for example, when upon occasion of some strange and deformed birth, it shall not be decided by Aristotle, or the philosophers, whether the same be a man, or no, but by the laws; the civil law containing in it the ecclesiastical, as a part thereof, proceeding from the power of ecclesiastical government, given by our Saviour to all Christian sovereigns, as his immediate vicars, as hath been said Part II chap. 7 sect. 10.

9. Martial law is civil law. But seeing it hath been said, that all laws are either natural or civil, it may be demanded, to which of these shall be referred that law, which is called martial law, and by the Romans, *disciplina militaris?* And it may seem to be the same with the law of nature; because the laws by which a multitude of soldiers are governed in an army are not constant, but continually changing with the occasion; and that is still a law, which is reason for the present and reason is the law of nature. It is nevertheless true, that martial law is civil law, because an army is a body politic, the whole power whereof is in the General, and the laws thereof made by him; and though they still follow and change as reason requireth, yet it is not, as the reason of every private man, but as the reason of the General requireth.

10. Written laws, Unwritten, &c. Customs, and Opinions, &c. When he or they in whom is the sovereign power of a commonwealth, are to ordain laws for the government and good order of the people, it is not possible they should comprehend all cases of controversy that may fall out, or perhaps any considerable diversity of them: but as time shall instruct them by the rising of new occasions, so are also laws from time to time to be ordained: and in such cases where no special law is made, the law of nature keepeth its place, and the magistrates ought to give sentence according thereunto, that is to say, according to natural reason. The constitutions therefore of the sovereign power, by which the liberty of nature is abridged, are written, because there is no other way to take notice of them; whereas the laws of nature are supposed to be written in men's hearts. Written laws therefore

are the constitutions of a commonwealth expressed; and un-written, are the laws of natural reason. Custom of itself maketh no laws. Nevertheless when a sentence hath been once given, by them that judge by their natural reason, whether the same be right or wrong, it may attain to the vigor of a law; not because the like sentence hath of custom been given in the like case, but because the sovereign power is supposed tacitly to have approved such sentence for right, and thereby it cometh to be a law, and numbered amongst the written laws of the commonwealth. For if custom were sufficient to introduce a law, then it would be in the power of every one that is deputed to hear a cause, to make his errors laws. In the like manner, those laws that go under the title of *responsa prudentum*, that is to say, the opinions of lawyers, are not therefore laws, because *responsa prudentum*, but because they are admitted by the sovereign. And from this may be collected, that when there is a case of private contract between the sovereign and the subject, a precedent against reason shall not prejudice the cause of the sovereign; no precedent being made a law, but upon supposition that the same was reasonable from the beginning.

And thus much concerning the elements and general grounds of laws natural and politic. As for the law of nations, it is the same with the law of nature. For that which is the law of nature between man and man, before the constitution of commonwealth, is the law of nations between sovereign and sovereign, after.

A DIALOGUE OF THE COMMON LAW*

Of the Law of Reason

Lawyer. What makes you say, that the study of the law is less rational than the study of the mathematics?

Philosopher. I say not that; for all study is rational, or nothing worth: but I say, that the great masters of the *mathematics* do not so often err as the great professors of the law.

L. If you had applied your reason to the law, perhaps you would have been of another mind.

P. In whatsoever study, I examine whether my inference be rational: and have looked over the titles of the statutes from Magna Charta downward to this present time. I left not one unread, which I thought might concern myself; which was enough for me, that meant not to plead for any but myself. But I did not much examine which of them was more or less rational; because I read them not to dispute, but to obey them, and saw in all of them sufficient reason for my obedience, and that the same reason, though the Statutes themselves were changed, remained constant. I have also diligently read over Littleton's book of *Tenures*, with the commentaries thereupon of the renowned lawyer Sir Edward Coke; in which I confess I found great subtlty, not of the law, but of inference from law, and especially from the law of human nature, which is the law of reason: and I confess that it is truth which he says in the epilogue to his book, that by arguments and reason in the law, a man shall sooner come to the certainty and knowledge of the law: and I agree with Sir Edward Coke, who upon that text farther says, that reason is the soul of the law; and upon section 138, *nihil, quod est contra rationem, est licitum;* that is to say, nothing is law that is against reason; and that reason is the life of the law, nay the common law itself is nothing else but reason;

*From *A Dialogue Between a Philosopher and a Student of The Common Laws of England* (Molesworth Ed. 1839, Vol. VI of English Works) pp. 3-34.

and upon section 21, *æquitas est perfecta quædam ratio, quæ jus scriptum interpretatur et emendat, nulla scriptura comprehensa, sed solum in vera ratione consistens;* i.e. <u>Equity is a certain perfect reason, that interpreteth and amendeth the law written, itself being unwritten, and consisting in nothing else but right reason.</u> When I consider this, and find it to be true, and so evident as not to be denied by any man of right sense, I find my own reason at a stand; for it frustrates all the laws in the world. For upon this ground any man, of any law whatsoever, may say it is against reason, and thereupon make a pretense for his disobedience. I pray you clear this passage, that we may proceed.

L. I clear it thus, out of Sir Edward Coke (I. Inst. sect. 138), that this is to be understood of an artificial perfection of reason, gotten by long study, observation, and experience, and not of every man's natural reason; for *nemo nascitur artifex.* This legal reason is *summa ratio;* and therefore if all the reason that is dispersed into so many several heads, were united into one, yet could he not make such a law as the law of England is; because by so many successions of ages it hath been fined and refined by an infinite number of grave and learned men.

P. This does not clear the place, as being partly obscure, and partly untrue. That the reason which is the life of the law, should be not natural, but artificial, I cannot conceive. I understand well enough, that the knowledge of the law is gotten by much study, as all other sciences are, which when they are studied and obtained, it is still done by natural, and not by artificial reason. I grant you, that the knowledge of the law is an art; but not that any art of one man, or of many, how wise soever they be, or the work of one or more artificers, how perfect soever it be, is law. <u>It is not wisdom, but authority that makes a law.</u> Obscure also are the words *legal reason.* There is no reason in earthly creatures, but human reason. But I suppose that he means, that the reason of a judge, or of all the judges together without the King, is that *summa ratio,* and the very law: which I deny, <u>because none can make a law but he that hath the legislative power.</u> That the law hath been fined by grave and learned men, meaning the professors of the law, is manifestly untrue; for all the laws of England have been made by the kings of England, consulting with the nobility and commons in parliament, of which not one of twenty was a learned lawyer.

L. You speak of the statute law, and I speak of the common law.

P. I speak generally of law.

L. Thus far I agree with you, that statute law taken away, there would not be left, either here, or any where, any law at all that would conduce to the peace of a nation; yet equity and reason, (laws Divine and eternal, which oblige all men at all times, and in all places), would still remain, but be obeyed by few: and though the breach of them be not punished in this world, yet they will be punished sufficiently in the world to come. Sir Edward Coke, for drawing to the men of his own profession as much authority as lawfully he might, is not to be reprehended; but to the gravity and learning of the judges they ought to have added in the making of laws, the authority of the King, which hath the sovereignty: for of these laws of reason, every subject that is in his wits, is bound to take notice at his peril, because reason is part of his nature, which he continually carries about with him, and may read it, if he will.

P. It is very true; and upon this ground, if I pretend within a month or two to make myself able to perform the office of a judge, you are not to think it arrogance; for you are to allow to me, as well as to other men, my pretense to reason, which is the common law, (remember this, that I may not need again to put you in mind, that reason is the common law): and for statute law, seeing it is printed, and that there be indexes to point me to every matter contained in them, I think a man may profit in them very much in two months.

L. But you will be but an ill pleader.

P. A pleader commonly thinks he ought to say all he can for the benefit of his client, and therefore has need of a faculty to wrest the sense of words from their true meaning, and the faculty of *rhetoric* to seduce the jury, and sometimes the judge also, and many other arts which I neither have, nor intend to study.

L. But let the judge, how good soever he thinks his reasoning, take heed that he depart not too much from the letter of the statute: for it is not without danger.

P. He may without danger recede from the letter, if he do not from the meaning and sense of the law; which may be by a learned man, (such as judges commonly are,) easily found out by the preamble, the time when it was made, and the incommodities for which it was made. But I pray tell me, to what end were statute laws ordained, seeing the law of reason ought to be applied to every controversy that can arise.

L. You are not ignorant of the force of an irregular appetite to riches, to power, and to sensual pleasures, how it masters the strongest reason, and is the root of disobedience, slaughter, fraud, hypocrisy, and all manner of evil habits; and that the laws of man, though they can punish the fruits of them, which are evil actions, yet they cannot pluck up the roots that are in the heart. How can a man be indicted of avarice, envy, hypocrisy, or other vicious habit, till it be declared by some action which a witness may take notice of? The root remaining, new fruit will come forth, till you be weary of punishing, and at last destroy all power that shall oppose it.

P. What hope then is there of a constant peace in any nation, or between one nation and another?

L. You are not to expect such a peace between two nations; because there is no common power in this world to punish their injustice. Mutual fear may keep them quiet for a time; but upon every visible advantage they will invade one another; and the most visible advantage is then, when the one nation is obedient to their king, and the other not. But peace at home may then be expected durable, when the common people shall be made to see the benefit they shall receive by their obedience and adhesion to their own sovereign, and the harm they must suffer by taking part with them, who by promises of reformation, or change of govern-

This is Hobbes speaking thru the lawyer!

nent, deceive them. And this is properly to be done by divines, and from arguments not only from reason, but also from the Holy Scripture.

P. This that you say is true, but not very much to that I aim at by your conversation, which is to inform myself concerning the laws of England. Therefore I ask you again, what is the end of statute-laws?

Of Sovereign Power

L. I say then that the scope of all human law is peace, and justice in every nation amongst themselves, and defense against foreign enemies. ⊛

P. But what is justice?

L. Justice is giving to every man his own.

P. The definition is good, and yet it is Aristotle's. What is the definition agreed upon as a principle in the science of the common law?

L. The same with that of Aristotle.

P. See, you lawyers, how much you are beholden to the philosopher; and it is but reason; for the more general and noble science and law of all the world, is true philosophy, of which the common law of England is a very little part.

L. It is so, if you mean by philosophy nothing but the study of reason; as I think you do.

P. When you say that justice gives to every man his own, what mean you by his own? How can that be given me, which is my own already? Or, if it be not my own, how can justice make it mine?

L. Without law, every thing is in such sort every man's, as he may take, possess, and enjoy, without wrong to any man; every thing, lands, beasts, fruits, and even the bodies of other men, if his reason tell him he cannot otherwise live *N.B* securely. For the dictates of reason are little worth, if they tended not to the preservation and improvement of men's lives. Seeing then without human law all things would be common, and this community a cause of encroachment, envy, slaughter, and continual war of one upon another, the same law of reason dictates to mankind, for their own preservation, a distribution of lands and goods, that each man may know what is proper to him, so as none other might pretend a right thereunto, or disturb him in the use of the same. This distribution is justice, and this properly is the same which we say is one's own; by which you may see the great necessity there was of statute laws, for preservation of all mankind. It is also a dictate of the law of reason, that statute laws are a necessary means of the safety and well-being of man in the present world, and are to be obeyed by all subjects, as the law of reason ought to be obeyed, both by King and subjects, because it is the law of God.

P. All this is very rational; but how can any laws secure one man from another, when the greatest part of men are so unreasonable, and so partial to themselves as they are, and the laws of themselves are but a dead letter, which of itself is not able to compel a man to do otherwise than himself pleaseth, nor punish or hurt him when he hath done a mischief?

L. By the laws, I mean laws living and armed. For you must suppose, that a nation that is subdued by war to an absolute submission to a conqueror, may, by the same arm that compelled it to submission, be compelled to obey his laws. Also, if a nation choose a man, or an assembly of men, to govern them by laws, it must furnish him also with armed men and money, and all things necessary to his office; or else his laws will be of no force, and the nation remains, as before it was, in confusion. It is not therefore the word of the law, but the power of a man that has the strength of a nation, that make the laws effectual. It was not Solon that made Athenian laws, though he devised them, but the supreme court of the people; nor, the lawyers of Rome that made the imperial law in Justinian's time, but Justinian himself.

P. We agree then in this, that in England it is the King that makes the laws, whosoever pens them; and in this, that the King cannot make his laws effectual, nor defend his people against their enemies, without a power to levy soldiers; and consequently, that he may lawfully, as oft as he shall really think it necessary to raise an army, (which in some occasions be very great) I say, raise it, and money to maintain it. I doubt not but you will allow this to be according to the law, at least of reason.

L. For my part I allow it. But you have heard how, in and before the late troubles the people were of another mind. Shall the King, said they, take from us what he pleases, upon pretense of a necessity whereof he makes himself the judge? What worse condition can we be in from an enemy? What can they take from us more than what they list?

P. The people reason ill. They do not know in what condition we were, in the time of the Conqueror, when it was a shame to be an Englishman; who, if he grumbled at the base offices he was put to by his Norman masters, received no other answer than this, *thou art but an Englishman.* Nor can the people, nor any man that humors their disobedience, produce any example of a King that ever raised any excessive sums, either by himself or by the consent of his Parliament, but when they had great need thereof; nor can show any reason that might move any of them so to do. The greatest complaint by them made against the unthriftiness of their Kings, was for the enriching now and then a favorite, which to the wealth of the kingdom was inconsiderable, and the complaint but envy. But in this point of raising soldiers, what is, I pray you, the statute law?

L. The last statute concerning it, is 13 *Car.* II. cap. 6, by which the supreme government, command, and disposing of the militia of England, is delivered to be, and always to have been, the ancient right of the Kings of England. But there is also in the same act a proviso, that this shall not be construed for a declaration, that the King may transport his subjects, or compel them to march out of the kingdom; nor is it, on the contrary, declared to be unlawful.

P. Why is not that also determined?

L. I can imagine cause enough for it, though I may be deceived. We love to have our King amongst us, and not to be governed by deputies, either of our own or another nation. But this I verily believe, that if a foreign enemy should either invade us, or put himself into a readiness to invade either England, Ireland, or Scotland, no Parliament then sitting, and the King send English soldiers thither, the Parliament would give him thanks for it. The subjects of those Kings who affect the glory, and imitate the actions, of Alexander the Great, have not always the most comfortable lives, nor do such Kings usually very long enjoy their conquests. They march to and fro perpetually, as upon a plank sustained only in the midst; and when one end rises, down goes the other.

P. It is well. But where soldiers, in the judgment of the King's conscience, are indeed necessary, as in an insurrection or rebellion at home; how shall the kingdom be preserved without a considerable army ready and in pay? How shall money be raised for this army, especially when the want of public treasure inviteth neighbor Kings to encroach, and unruly subjects to rebel?

L. I cannot tell. It is matter of polity, not of law. But I know, that there be statutes express, whereby the King hath obliged himself never to levy money upon his subjects without the consent of his Parliament. One of which statutes is 25 *Edw.* I. c. 6, in these words: *We have granted for us, and our heirs, as well to archbishops, bishops, abbots, priors, and other folk of holy Church, as also to earls, barons, and to all the commonalty of the land, that for no business from hence forth, we shall take such aids, tasks, or prizes, but by the common consent of the realm.* There is also another statute of *Edward* I. (34 *Edw.* I. stat. 4) in these words: *No tallage or aid shall be taken or levied by us or our heirs in our realm, without the good will and assent of the archbishops, bishops, earls, barons, knights, burgesses, and other freemen of the land;* which statutes have been since that time confirmed by divers other Kings, and lastly by the King that now reigneth.

P. All this I know, and am not satisfied. I am one of the common people, and one of that almost infinite number of men, for whose welfare <u>Kings and other sovereigns were by</u> <u>God ordained: for God made Kings for the people, and no people for Kings.</u> How shall I be defended from the domineering of proud and insolent strangers that speak another language, that scorn us, that seek to make us slaves, or how shall I avoid the destruction that may arise from the cruelty of factions in a civil war, unless the King, to whom alone, you say, belongeth the right of levying and disposing of the militia by which only it can be prevented, have ready money, upon all occasions, to arm and pay as many soldiers, as for the present defense, or the peace of the people, shall be necessary? Shall not I, and you, and every man be undone? Tell me not of a Parliament, when there is no Parliament sitting, or perhaps none in being, which may often happen. And when there is a Parliament, if the speaking and leading men should have a design to put down monarchy, as they had in the Parliament which began to sit the third of November, 1640, shall the King, who is to answer to God Almighty for the safety of the people, and to that end is intrusted with the power to levy and dispose of the soldiery, be disabled to perform his office, by virtue of these acts of Parliament which you have cited? If this be reason, it is reason also that the people be abandoned, or left at liberty to kill one another, even to the last man; if it be not reason, then you have granted it is not law.

L. It is true, if you mean *recta ratio;* but *recta ratio,* which I grant to be law, as Sir Edward Coke says, (1 *Inst.* sect. 138), is an artificial perfection of reason, gotten by long study, observation, and experience, and not every man's natural reason; for *nemo nascitur artifex.* This legal reason is *summa ratio;* and therefore, if all the reason that is dispersed into so many several heads, were united into one, yet could he not make such a law as the law of England is, because by many successions of ages it hath been fined and refined by an infinite number of grave and learned men. And this is it, he calls the common law.

P. Do you think this to be good doctrine? Though it be true, that no man is born with the use of reason, yet all men may grow up to it as well as lawyers; and when they have applied their reason to the laws, (which were laws before they studied them, or else it was not law they studied), may be as fit for and capable of judicature, as Sir Edward Coke himself, who whether he had more or less use of reason, was not thereby a judge, but because the King made him so. And whereas he says, that a man who should have as much reason as is dispersed in so many several heads, could not make such a law as this law of England is; if one should ask him who made the law of England, would he say a succession of English lawyers or judges made it, or rather a succession of kings? And that upon their own reason, either solely, or with the advice of the Lords and Commons in Parliament, without the judges or other professors of the law? You see therefore that the King's reason, be it more or less, is that *anima legis*, that *summa lex*, whereof Sir Edward Coke speaketh, and not the reason, learning, or wisdom of the judges. But you may see, that quite through his *Institutes of Law*, he often takes occasion to magnify the learning of the lawyers, whom he perpetually termeth the sages of the Parliament, or of the King's council. Therefore unless you say otherwise, I say, that the King's reason, when it is publicly upon advice and deliberation declared, is that *anima legis;* and that *summa ratio* and that equity, which all agree to be the law of reason, is all that is or ever was law in England, since it became Christian, besides the Bible.

L. Are not the Canons of the Church part of the law of England, as also the imperial law used in the Admiralty, and the customs of particular places, and the by-laws of corporations and courts of judicature?

P. Why not? For they were all constituted by the Kings of England; and though the civil law used in the Admiralty were at first the statutes of the Roman empire, yet because they are in force by no other authority than that of the King, they are now the King's laws, and the King's statutes. The same we may say of the Canons; such of them as we have retained, made by the Church of Rome, have been no law, nor of any force in England, since the beginning of Queen Elizabeth's reign, but by virtue of the great seal of England.

L. In the said statutes that restrain the levying of money without consent of Parliament, is there any thing you can take exceptions to?

P. No. I am satisfied that the kings that grant such liberties, are bound to make them good, so far as it may be done without sin: but if a King find that by such a grant he be disabled to protect his subjects, if he maintain his grant, he sins; and therefore may, and ought to take no notice of the said grant. For such grants, as by error or false suggestion are gotten from him, are, as the lawyers do confess, void and of no effect, and ought to be recalled. Also the King, as is on all hands confessed, hath the charge lying upon him to protect his people against foreign enemies, and to keep the peace betwixt them within the kingdom: if he do not his utmost endeavor to discharge himself thereof, he committeth a sin, which neither King nor Parliament can lawfully commit.

L. No man, I think, will deny this. For if levying of money be necessary, it is a sin in the Parliament to refuse; if unnecessary, it is a sin both in King and Parliament to levy. But for all that, it may be, and I think it is, a sin in any one that hath the sovereign power, be he one man or one assembly, being intrusted with the safety of a whole nation, if rashly, and relying upon his own natural sufficiency, he make war or peace, without consulting with such, as by their experience and employment abroad, and intelligence by letters, or other means, have gotten the knowledge in some measure of the strength, advantages, and designs of the enemy, and the manner and the degree of the danger that may from thence arise. In like manner, in case of rebellion at home, if he consult not with those of military condition; which if he do, then I think he may lawfully proceed to subdue all such enemies and rebels; and that the soldiers ought to go on without inquiring whether they be within the country, or without. For who shall suppress rebellion, but he that hath right to levy, command, and dispose of the militia? The last Long Parliament denied this. But why? Because by the major part of their votes the rebellion was raised with the design to put down monarchy, and to that end maintained.

P. Nor do I hereby lay any aspersion upon such grants of the King and his ancestors. Those statutes are in themselves very good for the King and the people, as creating some kind of difficulty for such Kings as, for the glory of

Vain glory

conquest, might spend one part of their subjects' lives and estates in molesting other nations, and leave the rest to destroy themselves at home by factions. That which I here find fault with, is the wresting of those, and other such statutes, to the binding of our Kings from the use of their armies in the necessary defense of themselves and their people. The late Long Parliament, that in 1648 murdered their King, (a King that sought no greater glory upon earth, but to be indulgent to his people, and a pious defender of the Church of England,) no sooner took upon them the sovereign power, than they levied money upon the people at their own discretion. Did any of their subjects dispute their power? Did they not send soldiers over the sea to subdue Ireland, and others to fight against the Dutch at sea; or made they any doubt but to be obeyed in all that they commanded, as a right absolutely due to the sovereign power in whomsoever it resides? I say not this as allowing their actions, but as a testimony from the mouths of those very men that denied the same power to him whom they acknowledged to have been their sovereign immediately before; which is a sufficient proof, that the people of England never doubted of the King's right to levy money for the maintenance of his armies, till they were abused in it by seditious teachers, and other prating men, on purpose to turn the State and Church into popular government, where the most ignorant and boldest talkers do commonly obtain the best preferments. Again, when their new republic returned into monarchy by Oliver, who durst deny him money upon any pretence of *Magna Charta,* or of these other acts of Parliament which you have cited? You may therefore think it good law, for all your books, that the King of England may at all times, that he thinks in his conscience it will be necessary for the defense of his people, levy as many soldiers and as much money as he please, and that himself is judge of the necessity.

L. Is there nobody hearkening at the door?

P. What are you afraid of?

L. I mean to say the same that you say: but there be very many yet, that hold their former principles, whom neither the calamities of the civil wars, nor their former pardon, have thoroughly cured of their madness.

P. The common people never take notice of what they hear of this nature, but when they are set on by such as they think wise; that is, by some sorts of preachers, or some that seem to be learned in the laws, and withal speak evil of the governors. But what if the King, upon the sight or apprehension of any great danger to his people, (as when their neighbours are borne down by the current of a conquering enemy), should think his own people might be involved in the same misery; may he not levy, pay, and transport soldiers to help those weak neighbors, by way of prevention to save his own people and himself from servitude? Is that a sin?

L. First, if the war upon our neighbor be just, it may be questioned whether it be equity or no to assist them against the right.

P. For my part, I make no question of that at all, unless the invader will, and can, put me in security, that neither he nor his successors shall make any advantage of the conquest of my neighbor, to do the same to me in time to come. But there is no common power to bind them to the peace.

L. Secondly, when such a thing shall happen, the Parliament will not refuse to contribute freely to the safety of themselves and the whole nation.

P. It may be so, and it may be not; for if a Parliament then sit not, it must be called; that requires six weeks' time; debating and collecting what is given requires as much, and in this time the opportunity perhaps is lost. Besides, how many wretched souls have we heard to say in the late troubles; what matter is it who gets the victory? We can pay but what they please to demand, and so much we pay now. And this they will murmur, as they have ever done, whosoever shall reign over them, as long as their covetousness and ignorance hold together; which will be till doomsday, if better order be not taken for their instruction in their duty, both from reason and religion.

L. For all this I find it somewhat hard, that a King should have right to take from his subjects, upon the pretense of necessity, what he pleaseth.

P. I know what it is that troubles your conscience in this point. All men are troubled at the crossing of their wishes; but it is our own fault. First, we wish impossibilities; we would have our security against all the world upon right of property, without paying for it; this is impossible. We may as well expect that fish and fowl should boil, roast, and dish themselves, and come to the table, and that grapes should squeeze themselves into our mouths, and have all other the contentments and ease which some pleasant men have related of the land of Cocagne. Secondly, there is no nation in the world where he or they that have the sovereignty, do not take what money they please for the defense of those respective nations, when they think it necessary for their safety. The late Long Parliament denied this; but why? Because there was a design amongst them to depose the King. Thirdly, there is no example of any King of England that I have read of, that ever pretended any such necessity for levying money against his conscience. The greatest sums that ever were levied, comparing the value of money, as it was at that time, with what it is now, were levied by King Edward III and King Henry V; kings in whom we glory now, and think their actions great ornaments to the English history. Lastly, as to the enriching now and then a favourite, it is neither sensible to the kingdom, nor is any treasure thereby conveyed out of the realm, but so spent as it falls down again upon the common people. To think that our condition being human should be subject to no incommodity, were injuriously to quarrel with God Almighty for our own faults.

L. I know not what to say.

P. If you allow this that I have said, then say, that the people never were, shall be, or ought to be, free from being taxed at the will of one or other; that if civil war come, they must levy all they have, and that dearly, from the one or from the other, or from both sides. Say, that adhering to the King, their victory is an end of their trouble; that adhering to his enemies there is no end; for the war will continue by a perpetual subdivision, and when it ends, they will be in the same estate they were before. That they are often abused by men who to them seem wise, when then their wisdom is nothing else but envy of those that are in grace and in profitable employments; and that those men do but abuse the common people to their own ends, that set up a private man's propriety against the public safety. But say withal, that the King is subject to the laws of God, both written and unwritten, and to no other; and so was William the Conqueror, whose right is all descended to our present King.

L. As to the law of reason, which is equity, it is sure enough there is but one legislator, which is God.

P. It followeth, then, that which you call the common law, distinct from statute law, is nothing else but the law of God.

L. In some sense it is; but it is not Gospel, but natural reason, and natural equity.

P. Would you have every man to every other man allege for law his own particular reason? There is not amongst men a universal reason agreed upon in any nation, besides the reason of him that hath the sovereign power. Yet though his reason be but the reason of one man, yet it is set up to supply the place of that universal reason, which is expounded to us by our Saviour in the Gospel; and consequently our King is to us the legislator both of statute-law, and of common-law.

L. Yes, I know that the laws spiritual, which have been law in this kingdom since the abolishing of popery, are the King's laws, and those also that were made before. For the Canons of the Church of Rome were no laws, neither here, nor anywhere else without the Pope's temporal dominions, farther than kings and states in their several dominions respectively did make them so.

P. I grant that. But you must grant also, that those spiritual laws were made by the legislators of the spiritual law. And yet not all kings and states make laws by consent of the Lords and Commons; but our King here is so far bound to their assents, as he shall judge conducing to the good and safety of his people. For example, if the Lords and Commons should advise him to restore those laws spiritual, which in Queen Mary's time were in force, I think the King were by the law of reason obliged, without the help of any other law of God, to neglect such advice.

L. I grant you that the King is sole legislator; but with this restriction, that if he will not consult with the Lords of Parliament, and hear the complaints and informations of the Commons, that are best acquainted with their own wants, he sinneth against God, though he cannot be compelled to any thing by his subjects by arms and force.

P. We are agreed upon that already. Since therefore the King is sole legislator, I think it also reason he should be sole supreme judge.

The King Is the Supreme Judge

L. There is no doubt of that; for otherwise there would be no congruity of judgments with the laws. I grant also that he is the supreme judge over all persons, and in all causes civil and ecclesiastical within his own dominions; not only by act of Parliament at this time, but that he has ever been so by the common law. For the judges of both the Benches have their offices by the King's letters-patent; and so as do judicature have the bishops. Also the Lord Chancellor hath his office by receiving from the King the Great Seal of England. And, to say all at once, there is no magistrate, or commissioner for public business, neither of judicature nor execution, in State or Church, in peace or war, but he is made so by authority from the King.

P. It is true; but perhaps you may think otherwise, when you read such acts of parliament, as say, that the King shall have power and authority to do this or that by virtue of that act, as *Elizabeth* c. I. "that your highness, your heirs, and successors, Kings, or Queens of this realm, shall have full power and authority, by virtue of this act, by letters-patent under the great seal of England, to assign, &c." Was it not this Parliament that gave this authority to the Queen?

L. No. For the statute in this clause is no more than, as Sir Edward Coke useth to speak, an affirmance of the common-law. For she being head of the Church of England, might make commissioners for the deciding of matters ecclesiastical, as freely as if she had been Pope, who did, you know, pretend his right from the law of God.

P. We have hitherto spoken of laws without considering

anything of the nature and essence of a law; and now unless we define the word *law*, we can go no farther without ambiguity and fallacy, which will be but loss of time; whereas, on the contrary, the agreement upon our words will enlighten all we have to say hereafter.

L. I do not remember the definition of *law* in any statute.

P. I think so: for the statutes were made by authority, and not drawn from any other principles than the care of the safety of the people. Statutes are not philosophy, as is the common-law, and other disputable arts, but are commands or prohibitions, which ought to be obeyed, because assented to by submission made to the Conqueror here in England, and to whosoever had the sovereign power in other commonwealths; so that the positive laws of all places are statutes. The definition of law was therefore unnecessary for the makers of statutes, though very necessary to them whose work it is to teach the sense of the law.

L. There is an accurate definition of a law in Bracton, cited by Sir Edward Coke: *Lex est sanctio justa, jubens honesta, et prohibens contraria.*

P. That is to say, law is a just statute, commanding those things which are honest, and forbidding the contrary. From whence it followeth, that in all cases it must be the honesty or dishonesty that makes the command a law; whereas you know that but for the law we could not, as saith St. Paul, have known what is sin. Therefore this definition is no ground at all for any farther discourse of law. Besides, you know the rule of honest and dishonest refers to honor, and that it is justice only, and injustice, that the law respecteth. But that which I most except against in this definition, is, that it supposes that a statute made by the sovereign power of a nation may be unjust. There may indeed in a statute-law, made by men, be found iniquity, but not injustice.

L. This is somewhat subtle. I pray deal plainly. What is the difference between injustice and iniquity?

P. I pray you tell me first, what is the difference between a court of justice, and a court of equity?

L. A court of justice is that which hath cognizance of such causes as are to be ended by the positive laws of the land; and a court of equity is that, to which belong such causes as are to be determined by equity; that is to say, by the law of reason.

P. You see then that the difference between injustice and iniquity is this; that injustice is the transgression of a statute-law, and iniquity the transgression of the law of reason. But perhaps you mean by common-law, not the law itself, but the manner of proceeding in the law, as to matter of fact, by twelve men, freeholders; though those twelve men are no court of equity, nor of justice, because they determine not what is just or unjust, but only whether it be done or not done; and their judgment is nothing else but a confirmation of that which is properly the judgment of the witnesses. For to speak exactly, there cannot possibly be any judge of fact besides the witnesses.

L. How would you have a law defined?

P. Thus; a law is the command of him or them that have the sovereign power, given to those that be his or their subjects, declaring publicly and plainly what every of them may do, and what they must forbear to do.

L. Seeing all judges in all courts ought to judge according to equity, which is the law of reason, a distinct court of equity seemeth to me to be unnecessary, and but a burthen to the people, since common-law and equity are the same law.

P. It were so indeed, if judges could not err; but since they may err, and that the King is not bound to any other law but that of equity, it belongs to him alone to give remedy to them that, by the ignorance or corruption of a judge, shall suffer damage.

L. By your definition of a law, the King's proclamation under the Great Seal of England is a law; for it is a command, and public, and of the sovereign to his subjects.

P. Why not, if he think it necessary for the good of his subjects? For this is a maxim at the common-law alleged by Sir Edward Coke himself, (I Inst. sect. 306), *Quando lex aliquid concedit, concedere videtur et id per quod devenitur ad illud.* And you know out of the same author, that divers Kings of England have often, to the petitions in Parliament which they granted, annexed such exceptions as these, *unless there be necessity, saving our regality*; which I think should be always understood, though they be not expressed; and are understood so by common lawyers, who agree that the King may recall any grant wherein he was deceived.

L. Again, whereas you make it of the essence of a law to be publicly and plainly declared to the people, I see no necessity for that. Are not all subjects bound to take notice of all acts of Parliament, when no act can pass without their consent?

P. If you had said that no act could pass without their knowledge, then indeed they had been bound to take notice of them; but none can have knowledge of them but the members of the houses of Parliament; therefore the rest of the people are excused. Or else the knights of the shire should be bound to furnish people with a sufficient number of copies, at the people's charge, of the acts of Parliament, at their return into the country; that every man may resort to them, and by themselves, or friends, take notice of what they are obliged to. For otherwise it were impossible they should be obeyed: and that no man is bound to do a thing impossible, is one of Sir Edward Coke's maxims at the common-law. I know that most of the statutes are printed; but it does not appear that every man is bound to buy the book of statutes, nor to search for them at Westminster or at the Tower, nor to understand the language wherein they are for the most part written.

L. I grant it proceeds from their own faults; but no man can be excused by ignorance of the law of reason, that is to say, by ignorance of the common-law, except children, madmen, and idiots. But you exact such a notice of the statute-law, as is almost impossible. Is it not enough that they in all places have a sufficient number of the penal statutes?

P. Yes; if they have those penal statutes near them. But what reason can you give me why there should not be as many copies abroad of the statutes, as there be of the Bible?

L. I think it were well that every man that can read, had a statute-book; for certainly no knowledge of those laws, by which men's lives and fortunes can be brought into danger, can be too much. I find a great fault in your definition of law;

which is, that every law either forbiddeth or commandeth something. It is true that the moral law is always a command or a prohibition, or at least implieth it. But in the Levitical law, where it is said that he that stealeth a sheep shall restore fourfold, what command or prohibition lieth in these words?

P. Such sentences as that are not in themselves general, but judgments; nevertheless, there is in those words implied a commandment to the judge, to cause to be made a fourfold restitution.

L. That is right.

P. Now define what justice is, and what actions and men are to be called just.

L. Justice is the constant will of giving to every man his own; that is to say, of giving to every man that which is his right, in such manner as to exclude the right of all men else to the same thing. A just action is that which is not against the law. A just man is he that hath a constant will to live justly; if you require more, I doubt there will no man living be comprehended within the definition.

P. Seeing then that a just action, according to your definition, is that which is not against the law; it is manifest that before there was a law, there could be no injustice; and therefore laws are in their nature antecedent to justice and injustice. And you cannot deny but there must be law-makers, before there were any laws, and consequently before there was any justice, (I speak of human justice); and that law-makers were before that which you call *own*, or property of goods or lands, distinguished by *meum, tuum, alienum.*

L. That must be granted; for without statute-laws, all men have right to all things; and we have had experience, when our laws were silenced by civil war, there was not a man, that of any goods could say assuredly they were his own.

P. You see then that no private man can claim a propriety in any lands, or other goods, from any title from any man but the King, or them that have the sovereign power; because it is in virtue of the sovereignty, that every man may not enter into and possess what he pleaseth; and consequently to deny the sovereign anything necessary to the sustaining of his sovereign power, is to destroy the propriety he pretends to. The next thing I will ask you is, how you distinguish between law and right, or *lex* and *jus*.

L. Sir Edward Coke in divers places makes *lex* and *jus* to be the same, and so *lex communis* and *jus communis*, to be all one; nor do I find that he does in any place distinguish them.

P. Then will I distinguish them, and make you judge whether my distinction be not necessary to be known by every author of the common-law. For law obligeth me to do, or forbear the doing of something; and therefore it lays upon me an obligation. But my right is a liberty left me by the law to do any thing which the law forbids me not, and to leave undone any thing which the law commands me not. Did Sir Edward Coke see no difference between being bound and being free?

L. I know not what he saw, but he has not mentioned it. Though a man may dispense with his own liberty, he cannot do so with the law.

P. But what are you better for your right, if a rebellious company at home, or an enemy from abroad, take away the goods, or dispossess you of the lands you have a right to? Can you be defended or repaired, but by the strength and authority of the King? What reason therefore can be given by a man that endeavours to preserve his propriety, why he should deny or malignly contribute to the strength that should defend him or repair him? Let us see now what your books say to this point, and other points of the right of sovereignty. Bracton, the most authentic author of the common law, (fol. 55), saith thus: *Ipse Dominus Rex habet omnia jura in manu sua, sicut Dei vicarius; habet etiam ea quæ sunt pacis; habet etiam coercionem, ut delinquentes puniat; item habet in potestate sua leges. Nihil enim prodest jura condere, nisi sit qui jura tueatur.* That is to say: Our Lord the King hath all right in his own hands; is God's vicar; he has all that concerns the peace; he has the power to punish delinquents; all the laws are in his power: to make laws is to no purpose, unless there be somebody to make them obeyed. If Bracton's law be reason, as I and you think it is, what temporal power is there which the King hath not?

Seeing that at this day all the power spiritual, which Bracton allows the Pope, is restored to the crown; what is there that the King cannot do, excepting sin against the law of God? The same Bracton, (*lib*. ii. *c*. 8, fol. 5), saith thus: *Si autem a Rege petatur, cum breve non currat contra ipsum, locus erit supplicationi quod factum suum corrigat et emendet; quod quidem si non fecerit, satis sufficit ei ad pœnam, quod Dominum expectet ultorem: nemo quidem de factis suis præsumat disputare, multo fortius contra factum suum venire.* That is to say: If any thing be demanded of the King, seeing a writ lieth not against him, he is put to his petition, praying him to correct and amend his own fact; which if he will not do, it is a sufficient penalty for him, that he is to expect a punishment from the Lord: no man may presume to dispute of what he does, much less to resist him. You see by this, that this doctrine concerning the rights of sovereignty, so much cried down by the Long Parliament, is the ancient common-law, and that the only bridle of the Kings of England, ought to be the fear of God. And again, Bracton, (*lib*. ii. *c*. 24, fol. 55), says, that the rights of the Crown cannot be granted away: *Ea vero quæ jurisdictionis sunt et pacis, et ea quæ sunt justitiæ et paci annexa, ad nullum pertinent nisi ad coronam et dignitatem Regiam, nec a corona separari poterunt, nec a privata persona possideri.* This is to say: those things which belong to jurisdiction and peace, and those things that are annexed to justice and peace, appertain to none but to the crown and dignity of the King, nor can be separated from the crown, nor be possessed by a private person. Again, you will find in Fleta, a law-book written in the time of Edward II, that liberties, though granted by the King, if they tend to the hinderance of justice, or subversion of the regal power, were not to be used, nor allowed; for in that book, (*lib*. i. c. 20, § 54) concerning articles of the crown, which the justices itinerant are to enquire of, the 54th article is this: You shall inquire, *de libertatibus concessis quæ impediunt communem justitiam, et Regiam potestatem subvertunt.* Now what is a greater hinderance to common justice, or a greater subversion of the regal power, than a liberty in subjects to hinder the King from raising money necessary to suppress or prevent rebellions, which doth destroy justice, and subvert the power of the sovereignty? Moreover, when a charter is granted by the King in these words: *"Dedita etc. . . . coram etc. . . . pro me et hœredibus meis"*: the grantor by the common-law, as Sir Edward Coke says in his Commentaries on Littleton, is to warrant his gift; and I think it reason, especially if the gift be upon consideration of a price paid. Suppose a foreign state should lay claim to this kingdom, (it is no matter as to the question I am putting, whether the claim be unjust), how would you have the King to warrant to every freeholder in England the lands they hold of him by such a charter? If he cannot levy money, their estates are lost, and so is the King's estate; and if the King's estate be gone, how can he repair the value due upon the warranty? I know that the King's charters are not so merely grants, as that they are not also laws; but they are such laws as speak not to all the King's subjects in general, but only to his officers; implicitly forbidding them to judge or execute any thing contrary to the said grants. There be many men that are able judges of what is right reason, and what not; when any of these shall know that a man has no superior nor peer in the kingdom, he will hardly be persuaded he can be bound by any law of the kingdom, or that he who is subject to none but God, can make a law upon himself, which he cannot also as easily abrogate as he made it. The main argument, and that which so much taketh with the throng of people, proceedeth from a needless fear put into their minds by such men as mean to make use of their hands to their own ends. For if, say they, the King may notwithstanding the law do what he please, and nothing to restrain him but the fear of punishment in the world to come, then, in case there come a king that fears no such punishment, he may take away from us, not only our lands, goods, and liberties, but our lives also if he will. And they say true; but they have no reason to think he will, unless it be for his own profit; which cannot be, for he loves his own power; and what becomes of his power when his subjects are destroyed or weakened, by whose multitude and strength he enjoys his power, and every one of his subjects his fortune? And lastly, whereas they sometimes say the King is bound, not only to cause his laws to be observed, but also to observe them himself; I think the King causing them to be observed is the same thing as observing them himself. For I never heard it taken for good law, that the King may be indicted, or appealed, or served with a writ, till the Long Parliament practiced the contrary upon the good King Charles; for which divers of them were executed, and the rest by this our present King pardoned.